FRANCES ELIZABETH WILLIS

Best wishes to
Marianne Maley

Mulile Willis

FRANCES ELIZABETH WILLIS

UP THE FOREIGN SERVICE LADDER— TO THE SUMMIT

Despite the Limitations of Her Sex

May 20, 1899 Metropolis, Illinois
July 10, 1983 Redlands, California

NICHOLAS J. WILLIS

CONTENTS

PREFACE

THIS is a biography of my aunt, Frances Elizabeth Willis, who was the third woman to join the U.S. Foreign Service, the first woman to make a career of the Foreign Service, the first woman to climb to the top of the Foreign Service ladder, the first career woman appointed ambassador, and the first woman appointed career minister and then career ambassador, which is the highest rank in the Foreign Service. She spent thirty-seven years in the Foreign Service, entering in 1927 and retiring in 1964. How she did it in the face of widespread bias against women in both the Foreign Service and State Department is the principal theme of this book.

I was drawn into Frances' biography when she visited us in Menlo Park, California over the 1975 Christmas holidays. Frances had retired from the U.S. Foreign Service and was living alone in the Redlands, California, family home. She consulted occasionally for the State Department and had become quite active in local affairs. And she had recently recovered from a hemorrhagic stroke, which had begun to affect her memory. Earlier family holidays had been spent at the Redlands home, but began to tail off after Frances' mother and my grandmother, Belle (James) Willis-Cairns, died in 1960. To continue the tradition we invited Frances to spend the holidays with us.

As was the family tradition, Christmas Eve dinner was festive, with cocktails before, wine with and brandy after the dinner. I don't recall seeing Frances in such an expansive mood. So I asked her to tell us about some exciting diplomatic escapades over her career as a U.S. Foreign Service Officer (FSO). And to our surprise, for the first time this most proper and reticent diplomat did just that.

One of Frances' stories happened in May 1940, just at the start of WW II when she was stationed as a second secretary at the American Embassy in Brussels. Frances' boss, Ambassador John Cudahy, was hosting a visit from Henry Luce, editor of *Time, Life* and *Fortune* magazines, and his wife, playwright and star reporter Clare Boothe Luce, when the Germans invaded Belgium wreaking havoc as they advanced. They bombed Brussels with their *Stuka* dive-bombers and then occupied the city with their *Panzer* tanks and *Heer Wehrmacht* troops.

Shortly after the invasion started, Clare suffered a nervous breakdown. When it became clear that she was not going to recover any time soon, Frances volunteered to drive the Luces in her own car from Brussels through German lines and on to a Paris hospital. Frances then drove back to Brussels, again through German lines, and resumed her duties at the (still neutral) embassy. Finally, Frances admonished us to not repeat the story until all principals were dead.

Frances died eight years later in 1983. Then Clare's posthumous diaries were published in 1997, which totally contradicted Frances' version of events: nothing about a breakdown, a different driver on the Brussels-to-Paris trip and a different Paris destination, the Ritz Hotel. Whom could you believe?

In an attempt to find out, I ordered Frances' Foreign Service *dossier*, or personnel record, through the Freedom of Information Act, which took two years to arrive. While there was nothing in it to resolve the Luce controversy, it did contain all her performance evaluation records, including her Annual Efficiency Reports and Rating Sheets, for the first twenty-eight years of her service. And in those early reports—said time after time, post after post—was the comment that she was doing good work, "despite the limitations of her sex." Furthermore, at a critical point in her career, the assertion was made that Frances recognized such a limitation.

And that was a stunner. I had never heard Frances say that; in fact many times she said just the opposite: "Sex has nothing to do with it." My first reaction was that Frances must never have reviewed her dossier because she was too busy in her short visits to Washington DC between foreign duty assignments and also during her one tour at the State Department to take a day off to do so. Second, it probably never occurred to her to review it, because many of her station chiefs had briefed (and occasionally even shown) their reviews to her, most of which were good, very good, even excellent. So why bother with known and encouraging information? Finally, if she had seen her dossier she would have at least commented about the sex limitation issue. But she never did.

In an attempt to resolve this dichotomy, I first studied the 800 pages in her dossier, subsequently augmented by hundreds of additional pages in her so-called 123 File, Decimal Files and Name Indexes accessible only through visits to the National Archives II facility in Maryland. Then I viewed thousands of letters, documents and photographs that Frances had bequeathed to Stanford's Hoover and Redlands' Smiley Libraries. Finally I communicated with the State Department's

Office of the Historian, the Diplomatic and Consular Officers, Retired (DACOR) and a few of her Foreign Service associates who were still around.

The answer is documented in this book and shows that the State Department and its sibling the Foreign Service (before they were combined in 1954) were bastions of male chauvinism. They erected not only the classic "glass ceiling" but also a much lower "glass table" for women, a table that discouraged young women from staying in the service. Then Frances and her fellow FSO traveler, Constance Harvey, shattered those barriers by simply ignoring them, doing good work and doggedly climbing the Foreign Service ladder. Even more astonishingly, both reached the top rung of their respective branches.

Incidentally, I did uncover circumstantial evidence, including passport entries, in the Hoover Library to support Frances' version of the Brussels story. In short, everyone —Cudahy, the Luces and even Frances—fibbed about Clare's breakdown in 1940 to "cover it up," as they say nowadays, in order to prevent embarrassment to such high-level national figures. Then Frances revealed the truth to us in 1975.

After Frances retired and at the urging of her brother (my father) Henry Willis, Frances began thinking about writing her memoirs in 1973. Dad became so enthused that he offered to help. He then wrote to George Kennan, who, after a distinguished career in the Foreign Service, had retired and was ensconced at The Institute for Advanced Study, Princeton. George wrote back saying in part:

> I was glad to have your letter and to know that there is at least a serious possibility that your sister Frances' reminiscences and impressions may be made available to the general public. I shall tell you quite frankly how I feel about it.
>
> In the case of a living person, memoirs should be written either by the person himself or by someone who is quite detached, emotionally and personally, from the person in question. But a near relative is apt, if only for reasons of delicacy, to idealize her; and that not only often embarrasses the subject, but bores the reader. Please give your sister my warm and respectful regards, and accept my thanks for your kind remarks about my own memoirs.
>
> Very sincerely,
> /s/ *George Kennan*

But before Frances could start her memoirs, she suffered the stroke, which effectively ended that effort. Then almost thirty years later I decided to write her biography, focusing on her struggle up the Foreign Service ladder. But I didn't run across the Kennan letter until I was almost done with the first draft, and it brought my effort to a full halt over the fear of becoming a flagrant hagiographer. That fear was exacerbated when I remembered that Frances was quite fond of the U.S. Navy all her adult life and I had spent eleven years in the Navy including five on active duty.

Then after more pondering, I decided to proceed because (a) Frances had died, so the pressure to idolize her was diminished; (b) the naval link between subject and author—and for that matter, author's opinions and biases—could be suppressed and if not suppressed, constrained to a footnote; and (c) her story was simply compelling—and I have never been a member of the Woman's Liberation Movement.

Unfortunately, a straightforward chronicle of Frances' Foreign Service struggle would, for the most part, consist of a dry recitation and explanation of the performance evaluation records for each of her ten Foreign Service posts, hardly enough grist for an entertaining biography. So I have included family anecdotes, letters and other digressions to describe her character, philosophy and social preferences, including the men in her life, all designed to enhance the chronicle.

Finally, in sorting through the material for this biography I picked up insights into the workings of the State Department, the Foreign Service and the people who populated them during the early twentieth century. These insights included how an FSO lived, traveled and worked when it really counted—when bilateral diplomacy was conducted person-to-person, on-site. Insights also captured changes in the Department's organization, operation and personnel policy for men and finally women, the latter closely paralleling the evolution of our species. And because Frances was the first woman to receive a full dose of these changes I included them in appropriate places.

So here is her Foreign Service saga:

Up the Foreign Service ladder—to the summit—despite the limitations of her sex.

ACKNOWLEDGEMENTS

I gratefully acknowledge the dedicated research and support of my wife Carlaine (Esmay) Willis, and the learned counsel of my sister Elaine (Willis) Mannon, daughter Sherene (Willis) Gravatte, fraternal cousins, Vivian (Vaughan) Cox and Frances Vaughan and maternal cousin Barbara (Hoxie) Van Hoven. Special thanks go to Barbara, Elaine and Carlaine for vigorously editing the manuscript, and to William A. Moffitt, a retired FSO who thoroughly vetted the Foreign Service world.

My gratitude also goes to Frank and Bill Moore, editor and publisher of the *Redlands Daily Facts*, who recorded Frances' career with precision, fidelity and humor over a span of fifty years, and to Mrs. Toni Momberger, current editor of the *Facts*, who granted permission to reproduce their record.

Finally I acknowledge the superb logistics support from the Redlands Smiley Public Library and its Chief Archivist Don McCue, the Monterey Public Library, Stanford's Hoover Archives, the Department of State's Office of the Historian, the Diplomatic and Counselor Officers Retired (DACOR) and the National Archives.

This biography of Frances E. Willis
is dedicated to her brother and my father,
Henry James Willis, whom we both admired.

1

CRISIS IN WASHINGTON

The Arrival

AUGUST, 1944: World War II was raging, a global nightmare, as Peter Jennings and Todd Brewster called it in *The Century*. While 1942 naval battles in the Coral Sea and at Midway had stunned Japan's expansion in the Pacific, and Italy had surrendered in June 1944, ferocious fighting faced allied troops in Europe following the largest amphibious invasion in history on June 6, 1944, D-Day. Monster battles lay ahead: the Bulge in Europe, Leyte Gulf, Okinawa—possibly Japan itself—in the Pacific.

Amid this turbulence a forty-five year-old Foreign Service Officer (FSO) reported for duty as night watch officer at the Department of State in Washington DC: Frances Elizabeth Willis, First Secretary and Consul Class IV, one of only three women in the U.S. Foreign Service. She had just finished sixteen years of continuous duty overseas with posts in Chile, Sweden, Belgium and Spain. She was stationed in Brussels when the German army invaded Belgium in May, 1940, ran the embassy when the ambassador was absent, was expelled after the Gestapo shut the embassy in July, 1940, then spent the next four years in Madrid helping to prevent Franco's fascist Falange party from joining the Axis.

The Department of State (or the State Department or just "the Department" as FSO's called it) decided to bring her home for two reasons. First, she had severely injured her arm in an automobile accident while delivering a diplomatic pouch to Lisbon and the Spanish doctors couldn't fix it, in fact made it worse. Second, sixteen years of Foreign Service duty overseas—four during wartime—is a good stretch even for a man, so why not bring her back for some rest and recuperation stateside?

Frances was delighted with her new assignment, writing Joe Erhardt, Director of Personnel at the Department:

AMERICAN EMBASSY

Madrid, June 16, 1944

Dear Mr. Erhardt:

After sixteen years outside the United States I can think of nothing [that] would make me happier than to be returning to stay for awhile, particularly at a time like the present. I do not know who is responsible for my great good fortune but I wish that whoever it is may know how pleased I am about it…

I hope to be able to go to California before I begin my work in Washington, not only to see my family, but also to see my doctors. I do not know whether you know that I was in an automobile accident over a year ago.

Again with my thanks to you and to all those who are responsible for my transfer, I am, sincerely yours,

/s/ *Frances E. Willis*

Frances did go to California to see her family. But the arm had finally healed enough so that further operations weren't needed.

Frances on home leave in Redlands, California, 1944.

She is posing on the front porch of the family home, sporting an elegant dress and new coif befitting a First Secretary and Consul Class IV FSO, about to report to the State Department for a tour of stateside duty. Frances' scarred left arm is hidden, probably done by habit at this point.

An earlier letter in her Foreign Service personnel file, or *dossier* as the Department called it, records who started the transfer:

DEPARTMENT OF STATE
DIVISION OF FOREIGN SERVICE ADMINISTRATION

November 9, 1943

FP

Mr. Erhardt:

I have a letter of October 21 from Miss Frances E. Willis at Madrid, Spain, in which she says, "I have regained the use of my arm up to about 90% of normal I should say. It still looks awful, but I am afraid it will have to continue to do so for the duration for two reasons, because I shan't let them touch it in Spain again, if I can help it, and operations partly for aesthetic reasons are too frivolous for war time."

As I believe I mentioned to you on a previous occasion, I retain the impression from my trip to Madrid that Miss Willis has long since earned a transfer to some easier post where her arm can be properly taken care of. She is doing a man-sized job at Madrid.

F. E. Flaherty

So the Director of Administration was the instigator, and of course knew about her arm. The letter had many initials on it, with the following handwritten note to Joe Erhardt in the upper left corner:

JGE
Joe, Secy says Miss Willis OK for night shift. How about it?

That note was not signed—and with handwriting distinctly different from all the others on the memo. But whoever wrote it had been talking to Cordell Hull, the current Secretary of State. And that's all it took: The transfer was started, but without Frances' knowledge, because she was not an addressee on the letter. And it took seven months to consummate the transfer, seven months to find a replacement, cut the paperwork and transport bodies, especially in wartime.

Traveling from Madrid to Washington DC in the 1930's and early 1940's was always a multi-day journey, even by air. And travel in wartime stretched it to a multi-week journey, as Frances recorded in her July 15, 1944, transfer report to the Secretary of State:

> July 1 Departed by air from Madrid; arrived Lisbon
> July 6 Departed Lisbon (10:55 a.m.) by Pan American Airways
> July 8 Arrived New York (1:55 p.m.)
> July 12 Departed by rail from New York
> July 12 Arrived Washington and reported to the Department for consultation [before taking home leave in Redlands]

Frances spent five days awaiting the Pan Am flight from Lisbon, which was not surprising because it first had to show up, then spend time on re-provisioning and maintenance, and finally wait until both the weather and German aircraft threats made it safe to fly again. Then it took over two days to fly from Lisbon to New York, stopping in the middle of the Atlantic Ocean, once in the Azores and again in Bermuda, just as the Pan Am Clippers did before WW II.

In fact it was a Clipper, as Frank and Bill Moore, editor and publisher of the *Redlands Daily Facts* newspaper, reported. Frank and Bill were old friends who followed Frances' career starting in 1927, usually in their weekly "With a Grain of Salt" column. They interviewed Frances after she arrived in Redlands for their July 19, 1944, column:

> For long distance travel, Miss Willis rates the trans-Atlantic clipper at the top of her list. The big flying boat, given fair weather, rides smoothly. It does not vibrate, as do some smaller airplanes. The passenger quarters are far more spacious than those in Douglas land planes. On the particular trip that Miss Willis came on, there were few passengers because of the heavy mail load. Everyone had plenty of leg room. Although the trip is long (31 hours elapsed time) she did not find it monotonous. There were too many things to break the passage of time—the first meal, conversation, sleeping, landing, eating, another landing, and then land fall.

So Pan Am kept a few of their massive, stately Clipper seaplanes—with first-class accommodations, some with sleeping bunks and a separate dining room—around for special flights during the war and Frances caught one of them. In fact one of the perks an FSO enjoyed in those days was traveling first class. But once they got to the new post, living was on their own nickel, and there weren't many of those paid to FSO's back in the 30's and 40's.[1]

Frances then spent four days in New York waiting for transportation. World War II was peaking in 1944, which meant that virtually all trains and airplanes were impressed for moving troops and supplies, especially on the East Coast. Not only that, but auto travel was severely restricted due to gasoline and tire rationing. So she was stuck in New York until a seat opened up.

She certainly didn't wait in Grand Central Station. She got a hotel, checked in with the train dispatcher a few times each day and then found her way down to Broadway for the current plays and shows, one of her favorite pastimes. That was called adaptive travel.

After about a month of more travel and home leave in California, Frances returned to Washington DC and checked in to the brand new, air-conditioned Statler Hotel on Connecticut Ave. near Rock Creek Park. But she could only stay there seven days due to wartime regulations. So she moved into an apartment on Corcoran St., NW, near DuPont Circle and a short hop to the Department, then started looking for a house to rent, large enough to host family members whenever they came to see her. Her search took the better part of a year. She finally found a rental on Fulton St., NW, just off the intersection of Massachusetts and Wisconsin Avenues in Washington DC, again in prime area.

Frances reported for duty at the "old" State Department building, which was described in a February 8, 1947, article from the *Redlands Daily Facts* newspaper:

DEPARTMENT MOVE BRINGS SIGHS, CHEERS

In this $10 million building of 900 column and chimney pots, American foreign policy has been formulated for 70 years. Now George C. Marshall, new secretary of state, is moving out—amid a howl of protest from career men. Sentimental diplomats of the old school love

---

[1] Nowadays FSO travel accommodations are quite different, according to the State Department's Office of the Historian: First class can sometimes be allowed for medical reasons; second (business) class, only for flights over twelve hours; third (economy) class, otherwise.

this old State Department building, a Victorian hodgepodge next door to the White House. The venerable home of the State Department represents a baroque compromise of French neo-classicist ideas, now called "neo-gingerbread" by Washington cynics. Begun in 1875 and designed by A. D. Mullet, then architect of the Treasury, the building was referred to as "Mr. Mullet's architectural infant asylum" by historian Henry Adams. Told the building was fireproof, Civil War Gen. William Sherman replied, "What a pity." Returning from a world tour, Gen. U. S. Grant described it as "a climax of all the curious construction" he had seen abroad. Apparently another famous general feels the same way about it. Marshall is taking his department to a new massive limestone building erected of "modern functional designs" which housed the War Department before it moved to the Pentagon. Move has been threatened since 1911, when an award was made for plans for a new State Department building.

This article was pasted into a scrapbook—actually six consecutive scrapbooks documenting Frances' career—initiated and kept current by Frances' mother, Belle (James) Willis-Cairns, until she died in 1960. The new State Department building is at the bottom of Constitution Avenue in "Foggy Bottom." In fact, most FSO's call the new building "Foggy Bottom," at least informally. Frances did too. But her office was here during her one permanent assignment to Washington DC in a thirty-seven-year career. A photo of the old building's front steps appears in the Foreign Service School chapter.

Preview of the Foreign Service's Attitude towards Women

The comment by Foreign Service Administrator F. E. Flaherty in his 1943 letter to Personnel Director Joe Erhardt, which said that Frances was "doing a man-sized job at Madrid," is certainly a flattering comment. But it seems to contradict an assertion in the title of this biography, "despite the limitations of her sex."

It turns out that the Foreign Service, in fact the entire State Department, was a bastion of male chauvinism during the first half of the twentieth century; actually, it didn't end until 1971. Specifically, no women were admitted to the Foreign Service until 1922 and it took ratification of the Women's Suffrage Amendment in 1920 to force that event. The first woman was Lucile Atcherson, but she soon became discouraged and resigned after three years. The second woman, Pattie Field, was admitted in 1925. She lasted just over four years. Frances was the third, admitted in 1927.

Then three more women were admitted between 1927 and 1930. But again, two of those three left after less than three years. The holdout of this group was Constance Harvey. Then between 1930 and 1941 no women entered the Foreign Service via examinations. (Two women, Margaret Hanna and Kathleen Molesworth, arrived via a lateral transfer from the State Department. Margaret arrived in 1937 and retired in 1939. Kathleen arrived in 1939 and retired in 1955.)

It wasn't because women didn't try to enter between 1930 and 1941: 126 women applied and took the Foreign Service examinations. None passed. In sum, between 1920 and 1941 a total of 214 women took the exams, with just six receiving appointments yielding a 2.8 percent success rate. In contrast, the men's success rate hovered around 20 percent. So that left Frances, her younger colleague Constance Harvey and newly transferred Kathleen Molesworth, as the women FSO residue entering WW II.[2]

But gender discrimination didn't abate for these women after they entered the Foreign Service; in fact it took on a heightened urgency, as Calkin reports: They must be deterred from pursuing a career that demanded so many male "technical qualifications," as one Old Guard FSO put it.[3] And of course marriage by a female FSO was out of the question, since such an arrangement "would bring ridicule" at a foreign post. Further, the position of her husband would "simply be intolerable." So to preclude such an event, one of the questions on the oral part of the Foreign Service entrance examination that was asked well into the 1960's was, "Do you expect to marry someday?" An affirmative answer by a female applicant could fail her. Thus the six successful women applicants must have persuasively hedged the question, and in fact none of the three women FSO's at the beginning of WW II did marry.

One of the Department's tactics for deterring the women who were admitted was to withhold promotions by doctoring the data considered for promotions.

---

[2] Further details are in Homer L. Calkin's well-researched book, *Women in the Department of State: Their Role in American Foreign Affairs*, 1978.

[3] "Old Guard" is defined by Merriam-Webster as "conservative members [of a group] who are unwilling to accept new ideas, practices or conditions." It is used that way throughout this book, particularly to characterize their aversion to women in their ranks.

In Frances' case, they discounted reviews submitted by her on-site supervisors or distorted their summaries, generated undocumented, disparaging comments, misfiled good reports so they weren't used and even worse, ignored good reports that were properly filed.

As a result, Frances spent over four years on the bottom rung of the FSO ladder as an FSO-unclassified, a grade even lower than an ensign in the U.S. Navy or a second lieutenant in the U.S. Army, whereas most of her male peers had been promoted to vice consul (ensign equivalent) within a year. Frances' next promotion was also slow: over three years to consul class VIII.

But that was swift compared to Constance Harvey who remained a vice consul for seventeen years! Constance persisted and only after she had won the nation's highest civilian award, the Medal of Freedom, was she appointed consul general, equivalent to a two-star, rear admiral or major general, in 1959. She retired in 1964, the same year that Frances did. Kathleen Molesworth's path was made a bit easier by these two ladies: She remained a vice consul for over six years and was promoted at about the same time Constance was promoted, possibly riding on her "skirt-tails." She retired as a first secretary in 1955.

Incidentally, the State Department—as in most other countries—sent two separate organizations to each overseas post: the Diplomatic Service for political work and the Consular Service for commercial and personnel work. Then in 1924 they were integrated into the new Foreign Service under the Rogers Act so that all jobs could be done interchangeably. That was a good plan on paper, but incredibly painful to implement.[4]

So, how did the first two career women survive—and ultimately prosper? Frances did it by dedicated work starting at her first post in Chile, which after a year or so began to impress her (male) supervisors. Consequently, she began to cleave the once-unified, Old Guard into two parts: The overseas group, who gradually got to know Frances and thought she was doing a good job—a man-sized job—and the home group, who didn't know Frances and had no reason to change their chauvinist opinions. Now Flaherty, even though he was a home-group-man, saw her work in situ and became a convert. But this powerful home

---

[4] As documented by Waldo H. Heindrichs, Jr. in his scholarly, 1966 biography of Joseph E. Grew, *American Ambassador*. Actually the diplomatic and consular services were merely amalgamated in 1924, since both retained their identities—and own ranks—for many years afterwards. These ranks, the arcane lexicon and early twentieth century history of the Foreign Service are outlined in Appendix 1.

group was full of Old Guard FSO's who held sway over her career for the better part of twenty years.

Constance Harvey called the overseas group *field dogs* and the home group *kennel dogs*. And these field dogs ran in a tight pack. The informal signal that a new FSO was found worthy of joining the pack was when he received birthday greeting cables from the other members. Constance probably did her share of Department-cleaving, again through dedicated work, although someone would have to pry her dossier out of the Department's archives to find out.

Night Watch Officer Duty

On August 14, 1944, Frances reported to the Department to start her night watch officer duty. Cordell Hull was Secretary of State ("SecState" as he was usually called in Department "despatches"—a variant spelling of dispatch, which the Department preferred.) Hull was at the end of his eleven-year reign as Secretary and retired in November, 1944. President Roosevelt then appointed Edward R. Stettinius, Jr. as Hull's replacement on December 1, 1944. About a month later Stettinius wrote a memorandum evaluating Frances' performance, starting with a description of her duties:

[Frances Willis is] one of three watch officers, one of whom is constantly on duty from the close of business until the following morning at 9:00 o'clock and on Sundays, holidays, et cetera. The night watch service has been in effect since September 1939, [following the German invasion of Poland, which started WW II] and it provides, in cooperation with the day force, a continuous 24-hour service.

At this critical time with a major war raging throughout the world, the responsibility resting upon the night watch officers is especially great. Each one, during the time he is on watch, is the "front" for the entire Department and it is his primary duty to see that all important messages requiring immediate action, no matter from what source, are communicated at once to the proper officer in the State Department or to officers of any other government department, which may have a direct or indirect interest in the matter, especially the War and Navy Departments. Likewise he is charged with the responsibility of seeing that the President and myself are informed promptly of emergency developments during his watch. For these purposes he has prompt access to incoming code messages and to him are routed telephone calls coming to the Department after office hours.

Note Stettinius' use of male pronouns. Frances lived with this gender bias all her career and, somewhat surprisingly, used it herself. Even though she was working in a male-dominated world she saw no need to distinguish women from men on the job—they all were FSO's. And as far as she was concerned that ended all gender policing discussions.

While each night watch officer was on duty for six hours, his time at the Department was probably more like eight hours, spending pre-watch time getting up to speed on previous and current action and then after the watch briefing the oncoming watch, just like a USN officer of the deck does when standing ship watch.[5]

Stettinius then reported how she performed as a night watch officer in the second part of his memorandum:

> It will be readily apparent that the efficient discharge of such duties requires a thorough knowledge of the Department and of the work of each division and subdivision of it, as well as judgment and discretion as to what immediate action, if any, to take on the hundreds of messages that come into the Department. From the very beginning Miss Willis applied herself diligently and conscientiously and very quickly familiarized herself with her functions. These she discharged in a very creditable manner and to my complete satisfaction. Her watches were characterized by a smooth-working efficiency.
>
> I should like also to make part of the record the fact that she showed deep interest in her work and took full advantage of the unique opportunity afforded her by this assignment to gain a close insight into the working of the Department and of the Department's policies generally. It is evident that she realized that her services here offered a splendid chance to equip herself for a field of enlarged usefulness on her reassignment to the field. In a personal way Miss Willis is of cheerful disposition, is very cooperative, and is, all in all, an excellent officer.

---

[5] As outlined in the Preface, Frances was fond of the U.S. Navy all her adult life, so this is an appropriate analogy.

Key phrases are "enlarged usefulness on her reassignment to the field" and "excellent officer." They carry extra weight because they come from the chief himself. And certainly no one can contradict the chief. Stettinius went on to say,

> Miss Willis terminated her services as watch officer upon December 25, at which time she entered upon new functions and duties in the office of the Under Secretary of State.

Frances' new boss was Joseph E. Grew, Under Secretary of State. He was originally an Old Guard but gave that up, becoming what George Kennan later called a "Wise Man." Grew looms large as the story unfolds.

Then Disaster

In the early part of the twentieth century an FSO came up for promotion roughly every two years. Promotions were initially made by a Personnel Board consisting of three assistant secretaries according to Heindrichs in his biography of Grew, then in later years by a Selection Board consisting of FSO's senior to the class being considered for promotion. In both configurations someone, probably a member of the board, would review material in each candidate's dossier accumulated over the past two years: memos, letters, newspaper clippings, performance reports from the Department and the very important Annual Efficiency Reports from the on-station supervisor, typically an ambassador or minister. He would then redact all this material into one paragraph and assign a rating of excellent, very good, satisfactory or unsatisfactory for the period. Finally he would add this new paragraph and rating to what was called a Rating Sheet, a running record of performance permanently kept in the candidate's dossier.

This process made the board's job much easier, because everything they needed to know about the candidate was neatly summarized in one new paragraph and rating. And they could immediately see whether the candidate was improving or slipping by scanning the past ratings. Speeds the selection process that way.

It also opens the door for mischief making if the redactor is biased or has a personal ax to grind. And the opportunity for mischief making is amplified when no signatures or even initials are required on the Rating Sheet. So an anonymous redactor is working a potentially vulnerable performance evaluation system.

Frances' Rating Sheet was included in her dossier and consisted of ten entries spanning 1933 to 1949: two years per entry, along with two one-year entries. And the first entry covered some, but not all, of her performance from 1927 to 1933. Frances was up for promotion in 1945 and had an entry for January 1, 1945, the seventh entry. (Her previous six entries were rated chronologically, satisfactory, satisfactory, very good, very good, excellent and very good.)

This 1945 entry consisted of two parts, the first for her last year in Madrid where she was administrative officer, and the second for her time as watch officer in Washington DC. As will happen in any career, you can get crosswise with your boss. And it happened to Frances in Madrid with Ambassador Carlton Hayes. This particular conflict arose when Frances, ever the stickler on regulations, refused to include ecclesiastical material from visiting Archbishop (and currently military chaplain) Francis Spellman in the "official-documents-only diplomatic pouch" sent from the Madrid Embassy to the State Department each week. The problem was that Ambassador Hayes, a political appointee and devout Roman Catholic, had offered this pouch service to Archbishop Spellman because it would be more convenient and faster than using the Papal Nuncio's pouch across town. But because Frances was in charge of the pouch, her decision held. Hayes was not happy.

Not only that, but Frances had fallen behind in the mission's administrative work because she insisted on doing all the important jobs herself. So she had some of those duties stripped away, which Hayes subsequently reported in her Annual Efficiency Report. He did balance this criticism by listing her better qualities—all quite proper and in accord with Department procedures. So far, so fair. But clearly exercised by the pouch conflict, Hayes saved his killing comment for last:

> Miss Willis is a very fine person, of good appearance and address, sterling character, thorough devotion to duty, loyal and dependable. She will be, I think, a faithful follower rather than a leader.

Simply put, the last sentence says she is not command, or as the military says, "flag-rank" material. And in the up-or-out Foreign Service promotion system, that kind of comment usually ends a career.

Hayes' report was duly summarized by the anonymous redactor in the first paragraph of Frances' 1945 Rating Sheet. He added terms like "altogether satisfactory" to the paragraph, suggesting that she had slipped a notch from the previous very good rating. But not to worry, because the second paragraph summarized Secretary Stettinius' memorandum with its excellent rating. So the redactor could be expected to weigh the two accordingly, possibly in favor of the big boss' comments, or at worst average the two for a very good rating. Not so:

Miss Willis welcomed her assignment to the Department and accepted cheerfully the rather unusual duty of serving as a watch officer in the Secretary's office. That she met adequately the requirements of the position was attested by a memorandum from the Secretary commending her for her interest in the work and the quality of her performance. Upon his appointment as Undersecretary Mr. Grew asked for her transfer to his office as executive assistant.

Her duties during the current review period were not of a character to test seriously the ability of an officer of her rank in the Service [equivalent to a Commander or a Lt. Colonel] and while she did well whatever tasks were assigned to her, it is felt that she should not be placed in line for advancement to Class III [Captain or Colonel] until she has demonstrated further her fitness for assuming the all-round responsibilities which ordinarily fall upon an officer of that class...

For the present period a rating of "Satisfactory" seems appropriate.

Not good; not good at all. In fact, her career is all but over. To start with, the redactor dismissed Secretary Stettinius' evaluation by denigrating her "unusual" night watch officer job, suggesting that it could—and should—have been done by a lesser-ranked FSO. So she got no credit for doing excellent work on a menial job. Not only that, but Stettinius' excellent commendation memo was downgraded to meeting "adequately the requirements of the position."

Surprisingly, the redactor omitted the two major—and polar opposite—comments from the Rating Sheet: Stettinius' "enlarged usefulness on her reassignment to the field" and Hayes' "faithful follower rather than a leader." It appears that he excised the highest and lowest comments, just as the highest and lowest scores are excised in calculating a golf handicap. That reduces the spread or standard deviation and makes it easier to come to a tidy average. Nevertheless, the bottom line heavily weighted Ambassador Hayes' evaluation over Secretary of State Stettinius' evaluation, with the result being an unmitigated disaster for Miss Willis.

How could that happen? Both Hayes and Stettinius were political appointees—non-career FSO's. If Hayes were a career FSO the redactor might assign more weight to his professional judgment. But he wasn't. He was a former Columbia University history professor with anti-Nazi credentials, appointed to his first post with a mission to keep Franco and his Falange fascist organization neutral.

Maybe the redactor had problems with Stettinius—and most of the senior FSO's did at the time. Specifically, Stettinius was a Department outsider, a former Board Chairman of U.S. Steel Corporation and then Administrator of the Lend Lease Program before Roosevelt appointed him Under Secretary and then Secretary of State following the eleven-year tour of insider Cordell Hull.

One of Stettinius' principal jobs was to reorganize the State Department, starting at the top: rearranging as well as adding deck chairs to the first-class section. He added seven assistant secretaries, twelve office directors, twenty division chiefs and eighty-eight assistant and associate chiefs, 190 new executives in all. That must have rankled the current senior Department members, because that's where they sat.

Then Roosevelt died and Truman immediately shipped Stettinius off to head the U.S. delegation to the United Nations. Because Stettinius was Secretary for a total of seven months, overlapping only one month with Frances, how could this trouble-making outsider really measure her performance? Not very well, obviously. So his evaluation must be discounted and adjusted accordingly: down—just as it was.

Even more devastating was the last comment on the Rating Sheet:

> Another factor meriting some consideration is the limitation imposed by her sex on her availability for any kind of assignment. Her frank recognition of this and of the consideration shown her up to this period in her career is further evidence of the good sense she has always displayed.

This wasn't the first time such "limitations of her sex" comments appeared in Frances' evaluations; indeed, they were widespread. But nowhere in the Hayes or Stettinius evaluations were they mentioned. And no other sources were cited on the sheet. So that comment must have been generated by the redactor. Not only that, but it appears that some senior, Old Guard FSO—maybe the redactor himself—had a heart-to-heart talk with Frances about this limitation, eliciting her agreement that it was indeed a limitation and that she was willing to live with it.

But that totally contradicts comments made by Frances about limitations of the female sex in the Foreign Service. Here are typical examples, first from a 1962 State Department press release announcing Frances' appointment as career ambassador, quoting Frances:

> It takes certain qualities to make a fair success in diplomacy. A diplomat's sex has nothing to do with it.

Next from a 1968 letter Frances wrote to Myrtle Thorne, Department of State, who had asked Frances to send biographic information for a book the Department was about to publish, then called *Women in the Service.* Frances turned down her request saying in part,

> I am "agin" articles about "Women in the Service." From the time I entered the Service I took the position that I wanted no publicity unless what I did would have been noteworthy if it had been done by any other Foreign Service Officer. I went into the Service as an officer, not as a woman...
>
> Throughout my career I proceeded on the assumption that sex had nothing to do with diplomacy, or with consular work, even when in charge of "seamen and shipping," which was part of my assignment in the second year at my first post at Valparaiso.

In fact, there was never any instance in Frances' files, letters, press interviews or records where she recognized a limitation of her sex. So it appears that someone was fussin' with the facts. And based on her tenacious comments about the subject, it's hard to assign the fussin' to Frances. In any case, Frances' Foreign Service career was in extreme jeopardy—*in extremis* as the USN calls it. The end was in sight, and the real tragedy is that because Frances never said she had reviewed her dossier, she would not have known about it.

One note before traveling back to see how Frances got herself into and then out of this pickle. In Frances' 1968 letter to Myrtle Thorne, she also said:

I went into the Service as an officer, not as a woman. I told the Department at the time that if I were ever given a job I could not do I would resign.

That comment was made to the Foreign Service Personnel Board during Frances' 1927 oral examination for the Foreign Service. Joseph E. Grew was chairman of that board, held that same viewpoint and was to be her next boss. Seeds of redemption may have been planted.

2

EARLY LIFE

The James and Willis Families

FRANCES' mother, Belle Whitfield James, was the youngest member of the aristocratic James family, who had lived in Memphis, Tennessee, since before the Civil War. Their life centered on the Southern Wagon Factory, which was acquired right after the war by Belle's father, Henry James from England, and co-owned by her maternal grandfather, James Roosa from Ohio, and future stepfather, William Graham from Georgia. They renamed it the James and Graham Wagon Factory after James Roosa died from yellow fever in 1879. Then in 1887 Henry James died in an accident at the factory, leaving it to be run by William Graham and subsequently by Belle's older brother, George James. They made fine wagons and buggies until about 1920, when automobiles finally did them in. All were devout Episcopalians, who worshiped at the Calvary Episcopal Church in Memphis.

And therein lies the link to the Willis family. The Calvary Episcopal Church was ministered by Dr. Fred P. Davenport, whose wife was Frances Neeley (Willis) Davenport. Frances was originally from Metropolis, Illinois, where the Willis family had lived since before the Civil War. Then in 1892, Frances' brother, John Gilbert Willis, came down from Metropolis to visit his sister and brother-in-law in Memphis and met the James family, most likely at the 11 a.m. Sunday service.

Almost immediately twenty-one-year-old Gilbert—who used his middle name—swept nineteen-year-old Belle off her feet. Even though Gilbert was a Northerner, whose father, Jonathan Clay Willis, had served as a quartermaster in the Forty-eighth Illinois Regiment during the Civil War, and Belle's future step-father, William Lafayette Graham was a captain in the Confederate army, who was captured at the battle of Vicksburg and threw his sword into the Mississippi

River rather than surrender it to "those damned Yankees," Gilbert and Belle were married the next year (1893) by Dr. Fred Davenport in the Calvary Episcopal Church.

But the James family extracted one concession from that filly-abductor: Only daughter Belle must stay close to home. So Gilbert settled in Memphis with his bride, apparently not too far from the James home, became a member of the Memphis Bar and hung out his lawyer's shingle. Three years later, first daughter Caroline was born—namesake of Belle's mother Caroline (Roosa) James. Following Caroline's birth, Belle kept a diary for about two years, which was cheerful, upbeat and full of news on both sides of the family, especially about Frances (Willis) Davenport. Belle and Frances became quite close.

Then around 1898, possibly 1899, Gilbert took his family back to Metropolis, Illinois, settling about two blocks from his father's home. While the reason for this move is lost, it is likely that Gilbert, a lawyer from the North, simply couldn't make a go of his new law profession in Memphis, a solid city of the South.

Consequently Gilbert talked Belle into trying a new life in his hometown, Metropolis. It appears that Gilbert also decided to give up his law practice altogether because his subsequent professions were stock farming, life insurance sales, lather and craftsman. This new life in Metropolis lasted five years, during which time Belle bore Gilbert two more children, Frances, named after Frances Davenport in 1899, and Henry, named after his grandfather, Henry James, in 1904.

Willis family in Metropolis, Illinois, circa 1901. From the left: Caroline, Gilbert, Frances and Belle. Caroline appears to favor her mother and Frances her father.

In 1905 Belle divorced her husband of twelve years because of infidelity. According to his contrite farewell letter, which Belle kept in her bible, Gilbert took full responsibility for the divorce, but didn't say who or why. He signed it "Mizpah, Gilbert." *Mizpah*, from Genesis 31:49, is an emotional bond between people who are separated either physically or by death.

That's ironic because a few years after the divorce was finalized, Belle—with collusion from her mother and two daughters—declared Gilbert dead. But Gilbert had not died; he had moved to Chicago, where he met and married Lynn Maise. Then he did die in 1943 without further progeny. He never saw his children again. Belle also ended, completely, further contact with the Willis family, including her sister-in-law and friend Frances (Willis) Davenport. Finally, Belle hustled her children back to Memphis at the first opportunity after the divorce was either broached or agreed to.

Upon arrival in Memphis, Belle received full financial support from her family. Furthermore, both stepfather William Graham, and brother George offered fatherly, Southern-type guidance to the Willis children. Because marital misconduct caused the divorce, both the State of Tennessee and the Episcopal Church declared it legal. Consequently, Belle was entitled to alimony, but did not receive any. While the reason is not documented, she could have rejected it or the court could have determined that Belle was reasonably supported and that Gilbert could not afford it, a finding typical of that time.

Saint Mary's Grammar School, Memphis

Frances was a model student at Saint Mary's Grammar School and her mother, Belle, was a model family librarian. Belle assiduously collected and saved everything from and about Frances' life—workbooks, reports, letters and press clippings—starting with her earliest school days. The most charming relics from St. Mary's are Frances' mathematics and English workbooks, consisting of loose-leaf pages bound in an early version of the modern three-ring binder. Each workbook is well organized and neat, nauseatingly neat from a boy's perspective.

Her penmanship is textbook correct, with no cross outs or erasures and very few inserts. Much of the work is recorded in ink. Some are original compositions. Others are copies of poems and passages from literature or the bible, complete with pictures that are either drawn as ink tracings or pasted into the workbook. Here is a typical composition from her English workbook when she was ten.

Her teacher, Miss Clark, did not add any corrections or, somewhat surprisingly, assign grades to any of the papers.

> Robert Louis Stevenson became a great man, but was always a boy in his heart. He was an invalid, constantly suffering pain, but he was most always cheerful in spite of his troubles. He loved to play with children, loved to be out of doors, and loved all of God's nature.
>
> His native land was Scotland, but on account of his poor health he and his brave family had to go and live on the Island of Samoa, a way out in the Pacific Ocean. They did a great deal to teach the people of the island how to take care of themselves, and to live a better life.
>
> Mr. Stevenson wrote many thrilling books, the sort that boys love to read. He also wrote many poems, several of which are given in "A Child's Garden of Verses."
>
> After living on the island for many years, the disease which had pursued him from Scotland mastered him and his body died. But Robert Louis Stevenson will never die as long as people read and love his books.
>
> Frances Willis
> April 12, 1910

Kemper Hall, Kenosha, Wisconsin

In 1912 Belle moved her family to Kenosha, Wisconsin, to get a fresh start and a little more breathing room in her life. She enrolled her children— including son Henry—in Kemper Hall, an Episcopalian parochial school for women. Religion was always a strong force in the James family, and grew even stronger following the divorce.

Kemper Hall was run by the Mother Superior, Sister Margaret Clare. Frances did fairly well under Sister Margaret, receiving eight A's and ten B's on her cumulative report card, where an A represented a year's work in English, for example. And she took just the basic courses from the parochial curriculum: English, Mathematics, Latin, Foreign Language (French), Chemistry, Bible History and (Secular) History.

She was appointed Head of the Preparatory Department, the VII Form and Honor Role in 1912. She won the Junior Class Prize in 1913. Then she was appointed Head of the Collegiate Department and Senior Class. She was also awarded First Prize in English in 1915 and co-awarded the St. Mary's Cross, equivalent to valedictorian, in 1916. Eleven women were in her graduating class.

Frances' 1916 graduation from Kemper Hall.

The parchment scroll Frances is holding announced that she had completed the College Preparatory Course with honors. It has a fleury cross and the Kemper Coat of arms at the top and was signed by Sister Margaret Clare and the Bishop of Milwaukee. Then each affixed their wax seals, complete with a ribbon, to the parchment. They certainly did things with a *fleurish* in those days.[6]

---

[6] Frances was a devotee of punning and head rhyming all her life. She would ply them on family and friends at most every opportunity, including her weekly bulletins to the family. That low-brow disease was so contagious that her audience caught it, responding with progressively worse puns or rhymes, leading to groans all round. For example, Frances would respond to the author's fleury-*fleurish* comment with, "That certainly makes me cross." The next response would be, "It's now time to cross out this kind of humor;" then "No, too soon; let's cross that bridge when we come to it;" finally, "That's a flurry of nonsense." So in the spirit of capturing Frances' spirit, the author beseeches the reader to join in.

Sister Margaret thought so highly of Frances that she penned the following letter to Belle a few months before graduation:

KEMPER HALL
KENOSHA, WISCONSIN

February 17, 1916

My dear Mrs. Willis:—
There are no words too strong for me to say in reference
to our dear Frances. In all her class work she is the head of the
School, and is perfect in deportment.
I always consult her and Marian Nichols in reference to
any puzzle that comes up in the Senior class. She is always fair,
always loyal; and each year she is getting a little stronger in her judgment.
Ever your loving
Sister Margaret Clare
Mr. Suf [Mother Superior]

As one might suspect, the three *R's* of parochial education, Refinement, Rectitude and Religion were important lessons at Kemper Hall. Sister Margaret summarized the first lesson, Refinement, on a little card titled "Kemper Hall Don'ts," which Frances saved. Here are samples.

Don't talk about yourself or your family affairs. It is a sign of verdancy.
Don't be inquisitive with either tongue or fingers, because curiosity is
    wholly vulgar and "common."
Don't forget your room-mate's rights; I am not afraid that you will over-
    look your own.
Don't announce your arrival at a neighbor's door by a knock like a black-
    smith's. Spare your knuckles and her nerves.
And don't be slovenly in speech. Sound your final d's and g's; treat your
    vowels with respect; make your verbs and nouns agree; don't use the
    present tense for the past, a participle for a verb, or an adjective for
    an adverb.
Don't use the following and kindred barbarisms:
    Those kind.
    But what.

Real nice.

He don't.

Kind of, sort of.

I don't feel very good.

Us girls are going.

You folks.

He asked she and I.

Don't talk loudly or laugh shrilly. "The loud laugh bespeaks the vacant mind."

Frances did violate one, possibly two of the "Don'ts" in her life. Her family parlor trick of asking children if they could touch their noses and then saying, "No, not with your finger, your tongue," and then doing it herself, had her being inquisitive with tongue, which would have rendered Sister Margaret uncomfortable. But a reasonable code of civility and certainly one that would serve Frances well in the world of diplomacy. (Her parlor trick was never performed there, of course.)

Frances kept scrapbooks during her time at Kemper Hall. She didn't have a camera, so pasted mementos of events into them, for example a flower or twig from some picnic, dance cards from parties, programs from plays, an auction bridge scorecard and a Hershey candy bar wrapper! Frances did like her chocolate.

Also included was a golf scorecard dated September 7, 1913, from the Kenosha Country Club. Frances played with Jeanette Robinson, who had a handicap of 7. Frances showed a 9 handicap. Their final score was not recorded. Then at the end of an interview in the June 27, 1954, *New York Herald Tribune* titled, "The Lady is a Diplomat" by Jean Block, Frances clarified her true golf interest:

"I still do some swimming and diving in the summertime. I played golf for a while, but I gave it up because I didn't like it." Suddenly she caught herself short. "Perhaps I'd better put that differently. Let's say I gave up golf because I wasn't very good at it." There spoke a true diplomat.

Kemper Hall closed as a school in 1975 after 97 years of continuous operation. The property became a Kenosha County Park, which now hosts music concerts, art exhibits, weddings, workshops and Christmas parties. The church and chapel remain in use. Incidentally, Frances wasn't the only notable alumna from Kemper Hall. Roy Rogers sent his daughter there, probably to sequester her from all the rogue movie stars.

University of Redlands, California

In 1915 the Willis family, including now twice-widowed matriarch Caroline James-Graham, traveled to Redlands, California, for the wedding of Betty Burns, the daughter of friends from Memphis. Caroline and Frances were bridesmaids.

Apparently the early twentieth century Southern California weather (before smog) treated Henry and his asthma-like symptoms much better than did the Great Lakes weather, especially the dank winter weather.[7] In any case, they found Redlands a quintessential, friendly, small American town. So they returned almost immediately after Frances graduated from Kemper Hall and bought a small house on Cyprus Court.

In her last year at Kemper Hall, Frances had identified Vassar, Smith and Wellesley as her three universities of choice, all women's universities—the only kind of school she had known. But she now was confronted with a large logistics problem: They were about three thousands miles and five to six travel days away from her new home. So she, along with Caroline, applied to Stanford University, which while new (founded in 1886) had a decent reputation.

Neither was accepted. Their rejection was likely caused by the cryptic reports written by Sister Margaret Clare, Kemper Hall, as part of their application to Stanford. In Frances' report, for example, when Stanford asked for "recommending grade fixed by school," she simply said, "B is passing grade"—and Frances had more B's than A's. Then when Stanford asked for "candidate's rank among the upper fifth, third, half; lower half, third, fifth of class," with instructions to "locate as definitely as possible by underscoring appropriate term," she just wrote "upper" and didn't underscore anything.

Finally, when Stanford asked for "additional information descriptive of the candidate's preparation, qualities and fitness" she wrote, "Average of two years work in church history and scripture." None of that could have done much to impress Stanford's Admissions Committee.

---

[7] Henry claimed it was actually typhoid fever, which he contracted when playing in the Memphis sewers. Typical humor from a bratty brother.

But what about all that adulation Sister Margaret wrote to Belle at almost the same time she wrote her report to Stanford? Comments like "head of school and perfect in deportment, always consult her, always fair, always loyal, getting a little stronger in her judgment"? Those would have made an impression. Why Sister Margaret didn't add those comments is lost in the heavenly ether.

Sister Margaret did show that Kemper Hall was accredited to Vassar, Smith, Wellesley, Mt. Holyoke, and the Universities of Madison, Michigan and Chicago. But there was nothing west of the Mississippi. Thus while the school had a reasonable track record, none of it was in Stanford's territory, which couldn't have helped much.

So both sisters applied and were accepted to the local college, the University of Redlands, a brand new, coeducational Baptist school founded in 1909. Thus while not Episcopalian, it was at least a Protestant parochial school.

Frank Moore described early campus living at the University of Redlands in his charming book, *Redlands, Our Town,* 1987:

> The character of the University was shaped at the outset by its parent, the Baptist denomination. With a strong emphasis on religion, it is not surprising that students were required to attend chapel every morning, Monday through Friday, like it or not.
>
> Furthermore, the Trustees swallowed the doctrine of 'In Loco Parentis' whole. The University would act in the place of parents, assuming full responsibility for the lives of the students.
>
> The Baptists of that period had an extremely strait-laced view of social behavior. Students were forbidden to play cards or to smoke. That they would be allowed to drink was absolutely unthinkable. The repeal of Prohibition in 1933 made no difference.
>
> And then there was dancing. That, too, was unacceptable. The policy became explicit in the first academic year, 1909-1910, and was seemingly cast in concrete forever.
>
> While the ban on cigarettes and alcohol was understandable to the townspeople, the ban on dancing was not. Indeed, this was identified as one of the important social graces by two of the most prestigious ladies in the community. They were Mrs. J. A. Kimberly and her daughter, Mrs. Elbert W. Shirk. For years they personally sponsored and chaperoned

dances for high school-age boys and girls each fortnight at the women's clubhouse.

More than any single thing about the University, the no-dancing policy marked the campus as a Baptist preserve, separate and different from the community at large. Redlands was not the happy hunting ground it should have been for Presidents in search of philanthropists who would finance new buildings and bolster the endowment.

It was not until World War II that the outdated bonds were broken. After Pearl Harbor the student body began to shrink at an alarming rate as the men either volunteered for military service or were drafted. To keep afloat, the U. of R. had to have more students. In 1943 a contract was signed with the government for the housing, feeding and educating of Navy and Marine officer candidates.

As to the bans on smoking and card playing, John Scott Davenport, who was one of the Marines, wrote an irreverent recollection in 1985 for "The Redlands Report." In it he remarked parenthetically:

"Mind you, there was always at least one poker game going on during off-duty hours in whatever dormitory Marines were occupying. Pipes, cigars, and cigarettes abounded. There was a beer route into the back of Grossmont Hall after dark—established in the fifth month."

Having set the stage with those remarks, he went on to Topic Number 1—Dancing. Let him tell it:

"Denied an official opportunity to celebrate on a balmy New Year's Eve in 1943, the Marines pulled out all stops. For starters they wired the memorial Chapel with loudspeakers connected to a record player, then passed the word to key coeds. That evening, between hourly musters, there was a gala dance on the University's holy of holies. Glenn Miller's Jersey Bounce could be heard all over Redlands and half way to Colton. Someone finally turned off the record player after midnight. All of Redlands was surely aroused, but no gendarmes appeared."

Two months later the Navy held a proper dance in the Commons. The Trustees now had a graceful out. They could discard a policy which had become quaint. In 1945 they did.

Leave it to the marines to shake the place out of its puritanical customs. Frances would have feigned shock at their shenanigans, but have been quite satisfied with the results, because she drank, smoked and danced all her life. Episcopalians are permitted such peccadilloes. In particular, Frances loved to dance, as she reported in bulletins throughout her career. And it probably started when she met the Kimberly and Shirk ladies at one of their clubhouse dances. Then when they discovered they had a common bridge interest (first auction, then contract), the social bond was cemented, lasting through their lifetimes. But none of these social indulgences were allowed on campus when Frances attended in 1916. And that was probably a major reason Frances and Caroline decided to try again for the more permissive Stanford environment—following a year of cloistered education.

Frances' University of Redlands transcript shows that she was admitted with an advanced standing in French. Her academic record for the year at Redlands consisted of thirty course hours in English, Latin, French, Mathematics and History and two course hours in Physical Education. She aced everything with high scores of 97's and 98's in Latin, French and History, and a low score of 88 for her second semester in Physical Education, the only score below 90. So that must have significantly advanced her standing with the 1917 Stanford Admissions Committee.

Two of Frances' extracurricular activities survived from this time. The first was recorded in a 1935 University of Redlands press clipping, announcing that Frances had arrived on a two-month Foreign Service furlough from Brussels. It said, in part:

> The career of Miss Willis has been an interesting one. She entered the U. of R. in 1916 and was an outstanding member of the woman's debate team.

Then upon request, the University of Redlands found a copy of their 1917 yearbook, *La Letra*. It shows Frances as an Initiate Member of the Pi Kappa Delta National Forensic Honor Society, which represented the University of Redlands in intercollegiate debates. Her debate record is listed on the following page, reporting that the Redlands Affirmative Team led by Frances won a 3-0 decision over the Pomona Negative Team, on the question:

Resolved, "That in California the present elective offices—governorship and lieutenant-governorship excepted—should be filled by gubernatorial appointment rather than by popular election as at present."

That was the only girl's debate recorded in the yearbook, which is not surprising considering that there weren't many colleges with a girl's debate team nearby. Not only that but travel was time consuming and complicated in those days, including obligatory chaperones. But even though Frances and her team won the debate, California continues to elect their Secretary of State, Controller, Treasurer and Attorney General, thereby confirming that populace's votes usually trump judge's votes.

The second extracurricular activity was her romance with Harry Cook, whom she had met after moving to Redlands in 1916. The Cook and Willis families became close and the two youngsters became informally engaged in 1917. Soon afterwards Harry was commissioned a second lieutenant in the U.S. Army and then shipped off to France to fly fighter aircraft during WW I. He was killed in a French train accident returning home in 1918. Sad details are in the Men in Her Life chapter. So after the obligatory year of California academic and (tough) coeducational seasoning, Frances reapplied to Stanford and was admitted.

Stanford University—Undergraduate

The academic transcript for Frances' Stanford career shows that her three undergraduate years at Stanford included courses in History (her major), English, Romance Languages, Economics, Education, Political Science, Law, Zoology and Military Training (War Issues.) Frances earned thirty-one A's, three B's and two C's, based on a curve grading system where an A was only given to the top ten percent of a class. Her course load appeared normal, between 14 and 16 hours per quarter. Frances reported in a 1970-era letter that she lived in Roble Hall in 1917, the first year it opened.

Catalogued among Frances' records at Stanford's Hoover Archives are about 400 pages of typed papers and handwritten notes from her history and political science courses. They include course outlines, detailed lecture notes, term papers and exams and—continuing her St Mary's workbook tradition—are fastidiously neat, almost perfect.

One of Frances' term papers is forty-three typewritten pages and appears to be her 1920 Senior Thesis, titled "Sino-Japanese Relations 1914-1915," a most scholarly work but with no grade attached. A second paper, which received an A-grade, is twenty-three hand-written pages probably for a senior year political science course, and titled "Woodrow Wilson: Theory of Party Government." She analyzed Wilson's views on such topics as liberty, justice, a just and lasting peace, a government founded on the consent of the governed, and equality of opportunity, but did not elaborate on the last point.

In fact, nowhere in that paper, nor in any other paper, did Frances advocate or lobby for women's suffrage, a new, hot topic in those days. Apparently, it didn't ring a resonant bell with Frances. She was doing fine in academe and didn't need to become assertive about the subject. Not only that but it probably would work against her if she happened to encounter male chauvinists in her path. In short, achieve your equality through equal—or superior—performance, in this case grades. And except for the one big slip with Ambassador Carlton Hayes in Madrid, that attitude served her well.

Frances expanded this attitude in a 1933 letter to the American Association of University Women, which was conducting a study on the adequacy of college training for women:

> I believe women have in the past been handicapped by the fact that they have been educated as "women," and therefore I have no sympathy for undergraduate offerings for women" as such. The things in education which I consider worth while are equally valuable to men and women.

So Frances wasn't about to cut women any slack in their competition with men. Keep that playing field level at all times—no need for such modern (post-1965) mandates as affirmative action, offsets or preferences.

Only one letter from Frances to the family survived this period. It was posted May 9, 1920, just before graduation and reported a date to the Junior Opera with Phil.[8] She said they enjoyed the oranges that Belle had sent from the home grove. Then Phil vanished.

Frances was a member of the YWCA Board of Directors and its President in her senior year. Frances reported in that May 9 letter that she had asked Mrs.

---

[8] Of no last name. In fact most of her letters to the family used only first or last names for her friends and associates, which made it hard to sort out people eighty years later.

Cottrell, wife of Professor of Political Science Cottrell, to serve on the YWCA's Advisory Board. Mrs. Cottrell accepted and was then elected.

Apparently Frances and the Cottrells were close. So close in fact, that when Frances announced she wanted to go to Columbia University for her graduate work, Professor Cottrell talked her out of it with an offer to stay at Stanford. Because he was the acting head of the Political Science Department while Professor Victor J. West was away, he had no trouble with the approval process, and Frances accepted after she finished her one-year fellowship in Brussels.[9]

Frances also admired Professor West, as she said in a 1961 letter to Stanford, which requested her reminiscences:

> Certainly no course had a more lasting effect on me than Victor J. West's "Poly Sci I." It was a lecture course, but in the midst of a lecture he would fire a question at a student who was not allowed to "get by" with a slipshod answer. Mr. West would pursue the subject and his supplementary questions showed up the weakness of the original answer, or led the student on to more profound probing, yes, even in Poly Sci I. It was in that course that I became aware of the fact that a student was expected to think for himself. The demonstration of ability to memorize and retain facts was not enough. From then until this day "figuring things out for myself" has proved to be one of the most stimulating things in life.

Frances then reported other favorite professors:

> Another thing about my days, and years, at Stanford that I treasure was the keen intellectual competition. I hesitate to use the word competition because it may be misunderstood, but I can find no other word. It was good to be in a world where many had as good and better minds than your own. You had to do your best to keep up with them and more and more you came to appreciate a fine piece of work. I can remember vividly the impression it made on me when Professor Adams would read

---

[9] If Frances had gone to Columbia, she most certainly would have run into Carlton Hayes, professor of history, who could have seized an even earlier opportunity to end her career aspirations, as he did in Madrid. So Professor Cottrell must be credited with salvaging Frances' Foreign Service career—before it started.

to the whole class samples of what he regarded as the best answers to questions on the last written test. I also remember my admiration for some of the briefs that were presented in Professor Cathcart's course in Constitutional Law.

But life was not just study, as Frances reported later in her 1961 letter:

The things that made a lasting impression and that I enjoyed at Stanford were not all intellectual. A canoe on [Lake] Lagunita could be wonderful fun, particularly if the right man was wielding the paddle. Then there never were better chocolate malted milks (or "rocky roads") than those made at Stickey Wilson's. I still have a weakness for them and lamented the passage of Stickey's until Blum's came on the scene.

Frances was also a member of the Woman's Council, the Woman's War Service Board, Chairman of the Stanford Clinic Board and President of Cap and Gown, a woman's honorary society. The 1919 and 1920 *Stanford Quad* yearbooks show that Frances was a member of the Wranglers Society and was its vice president during the first quarter of her junior year. Surprisingly, the *Quads* didn't say what the Wranglers did. But because it is the only group of women shown in an extensive debating section—and the last entry in that section—it is obviously the women's debating team. While the *Quads* spent tens of pages describing each of the men's debate, complete with photos of each debater, there is nothing about the Wranglers except their names. No real surprise in these early days of women's suffrage.

According to her graduation program Frances was elected to the Phi Beta Kappa Society November 26, 1919, the first quarter of her senior year. She graduated with an AB in History June 21, 1920. At that time Stanford did not award graduation honors for scholastic achievement.

Frances' 1920 graduation from Stanford.

Universite Libre de Bruxelles

Frances was listed in Stanford's twenty-ninth Annual Commencement Program as winning one of four, one-year fellowships to the Universite Libre de Bruxelles. The amount was not specified, but probably was enough to cover room and board, tuition and maybe even transportation. The fellowships were awarded by the Belgium Relief Commission, headed by Secretary of Commerce Herbert Hoover, with the following citation:

> Established by the Commission for Relief in Belgium, as a memorial to the work of America in aid of Belgium during the world war [WW I] and for the further maintenance of good relations between the peoples of the two countries.

Mother Superior Margaret Clare and all sisters at Kemper Hall sent Frances a telegram of congratulations on her graduation and fellowship award. They obviously kept track of their girls, even if they were a bit short in their college admission support.

In September, 1920, Frances traveled to Brussels on the Red Star's SS Finland in an outside stateroom with a lady roommate, Miss Brown, who remains unidentified but probably was another Belgium Relief Commission fellowship recipient. Frances then checked in to the Maison des Etudiantes in Brussels, her quarters for the next eight months or so.

Her time in Brussels was sweet. Classes didn't start for almost a month, so she took off with other students on sightseeing trips to Paris, Rome and their environs. The travel didn't stop when classes started: more trips to Paris, London, Amsterdam, augmented with social dates and evenings at the symphony and opera in Brussels. Studying appeared to be a distinct afterthought.

Frances kept an informal diary of all this excitement, which she would send to Belle every week or two as an enclosure to her current letter. In one letter Frances asked Belle to send her more calling cards, because she had used up the current batch in the first four months of social events.

In another letter Frances mentioned that Harry Cook would have been twenty-nine, and that she was seriously thinking about visiting his grave in France. But she decided not to. In a December letter she said she was having trouble with the cold and slush—like Memphis weather, and then reported, "Brussels is not a very clean city anyway." That was one of the few undiplomatic remarks in any of Frances' public or private correspondence. Then in a March letter to big sister Caroline, Frances reported:

> I fear I'm going to have your trouble [of relearning to study after a year's layoff] when I try to work next year—of course I've studied some this year but never so little in my life.

She then added that it's all right because "the Commission seems to approve this [student/tourist] plan." Her academic record—if recorded—is not available.

Finally, Frances told her mother about a classmate John that "I liked awfully well —but I'm not crazy about him." She said that John made fun of her serious discussions and called her a feminist, and after that she "went dumb and self-conscious." And that was the last of John in her letters. Then it was back to Redlands and graduate work at Stanford.

Stanford University—Graduate

In the fall of 1921 Frances returned to Stanford for her PhD program, complete with a $750 graduate fellowship, which was renewed for a second year. The fellowship was enough to cover tuition and part of her room and board. She didn't need a third year because she finished her doctorate in two years. So her year in Brussels must have counted as a Masters degree and then some.

Her academic record for the two graduate years at Stanford consists of courses in Political Science (her major), Economics, Law, German, and the History of Philosophy. She earned seventeen A's and five +'s, which meant passed without defining grade. Three of the +'s were in German. Then to cap that record, in the spring quarter of her first year she scored three As, one + and an A+ in Political Science Theory, with the instructor, Dr. Fearing writing on her transcript with an arrow pointing to the A+: "Look me over, kid, my name's Willis."

Frances wrote her PhD thesis, "The Belgian Parliamentary System," at Stanford's Hoover War Library. It is obviously of interest to a political scientist, but not many others. Why she picked this subject, other than the fact that she had just spent a year in Belgium and could speak French, is summarized in the Introduction:

> The Belgian Parliamentary System offers an almost totally unexplored field to the investigator. Occasionally English and American writers have mentioned phases of it by way of comparison, but no effort has ever been made to present anything like a complete description of it in English. Nor has the treatment of it by Belgian and French writers been much more extensive. If one is really to understand the system he will have to turn to an examination of the legal texts on which it rests and to an observation of the practices which have developed. Both of these things have been done and the results of the investigation are presented in this volume.

She then analyzed powers and prerogatives of the three elements of Belgium's system, the Parliament, the Crown and the Ministry. Finally as all theses should, she drew conclusions. At this point the reader is excused, except for the following paragraphs, which show Frances' view of political science and

American implementation of democracy—surprisingly bereft of any modern-day, minority-rights caveats:

> There is, however, no universally accepted body of principles in the realm of political science and any proposition that is advanced will be attacked by some one. Faulty as so-called democratic governments have been in the past, it is still believed by a large group of people that more rather than less democracy is necessary. To be of this opinion does not necessarily mean that one thinks that democratic government is the ultimate form of state organization nor that it will furnish the solution to all the social, economic, or even political problems. But true democracy does mean that the people will have the machinery at their command by means of which they can satisfy their political desires.
>
> Democracy was not, and in modern states never can be, secured by participation in government. The will of the people can prevail only where the organization of the government makes popular control possible. Moreover, as long as human wills conflict, popular control means only majority control. Nor is this altogether unjust, for who will say that the few rather than the many should be satisfied?

Frances will side with the British government and ram this "only majority control" axiom down the throats of striking British miners—who were in the minority—when she starts teaching political science at Vassar College.

Frances mentioned in one of her letters that she met Herbert and Mrs. Hoover at Stanford, but without elaboration, except to imply that she had been to their home. The connection almost certainly came through his War Library, but can't be pursued because nearly all of her letters from Stanford, Goucher, Vassar and the first few years of her Foreign Service career are lost. Incidentally, Frances' PhD was the first awarded to anyone—man or woman—in Political Science at Stanford.

To continue the Belgian connection, while Frances was doing her graduate work the Belgian government presented a statue of Isis (goddess of plenty, nature, motherhood, fertility and navigation) to Herbert Hoover as gratitude for the U.S. relief work after WW I. The ceremony at Stanford was reported in an un-attributed December 5, 1922, press article:

The strings that unveiled the statue were pulled by a Belgian and an American girl: Mille Germaine Colette, a student at Stanford University from Belgium and Miss Frances Willis, a Stanford student who formerly attended the University of Brussels.

Frances' next Belgium connection was her Foreign Service posting to Brussels in 1934, which lasted through the beginning of WW II. In 1946 she was appointed Belgium/Luxembourg Desk Officer in the State Department's Division of Western European Affairs, an assignment lasting eight months, after which she was promoted to Assistant Chief of that Division.

Finally, in 1955 Frances was elected a Fellow in the Commission for Relief in Belgium (CRB). Her election notification said she was one of just ninety members, and enclosed their names and vital data. Frances was the oldest member by twenty years! Subsequently, she was elected a Director of the Belgium American Education Foundation, Inc., which was established by the CRB. The CRB was one of the very few organizations Frances joined, mostly because she perceived conflicts of interest with the others.

Teaching at Goucher and Vassar Colleges

Unfortunately, the missing files and letters from the family, Hoover and Redlands archives leave a large void in Frances' college teaching life. Nothing is known about her year at Goucher College as a history instructor, and only a little about Vassar College as a political science instructor and then an assistant professor. And these colleges have been no help in filling the voids.

A circa 1927 news article in one of Belle's scrapbooks said that while at Vassar

Miss Willis was well known in Poughkeepsie as a member of the Hudson Valley Branch of the American Association of University Women and as leader of its study group last winter on international relations.

Then at the urging of her boss, E. D. Fite, Chairman of the Political Science Department at Vassar, she joined the Political Association, apparently a school-sanctioned organization that kept track of both domestic and foreign political events. A lead article in the May 15, 1926, semi-weekly *The Vassar Miscellany*

News, details one of their meetings and supplies the rest of what is known about Frances' Vassar tour:

ISSUES OF BRITISH STRIKE DISCUSSED

Professor Smith and Assistant Professors
Willis and Gibson Speak;
Present Facts for Both sides of Questions;
Describe Action Taken

On Monday afternoon the Political Association held an open meeting to discuss the issues of the General [Coal Miner's] Strike in Great Britain. Katherine Fite [likely the wife of Professor E. D. Fite] spoke of the purpose of the meeting, then introduced the three speakers...

Miss Smith opened the discussion with a short talk on the situation. She stressed the importance of reading more than one newspaper in order to obtain unprejudiced information.

She was followed by Miss Gibson, who explained the strike in relation to its historical background.

Miss Willis, who spoke last, reiterated the fact that when the worker used the strike weapon for [*sic*; more likely against] wage reduction, no one dreamed of the far reaching results of a general strike. As 5,000,000 workers out on strike are only one-fifth of the British population, the government feels that it represents a majority, and so can take every necessary precaution to preserve and assure order and British rights.

Frances described these precautions under the 1920 Emergency Powers Act, which allowed the English government "by any methods necessary, to supply the essentials of life to the people." They included the use of troops, taking and paying for food, property or fuel, coal control, billeting troops without permission, arrest without warrant, searching houses for food conspiracies, e.g., hoarding, suppression of treasonous publications, and quelling of riots. She then concluded that

Although the government has gone a long way under the Emergency Act, it might go much further in the line of army and navy aid and lawsuits. Nevertheless the English government considers the strike as an attack on the fundamental rights of Englishmen, and it will use all the means in its power to restore order. The strikers' answer [is] that as striking in itself is a recognized industrial weapon and involves no political issues, they will continue to suspend work until the government yields.

The article finished with the following:

There are five possible outcomes, as Miss Willis sees the situation:
1. The general strike may be a failure, in which case the government wins.
2. The present conservative government may resign, and a labor ministry more in sympathy with the workers may be called. This would mean a subdivision of English conservative law.
3. A die-hard conservative government might be put in who would force the strikers to yield.
4. If sufficient sympathy with the workers is shown, parliament might be dissolved and a general election would show the trend of public opinion.
5. A compromise, in which case neither side gains anything.

Frances wrote along the margin by these five outcomes, "Obviously very weak," meaning that while she had all the possible outcomes covered, she didn't step up to the task of positing which outcomes were more likely than others. In short, she didn't complete the analysis. But that is precisely the kind of work required of a junior Foreign Service Officer: assemble the facts and leave conclusions to the senior Foreign Service Officers. E. D. Fite was probably at the meeting with his wife and saw that potential. So he proposed a Foreign Service career to Frances when she complained to him that she felt uncomfortable teaching Political Science without any practical experience.

Frances elaborated on this frustration in a 1962 press release by the State Department, titled "Frances E. Willis, United States' First Woman Career Ambassador:"

The more I taught, the more I realized how little I actually knew about Government. I decided to find out firsthand what it was like.

Newfoundland—First Foreign Tour

In 1926 Frances volunteered to the International Grenfell Association for a summer of school and public health work in Labrador, Newfoundland. About half a dozen letters written by Frances in Labrador survived in the family collection, along with this May 10 letter to Belle from Frances at Vassar College, describing her jobs:

> You asked what I have to do. The chief thing is teach an un-graded school and adults who want to learn to read or write. Also, any first aid we are capable of and community health work. They are putting us through a course of lectures for that part now. Also we are supposed to get in touch with the people so when Dr. Grenfell and some of the other doctors come around they can have medical care. That's all I know about our duties.

Frances asked if "Hen's old sheepskin coat [was still] in the land of the living," and accepted Belle's offer to knit her a sweater.[10] Then she boarded a train to Montreal for a few days of sightseeing. Finally, she took the steamer Northland to Labrador with many stops in between. Apparently there were more stops than usual because the bishop was on board for his annual visit through the province, which required stopping to confirm his subjects in all villages accessible by boat. Her destination was L'Anse au Clair, a small port on the Strait of Belle Isle., the Gulf of St. Lawrence's northern entrance, with "a real iceberg to greet me just off the point and quite a few pieces of ice in the harbor."

Frances was assigned to live with the Deumaresque family of six in their home. She described her quarters and then her classes in a July 30, 1926, letter that went out on the (almost) weekly mail boat:

> I have a wonderfully comfortable place to live—and <u>clean</u>. I have one tiny room to sleep in, on a feather bed; room is not much bigger than the bed; has a wash stand, chair and what serves as a dresser—all touching each other in their proximity.[11] The room where my trunk is

---

[10] *Hen* was a nickname she used for her brother Henry, which was far better than the ones Belle used for him: *Henny Penny* and *Presh Lamb*.

[11] Obviously with no private toilet. And since a washstand and indoor plumbing are usually

and where I have my meals in solitary state is somewhat larger, and I look right out over the water as I eat. The food has not been half as bad as I expected.

I have thirteen children of all ages up to about thirteen years. A few can clearly read but most of them are near the very beginning. Some can't even say their abc's or count. We have school in a room about twelve feet square and it makes it somewhat difficult. Children mind pretty well though—don't think I was cut out for a kindergarten school teacher however. When things get too bad we have recess and play games.

Frances then added more detail about her students:

I try to keep them till four [p.m.] because they are rather wild and don't know what to do with themselves. Never saw such undisciplined children—that is on the whole. The children from the slums of San Francisco who used to be at the [Stanford] convalescent home could hold a candle to these. But they are cute at the mischief and one at least I'm sure has an unusual mind. He's never been to school before, but learns just as fast as I can teach him—knows more now than some who've been going a year. That's not much though, I'm afraid.

Frances described some of the Newfoundland sights: "the most gorgeous northern lights, moonlight and phosphorous water, the beautiful sled dogs roaming the town." Incidentally, these dogs zeroed out the town's cow and goat population. She remarked on how warm the weather was, so warm that she went swimming—one of her favorite sports—off a sandy beach. It was also an alternate way of bathing. In subsequent letters she reported swimming many times until the fishermen spotted a dogfish, a small shark, in the bay and wouldn't let her swim until it was gone.

Frances observed that "everybody's time in the village is different, some by as much as an hour." That of course was a throwback to local time keeping, the way time was kept before the advent of railroads in the nineteenth century with their Standard Time Zones. Because there were no trains and few roads

---

mutually exclusive, she may have been stuck with the communal privy and bathtub.

in Labrador—even today—there was no need for such zones. So these people continued to keep their own local time even when they traveled away from home.

Then Frances reported a death in the family:

> Thursday Aunt Emily died and I spent most of my time out of school down there doing what I could. Every night they have had a wake—everybody in black down in their kitchen parlor just sitting or singing hymns in the most ear-splitting tone. And some of the hymns they pick! "Rejoice, rejoice again, Jesus is King," being the oft repeated refrain of one of them.
>
> Friday I helped her two grand daughters whom I have in school make a wreath of hemlock and wild sweet peas. That was fine until the mother of one of them asked me [for] a verse to put on it. That nearly finished me—like being called in a week ago Saturday night, half the women of the town looking on, to make a mustard plaster and I'd never even seen one. Both got done somehow. I'm glad not more than a fourth of the grown-ups can read.

Frances' last letter was undated but was probably written around August 20, 1926. She planned to leave near the end of August for New York via St. John's and Halifax if possible, and then directly to Vassar. She finished with the following summary.

> Summer hasn't seemed a bit long. Don't think I have accomplished much but have thoroughly enjoyed it and it has agreed with me. Everybody tells me I've gotten fat and I have gained seven pounds.

That ended Frances' first out-of-country tour. She was destined to have ten more with the Foreign Service starting in 1928, spanning thirty-seven years.

3

FOREIGN SERVICE SCHOOL

The Application

FRANCES took the advice of E. D. Fite, Chairman of Vassar's Political Science Department, and applied to the Foreign Service in November, 1926. That required sending an application to the U.S. Foreign Service, along with five letters of recommendation, birth certificate and photo to the State Department's Board of Examiners.

As might be expected in 1926, the application was totally male-dominated. For example, nowhere did it ask for the applicant's sex. Line 5 asked, "If married, give names of wife and children," and then two more questions about wife. Then Line 10 asked for the name and permanent address of father. Frances just put Gilbert Willis, with no address. She listed "Reading, writing and speaking knowledge of French (all my work at University of Brussels—including the oral examination in French.) Reading knowledge of German." [12]

She was notified by return mail that she qualified for the next step: a written examination, scheduled for January 10 and 11, 1927, given in thirteen locations throughout the U.S.—her choice. Frances chose New York City, which was closest to Vassar.

The five letters of recommendation are filed in her Foreign Service dossier; the first is from her Uncle George James, a man of imposing stature and status.

---

[12] That German assertion, while true, would return to bite her during the oral exams.

George Roosa James, circa 1920.

George Roosa James, 1866-1937, had a rather illustrious career, starting in Memphis, Tennessee. In 1889 he was appointed president of the James and Graham Wagon Company. In 1892 he was elected to the Memphis City Council. In 1910 he became president of the State National Bank and in 1915, president of the William R. Moore Dry Goods Company, all in Memphis. He was then appointed to the War Industries Board in Washington DC during WW I and subsequently to the Federal Reserve Board in 1923, serving through much of the Great Depression. When he retired in 1936 a press article called him "crotchety but wise."

George was a good friend of Bernard Baruch, Chairman of the War Industries Board. Both were 6' 4" Southerners. Incidentally, Bernie kept a mistress between 1932 and 1935, Clare Boothe, but then dumped her when she besotted Henry Luce, saying, "The eagle never shares his mate with another." Courtesan Clare joins Frances in a later chapter. Another member of the War Industries Board was John Foster Dulles, who as Secretary of State would recommend Frances for appointment as Ambassador to Switzerland in 1953 and then Norway in 1957.

Neither George nor his sister Belle went to college; in fact George left school at the age of fourteen! While that is a surprise by today's standards, it wasn't one-hundred years ago. For example, a September 3, 2003, *Wall Street Journal* article by Cynthia Crossen on nineteenth century schools in America reported that in 1900 less than ten percent of 14-17 year-olds attended high school and of those, only about ten percent attended college. So roughly one percent of these youngsters went to college in 1900. This was simply a manifestation of the prevailing attitude that formal schooling was needed to teach the child to read and write, making them literate. Then education was switched to on-the-job training, which was considered more valuable than book-learning for most people in those days.

Because George was a member of the Federal Reserve Board, he wasn't about to communicate with some lowly Chairman of the Foreign Service Board of Examiners; his letter—with Federal Reserve Board letterhead—went right to the top: The Hon. Frank B. Kellogg, Secretary of State. He identified Frances as his niece, summarized her qualifications and finished with,

It is a pleasure to me to assure you that the young woman is eminently qualified for such work [and that] her record as a member of the faculty of Vassar College bears me out in this opinion.

The other four letters are from West and Cottrell, Stanford Professors of Political Science, Kirkwood, Dean of Stanford's Law School, and E. D. Fite, himself. All are effusive in their praise of Frances. For example, from Fite and then from West:

She has the best of education, has had a most distinguished record as a teacher in Vassar College in the department of Political Science, and she has personal qualities of the very first rank.

There can be no possible doubt about her character and integrity; her standing as a member of the Stanford community is the highest. Her ability is amply evidenced by the scholastic distinctions achieved by her. If I have a just conception of the kind of person wanted in our foreign service Miss Willis fully meets it.

The Examination(s)

Frances took the written Foreign Service examinations in New York City starting on January 10, 1927. A record of the 1927 exams is not available, but The Department of State's 1931 edition of *The American Foreign Service* published a sample of exam topics and questions, and although they may have been slightly different from the 1927 set, shows how formidable they were:

> The written examinations will consist of general examinations in American history, government, and institutions, history of Europe, Latin America, and the Far East since 1776, elementary economics, including the natural, industrial and commercial resources of the United States, political and commercial geography, elements of international, commercial, and maritime law, and arithmetic, and of special examinations in law, economics, history, and modern languages.

These examinations lasted three days at five to six hours each day. The general examinations required true-false, multiple choice or single-sentence answers. The special examinations were essay-type. Here are sample questions.

> A rectangular tank, with vertical sides, measures 4 ft. x 2 ft. 6 in. x 2 ft. 6 in. internally. Find to the nearest second, how long it will take to fill the tank from a tap delivering 3 3/4 gallons a minute. (1 gallon = 231 cu. in.)

> The Reform Bill of 1832 was passed by the Tories in the endeavor to win the support of the middle class.
> T__ F__

> Contrast the problems involved in maintaining an adequate water supply for the cities of New York and Chicago.
> 30 minutes

> Give a brief history of the trade balance of the United States since 1850. Account for the changes noted.
> 30 minutes

Despite their popularity today it is apparent that the sound doctrines of Hamilton did not command the approval of the American people during the period 1800-1860. How do you account for this short-sightedness? 1 hour

Write in French, Spanish, or German, a letter of approximately 200 words in length, describing in as much detail as space will permit, the events of one day of travel on some journey which you have recently taken.

Then on January 21, 1927, the State Department sent Frances a letter informing her that one of the candidates was caught cheating with an advance copy of the examination. Thus all the exams on those dates were annulled, and she would have to take it over again; sorry about that.

She took the second set of exams starting on February 28, 1927, again in New York City. Frances reported in a January 8, 1974 *Riverside Daily Press* interview that:

> The head of the department [Fite] took over my classes [twice] so I could take the exams. He agreed that it would not be in the best interest of the faculty or myself if it became general knowledge that I was doing any such thing—especially if I failed.

On April 16, 1927, Frances was notified that she had passed the written exam with an average score of 81.94, where passing was an 80, and that the oral examinations would be held in Washington, "beginning May 18, 1927, and to inform the Department promptly whether or not you will present yourself."

The score sheet was also attached to that letter and showed that Frances aced Arithmetic, Political Economy and Modern History; did well on Political Geography and American History; but stumbled on International Law, U.S. Commerce and Modern Languages. How could this be, because she was fluent in French? Well, maybe she didn't give herself a choice, which will be covered shortly.

Even more surprising was the examiner's own arithmetic: Frances' score sheet showed a 78 for U.S. Commerce, which with a weight of 4 was the most important topic, yielding a weighted score of 4 x 78 = 312. Except that the weighted score was recorded as 316. So if the correct score were used, Frances' average would have dropped to 81.73, fortunately still above the passing threshold. Because no one caught the error Frances proceeded with an 81.94 average score.

Frances then wrote a letter to the Board informing them that she would indeed present herself, and asking exactly when the orals will take place; how long they will last; how soon the results will be known; and how soon after that would one receive an appointment? Answers came back in an April 21, 1927, Department letter filed in Frances' dossier:

> About the first of May you will be notified of the exact date on which you are to appear for your oral and physical examinations...
>
> It is expected that the final results will be announced early in June, when the names of the successful candidates will be placed on the list of those eligible for appointment as Foreign Service Officers. It is not possible, however, for the Department to forecast when a successful candidate might receive an appointment, nor can it give any definite assurance that an appointment will be received during the two-year period of eligibility.
>
> I am, Madam,
>
> Your obedient servant,
For the Secretary of State:
/s/ T. J. Norton
Member, Executive Committee,
Foreign Service Personnel Board

To paraphrase and extrapolate, "If you pass all our examinations we will place your name on a list and then let you know when an FSO appointment *might open up* in the next two years. So please, successful applicant, stand by; never mind how that disrupts your plans or job continuity." Fortunately, her boss, E. D. Fite, was responsible for this situation, so he had to be accommodating.

Frances annotated the letter and sent it to Belle with the following note at the top:

> Read this and tell me what I'm going to do next winter.

Then along side "About the first of May," she wrote, "I thought that was settled once, but the D.O.S. seems to me like the sovereign." She underlined two-year period twice. And in a complete pique of frustration, she crossed out the Department of State letterhead and wrote in "Dictatorship of Laughter," adding the following comment to the closing, "Your obedient servant,"

—LIKE HELL—

That is one of the few times Frances became so upset she used profanity. But Frances will exact exquisite retribution during her Foreign Service School play, which appears in the next chapter. Remember the name, "Foreign Service Personnel Board."

Next to arrive was this undated memorandum from the Department directing

Candidate Number 996 to report to Room 201, Department of State, at 11:30 o'clock on May 18 for his oral examination, and at the Naval Dispensary, Wing 9 New Navy Building, Foot of 17th Street, N.W., at 9 o'clock on May 19 for his physical examination. N.B. Immediately after the oral examination each candidate will report at Room 102, Department of State, for his oral language examination. No change can be made in this schedule.

Note the male gender orientation three times. Incidentally, the "New Navy Building" was a truly ugly structure erected right on The Mall between the Washington Monument and Tidal Basin during WW I as an emergency measure. It and similar structures were supposed to be temporary but stayed there another fifty years before migrating across the river to Crystal City, Virginia.

Frances reported that the Naval Dispensary was an all-male operation. So for her exam the government surgeons cordoned off a wing of the facility and posted guards at the doors. Frances reported that she escaped unscathed, except that she had to go back again in June for the vision retest, this time with a new—maybe even a first—pair of glasses. That made two trips to New York and two trips to Washington D.C. for all these exams.

According to Calkin's *Women in the Department of State,* the oral test amounted to a fifteen-minute interview in 1925. It was then expanded to a full day in 1927, according to Frances in a 1932 Swedish press interview. And it counted for half the total score, while the written test and oral language test counted for a quarter each. Calkin listed twenty-two questions used in the 1924-1925 oral test. Typical questions are:

1. Do you think Germany ought to be required to pay the entire cost of the war incurred by the Allied Nations? Why?
2. What do you consider to be the reason for the present high cost of living?
3. Is there any difference between Bolshevism and socialism and if so in what respect?
4. What, in your judgment, will be the effect of aerial navigation upon other modes of transportation?
5. How can disarmament of nations best be brought about?
6. Discuss the advantages and disadvantages of cold storage from an economic point of view.
7. What has been the effect of the tendency of capital to seek employment abroad upon the standardization of commercial and industrial process of the world?
8. What do you understand to be the "Shantung Question"?
9. Has the steel industry in the United States any reason to apprehend disadvantageous competition from similar industries in Japan or China or both? Give your reasons.

These were preceded by sixteen basic questions, including, "Where were you born? Are you married? Have you ever been married? If you should be appointed, to what country would you prefer to be assigned? Give the reasons for your preference." One critical question that wasn't on Calkin's 1925 list—probably because only two women had ever made it past the oral gate by then—was flagged by Ann Miller Morin in her book, *Her Excellency, An Oral History of American Women Ambassadors,* 1995: "Do you expect to marry someday?" Ann reported that question was asked well into the 1960's and an affirmative answer could fail a woman![13]

---

[13] Ann Morin started work on her book around 1984. Frances' interview wasn't included because she had died in 1983. She is mentioned throughout the book, using recollections of succeeding women ambassadors and also Frances' first cousins once-removed, Margot (Child) Pomeroy and Marion (Child) Sanger. All this occurred before the author began work on this book.

All of this terror was captured in the following sketch from a small book, *The Road to Success, or The Career of a Diplomat*, by M. C. Perts, published in Germany, 1924. The book was number 168 of 200 copies, signed by the author and stored in Frances' effects.

"The Oral Examination" from M. C. Perts' 1924 book.

The question about which country the candidate prefers is particularly important, because it will emerge in a slightly altered form as part of Frances' retribution during the Foreign Service School play.

Ann Morin reported Constance Harvey's recollections of her 1930 oral tests:

You had to know one [language], and you had to take a written as well as an oral. Then you were given oral exams in the others.
I didn't do very wonderfully on the written, but I got through it. I did very well on the oral. I remember sitting with a couple of people in the outer room waiting to be called in. There were five examiners [just as in the sketch]. The young man who was sitting next to me said something marvelous just before the door opened and I was beckoned in. He said, "Miss Harvey, walk in very slowly." And I did. I just sort of strolled into the room and sat down. I heard later that the next man that had gone in to take the exam had fallen over the rug—flat down on his face. And

they flunked him! So I was very grateful to my neighbor for his good advice.

Those five men were sitting with their backs to the light. I think it was sort of towards sunset, so I couldn't see their faces very well. I don't remember many of the questions they asked me, but one was—and this was in 1930—"What do you think, Miss Harvey, about the advisability of the United States recognizing Russia?" I remember I answered, "Well, I know that you gentlemen have a lot more information than I have." They looked with real pussycat grins across their faces at that. "I believe that we should. We should be very careful that there is a complete understanding that they do not try to impose their system on us." Well, they gave me a pretty good rank.

Then I took orals in languages, and a young FSO gave me my exam in oral German. Imagine! I remember he said to me in German, "Speak a little German." So I said back to him in German, "What do you want me to say?'" And he laughed and gave me 100! I did not take an exam in Spanish. I'd gone to Spanish summer school at Cornell, and I'd carefully concealed the fact I knew any Spanish. I did not want to go in that direction.

So that's probably why Frances didn't do so well on her oral language test: She listed all the languages she could on her Foreign Service application, including German, thinking the more the better. Then the examiner likely selected German for a second oral, which she could read a little but not speak.

The next entry in Frances' dossier is a June 2, 1927, letter from Board Chairman Joseph C. Grew notifying Frances that she "passed the written and oral tests with a rating of 80.95 percent." And again, they had made a calculation error, so that the final rating should have been 80.68, over a quarter-point lower! But because these errors favored Frances, they couldn't have been prompted by gender bias. They were simple calculation errors, suggesting that diplomacy and mathematics are mutually exclusively professions. In any case, all scores were above the passing threshold of 80—just barely, which in turn will severely disrupt Frances' life for the next four months.

The Wait

By June 26, 1927, Frances had not heard from the State Department, and was concerned about her teaching commitments at Vassar that fall. So she queried Mr. E. A. Shreve at Personnel Bureau about her status:

> May I trouble you to let me know if the report about my eye test came through from the naval dispensary and whether or not my name is now on the list as eligible for appointment as a Foreign Service Officer without any reservation?
>
> I should also appreciate any further information about the possibility or probability of an appointment, if any can be given at this time, as I should like to make plans for next winter as soon as possible.

Back came the reply on July 2:

> My dear Miss Willis:
>
> I have received your letter of June 28, and in reply I take pleasure in saying that under date of June 18 the Naval Dispensary reported that after a reexamination in regard to your vision you were found to be physically qualified for the Foreign Service. Your name, therefore, appears without condition on the list of those eligible for appointment as Foreign Service Officers.
>
> I am unable, however, to give you any information as to when you may expect to receive an appointment, as I do not know how many appointments will be made before the beginning of the next session of the Foreign Service School.
>
> Very sincerely yours,
> /s/ *Edgar A Shreve*

Now Frances had both her feet stuck to the *Tar-Baby* and was no closer to resolving her Vassar winter commitments than before. So she waited.[14]

By August 16, 1927, the clock was ticking away and she had heard nothing.

---

[14] Uncle Remus' 1881 Tar-Baby was a doll made of tar and turpentine. Br'er Fox used it to entrap Br'er Rabbit. The more that Br'er Rabbit fought the Tar-Baby, the more stuck he became. The author often heard that story from his grandmother Belle.

So she decided to take a page out of her Uncle George's book—in fact, Uncle George likely suggested it to her—and go right to the top with a letter, this time a typed letter, to the Secretary himself, The Honorable Frank B. Kellogg. The letter was most respectful, with phrases like "May I ask," and "I do not wish to appear to press the matter, but" how about a solid answer? And if not that, what else do you have to offer?

That prompted the following reply from the Assistant Secretary of State, Nelson T. Johnson, on September 2:

> While the Department is unable to give you any definite informa-tion at the moment, you are informed confidentially that it appears quite probable that your name on the eligible list will be reached in the very near future. As soon as possible the Department will advise you definitely regarding this.

The letter was sent to Frances in Redlands, so she must have made the deci-sion to stick it out and not start the new Vassar school year in New York. And then more silence from the Department.

Then on September 17, 1927, *The Woman Citizen* magazine inserted itself into the act, with this telegram to the State Department:[15]

> HAS MISS FRANCES E. WILLIS WHO SUCCESSFULLY PASSED RECENT DIPLOMATIC EXAMINATIONS BEEN ASSIGNED POST? PLEASE WIRE ANSWER COLLECT TO WOMAN CITIZEN, 1712 MADISON AVENUE, NEW YORK CITY

And penciled in at the bottom of this telegram was the following:

> *Ans'd Sep 19 / 27.*
> *Miss Frances E. Willis commissioned Foreign Service Officer-unclassified, and directed to report for For. Ser. School requisite training of new appoin-tees before being assigned to field.*

---

[15] In 1870 the American Woman Suffrage Association founded a magazine, *Women's Journal*, edited by Lucy Stone. It was published for forty-seven years before being replaced by *The Woman Citizen* magazine in 1917.

That was followed by this telegram:

SEPT 20, 1927
MISS FRANCES E WILLIS
12 EAST CYPRESS AVE, REDLANDS, CALIF
YOU HAVE BEEN APPOINTED FOREIGN SERVICE OFFICER
-UNCLASSIFIED INSTRUCTION FOLLOWS
                              WILBUR J CARR
                              ACTING SECY OF STATE[16]

So there it was: about four months of constant prodding to find out her status, with a final poke from *The Woman Citizen*. It's not clear how they got involved. It was probably initiated by her big sister Caroline, who was a member of the woman's suffrage movement at the time and certainly familiar with *The Woman Citizen*. The telegram was preceded by a formal appointment letter, which arrived after the telegram:

                                                        Sept 17, 1927

Madam:
    The Department takes pleasure in informing you that you have been appointed a Foreign Service Officer-unclassified, with compensation at the rate of $2500 per annum beginning on September 29, 1927. You are further informed that, in compliance with the Executive Order of June 7, 1924, a Foreign Service School for the instruction of new appointees has been established in the Department of State. The term of instruction in the Foreign Service School is considered a period of probation during which the new appointees are to be judged as to their qualifications for advancement and assignment to duty. While the probationary period is one year, the Foreign Service Officers found qualified may be assigned to duty for further training in the field before the expiration of that time.
    The fourth term of the Foreign Service School will commence September 29, 1927, at 9:00 A.M., and you are instructed to report for duty on that date at the Department in Room 100.
    You are requested to advise the Department as soon as possible

---

[16] Wilbur Carr and Nelson Johnson appear in a subsequent photo.

whether or not you accept appointment and will be able to report for duty on September 29. An early reply is particularly necessary for the reason that the number of vacancies is limited, and if for any cause you should find it impracticable to report by September 29, the Department would desire to fill the vacancy from the eligible list.

I am, Sir, your obedient servant,

For the Secretary of State:

/s/ Unintelligible

Note that the appointment letter started off with Madam and ended with Sir. But at least the Department was trying to accommodate this new gender problem. M. C. Perts captured the moment:

"The Arrival of the Commission" from M. C. Perts' 1924 book.

As a result, Frances had just eight days to get herself from Redlands to Washington DC. But even more surprising is that the official biographies from her dossier show August, 1927, as her appointment—a month before the State Department's telegram and letter were dated.

It appears that Frances got one of the last appointments—if not the last appointment—to the Foreign Service and its school. Certainly pressure from *The Woman Citizen* didn't hurt her cause. In any case, the Department decided to shoehorn her in at the last moment and then backdate the commission. What a way to start a thirty-seven-year career!

Frances reported in a 1968 letter to the Department that twenty-six students were accepted to her Foreign Service School class. And Calkin reported in his book, *Women in the Department of State,* a total of forty people were offered appointments to the Foreign Service in 1927. So up to fourteen men must have refused appointment, or otherwise dropped out along the way, before they got to Frances, which explains most of her appointment delay. Furthermore, Calkin reported that of those forty, three men failed the orals but received appointments anyway—probably ahead of Frances. The rational for those actions is lost in the Foreign Service ether.

Now to revisit Frances' true exam score: 80.68. Would that have been enough to drop her below the threshold of forty offers, thus slamming the door on the current class? And speaking about school slots, why were there 26 rather than a more typical 25 slots? Neither the State Department's Office of the Historian nor the National Archives and Records Administration could identify a Department policy or rationale for this unusual number. Nor could the 1961 book by Barnes and Morgan, *Foreign Service of the U.S., Origins, Development and Functions.* Possibly that *Woman Citizen's* telegram was responsible for the extra one. In any case, there was no slack left in the appointment queue, even with her official score.

Incidentally, both Lucile Atcherson and Pattie Field, the first and second women admitted to the Foreign Service, scored much higher on these examinations than Frances did. Lucille attributed her success to attending the Crawford Foreign Service Cram School before taking the examinations. Constance Harvey also attended, and Pattie probably did too, whereas Frances walked in cold. So Frances either didn't know about the school or found that it conflicted with her teaching duties at Vassar and didn't attend.

After Frances arrived in Washington DC, the Department's Comptroller General (CG) took issue with her Redlands-to-Washington DC travel expense report. He deducted a total of $11.50 from her claim: a $0.75 error in addition, a $0.75 disallowance for an excessive porter tip, and a massive $10 because he determined that Frances didn't take the most economical train to Washington DC—that the one leaving two days earlier was cheaper.

Frances immediately sent the U.S. Treasury a check for $1.50, which must have been embarrassing considering her score in arithmetic, but was incensed over the fare disallowance. She wrote a rebuttal showing that she was notified on a Saturday when the banks were closed. Thus she couldn't draw the necessary funds from her own account to buy the ticket until Monday. By that time it was too late for the earlier train, and she had to take the one she did—or be late arriving for school. After two more rounds of letters, the CG relented and allowed the extra $10 charge.

This was Frances' first encounter with the omnipotent Comptroller General. She will have many more during her career, including a gleeful—only because it was imaginary—encounter on precisely the same subject in the Foreign Service School play.

The School—and Beginning of Gender Bias

Frances attended the Foreign Service School in Washington DC from October, 1927, to March, 1928. A Record of Work at the school, filed in her dossier, consisted of grades and comments by the instructor in each subject, including Passport, Visa, A-C/C (relating to commerce), Accounts, Index, Shipping and Seamen, Notarials (notary public work), and Invoices—topics certain to excite a back-office clerk. Both qualitative and quantitative grades were posted.

She was rated qualitatively on mental keenness, practical judgment, effectiveness and general attitude and quantitatively by a written exam in each subject. Her average qualitative score was 88.84, with a fairly tight standard deviation. Her high score was a 94 for general attitude in Invoices, and her low score was a pair of 86's in Accounts and Indexes. She ranked fourteenth in the class of 26: 25 men and Frances.

Her average quantitative score was 90.88, with a high of 96 in Invoices and a low of 84 in Passports, yielding a ninth rank in class—which exposed a qualitative gender bias in the grading system. Her general rating was 89.86 for an eleventh rank—with all averages calculated correctly this time.

The instructors' comments were generally favorable, except for their aversion to having a woman in their midst. For example, this from her Visa instructor, who gave her a 90.25:

Miss Willis has unusual intellectual qualities, grasping quickly both fundamentals and details. She is sensitive to the legal aspects of a case and has an excellent memory, although she cannot always be depended upon to maintain a uniform standard of excellence in arriving at her final conclusions, through a tendency to be unduly influenced by an inflexible, though often keen, logic.

This from the Passport instructor who gave her an 88—while exposing his gender bias:

Miss Willis showed excellent judgment and other qualities, which in a man would have called for a high rating.

Then this from her A-C/C instructor, who gave her an 87:

Should make a good officer if a place adapted to a woman can be found. Consul General Skinner while at Paris suggested the great field in commercial work in that office which was open to a woman of judgment and common sense in investigation and reporting on articles for woman's wear. His suggestion is worthy of consideration.

Consul General Skinner appears in the next chapter. Finally this from Chief Instructor Dawson:

Miss Willis is a young woman of considerable poise, determination and force. She has a very keen mind and her educational and intellectual qualifications are well above the average. Personally, she is very attractive and has much charm. While distinctly feminine, she seems able to work and associate with men on terms of complete equality. Qualified for diplomatic work within the limitations of her sex.

So this is where it started: the first "limitations of her sex" comment in her dossier. But that's probably the best she could expect from trying to break into the WASP-male bastion in 1927. Now Frances was a WASP—White-Anglo-Saxon-Protestant—herself, which was certainly a good start. Her chances would have been greatly diminished otherwise.

These instructor comments provide a deeper insight into the Department's attitude towards women: They range from a critical-but-fair evaluation to an institutional gender bias to a perverse gender bias. The Visa instructor's "inflexible though often keen logic" comment is critical-but-fair. The Chief Instructor's "limitations of her sex" comment represents a widely held, institutional gender bias that, when used indiscriminately, can delay a career. But the Passport and A/CC instructor's comments about assigning lower ratings and trivial jobs to women—simply because they are women—flag perverse gender biases that are usually designed to terminate a career. A particularly nasty perverse bias was detailed in the first chapter.

Institutional gender bias was implanted into most male members of the State Department and Foreign Service up through the early twentieth century, because the male-only service had always been—and should always stay—that way. It is described in The Other Woman chapter, and when taken to the extreme resulted in the "keep 'em out" tactic. And if they couldn't do that, they would "ease 'em out" at first opportunity, which characterizes the perverse gender bias.

Institutional gender bias can manifest itself in ways beyond formal evaluations. One version occurred when Frances would report to a new post and be greeted with both concern and skepticism: Can she do a man's work as well as an FSO's work? That extra requirement is characterized as an arrival gender bias, forcing her to start at "square zero," rather than "square one," where most men would start. It was also laid on her whenever a new boss would arrive. Frances was aware of this type of bias and reported it in her bulletins during the first part of her career. With dedicated, hard work on her part, she could usually—but not always—banish it in a month or two, which was her first step in cleaving this Old Guard, overseas group.

Another version was invented when Frances reached flag rank and was designed to keep her out of harm's way: She must not be assigned to posts where her life could be endangered, which reflected the prevailing national view that women—excepting nurses—were not allowed in combat zones. That is characterized as a protective gender bias. Frances would encounter this full range of gender biases throughout her career, and because she only reported the arrival one, she was likely unaware of the others. Here is the graduation photo.

The graduates are standing on the front steps of the old State Department building, behind seven members of the Personnel Board in the front row, including Wilbur J. Carr, recently appointed Chairman of the Personnel Board, front row center, Assistant Secretary William R. Castle, Jr. on his right and Assistant Secretary Nelson Johnson on his left. Seven school instructors are standing in the back row. Frances is conspicuous in the center of the second row.

Remember Wilbur J. Carr because the class will tease him unmercifully in their school play.

Graduates of the 1928 Foreign Service School
(courtesy Department of State.)

One of Frances' classmates was Paul Daniels. Paul was the first in this class to make ambassador. He also had a special interest in Frances—according to Findley Burns in a May 13, 2003, phone conversation with the author. Findley, a young FSO in Madrid during WW II, was mentored by Frances and subsequently became good friends with her. He said that Frances told him Paul filled out his post preference request after graduating from the Foreign Service School: "Where ever Frances Willis is posted." Not only that, but Frances said that Paul proposed marriage to her!

Even if that is hearsay, it makes a fine tale. Now Frances probably told her mother Belle and big sister Caroline about it—apparently girls do that sort of thing. And that tale coupled with her subsequent encounter with another young FSO, John Cabot in Peru provided grist for an old family story, "Safety in Numbers:"

Because the Department's Old Guard was not happy about women trespassing on their territory back in the 1920's, they assigned them to the most dangerous outpost in the world, preferably one that had a revolution or war going on. Then they assigned the most eligible Foreign Service bachelor to the same outpost, in hopes that the woman in her terror would be thrown into the bachelor's arms, fall instantly in love with him, marry, and become the perfect Foreign Service wife. Apparently, that's what happened to the first woman. So, if it worked once...[17]

Chile was sort of at war with Peru over the Tacna-Arica land dispute at the time and so Frances was sent there. Well, that was sufficiently frightening to Frances' mother, Belle, that she immediately ordered Frances' older sister Caroline to accompany Frances to Chile, in the misguided hope that there was safety in numbers: One would protect the other.

Fortunately, little physical protection was needed, so both survived. But the outcome was hardly as expected for either Belle or the Foreign Service. First, Caroline-the-Protector met, fell in love with and married an Englishman, Fredrick V. Vaughan. They then stayed in Chile for the next forty years, raising both their children, Vivian and Frances, there. So Belle lost both daughters and two granddaughters in one shot, so to speak.

Second, the Foreign Service failed in its mission of marrying off Frances: She did indeed meet the eligible bachelor and remained good friends with him the rest of her career, but apparently the attraction never clicked—much to the Old Guard's and the family's chagrin. You see, he was John Cabot, a Boston Brahmin. (Recall the old ditty: Boston, home of the bean and the cod, where the Lowells talk only to Cabots,

---

[17] That was embellishment #1 to the story, since while the first woman, Lucile Atcherson, did fall in love with and then marry an American bachelor she met at her first post in Bern, Switzerland, he was doing post-doctoral medical research at a university and was not in the Foreign Service. And Bern was hardly a dangerous outpost. Details are in The Other Women chapter.

and the Cabots talk only to God.) The law of unintended consequences continues to reign.[18]

To connect the dots: smitten FSO suitor (Paul Daniels), dangerous outpost, (Chile) near-on-site FSO bachelor (John Cabot), falling in love, concluding in the perfect Foreign Service wife; it is not difficult to see how the story evolved with John subbing for Paul.

Findley Burns also reported that Frances put on her post preference request: "Wherever the British Navy is." What a flip bunch of graduates they were; nothing was sacred, which will be confirmed in the school play. By the way, Paul is probably the tall one standing behind and to the right of Frances, because someone that tall should normally have been assigned to the back row.

---

[18] And that was embellishment #2, since John Cabot was stationed in Peru, not Chile, at the time. But they did meet and socialize when Frances and Caroline's ship stopped at Lima on the way to Valparaiso, and possibly again over the Peru/Chile Tacna-Arica dispute, all of which Frances likely reported to the family in her (now lost) letters. So this embellishment could have been "almost true." Incidentally, Frances will join John again in Finland when she is appointed his deputy chief of mission.

4

THE SCHOOL PLAY

O N March 6, 1928, the graduating class of the Foreign Service School performed the play titled "HOW MUCH DID YOU PAY FOR YOUR JOB? An Obsolete Mystery Play" at the Wardman Park Theater in Washington DC. The theater, apparently part of the old Wardman Park Hotel, is long gone and there is no record of this play in public archives, including book or play indexes, the Library of Congress or on-line sources.

A copy of the play's manuscript was buried in Frances' effects in the Hoover Archives. The playbill and accompanying list of cast members later turned up in the Redlands Smiley Library, with Frances playing *Miss Phyllis* and then *Consul Phyllis*. A 1927 *New York Times* article shows that nineteen of the twenty six students in the graduating class were cast members. The manuscript is typical play-length, lasting the better part of two hours. It was typed in final form but had been annotated with changes and comments in pencil, which usually occurs during rehearsal.

The State Department's Office of the Historian was not aware of the play and reported that it was highly unlikely such plays were still being performed. Subsequently, Mr. Evan Dawley of that Office requested a copy of the play for possible use in his training of new FSO's at the renamed Foreign Service Institute, "focusing on diplomatic history and the history of the Department and Foreign Service."

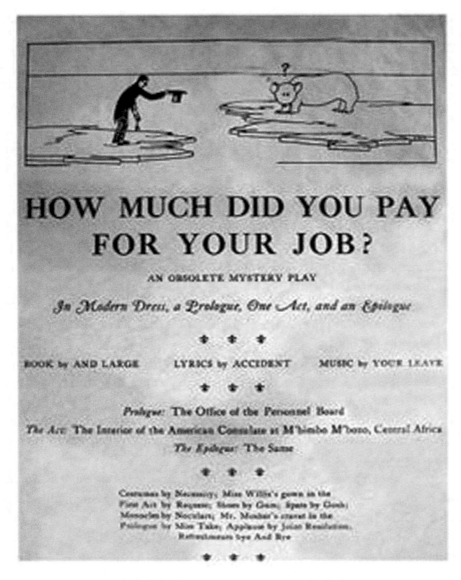

Playbill for the 1928 Foreign Service School play
(courtesy Department of State.)

The manuscript's credit page shows that the play was based on a book by Mosher and Browne, with lyrics by Browne and piano music by Abbey, but with no first names attached. And the score has yet to appear. The identity of these people is researched at the end of the chapter.

The audience was likely the school faculty, friends and relatives, and maybe a few members from the State Department. The plot is simply to spoof the State Department in the Prologue and then the Foreign Service in the Act. Here are roughly half the passages from the play, focusing on Frances' part. Annotations by the author are in brackets. The full manuscript continues to reside at the Hoover Archives.

PROLOGUE

(The scene is the Office of the Personnel Board. As the curtain rises it discloses a room devoid of decoration or furniture except for one framed picture and a long table with five chairs behind it. The picture is a framed portrait of Silver J. Barr, and it hangs in the center of the rear wall. A group of small American flags are draped about it, their shafts meeting behind it. Three of the chairs are behind the table and face the audience, with the other two at the ends of the table.)

[The Department of State's Office of the Historian has no record of a Silver J. Barr. But they recalled that Wilbur J. Carr was an assistant secretary at that time. Carr was an Old Guard FSO: former Director of the Consular Service, current Assistant Secretary and Budget Officer, a major force behind the Rogers Act and current Chairman of the Personnel Board, as the last photo in the previous chapter shows.

[At this time the U.S. was considering going off the gold standard and leaving it on the silver standard, which in turn would seriously reduce the disposable income of overseas FSO's (Constance Harvey's field dogs.) So Silver J. Barr is likely a play on Wilbur J. Carr's name, as a not-so-subtle reminder of these ugly consequences. Then the U.S. went off the gold standard in 1933, and all the field dogs did take a large hit to their disposable income, as Frances will report in the Sweden chapter.]

(A pompous clerk is standing in an attitude of rigid attention side the door of the room, which is situated down left in the wings. Enter Mr. Colds.)

CLERK   (Bowing, and with a flourish of his hand toward the table.)
               Good day, Mr. Colds.

COLDS   Good day to you, my boy. (He goes to the middle seat and sits down.)

CLERK   Good morning, Mr. Barr. (Bows and flourishes.)

BARR   (Entering.) Good morning, Sir, good morning. (To Colds, as he takes his seat at the latter's right hand.)—Good morning, Sir, good morning. I hope you are well?

CLERK   Greetings, Mr. Snorton. (Bows and flourishes.) You, too, are well?

SNORTON (Entering.) Oh, yes, indeed, thank you very much indeed. I have just had my walk around the circle with my Spanish grammar. I am well. (Sits in the chair on Cold's other hand.)

BARR   I didn't know your grandmother was Spanish, Mr. Snorton.

SNORTON I said grammar, Mr. Barr. I may add, for self-protection, that, although it is a Spanish grammar, it was printed in the United States. So, you see, there is no danger of my becoming interested in the Spanish-speaking countries through study.

COLDS   I rejoice with you. I, too, am fond of American libraries.

CLERK   How do you do, Mr. Wrastle. (Bows and flourishes.)

WRASTLE (Entering.) Good morning, dear old fellow. Charming morning, isn't it? (Walks blithely to chair at end of table nearest the door.) Good morning to you all, my dear old fellows. How well you all look! (Flings himself gracefully into chair.)

BARR   Shall we proceed to business? As usual, Mr. Wrastle you are just on time. That makes Mr. Jawson late, also as usual. We really must proceed.

WRASTLE   Good fellow, Jawson, but unpunctual. When I was dean at Harvard we used to put people like that on probation. Tell you what! —let's put Jawson on probation! Ho-ho!

COLDS   Where is the candidate? Let's get this over with—I have some work to do. Mr. Barr, where is the candidate?

WRASTLE   The candidate, who is charming, is outside. Shall I call the candidate?

COLDS   If Caligula could make consul out of a horse, there's no telling what this Personnel Board can do with a mere female.

ALL TOGETHER   CANDIDATE! CANDIDATE!!

[The last member, JAWSON, finally shows up and is harassed for being late.]

COLDS   But had we not better tell the world just who we are, before going any further?

ALL TOGETHER Right! (They rise, come forward, stand in a line in front of the table, and sing :)

> We know all about punctuality,
> We got lots of personality,
> Firmness, force, co-operation,
> Self-control, subordination—
> For we are the Personnel Board!
> We are tactful, calm, and circumspect,
> We got common sense and intellect,
> Culture, knowledge, education,
> Breadth of view, sophistication—
> For we are the Personnel Board—we are!

We are the Personnel Board!

We got great command of languages,
Russian, Danish, Hebrew, Portuguese;
We speak English with intelligence,
Oriental style and elegance—
For we are the Personnel Board!
We know all the Regulations,
We got all the qualifications
For executive ability,
Moral courage and virility—
  For we are the Personnel Board—yes, we!
We are the Personnel Board!

We feel our responsibility;
We know our dependability,
Candor, fairness, and sincerity,
Accuracy, love of verity—
For we are the Personnel Board!
We are free from eccentricity,
We are lavished with felicity
And promoted with rapidity
For good morals and solidity—
  For we are the Personnel Board—are we!
We are the Personnel Board!

We are handsome, upright, generous,
Devoted to our duties onerous;
We got judgment and ambition,
Industry and erudition—
  For we are the Personnel Board!

We got truthfulness and honesty,
Social balance, poise and mannerism,
Snappy clothes and magnetism—
  For we are the Personnel Board—ah oui!

We are the Personnel Board!

(All return to their chairs and sit down.)

COLDS   Now, shall we call the candidate again, and get this over with? I have some work to do, you know.

BARR   Very well. Let us go, to use a vulgar expression.

ALL TOGETHER
    (With Barr acting in the manner of a cheer leader)—
    Candidate! CANDIDATE!! CANDIDATE!!!

PHYLLIS   (Entering quietly by the other door, which is in the wings down right.) Did you want to see me? (Everyone turns in his chair.)

COLDS   (Promptly.) What are the two capitals of Australia?

BARR   (Immediately, without giving her a chance to reply.) Name two thousand functionaries of the Comptroller General's Office.

SNORTON (Following suit.) How many Victrola records are required in the study of Spanish grandmother—I mean, grammar?

JAWSON   (On his heels.) Can you read and write? Are you fond of examinations? Do you realize your insignificance? Which places in the world do you dislike most? Please answer in writing, if any. Yesss, most decidedlay.

WRASTLE (After a short pause, during which she stares bewilderedly from one to the other.) Pardon a personal question, my dear young lady, but might one learn how young you are? And after that, would you delight us all with a reply to the question: "Do you prefer to be a clerk in the Diplomatic Service or Consul General to Chicago?"

[Here are questions, transmogrified straight from the oral examination.]

COLDS   (Pounding the table.) Order, order, I asked her first.

BARR   You did not. I asked her first.

COLDS   Do you mean to call me a liar?

SNORTON, WRASTLE, JAWSON
          Yes, do you mean to call him a liar?

BARR   I never specify charges. I do not choose to call him a liar.

PHYLLIS   Oh, for heaven's sake, shut up and get down to business!

JAWSON   Madam do you realize that we are the Personnel Board?

PHYLLIS   I begin to realize that I am the bored personnel. If talking
          is the important thing the entire Foreign Service should be
          composed of women.

[Frances probably had a hard time keeping a straight face when she recited
those lines.]

WRASTLE   Oh, no, that would never do, my dear young lady. Who would
          protect our brave sailors in foreign ports?

PHYLLIS   The women could do that just as well as the men—they
          could do it better. Just think of the advertising possibilities!
          "Your girl in every port now furnished by the Government!
          Enlist today!" Why the United States would have the largest
          merchant marine in the world in two months.

[These lines are prescient—with one small modification: Substituting the
British Navy for merchant marine identifies Frances' first choice in foreign posts.

Then starting in Stockholm, the U.S. Navy will become a quite satisfactory replacement for the Brits.]

BARR   It's a wonderful idea, but I fear the Comptroller General would never allow it. (Shaking his head.) He's such a <u>moral</u> man... yes, yes, nice—but moral.

COLDS   See here, are we conducting an examination, or a Congressional investigation? I have some work to do, you know.

JAWSON   Yesss, yesss—most decidedlay. To work, to work. Er, Miss Phyllis, what types of vaccination do you prefer? What was the output of jumping beans in the province of Chihuahua in the year 1896?

PHYLLIS   I can answer that last one. Four million, five hundred thou- sand, six hundred and seventy-eight—and four beans that couldn't tell which way to jump.

JAWSON   (Astonished) Why, why, how did you know?" (Very disap- pointedly.) I thought I was the only one who knew that. It was so long ago! Surely you weren't born in 1896?

PHYLLIS   While I was waiting this morning in Room 109 I read some of the magazines there. The rest was easy.

SNORTON It's my turn to ask questions. I haven't had a single chance. Miss Phyllis, do you like buttercups?

PHYLLIS   Yes. Is that the right answer?

SNORTON (Grudgingly.) Yes. I think you're just as mean as you can be. You're a big meany, that's what you are. I don't care.

COLDS   Do you like onions?

PHYLLIS   NO!

COLDS   (Triumphantly.) Ha, ha! I got you there! Now you can't be sent
            to any of the consulates in Italy!

PHYLLIS   I don't want to be sent to any of the consulates in Italy or
            anywhere else. I am interested only in the Diplomatic Service.

WRASTLE   But, my dear child, nowadays you have to be a good consul for
            years before you can get into the Diplomatic Service. In fact,
            you have to be a <u>very</u> good consul.

PHYLLIS   What happens to the bad consuls?

BARR   (Emphatically.) They become bad diplomats.

PHYLLIS   Oh, I see.

BARR   (Angrily.) No you don't! Nobody sees! It's an outrage, that's
            what it is!

JAWSON AND SNORTON
            Hear, hear!

WRASTLE   It is not an outrage. It's just as it should be.

BARR, SNORTON AND JAWSON
            It is NOT! It is NOT!

COLDS   Don't fight that all out again. Of course it's as it should be.
            How else could we have an efficient Diplomatic Service? I
            should think it was perfectly obvious. You must have diplo-
            mats with <u>some</u> training.

BARR   I don't see why they have to be the only ones with diplomatic
            immunity.

COLDS   It's the only way we can keep them out of jail.

[The Department of State's Office of the Historian suggested a book, *Mr.
Carr of State* by Katherine Crane, 1960, to help resolve the Carr/Barr riddle.
And indeed Crane provided much needed background. She also described
the continuing schism between the Consular and the Diplomatic Services—
integrated only by law via the Rogers Act. In truth, social integration lagged
considerably behind professional integration. Crane observed that diplomats
were usually financially independent via old money, whereas consuls were usually
dependent on their meager salaries. That in itself created a strain in the new
service. Add to that Crane's following observation:

> To be sure consular officers knew well enough that some members of
> the Diplomatic Service—and their wives—were believed to look down
> on the Consular Service, because it was "in trade."

[Waldo H. Heindrichs, Jr. in his biography of Joseph Grew, *American
Ambassador,* spent almost two chapters detailing this schism. Consul Carr even-
tually won the battle with diplomat Grew and the service became professionally
integrated in 1927.
    [That seems to be exactly what's playing out here. Barr, Snorton and Jawson
are in the consular camp, and Wrastle and Colds are in the diplomatic camp—all
nattering about doing apprenticeship in the Consular Service before graduating
to the elite Diplomatic Service.[19]]

PHYLLIS   (Interrupting.) Is the examination over? Can I go now?

BARR   Just a minute, just a minute. We haven't decided where to send
            you yet. (The members of the Board all rise and go into a foot-
            ball huddle. Murmurs of Punta Arenas, St. Helena and Devil's

---

[19] Not unlike Dr. Seuss' story of the *Sneeches:* the *plain-bellied* Sneeches and the ones with
stars-upon-thars. And Frances remained a plain-bellied Sneech for over four years before
getting her secretary star.

Island are heard. Finally they break away and take their places behind their chairs, in imposing and solemn postures.)

COLDS   (With the solemnity of a judge pronouncing a death sentence.) Jawson, will you make known to the candidate the consensus of opinion?

JAWSON   (Briskly rubbing his hands with delight.) With pleasure, wi-i-thh pleasuah. (He fumbles in his inside coat pocket, producing at length a large sheet of paper with a red seal in one corner.) Harr-humm! (Clearing his throat, preparatory to reading the contents of the document.)

PHYLLIS   (Suspiciously.) What's this, the hidden ball play? You've had that all the time!

JAWSON   Not at all, not at all. Nono, nono. Deecidedlay not. No.

PHYLLIS   You have, too. You decided where I was going before I even came in here. (To the others.) Didn't you? Do you think that was fair? (They all hang their heads, and grind their toes into the floor, too shamefaced to answer.) How dare you? You haven't consulted my wishes at all. (They are even more ashamed.)

[The Board tries to extricate itself from this predicament for another couple of pages, with Phyllis at one point correcting Barr who has again called the Comptroller General "a little moral."]

PHYLLIS   A little moron, you mean.

[Finally the Board announces that Phyllis is to be assigned]

> ...to a term of an indefinite number of years at hard labor in... in... (With great effect.) in M'bimbo M'bozo, Central Africa!

[The rest of the Prologue is spent by the Board trying to convince Phyllis to accept M'bimbo M'bozo. She steadfastly refuses, so the Board sedates her with chloroform, and ships her out, "dead or alive, she will be welcome there." The act ends with:]

COLDS   Stop them, stop them! We forgot something! We never asked her whether she had bribed anybody to get this job. (Tableau of despair.)

[A few liberties were taken with actions of the *faux* Personnel Board. They assembled first to conduct oral exams of candidates for the Foreign Service, and then morphed into a board for the assignment of officers who had just completed the Foreign Service School. In any case, a cleverly written roast in the style of a Gilbert & Sullivan operetta. Except that truth leaked through just enough to make it a fascinating read—an insider's look at the State Department in the 1920's.

[Colds' question about "whether she had bribed anybody to get this job" is, of course, a paraphrase of the play's title, "How Much Did You Pay For Your Job?" According to the State Department's Office of the Historian, those questions refer to the long-established process, starting in the nineteenth century, of appointing consuls based primarily on the political spoils system and then paying them out of fees on passports, visas, bills of health, etc. collected at the consulates. C. L. Jones, in his book, *The Consular Service of the United States: its history and activities*, 1906, reported that such consuls could appoint consular agents and commercial agents to actually collect the fees, and then split the proceeds with them as their remuneration.

[Such a back-door process was open to corruption, including bribery: political bribery for the consul's job and consular bribery for the consular agent's job. Jones reported many attempts to reform the system by the President and Congress but nothing stuck until the turn of the century when President Roosevelt established entrance exams for the Consular Service. Apparently enough progress was made in controlling the corruption because the 1928 play was billed as "obsolete."

[The *Act* is set in M'bimbo M'bozo, with scenes of the current vice consul and consul selling visas to the highest bidder; selling code books to the Bolsheviks and Mexicans; drinking on the job; "reading a penultimate Instruction of April 1, 1889, from Silver J. Barr, Consul General at Large, or even Larger," which consisted of a twenty-six line first sentence full of bureaucratic jargon and Latin phrases; attending to six American seamen who mysteriously show up in Central Africa;[20] servicing Senator Pester and Congressman Bullivan, who are investigating visa matters. (Congressman Bullivan spits a lot and grabs a bottle of Gordon's gin offered by the vice consul, "takes a terrific pull at it, emits a piercing yell and staggers out.")]

CONSUL   Good God! What was that tankage you gave him?

VICE CONSUL
          Best American synthetic. Called block and fall: You drink it, walk a block, and fall. Guaranteed no preliminary blindness— made in Baltimore. (Looks at watch.) Yes, he's dead by this time.

[The *Act* ends with the following:]

CONSUL   Gosh Joe, if that Consul doesn't relieve me soon… (Mops his brow. The doorway suddenly frames the figure of Consul PHYLLIS. She is dressed in sport clothes and carries a hatbox and a tennis racket. Everyone concentrates his attention upon her.)

PHYLLIS   This is the American Consulate, I presume? I am Frances Phyllis, the new Consul.

ALL TOGETHER
          <u>WHAT</u>! <u>CONSUL</u>?

PHYLLIS   You heard me. (To CONSUL.) Well, I suppose I had better begin by reading the archives and correspondence. Where are they?

[At this point everyone gets the message that a straight arrow FSO has

---

[20] It is well known in maritime annals that every tourist site in the world is populated by at least one sailor at all times.

arrived on the scene, and they all hastily depart the country: consul, vice consul, messenger, clerk, even the British consul, with comments like, "The most money is in visas."]

"Reporting at His First Post" from M. C. Perts' 1924 book.

[This sketch captures the essence of M'bimbo M'bozo. The only required modifications are to change the sex and to eliminate the perspiration. Frances was never affected by the heat.]

PHYLLIS   Good gracious! (She sits down in the Consul's chair, where-
           upon some of the mob [people wanting visas] start for her
           with cries and gesticulations. She raises a hand and quiets
           them.) One moment, please! Now, get this: From now on this
           office is going to be run <u>efficiently</u>. That's what I'm here for.
           All interviews will be given <u>one at a time</u>, and by appointment
           made <u>in advance</u>. Understand? (Glances down at her desk. The
           crowd remains silent, but takes one step forward. She jumps
           to her feet, waving a sheet of paper.) Wait till I read this, after
           which I will begin making appointments. (Reading.)

"The Comptroller General presents his compliments to Consul PHYLLIS and begs to inform her that, because her taxi across New York went one block out of its way, her trip from Washington to M'bimbo M'bozo cannot be deemed to have been made by the shortest and most direct route, wherefore her traveling expenses in the amount of $1,440,000.87 are disallowed."

(She falls back into the chair. The waiting mob, as if a signal had been given, swirls around her, shouting and waving arms. Nothing can be seen of her but her two hands raised above the turmoil, like the hands of one who drowns in angry waters.)

CURTAIN

[The Comptroller General with all his regulations was a force to be reckoned with back in the 1920's. His empire continued to grow, especially after WW II, as entries in Frances' dossier confirm. The only good news is that he's not talking about those seven-figure expenses, because Frances' passage from New Orleans to Valparaiso was only $75. And her comment about running an efficient office is truly prescient. Finally, the last scene of Phyllis being consumed by the mob augers ominously for Frances' career-to-come, as it did for the two previous ladies through the Foreign Service School.]

EPILOGUE

(The curtain goes up on the entire company, which forms into appropriate lines and sings the finale, as follows:)

Now give a shout, for school is out
  We're off for foreign lands;
To sit and freeze by the Arctic seas
  Or fry on tropic strands.
We've had enough—we know our stuff—
  This is our farewell song;
So give a cheer for wine and beer,
  And, teacher dear—so long!

They kill a man in far Durban
    Every day in the week;
The Caracas smell is simply—well,
    Like the great Calcutta Reek!
Havana's nice, if you've got the price;
    Valparaiso takes your dough—
So shout 'Hurray !' for old Bombay
    Where the typhus microbes grow!

In rich B.A. your hair turns gray
    At sight of your monthly bill;
The roaches feast in that near East,
    And there's garlic in Seville!
The Jo'burg air will curl your hair;
    Sao Paolo's not so hot—
Come, give a roar for Singapore
    Where the strongest Consuls rot!

[Note that the troupe has cited specific post assignments in the Epilogue and that Frances' first assignment was Valparaiso.]

The authors of this play, Mosher and Browne, certainly knew where the State Department skeletons were buried, and the best way to know that was if they were part of the organization. So ever responsive, the Department's Office of the Historian searched their files and identified two candidates: Robert B. Mosher, a former consul who retired from the Consular Service on July 1, 1924, and Julius Basil Browne, a British consul in Galveston, Texas from 1924 to 1926. No further data is available on either one, except that both names, Mosher and Browne, show up in the cast, along with a Mrs. Mosher.

To complicate matters, according to the 1927 *New York Times* article, one of the students was Sidney H. Browne, Jr. While he doesn't appear to be related to the other (Julius Basil) Browne, he could be the author. He certainly had opportunity and motive. But did he have means? If so he would have been prodigiously productive: both a full time student and author.

In contrast, Mosher while not listed a student, could have signed on as an instructor at the school after his retirement. Then in that capacity he became a co-author and player, along with his wife. But that's about as much as rational speculation allows.

The sketch on the playbill looks suspiciously like Perts' sketches. But it is not because it has a small *JSM* initial near the bottom. Now a student listed in the 1927 *New York Times* article was J. S. Moose, Jr., aka *Shti Shtikootski* (pronounced very carefully) in the play. So he is the likely culprit, aping Perts' characters from Frances' book into the Playbill.

Finally, of the twenty six graduates five became ambassadors, and all five were in the play: Paul Daniels as *Simian Emulsian*, Gerald Drew as *Mr. Snorton*, Frances as *Miss Phyllis* then *Consul Phyllis*, James Bonbright as *The Trade Commissioner*, and Vinton Chapin as *British Consul*. So, unlike mathematics, acting—at least satirical acting—and diplomacy appear to be mutually inclusive.

5

THE OTHER WOMEN

Some Statistics

WHEN Frances entered the Foreign Service in 1927 she was breaking into an all-but-one male bastion. Two women, Lucile Atcherson and Pattie Field, preceded her but Lucile had already resigned, so that left Pattie as the "other woman." The U.S. Department of State's Website, *Frequently Asked Historical Questions, Women in Foreign Service* provides their official Foreign Service biographies:

> Lucile Atcherson passed the Diplomatic Service examination in 1922 with the third-highest score, and was appointed a secretary in the Diplomatic Service on December 5, 1922. She was assigned as Third Secretary of Legation in Berne, Switzerland, on April 11, 1925. She resigned September 1927 in order to get married. Pattie H. Field was the first woman to enter the Foreign Service after passage of the [1924] Rogers Act. She was sworn in on April 20, 1925, served as Vice Consul at Amsterdam, and resigned on June 27, 1929, to accept a job with the National Broadcasting Company.

Left unanswered are the "unofficial" reasons for their resignations. An answer to that question lies in the State Department's solution to their new gender problem, starting with a quantitative assessment of their solution.

As outlined in the first chapter, a woman entering the Foreign Service in the 1920's and 1930's was a low probability event. Calkin in his well documented book, *Women in the Department of State*, reported that Wilbur J. Carr, Director of the Consular Service, responded to a 1922 query from the National Civil

Service Reform League that two women had taken the exam prior to 1922 but failed, and that three women had taken the exam in 1922, but that he didn't have results yet. Lucile Atcherson was one of these three women and the only one who passed. Twelve men passed the test with her.

Calkin then reported that two women took the exam in 1923, zero in 1924, eight in 1925 and seven in 1926, with Pattie Field being the loan survivor from this group. (856 men took the exam during this period, with 148 appointed.) In 1927, seventeen women took the written test, three passed and one (Frances) passed the orals and was appointed.

To finish the numbers, the peak of women entries occurred in 1928 and 1929: Forty nine women took the written test and three were appointed, the last of which was Constance Harvey, who became Frances' fellow traveler for the next thirty-four years. This peak was followed by an astonishing nadir; 126 women took the written test between 1930 and 1941 and none were appointed! Calkin expanded on the 1941 exams:

> Some 440 persons took the examinations in 1941, of whom thirteen were women. Eighty-two men and no women passed the written examinations whereupon the Foreign Service Journal commented: "That's one time feminist would-be-diplomatists can't blame that august body—the Examining Board." As might be expected, the Board of Examiners had been viewed by many as being anti-women for several years.

The State Department's Dilemma and Solution

The Department's gender solution was more complicated and nuanced than just numbers. Calkin again becomes the source for much of this development. He reported that between 1922 and 1925 the Department was in a hand-wringing snit over the early women Atcherson and Field, and the threat of more to come. Principal players were Director of the Consular Service/Assistant Secretary Wilbur Carr, Under Secretary Joseph Grew, Minister to Switzerland Hugh Gibson, and Secretary of State Charles Evans Hughes, along with President Harding. It actually started in 1921 with communiqués between Wilber Carr and Robert P. Skinner, Consul General in London, who in the last chapter suggested "a great field for new female FSO's in Paris was commercial reporting on articles for woman's wear:"

The position of the Department in late 1921, as conveyed by Carr to Skinner, was that only the youngest unmarried [women] candidates were selected for the corps of consular assistants. However, women were to be admitted to "future examinations [for career officers] upon the same terms that are applicable to men."

Skinner complied with the instructions [but] thought it was conceivable that a young woman of the "highest intelligence and personal qualifications" might become a consul, having in the meantime acquired a husband and family. [He then] questioned if her position in a foreign community as the head of a U.S. government office would not "bring the whole arrangement into ridicule, destroy her usefulness and render the position of her husband intolerable." As one solution he suggested that rules be adopted before women were permitted to take the examinations which would automatically terminate appointments upon a woman's marriage.

Calkin reported that this non-marriage rule was to prevail for fifty years. Ann Morin in her 1995 book, *Her Excellency,* detailed the first crack in the thirty-seventh year:

Elinor Constable, an FSO who married, challenged the system in 1958. Constable questioned the legality of being asked to resign, demanding to be shown the written rule. She was right, there was no rule; the entire practice rested only on custom. Although Constable left the service, she had proved there were no legal grounds for the custom. (She worked outside the service, reentered in the 1970's, and rose to become an ambassador and then an assistant secretary.)

It was not until August 16, 1971, that a Departmental Notice established equal opportunities for women, finally obliterating that unwritten rule—long after Frances and her lady fellow travelers had either resigned or retired from the Foreign Service.

Then after passage of the Rogers Act in 1924, Wilbur Carr corresponded with a woman and her mother about the feasibility of a career in the Foreign Service. Calkin quoted Carr as worrying about adverse conditions of health and climate for women overseas. Furthermore,

"There arise other problems due to custom and convention prevailing in many countries with respect to the employment of women in public positions; the practical inability of women to perform a large number of services required of all commissioned officers in the Foreign Service, as for example, the shipping and discharging of seamen, the inspection of vessels; the contact work in dealing with certain types of immigrants."

Carr thought it was virtually impossible for women to adapt themselves to these conditions and render the kind of service "all right minded women would wish to render." Carr commented candidly that, if his own sister came to him with the question being discussed, "I would advise her in no circumstances to enter the Foreign Service."

This informal statement appears to be the first exposition of limitations that women would encounter in an overseas assignment.

All this informally generated policy fell under the purview of the newly established Foreign Service Personnel Board, chaired by Joseph Grew. Calkin reported that it convened on November 6, 1924, to consider the admission of women to the next Foreign Service examination and the assignment of Lucile Atcherson to an overseas post.

Carr thought that the Board could make no rule that would exclude women. Therefore, "the most feasible way to deal with the question was to defeat them in the examination on the basis that they were not fitted to discharge the exacting and peculiar duties of an officer in the Foreign Service."

Under Secretary Joseph C. Grew felt this "would be a subterfuge, and would not meet the situation as fairly and squarely as he would like to have it met." If the Foreign Service Personnel Board were to defeat women who were qualified by education to pass the examinations successfully, "the whole thing will sooner or later come to a head with a 'bang,' and we will find ourselves confronted with the problem more serious than it is now."

Some Board members were concerned about the way in which women could be discouraged from taking the examinations. Although it might be comparatively easy to do this in conversation with them, there needed to be some formula to follow in writing to female applicants.

Grew was of the opinion that the Board should first ask the President to sign an Executive Order that would exclude women from the examination. If this failed, the Board could then adopt Carr's idea of defeating the women in the exam. Meanwhile, the decision of Lucile Atcherson's overseas assignment was deferred.

The Executive Committee of the board prepared a memorandum on how it might be "possible to relieve the Government of the necessity for the appointment to the Foreign Service" not only of women, but Negroes and naturalized citizens as well.

Then off Grew went with these alternatives to see Secretary of State Hughes. Calkin reported the response:

A few days later Secretary Hughes emphatically stated that the President would not issue an exclusionary Executive Order, and "I should not be willing to recommend it." If women, Negroes, and naturalized citizens were admitted to the examinations, "they are entitled to fair and impartial treatment and should not be rated so low that they cannot obtain a passing mark merely because of the fact of sex, color or naturalization."

Hughes did more than emphasize to the Board of Examiners that no woman should be prevented from passing because of sex. He went so far as to say that he thought "it would only be a question of time before women would take their place in diplomacy and consular work just as in other professions." He saw no reason for "creating friction by attempting to stem the inevitable tide temporarily."

So Charles Evans Hughes, likely with the blessing of President Harding, took the Department's Old Guard to the woodshed and stomped on their recidivist policy.

Then Hugh Gibson, Minister to Switzerland, jumped into the fray. In addition to calling women in the Foreign Service "a very radical experiment," which may require revising Secretary Hughes' current policy,

Gibson suggested that it would be wise to refrain from taking in any more women until some idea of their "possible usefulness" could be formed. It would be more difficult to eliminate 10 or 15 than 1 or 2. "Why incur this risk needlessly."

Calkin reported that William R. Castle, Chief of the Division of Western European Affairs, agreed with Gibson's position and wrote Secretary Hughes, apparently receiving his agreement, which is somewhat surprising given his previous decision.[21] But Carr disagreed and literally put an end to that discussion in a memorandum to J. Butler Wright, Third Assistant Secretary:

If the members of the Service are to persist in carrying on discussions by correspondence in regards to ways and means for preventing women from being admitted into the Foreign Service and creating an impression that the Board is excluding them through arbitrary use of its powers rather than through orderly processes of an examination and a judicial determination of their fitness for appointment, a charge of discrimination is almost certain to by made and so much political pressure focused upon the Board of Examiners as to make the honest performance of its duties well nigh impossible.

Finally, Calkin reported that Grew codified the Department's solution—with a clearly demonic twist:

Grew saw only one course of action that could be followed. The examinations of both men and women must be thorough so that "no one not clearly possessing fitness for the Service shall be certified as eligible." Appointments for both sexes should be made in the same manner. There would be the tendency, once women were sent to the field, to protect them by giving them inside work or clerical duties and by shielding them from difficulties in which their positions would place them. Grew did not believe this should be done. Instead, every woman should be rated for her efficiency the same as any male employee. "Otherwise there would be no equality of treatment and my understanding is that first

---

[21] Castle, now an Assistant Secretary, is standing next to Carr in the graduation picture of the Foreign Service School chapter.

and foremost the claims of women are that they shall be treated exactly as men are treated."[22]

The first women to get a dose of the "equal treatment policy" were Lucile and Pattie.

Lucile Atcherson's Saga

Lucile Atcherson's life was summarized by Marilyn Greenwald in her 1999 book, *A Woman of the Times, Journalism, Feminism and the Career of Charlotte Curtis*. Charlotte Curtis was Lucile's first daughter and the first part of Greenwald's book covered Lucile's life. Calkin added information about Lucile's short FSO career. Here is a summary of those summaries.

Lucile (b. 1894) was a bright young woman, nurtured by wealthy parents in Columbus Ohio, complete with horses. She graduated from the prestigious Columbus School for Girls at fourteen and Smith College at the exceedingly young age of eighteen. After graduation she returned home and worked at secretarial jobs in Columbus. She found that boring, so took up volunteer work including the Woman's Suffrage Society and National Women's Party. After WW I she went to France to work for the American Committee for Devastated France, which tweaked her interest in the Foreign Service.

Calkin, in a 1978 interview with Lucile, filled in details about her preparation for the Diplomatic Service examination, as it was called then:

> While in Washington [Lucile] learned of a cram school for men who wanted to enter the Foreign Service. The director was horrified when she asked to enter the class. It would "destroy the morale of the young men." Since it was hot weather, they would want to loosen their collars and remove their ties. He did accept her as a private student, though, letting her attend only the last session with the men.
>
> Atcherson took the Diplomatic Service examination in July 1922. She was glad that no examination had been held sooner, knowing that she could not have passed with only the knowledge she had gained in college.

---

[22] Mark this last sentence, because it will become Frances' salvation twenty years later.

Lucile Atcherson, circa 1920, wearing the uniform of the American Committee for Devastated France (courtesy Department of State.)

So that's how she passed with such flying colors—and why Frances just squeaked by. Calkin also reported that

In 1924 Joseph Grew, Under Secretary of State, noted in his diary that he thought Lucile Atcherson "was let into the Service through the direct intervention of President Harding, and it has established a very unfortunate precedent."

Apparently all sorts of political lobbying from Lucile's Ohio constituents—from Senator Willis (no direct relative) and Attorney General Price, to the Columbus Women's Association of Commerce—was laid on Harding to give her a political appointment as a secretary to the embassy in Paris. But Harding, heeding recommendation from State, wrote Lucile that

I think it will be the better for the service and better for you when you enter the service if we proceed along regulation lines.

So she did it by the book—successfully. Thus Grew, to put the modern spin on it, was misinformed. Calkin continued:

Following her appointment [as secretary] in December 1922 she had been in the Division of Latin American Affairs doing research on U.S.-Haitian relations under the direction of Dana Munro. Meanwhile, male officers had been in the office for a short time, receiving training in political affairs for a month or two and then being assigned to overseas positions.

In December 1924, J. Butler Wright [Third Assistant Secretary] suggested keeping her in Washington as long as possible [beyond the two years she had already served] and then appointing her to a post, such as in Scandinavia, which would prove the least embarrassing and difficult for her. The [Personnel] Board should then reappoint her to the Department as soon, and for as long a time, as possible under the law.

On March 25, 1925, Under Secretary Grew wrote Hugh Gibson regarding the assignment of Atcherson. He said that the Personnel Board had "scanned the field fully and finally came to the conclusion that the best possible post and the best possible Chief for her first foreign assignment were Berne and your good self."[23] The decision to send her to Switzerland "is in fact a compliment to that country and a recognition of its progressiveness."

Grew's last sentence was obviously ironic, because Switzerland was the last of the major western countries to pass woman-suffrage legislation—in 1971. Only Liechtenstein remained a woman's suffrage holdout. (In a 1984 referendum, their women were finally given the right to vote in national, but not local, elections.)

Gibson replied that he thought she should be assigned to a large embassy rather than to a legation. He also thought that she would find herself in an "unenviable and conspicuous position after the first ripple

---

[23] Not too different from the process used in assigning Phyllis to M'bimbo M'bozo in the Foreign Service School's play of the last chapter.

of excitement after her arrival had subsided." Gibson's protest arrived too late. The Department had assigned Atcherson as Third Secretary of the Legation at Berne on April 11, 1925.

None of this action stopped Hugh Gibson:

In the meantime Gibson was raising other objections to the appointment of women. On April 20, 1925, he wrote Secretary Hughes and Under Secretary Grew regarding the establishment of precedents for governing activities of women in the Diplomatic Service. Many of the problems he raised were protocol matters:
- Should Atcherson call on all gentlemen representatives of the [other] countries?
- Where would her place be at official dinners?
- Should she remain at the table over a glass of port or retire to the drawing room alone and wait until the President of the Republic rose and said, "Gentlemen, shall we join the lady?"
- And what dress should she wear on official occasions: a dress suit and top hat?

Another problem facing Gibson was office space for Atcherson. It would be necessary to place her desk in a room that had been used for the storage of old files. Gibson ventured "to point out that anything once put in the file room has never been found again."

The Department must have received these messages that Hugh was not thrilled to receive Lucile. So Grew talked to her about these types of problems,

...and told her that without doubt there would be times when "her sex would make it difficult and embarrassing for her to take part in all the official activities of the Diplomatic Corps on an equality with her male colleagues." He referred to two dinners given by the Swiss Government and the Diplomatic Corps at which she would be the only woman "in a room with a hundred men smoking cigars and drinking beer." Atcherson replied that on such occasions "a temporary absence from Berne would come in very conveniently [and that she would follow the]

line of least resistance in the face of possible embarrassments to herself
or the Legation when circumstances arose such as dinners."

In retrospect, that decision would be the *kiss of death* for Lucile, as will
become apparent shortly. Following this discussion, Grew notified Gibson that
Lucile would likely "settle into her niche with the least possible splash," and that
she would "probably prove to be a quiet, dignified and hard-working member"
of Gibson's staff.

Marilyn Greenwald reported that Lucile did arrive at the Berne Legation as
a third secretary and soon met George Curtis, an American doctor of anatomy
studying iodine metabolism at the University of Berne. They became engaged
within the year.

Greenwald also pried Lucile's Foreign Service dossier out of the Department,
complete with early versions of her Annual Efficiency Report and Rating Sheet
for her time in Berne. Her reviewer was, of course, Hugh Gibson. Things started
off well enough:

> The appointment of a female diplomat amused the Swiss, "and they
> have not always been kindly in their comments. [But] Miss Atcherson
> has conducted herself with dignity and good sense by showing a desire
> to be inconspicuous and has done a good deal to disarm criticism."

Then it turned ugly. By October, 1926, Gibson reported:

> Lucile's inability to mingle with her male colleagues was devastating
> to her career. Her status as a woman officer was a novelty and made her
> conspicuous: "She is by nature reserved and formal with little facility in
> personal relationships. She does not possess the savoir vivre necessary
> to meet a difficult situation." Further, Lucile received substantial help
> from her colleagues—much more than any man in her position would
> receive.

While these comments are indeed ugly, they also define necessary attributes
for a diplomat and if not met, must be so stated. To this virtual *death-kiss*, Gibson
added the following generalization:

A woman diplomat can never be successful simply because she does not have the access to and personality of the men with whom she works: [A male secretary] cultivates the society of colleagues and officials of the Government. He frequents their company in spare time, encourages them to come to his home and otherwise seeks to cultivate their confidences. A woman secretary is at a disadvantage.

Finally, this blow dealt by the Personnel Board:

By 1927, her ranking of seventy-six made her eighty-fifth in her class of ninety-two officers. Further, she lacked character ("Lacks initiative and has little sense of responsibility"), ability ("Lacking in resource, tact, judgment and sense of what is fitting"), and a positive personality ("Egotistical; has harmed prestige of Legation with her actions. Her sex a handicap to useful official friendships").

In this case, the Department didn't have to distort or disparage much of anything because Gibson's on-site Annual Efficiency Report was discouraging enough.

Marilyn Greenwald reported that Lucile was then transferred to Panama in 1927, where she found the "bugs and heat difficult." Besides that, she had not been promoted whereas most of her contemporaries had. She complained via a courteous letter to the legation's personnel chief in the summer of 1927. In response she was told that her performance record did not merit promotion. So that, plus her transfer to Panama, plus her "deepening relationship with George Curtis," prompted her to resign in the fall of 1927. She and George were married in January, 1928, moved to Chicago and immediately started a family.

Lucile's saga identified the Old Guard's second tactic: If you can't keep 'em out, ease 'em out—at first opportunity. This tactic can be called the *glass table* policy, which has a much lower bar to advancement than does the modern *glass ceiling* policy. "So there you have it," as Mark Twain liked to say. The glass table was set; the glass ceiling was far out of sight.

Pattie Field's Saga

Both Lucile and Pattie were assigned overseas within months of each other in 1925, with Pattie's saga initiated by Calkin with a quote from Grew:

In the case of Miss Field, who enters subsequent to the passage of the Rogers Act, we shall probably send her first to a consulate where she will have rough and tumble work to perform and see if she can get away with it. If she fails, it will be an indication that no woman is capable of carrying out all the duties of a Foreign Service officer and this would probably make it more difficult for women to pass in the future. The principle must have a fair test.

Calkin then reported:

After several months at the Foreign Service Institute in Washington, Pattie Field was assigned as vice consul at the consulate general in Amsterdam and reported for duty on November 2, 1925. William H. Gale, Consul General, had read newspaper reports of the appointment before he received notification from the Department. In a telegram to the Department, he said, "If true, earnestly advise reconsideration and suggest assignment to a post having larger staff where appropriate duties could be arranged. A woman would not fill the requirements here and would be worse than useless."

Grew responded:

[Field] passed such an excellent examination and impressed the Board so favorably by her general qualifications that it could only, in all conscientiousness, give her a passing mark. Miss Field is particularly fortunate in going to such a Chief as yourself, and I know that whatever may be your personal views with regard to the principle involved in the admission of women to the Foreign Service you will none the less give her the same sympathetic advice and support that you would give to any young man on your staff.

Patti Field, second woman Foreign Service Officer, circa 1924
(courtesy Department of State.)

Pattie's vice consul appointment was flippantly reported in the September 14, 1925, edition of *Time* magazine:

> [Pretty,] dimpled Miss Pattie Field, age 24, of Denver, was last week assigned as Vice Consul at Amsterdam, Holland... Although the consular service to which she is assigned is still not quite so selectable as the diplomatic [service,] nevertheless pretty Miss Field was all smiles when Washington newspapermen came to report whatever she had to say:
>
> > "I am sure women will be useful in the foreign service. Just as in other callings, there are some things in this career that women can do better than a man, especially in the large consular offices."

That quote must have stirred up the Old Guard in Amsterdam, with comments like, "Well, let's see just what things she can do better than we can." *Time* continued the story in its January 25, 1926, edition:

At Amsterdam there arrived Miss Pattie Field, 24, of Denver—and her mother and many trunks... With gracious feminine evasiveness she parried all efforts of the correspondents to draw her out into some statement that could be revamped as "copy."

With incisive, feminine neatness she ordered her trunks unpacked, and though no prying reporter saw, her U.S. friends well knew that there came forth: a Paris wardrobe... skins of wild Colorado animals... riding habits... perhaps a ravishing orange skin-tight swimming costume (it was seen many a time last summer in the tank [swimming pool] of the Wardman Park Hotel, Washington, D.C. [where she was staying while attending the Foreign Service School]).

With resolute feminine determination, she settled down at her desk in the American Consulate at Amsterdam...

Apparently Pattie's subsequent work was uneventful, with no reports of anything she did better than the men. But the potential was there, according to a 1929 despatch to the Department:

Pattie Field, according to Gale's successor, Charles L Hoover, was a "charming young lady," possessed a "good mind," and gave some promise of developing into an "officer of considerable talent along certain lines." She performed well enough that Alexander Goldstein, Export Manager of the Everseal Mfg. Co. of New York City, wrote the Department of State that he had been assisted by Pattie Field in the absence of the Consul. "It affords us considerable pleasure to state that we were courteously received and Miss Field assisted us greatly in important commercial matters."

Calkin then reported the ending:

On July 3, 1929, after almost 4 years of employment, Field submitted her resignation. Consul General Hoover suggested that the principal reason for Field's resignation might have been that "she has not found life abroad to be as pleasant as she had anticipated it would be." She seemed to be apprehensive of losing contact with "her relatives and countrymen, to whom she is sincerely devoted." On the other hand,

Hoover added, "it may have been purely a question of obtaining a more lucrative position and greater financial advantage than she could have gained by remaining in the Service."

What really happened to Pattie can be surmised from data in Lucile's and Frances' Foreign Service dossiers. First Pattie had not been promoted during her time in service, whereas many of her male peers had—just as with Lucile and Frances. So she must have received a strong message there. Second, the 1929 despatches likely mirrored Pattie's latest Annual Efficiency Report, which should have been written by Consul General Hoover. Because his words were similar to words Frances received in her first post in Chile, which in turn drew a satisfactory rating from the Department, Pattie probably drew one as well. Now satisfactory was, at best, middle of the pack and nothing to write home about. And while it was significantly better than the one Lucile received, it was still not particularly encouraging. So another message was sent.

Finally, all of Hoover's reasons for Pattie's resignation were Pattie's personal problems and certainly not of his or the Department's making, except for the low pay, which obviously was for menial work—except when Consul was out of town. It appears that Hoover was applying a little self-serving spin to protect the Department from the ever-vigilant eye of the Woman's Rights (now Liberation) Movement.

Unfortunately, Pattie's own reasons for her resignation are not available; in fact they may never have been recorded. The latter possibility is understandable given that Pattie may not have wanted to burn bridges before joining NBC, where she might need those diplomatic contacts in her new job. That would have been a smart move on her part. In any case that's the last news of Pattie.

Constance Harvey's Saga

Constance Ray Harvey was the sixth woman to enter the Foreign Service in 1930. Frances was the third. The fourth was Margaret Warner, a graduate of Radcliffe, and the fifth was Nelle Blossom Stogsdall, a graduate of Wellesley. Both lasted less than three years before resigning. While information about these two women is not available, reasons for their leaving again fit the "ease 'em out" tactic: Assign them menial tasks; give them a reasonable trial; discourage them with nothing more than average reviews and no promotions; then wait for them to resign. And because they all were very bright women, they would have been bored to death with that kind of work—except for Constance, who while bored, gutted it out for seventeen years.

Calkin reported that the *New York Times* said after Constance's entry in 1930, "The appointment of women to the Foreign Service, while a novelty only a few years ago is no longer unusual." They were also misinformed, because hers was the last entry from outside the State Department for the next eleven years. (As outlined in the first chapter, two women joined the Foreign Service in a lateral transfer from the State Department: Margaret Hanna arrived in 1937 after nearly forty two years in the Department. She started in 1895 as a confidential clerk, rose to the rank of drafting officer, was appointed chief of her division in 1924 and retired in 1939. Kathleen Molesworth took the same route in 1939, retiring in 1955 as a first secretary. She served with Frances in London.)

Constance was born in Buffalo, New York, and had an extensive education: Franklin School, Lycee de Beauvais and Sorbonne in France, an AB from Smith College in 1927, the School of International Studies in Geneva, the Williamstown Institute of Politics and an MS from Columbia in 1930. She then attended the Crawford Foreign Service Cram School, likely the same one that Lucile Atcherson attended.

She was first appointed vice consul in Ottawa, Canada in 1930 and was stationed in Lyon, France, during WW II. She was interned first by Vichy France in Lourdes hotels after the American invasion of French North Africa in 1942 and then by the Germans in a Baden Baden prison camp from 1943 to 1944. And like Frances in her later career, Constance had her mother with her between 1931 and 1940 when she was posted to Switzerland and France. Her mother died in Switzerland in 1940.

Constance's promotion track was agonizingly slow. She remained a vice consul for seventeen years. Then her career accelerated, culminating in the first woman appointment as consul general (to Strasbourg) in 1959. She retired in 1964—the same year as Frances—and is the first woman interviewed in Ann Morin's book, *Her Excellency*.

In 1945 Constance was awarded the Medal of Freedom, one of the first Medals of Freedom honoring citizens who aided the war effort, in her case for undercover work in Lyon before her internment in 1942. She was recruited for this work by Gen. Barney Legge, military attaché in Berne during the war. Unfortunately, but not unexpectedly with such secret matters, the nature of her work is not available. But it must have been extraordinary, given the medal's lofty status and the short time in which it was awarded.

Constance Harvey with Gen. Barney Legge in Zurich, Switzerland, circa 1945, upon receiving the Medal of Freedom (courtesy, U.S. Government.)

All this happened while Constance was still a lowly vice council. Then shortly afterwards, her career took off, reaching its peak fourteen years later as a consul general. So it took a massive, Medal of Freedom jolt to the Old Guard's personnel review system to finally break Constance's career loose. Although not recorded, General Legge was certainly the key player in this action. As will be seen, Frances' career was similarly jolted loose—actually salvaged—by Joseph Grew.

Ann Morin made the following observation in Constance's chapter:

There are many reasons why Harvey did not achieve Willis's distinction. Two are probably important: Willis had as her mentor the very influential Under Secretary of State Joseph Grew, and she was much more of an establishment player who went by the book. Harvey had no mentor and was more of a risk taker.

Those are accurate observations as far as they go. While Grew indeed became Frances' mentor, it wasn't until he had thoroughly vetted her performance as his executive assistant in Washington DC in 1945, exactly half way through her career. Before then her career was *in extremis,* as outlined in the first chapter. Other reasons could be added, such as the enormous effect Hugh Gibson also had on her career, her ability to interact with all types of people and her total dedication to duty, but Morin's comments capture the essence of her success.

At the end of her recollections in Morin's book, Constance Harvey had this to say about Frances:

> [Frances Willis] was regarded with the greatest admiration by her colleagues, including me. She was, to me, "the" great lady of the Foreign Service so far. She got ahead very fast. She didn't let herself be vice consul very long. She got herself out of any kind of job that was really menial. I spent the whole of my youth in the Foreign Service doing things that I felt were beneath my abilities, to tell you the truth. That was true for many men also.

Frances and Constance met for the first time in Berne, Switzerland, during the early part of WW II. Constance was posted to Berne and Frances stopped there after the Gestapo expelled her from Brussels, Belgium. After a few days in Berne, Frances continued on to her next post in Madrid, Spain. They may have met again in Madrid in 1944 when Constance was released from the Baden Baden prison camp and sent through Madrid to the United States. Both meetings are covered in the Spain chapter.

Constance sent Frances a fine letter of congratulations on her appointment as career ambassador, which is in the Ceylon chapter, but that is all the correspondence that survived. So they were like two ships at sea, occasionally passing—and signaling—each other en route to separate ports.

Related Photos

The following photos extend the context of this chapter.

Frances, circa 1935 (courtesy American Foreign Service Journal.)

This photo followed ones of Lucile Atcherson and Pattie Field, shown earlier. It appeared under a new paragraph, titled "Four More Successful Women, 1926-1929." They were of course successful in the sense that they received FSO appointments, and the last to do so until 1941. But only two out of these four women stuck it out for a career: Frances and Constance Harvey.

This photo ties together some of the protagonists in this chapter.

Retirement award ceremony for Ambassador Clifton Wharton
on Foreign Service Day, May 19, 1978 (courtesy Department of State.)

People are from the left: Deputy Under Secretary for Management, Ben H. Read, Deputy Assistant Secretary, J. A. Burroughs, Ambassador Clifton R. Wharton, Mrs. L. A. Curtis, Ambassador Frances E. Willis. Mrs. L. A. Curtis is better known by her full name: Mrs. Lucile Atcherson Curtis. So she returned to visit the Foreign Service fifty years after she left it. This is the only record of Lucile and Frances meeting, and documents a confluence of firsts:

> First woman in the Diplomatic / Foreign Service
> First woman up the Foreign Service ladder
> First career woman ambassador
> First woman career ambassador.
> First black in the Foreign Service
> First black up the Foreign Service ladder
> First career black ambassador.

That was an awesome assembly, with delayed apologies to Clifton from the women who are greeting each other and totally ignoring him on his day of adulation. It is also the last photo taken of Frances. She died five years later in 1983 at the age of 84. Both Clifton and Lucile outlived Frances, each lasting until 91.

Clifton Wharton was born in 1899, the same year as Frances, and entered the Foreign Service in 1925 with Pattie Field. He subsequently was appointed Ambassador to Romania, then to Norway—relieving the current ambassador, Frances E. Willis. Clifton appears again in the Frances and Julia chapter.

Both Clifton and Frances were honored by the U.S. Postal Service, which issued a six-stamp pane of Distinguished American Diplomats in 2006. The six diplomats are:

> Hiram Bingham IV   (1903-1988)
> Frances E. Willis   (1899-1983)
> Robert D. Murphy   (1894-1978)
> Clifton R. Wharton, Sr.   (1899-1990)
> Charles E. Bohlen   (1904-1974)
> Philip C. Habib   (1920-1992)

The accompanying brochure said that they are remembered for "their contributions to international relations, not only as negotiators and administrators but also as trailblazers, shapers of policy, peacemakers and humanitarians." Frances' stamp appears on the front cover.

6

FIRST POST: EXILED TO CHILE

Getting to Valparaiso

AFTER graduating from Foreign Service School in March, 1928, Frances sailed off to her assigned post Valparaiso, Chile, following twenty-six days of home leave in Redlands. Because Chile was not on the scheduled routes of major ship or air lines, the only offerings were merchant ships with a few cabins set up for passengers and nearly always requiring transfer to another ship in Panama. Because these ships stopped in many ports along the way to exchange cargo, which was their first priority, the total trip usually took a month, possibly longer.

No wonder Mother Belle was nervous about her young, attractive daughter taking off for the other end of the world, 7,000 miles away, the only female passenger on some cargo ship populated by uncivilized seamen—deck-apes they were often called—who only saw women when they got to port. It was more like terrified and for pretty good reasons.

Then when she got to Chile, where Spanish—a language foreign to Frances—was spoken, only God knew what could happen. Apparently the Department's Old Guard was at it again: If Panama worked for Lucile, why wouldn't Chile work for Frances? So Belle exercised about the only option left in her mothering kit: She sent big sister Caroline along for protection. The one bit of good news is that the Willis sisters, holed up in their cabin for most of the long trip, had time to learn some Spanish.

One of their port calls was Lima, Peru, according to Frances in a 1963 bulletin to the family. She was commenting on an article by Ellis Briggs, a fellow career ambassador appointed in the group ahead of her, who had just retired. She then said:

I have known him practically ever since I entered the Service—
Caroline, he was the third bachelor sharing the house with Sam Reber
and Jack Cabot in Lima when we stopped there in 1928.

Jack, aka John, Cabot was the eligible bachelor in the family's Safety in
Numbers story. Even though Frances' letters from that time are lost, it's likely
that the bachelors coached Frances on a fallout of the War of the Pacific, the
Tacna-Arica dispute between Peru and Chile.

Graham Stewart, one of Frances' political science professors at Stanford and
an early admirer of hers, had just given Frances a copy of his report, "The Tacna-
Arica Dispute," signing it, *With sincere regards, G.H.S.* The dispute arose from
provisions of the Treaty of Ancon (1883), which ended the War of the Pacific.
Chile won that war and was ceded Tacna and Arica, the southern provinces of
Peru. Then they squabbled over those provinces for the next twenty or so years,
complete with a severing of diplomatic relations in 1911. Calvin Coolidge got
into the act in 1925 to no avail, and that's where it stood in 1927.

Consequently that was a hot topic when Frances arrived in Chile and she
was going to know all about it, thanks to Graham Stewart and the bachelors.
Ultimately Herbert Hoover settled things down in 1929, with Chile retaining
Arica and returning Tacna to Peru, plus $6,000,000.

Frances and Caroline arrived safely in Valparaiso on May 3, 1928, found a
place to live and Frances started her Foreign Service career as an FSO-unclass.
and acting vice consul.[24] But that living arrangement didn't last very long because
Caroline immediately succumbed to the charms of Fredrick V. Vaughan, who was
currently working as the export manager of Gibbs & Co. in Santiago. Freddie,
as he was called, was a retired British naval officer who fought in WW I. He
missed the Battle of Jutland because his cruiser had been torpedoed. He was then
appointed British Naval Attaché to Chile and received the Order of the British
Empire in 1954.

Caroline and Freddie were married in September 1929, settled in Santiago,
raised two children there and finally, thirty-three years later, retired to the
Redlands family home in 1962. So the big-sister protection ploy lasted about
seventeen months, then leaving Frances to fend for herself.

A glimpse of how Frances was living in Valparaiso after Caroline abandoned

---

[24] FSO-unclass. designates a newly appointed FSO on probation for a year—or longer for
women. See Appendix 1 for all the FSO classes in these early days.

her appeared in a Department Transfer Record, which Frances was required to submit in July, 1930. Here are excerpts:

RESIDENCE QUARTERS.

Address and general location of rooms now occupied: 70 Calle Valparaiso, Miramar, Vina del Mar. The house is one block from the railroad station of Miramar, which is a suburban residence district, six miles from the center of Valparaiso.

Number and size of rooms; number of baths: One medium sized room, no private bath. If there were small apartments available the officer would prefer one, but there are none available.

Heating facilities: None. Officer owns a kerosene stove.

Cost of boarding accommodations of the officer: Approximately fifty dollars a month.

So Frances had been renting a furnished but primitive room—no heat and no private bath—and likely sharing the kitchen in a private home for more than two years. But at least she was immersing herself in the country's culture and language, all for fifty dollars a month, which must have been a bargain.

Well it wasn't, because $600 per year was a quarter of Frances' total salary, and probably over a third of her take-home pay. But not to worry, Assistant Secretary Wilbur Carr came to the rescue of FSO's with "a post allowance by way of additional compensation at annual rate of $250," starting July 1, 1931. Then the Great Depression really kicked in, and the Department had to tighten its purse strings. So about four months later Wilbur sent another directive reducing that allowance to $200. But at least FSO's didn't have to cough up the excess allowance over that four-month period; they just had to live with less. So it goes, except it didn't go away; it reared up again in Santiago.

Frances detailed her desire for a transfer in the second part of the Transfer Record:

The officer has been serving for over two consecutive years at this post, her first, and it is felt that especially during the first years in the service the more varied the assignments the better the training.

Any post in the Orient or in Europe (including England) [would be preferred.] A transfer to the Diplomatic Branch of the service would not be unwelcome.

After two years of a rather basic (and primitive) life in Valparaiso, Frances was ready for something more challenging. This was her first request for a post in the Orient, which would finally be granted at her last post, Ceylon.

Work

Frances' FSO performance in Chile was recorded in a set of Annual Efficiency Reports filed in her dossier. Four of the reports, each one page long, were prepared by Consul General Carl F. Deichman, her supervisor in Valparaiso. Here is part of Deichman's first report of February 11, 1929, nine months after she arrived:

> I have much pleasure in informing the Department that Miss Willis has shown marked ability in acquiring a practical knowledge of the routine work of the Consulate-General, and with it a fair working knowledge of the Spanish language. She has also a good knowledge of the French language, and a smattering of German.
>
> She is possessed of good judgment, common sense, ambition, balance and poise, and a determination to succeed. She has a good command of the English language and marked literary ability, as well as an analytical turn of mind.
>
> At present she is in charge of the visa work of this office for which she has a special aptitude, and also takes part in statistical compilation and other reporting work.
>
> She will make a very good consular officer, subject to sex limitations of course, and I can recommend her highly for the thoroughness and accuracy of her work. I believe, however, that the countries of Northern Europe, or Canada, instead of a Latin country would be more suitable for her. She has not [yet] expressed any desire for such a change and so far as known to me is content with her present assignment.

Here is the second, institutional gender bias comment. Deichman's second evaluation, just six months later in August, 1929, was even more complementary:

...has continued in her very efficient and reliable way especially in the passport and visa work in which she has become quite expert.

...progress in her knowledge of Spanish and can carry on a limited conversation in a fluent manner.

...a most efficient Vice Consul, and entitled to promotion on account of her efficiency, common sense, service spirit, and all around adaptability to the different branches of Consular work. I trust, in all fairness and justice to her excellent work and efforts, the Department will grant her a promotion in recognition of her services at a <u>very early date</u>.

Someone had underlined that last phrase. The third, August, 1930, evaluation got even better:

...most remarkable progress ...most efficient and expert officer in all that pertains to a seaport office, having demonstrated her efficiency in the shipping and seaman work to an unusual degree, especially in handling disputes between Master and members of crew, destitute and straggling [i.e., drunk] seamen.[25]

In addition to this work she has had charge of the accounts, citizenship and immigration, and has performed all these duties in the most efficient and capable manner ...excellent progress in her studies in the Spanish language, and can now converse in a fluent manner on all topics of the day ...and writes it very well ...spending many hours after closing time to keep the routine work up to date.

In view of her efficiency in all lines of consular routine, her all around adaptability, her common sense, service spirit and capability, I hope it will be possible for the Department to promote her to the $3000 grade [vice consul] in the very near future, in recognition of her very excellent services.

In contrast to Lucile Atcherson's first evaluations, which went down, Frances' were going up. Even more significantly, these last two reports said nothing about limitations of her sex. It appears that Frances has cleaved her first convert.

---

[25] That had to be a test of fire for a woman, especially in a port like Valparaiso.

Much of the difference between Frances' and Lucile's evaluations can be ascribed to the nature of their work: Frances was doing consular things and Lucile was doing diplomatic things. The former worries about visas, notarials, shipping—quantitative tasks that have a beginning and an end, all of which are relatively easy to quantify and grade. The latter is qualitative, based on person-to-person contacts and relationships that are much harder to grade objectively. And with Lucile's boss, Hugh Gibson, the opportunity for perverse bias to creep into the evaluation was a given. So Lucile started with a major disadvantage.

Both jobs were important, as Frances wrote in a 1971 letter to the *Foreign Service Journal*: "Every FSO needs the experience of serving as a consular officer." Specifically, Frances was suggesting that consular work was a good way to break into the Foreign Service, just as Wrastle and Colds advocated in that Foreign Service School play.

Inspection of Miss Willis

These improving reports must have alarmed the Department's Old Guard: a young woman making the best out of her first Foreign Service assignment, as tough as they come, close to exile. And what's wrong with Deichman anyway? Maybe she had cast a spell over him. So after Deichman's second report, they decided to generate a second opinion and sent Consul General George S. Messersmith, now detailed as Foreign Service Inspector, to conduct an "American Foreign Service Inspection Report on Miss Willis." Because Messersmith was later appointed head of mission to Uruguay, Austria, Cuba, Mexico and Argentina, along with a tour as assistant secretary of state, he was certainly qualified to inspect her.

Messersmith's Inspection Report, dated June 14, 1930, is three, legal-sized pages long—the longest report in her entire dossier—with sections on Personality, Mode of Living, Contacts, Cooperation, Standing, and the last, which took up half the report, Professional Attributes. It started out:

> PERSONALITY. Miss Willis is a young woman of very pleasing personality and makes a very good general impression. …dresses neatly and becomingly …education and cultural background are excellent …natural poise and dignity …tactful and patient …good address and her manners are excellent …above average intellectual capacity …interested in her work …considerable initiative …considerable force of character without, however, losing her feminine qualities. Her personal life and

habits have been above reproach. She has the quality of retaining her feminine characteristics and attractiveness and yet at the same time possessing those masculine qualities without which she would not be able to perform even in a mediocre fashion consular function. As the inspector was able to observe, her sex has so far not been a handicap to her.

That last comment about being able to do her work without sex being a handicap is a first and a significant breakthrough—for a brief moment. Messersmith continued:

REPRESENTATIVE CAPACITY. She is superior, in the opinion of the inspector, to many career Vice Consuls of his acquaintance. She has a real ability to meet people easily and to arouse confidence and the general impression which she makes is pleasing. While her sex imposes certain limitations, it would appear that Miss Willis has shown in her work at Santiago [sic; she was actually working in Valparaiso, but she probably went to Santiago for the interview] that a woman can do certain work in the Consulate which it was assumed she could not do acceptably.

On second thought, sex does have some limitations, not defined but limitations nevertheless. That Old Guard's institutional gender bias just couldn't be suppressed, even when buried in accolades. Messersmith went on:

COOPERATION. Miss Willis apparently feels that she has been treated with every consideration by the Department. It is evident that she feels a certain discomfort in the Service as she is of the opinion that the Department is in principle against women officers but at the same time she feels that she has not been discriminated against.

Frances clearly scored points with that restrained attitude. Then Messersmith, now with his Old Guard hat firmly on, came to the critical part of the report:

PROFESSIONAL ATTRIBUTES. Her general professional equipment so far is only fair and she had no particular training which would fit her for the work of the Service. She has, however, certain natural aptitudes for the Service which can be much developed. She apparently has the capacity to become a good consular or diplomatic officer. Her background is such that she can serve in either branch. She has a good capacity for work and is at present carrying on her own shoulders at least half of the work of the office in spite of the fact that there are three other officers on the staff.

She has so far had no training, and has shown no capacity for political and economic reporting. It is possible that in this field her sex may impose certain limitations to her usefulness but this observation may be unjustified and the inspector refrains to pass judgment.

While the inspector believes that Miss Willis could serve acceptably as a diplomatic secretary, he is of the opinion that it would be better for her to continue for at least several years more in the consular branch.

So Messersmith's report started on high notes of adulation and then descended into rumblings of unease about her fitness, with the last paragraph literally overwhelming everything else. Specifically, that "keep her locked up in the consular service" recommendation was exactly what the Department's Old Guard wanted to hear. And they did just that for the next eighteen months. Messersmith finished with the following:

She is single and while interested in the Service evidently has no objections to matrimony. She apparently desires to spend some more years in the Service but as she is feminine in her major instincts and attractive to men, it is of course a question as to whether she would remain indefinitely in the Service. It is the opinion of the inspector, arrived at only after careful consideration, that as long as she desires to remain in the service, she will be a useful member of it.

Finally a Promotion

Now back to Carl Deichman, Frances' supportive boss, who was becoming increasingly frustrated over her lack of progress. His fourth report was submitted March 11, 1931, just after Frances was transferred to Santiago, and was an impassioned plea for a little recognition:

I can but reiterate the words of commendation and praise for her work as stated in my report on her efficiency dated August 1, 1930, and her service spirit is as keen and active as ever. She has taken part in every detail of the work of this office and demonstrated her unusual ability in every emergency.

I would strongly recommend that Miss Willis be promoted in grade as I think she feels keenly that so many of her class have been promoted, some of them some time back, and she might come to think that her efficiency is not recognized. It would seem a pity to discourage so efficient an officer when a sign of appreciation in the way of an infinitesimal promotion would encourage her to even greater effort and at the same time give her pleasure and satisfaction in knowing that the Department recognized her ability. She was in charge of the shipping and seamen work of this Consulate for one year and performed this disagreeable duty as well as any man could have done, and in addition had charge of the accounts and the visa work. I hope it may be possible to promote Miss Willis at an early date.

And that did the trick. The Department promoted Frances from FSO-unclass. to vice consul with a raise from $2500 to $3000 per annum in February, 1931, backdated a month from Deichman's letter.

A major reason for the delay in promoting Frances lay in the evaluations generated by the Department itself. During this time the Department hadn't started using its Rating Sheet. Instead, the Consular Service used short, unsigned reports called Efficiency Rating, covering Passport, Visa, Accounts, Notarials, Commercial, Shipping, etc. They ranged from one word to several lines, with some—astonishingly—handwritten at the bottom of her Foreign Service School record. That was such an informal, haphazard way of recording entries that they could easily be overlooked. And indeed they were at her next post, Stockholm.[26] These Efficiency Ratings continued to be used after the Rating Sheet was introduced in the early 1930's, then mercifully faded away after a few years. They were resurrected after WW II, but now in a well structured format.

Three Efficiency Rating topics were filed in Frances' dossier: Passport, Shipping and Commercial, starting out as follows:

---

[26] But maybe the Old Guard thought it wouldn't make any difference where they were recorded because none of these women were going to last very long anyway.

- Passport simply reported satisfactory but with no date or explanation.
- Shipping reported the following for 1928: "Drafted practically all shipping reports, which were better than Average and show steady improvement; deserves very close to a VERY GOOD rating. Rating: HIGH AVERAGE." Then Shipping boosted it to a VERY GOOD rating for 1929.
- Commercial reported the following for 1928: "This officer's commercial work gave evidence of careful study and unusual grasp of economic questions. She submitted 1 report Very Good and 2 Good, besides commendable shipping reports. Volume should increase as she extends her knowledge of the district. HIGH AVERAGE."

In 1930 Commercial dropped the rating to AVERAGE "due to the decrease in volume of work submitted." Finally, Commercial dropped it to a NO RATING because Frances submitted an "insufficient quantity of commercial work upon which to base a rating." That is understandable because she had been transferred to other jobs for part of that reporting period. But the evaluator either didn't know about that transfer or chose to ignore it.

Thus a satisfactory Passport rating plus a steadily declining Commercial rating overwhelmed the very good Shipping rating. So, apparently based on the Department's own assessment of work submitted, Frances was performing no better than any of her female predecessors and didn't rate a promotion—never mind Deichman's glowing words.

Ultimately, Deichman broke through the Old Guard's inertia with his persistent recommendations, which resulted in the following entry in her Efficiency Rating report:

> November 13, 1930—Consul General Deichman calls to the Department's attention the excellent work performed by Miss Willis at Valparaiso, and recommends that she receive a promotion in recognition of her "demonstrated ability, efficiency, tact, and service spirit."

That comment followed by Deichman's impassioned March 11, 1931, report finally turned the tide for Frances.

Then to add a little whimsy to her working life, Frances received this hand-written note from Richard Halliburton, explorer, raconteur and author, dated January 3. No year was given, but it was probably 1929:

> *at sea*
> *Dear Miss Willis,*
>   *The enclosed cable awaited me in Rio—so that my long anxiety in regard the Para[guay] mail was somewhat allayed—especially as I know that once if ever, the package reaches <u>you</u>, it's good as in my hands, c/o Bolebs-Merrill Co., Indianapolis, Ind…*
>   *Had a most rollicking time in Buenos Aires—bought a monkey and hand organ & begged my way overland to Rio—via the Iguazu [Portuguese spelling, or Iguacú, Spanish spelling] falls. They are superb—be sure to include them on your way home.*
>   *My sincere compliment to you, and my appreciation for your many courtesies—*
>
>   *Cordially,*
>   *Richard Halliburton*

Richard Halliburton wrote adventure stories, including *The Royal Road to Romance, Glorious Adventure* and *The Complete Book of Marvels*. The Travelers' Tales Website provides more details of his life:

> Halliburton is known for having paid the lowest toll to cross the Panama Canal, which he swam in 1928, paying 36 cents.[27] Born in Tennessee in 1900, Halliburton died in 1939 as he and his crew attempted to sail a Chinese junk, the Sea Dragon, from Hong Kong to San Francisco as a publicity stunt. The vessel was un-seaworthy and went down in a storm, apparently shortly after Halliburton sent out his last signal. "Southerly gales, squalls, lee rail under water, wet bunks, hard tack, bully beef, wish you were here—instead of me!"

That's going out with panache. Clearly one Foreign Service perk is rubbing elbows with the rich, the famous and the eccentric to hear first hand about their monkeyshines.

---

[27] Then he traveled on to Chile where he met Frances.

The Smoker

The most notable event of Frances' tour in Chile occurred in 1928 when she was invited to a "smoker" aboard the battleship USS Maryland. The ship was carrying President-elect Herbert Hoover on a good-will tour around South America and had just put in to Valparaiso. The story goes as follows.[28]

Apparently, Frances' boss, Consul General Carl Deichman, had to leave town for a short while. And because his consulate then consisted of just two FSO's and a support staff, Frances, still a FSO-unclass., found herself as acting consul general, which sets the scene for the arrival of the USS Maryland.

Whenever a USN ship enters a foreign port, she radios ahead to notify the senior US official in that port. The official is also invited aboard to brief the ship's officers on local customs and conditions, schedule meetings and events with the local dignitaries and maybe enjoy a smoke, because liquor was—and still is—proscribed aboard USN ships. So Frances, listed as F. E. Willis, Acting Consul General, Valparaiso, was duly invited aboard the USS Maryland.

The captain's gig was sent to pick up the acting consul general. It then returned to the battleship where this official was piped aboard by the boatswain mate of the watch. And who should emerge on the quarterdeck? A girl, to the utter astonishment of the officer-of-the-deck and probably everyone else on board including Hoover.

The smoker was immediately cancelled, to be replaced with on-deck tea. But Frances would have none of that and the smoker proceeded as scheduled! There is no record of Frances actually smoking a cigar, although it is quite possible she did—if it were a small one.

There is also no record of Frances meeting Hoover, but it would have been another stunner if she had, because she could have said, "Good to see you again, Mr. President!" In any case, this was the first time in the annals of U.S. Naval history that a woman FSO was piped aboard a capital ship. (Ruth Bryan Owen

---

[28] This story was patched together from two badly distorted news articles and a letter from her old friend Scott Burns, of 1915 Redlands wedding fame, along with the author's experience from tours aboard battleships and destroyers. For example, one article had the USS Maryland dropping anchor in Santiago, which would be a neat trick, since Santiago is 50 miles inland. Another put the U.S. Legation in Valparaiso, which just had a Consulate there. Another called Frances a "Ranking Vice Consul," a fictitious title. Finally, the USN gave Frances an 18-gun salute when she was piped aboard the USS Maryland. That of course is reserved for deputy heads of state, cabinet members and five-star generals.

Rohde was politically appointed Minister to Denmark a year later in 1933, thereby becoming the first U.S. woman chief of mission. So she would be the second woman to receive such honors whenever USN ships visited Copenhagen.)

A reception followed the smoker the next day.

Reception aboard the USS Maryland in Valparaiso (courtesy U.S. Navy.)

People are from the left: Mr. Carl F. Deichman, Consul General; Mrs. W. A. Murphy; Miss Frances Willis, (Acting) Vice Consul; Capt Kimberly, Commanding Officer. Apparently Deichman hustled back to town in time to resume command of his consulate and then visit the President aboard the Maryland, with Frances reverting back to bottom-rung (acting) vice consul. In fact, the entire staff in Santiago probably showed up for the same reason, but no other photos of the visit, including any of Hoover, survived. Mrs. W. A. Murphy's identity remains a mystery.

Incidentally, there was nothing in Frances' dossier about this acting consul general position, and it wouldn't be the last time such an omission happened. But one thing is certain: This was the first "naval event" recorded in her career. She would have many more.

Short Transfer to Santiago

Frances, as a newly minted vice consul, was ordered to Santiago on February 24, 1931, reporting to the consulate there on March 4, 1931. Then she received orders dated March 3, 1931, assigning her to a new post in Stockholm! Clearly, the consul general made his decision to transfer Frances from Valparaiso to Santiago without any knowledge of the Stockholm assignment from Washington.

That's not surprising because long-distance telephone or telegraph service was both expensive and tenuous in the early thirties, especially to remote places like Chile. And mail traveled over the same 30-day route most people did—by steamer. So foreign service outposts were pretty isolated from the mother station, i.e., the left foot had no idea what the head was doing at the moment, and vice versa.

But Frances didn't leave Chile for another seven months. While there is nothing in her dossier about this delay, she was probably waiting for her relief to show up. This extra time allowed Consul General Thomas Bowman to file an Annual Efficiency Report on Frances, dated August 1, 1931. His report is almost identical to Deichman's first report:

> It is a pleasure to be able to report that Miss Willis has proven to be a very highly intelligent officer ...shown excellent judgment ...very good speaking, reading and writing knowledge of Spanish ...entirely dependable, exceedingly industrious, ...capable of any function in the consular office ...English composition beyond criticism ...but her only handicap would be one entirely due to her sex which makes certain contacts out of question.
>
> I believe her competent for any administrative work ...has a pleasing but amply dignified manner towards callers, with ample self assurance. Complimentary remarks regarding her have been received on the outside in abundance.
>
> She deserves special credit for the long hours freely and uncomplainingly devoted to assisting in the onerous work of organizing a new officer and training clerks. In appearance and dress she is beyond criticism. Her work is neat. She moves in the best social circles and appears to be popular. She enjoys the best of health and is amply energetic.
>
> She would prefer a diplomatic assignment. Aside from the question of sex I should say she is amply qualified for such work.
>
> I consider her an excellent officer.

Like Deichman's first report, Bowman used glowing words about her—interspersed with that institutionalized gender bias. And, like Deichman, it appears that Bowman was beginning to join the cleaved FSO camp.

Frances and Bowman became good friends during her short stay in Santiago. Their friendship was documented in a long, chatty letter she wrote to him April 1, 1932, after arriving in Stockholm, now as a third secretary in the Diplomatic Corps. She commented that it was "too soon to know whether or not I like the consular or diplomatic work better—anyway ten o'clock instead of nine in the morning is some improvement." That comment suggested she was an evening person when much of the important foreign service work was done, via dinner, parties, bridge, etc. Perts documents this kind of work in the following sketches. Frances would have avoided the first one. But she was comfortable in the second, scoring many of her career points in this kind of "work environment," as they say today.

"Overtime" and "More Overtime" from M. C. Perts' 1924 book.

Frances' letter was in response to Bowman's January 20, 1932, letter, which reached her in Redlands while she was on home leave. The exchange was initiated because the Comptroller General had disallowed some of Frances' expenses in Chile and Bowman had gone to bat for her—to no avail.

The problem was that old Valparaiso post allowance compensation issue: Carr granting $250 per year in July, 1930, then rescinding $50 of it in November,

1930, but magnanimously forgiving the overpayment for those four months. But Chile (and other out-back posts) didn't get the rescinding word soon enough; so payments at the $250 rate continued beyond November. Consequently Frances was on the hook for those overpayments, an unwelcome claw-back anytime but especially in the Great Depression. Here is most of Bowman's letter.

PERSONAL

Santiago (Not Chilly now) on January 20th

Dear Miss Willis:

It was a relief to get your cable reporting a happy landing; a delight to get your equally kind and thoughtful letter from Buena Ventura and a pleasure to read of your appointment to Stockholm. But only grief attends the necessity which impels me to transmit the attached copy of an Instruction regarding your post allowance. I presume you have already received a copy. I tender no comments. Paper is too inflammable and I am rapidly developing a complex—if I have not already done so—upon certain subjects.

The other day I was riding home from a business trip to Valparaiso; I was hot, tired and in just the mood to brood upon certain aspects of my daily routine so I delivered myself of this:

> In the olden, golden, early days
> We earned our salaries various ways.
> Tough, fighting seamen added a zest
> To days that granted infrequent rest;
> Destitute countrymen, seeking relief,
> With explanations taxing belief;
> Missing husbands to be discovered;
> Missent baggage to be recovered;
> Many a message from the hoozgow:
> 'Consul, you must get me out somehow;'
> Bashful pride in the birth of a child;
> Joy of the wedding bells ring wild;
> Anguishing notes of death's sombre chord;
> All these were ours to share and record.
> Work was abundant and staffs were small

But joy of service repaid it all.

Now what do we do to earn our pay?
We fill out blank forms most of the day;
Replies to exceptions, these consume
Most of our time and much of our room;
Monthly accounts, ten days to prepare,
(And not a day too much, I swear)
Sign here you didn't, here that you did,
Of signing you may not hope to get rid,
Now turn over and sign the reverse,
G.A.O.'s demands grow worse and worse;
Upon growing index cards we frown,
Swarming like rats of Hamelin Town;
Consular Regulations must be
Annotated and checked up to see
If pages are missing. When that's done
The rest of the month we spend upon
Visa reports, eight, ten, twelve or more,
Well filled up with statistics galore.

We don't begrudge work but the routine
Leaves us scant time for things in between.

After which I felt better. We have too many officers and not enough clerks in the office. I am going to offer to swap an officer for a clerk. There are several men that do not seem to have so much business with us since you left. I use the adjective "several" only in the interest of moderation of which I am a strong advocate.

My wife joins me in very kindest regards to you. We sincerely hope you have a pleasant voyage, like your new work, enjoy Stockholm and don't have any troubles. Don't fall overboard.

Cordially yours,
/s/ *Thomas Bowman*

[PS] Did you not pick up any juicy morsels of gossip in the Department?

So Frances had become a magnet for men in Santiago, as she will be in later posts, starting with the U.S. Navy in Stockholm. And the poem: as clever as the Foreign Service School play, but now tragic. The Consular Service has gone from a place of action officers to paper-pushing bureaucrats, all under the watchful eye of the G.A.O., the General Accounting Office established in 1921 under the Comptroller General with the principal mission in the 1920's and 1930's of voucher checking! What a sad stroke for someone like Bowman.

7

SWEDEN AND DIPLOMACY

Settling in as a Diplomat

FRANCES spent the next four months, between October, 1931, and February, 1932, on one-month home leave, one-month temporary assignment in Washington DC and the rest on first-class travel: Santiago to New York to Washington DC, then to Redlands, back to New York and finally to Stockholm.

Frances was informed via an official letter of December 29, 1931, from Wilber Carr (of State) that she was nominated "Secretary in Diplomatic Service of the U.S." and confirmed by the Senate on December 17, 1931. Now she must take the oath, which she did as part of her duty in Washington DC. So Deichman's impassioned pleas, bolstered by Bowman's excellent review, reduced Messersmith's (minimum) two-year consular sentence to 18 months when she was finally admitted to the diplomatic service. She arrived at the American Legation in Stockholm on February 2, 1932.

Frances' April 1 letter to Bowman from the last chapter, recounted her first impressions of Stockholm and the American Legation there:

> Mr. Tredwell, the new C.G. [Consul General] here, is rabid on the subject of routine. He impresses me as being very able, and also very likable. His wife is very young and very pretty—they have only been married three years I believe. Dunlap is the only other officer at the Consulate, but they have a large staff of clerks, and of course their immigration work, which used to be tremendous, has practically evaporated.

Here at the Legation Mr. Crocker, the other secretary, is the only other career person, Mr. Moorhead being very much the political appointee.[29]

I'll have been here just two months tomorrow and so far am very favorably impressed. Lots of people tell me Sweden is a very depressing place to live, but at least I missed the worst of it, November, December and January being the really gloomy months. People and entertainments are very formal but taken individually I find the Swedes charming and hospitable. They are terribly proud and independent, and things must be done their way, but on the whole it's not such a bad way, so far as I have discovered so I've no objections to conforming.

I'm still living at the Grand Hotel, but am looking quite vigorously for an apartment. I hoped to find a furnished one, but that breed doesn't seem to grow here, at least not the kind I want, so now I have just about decided to take one unfurnished and begin to accumulate a few household goods and chattels of my own. The difficulty is that I don't particularly admire the type they have in Sweden, and things here are expensive.

I'm afraid I didn't hear any really "good" gossip while in Washington. The people I know in the Department were all very much taken up with the "Manchuria Affair" when I was there, and that is such ancient history now that it is ridiculous.

The Manchuria Affair started with Japan's invasion of Manchuria in 1931. The League of Nations failed to respond. Neither did the U.S., because it was still steeped in isolationism and of course was not a member of the League of Nations. So Japan got away with it—with ominous portents for events ten years later.

Her housing problems were solved when a member of the legation staff was temporarily transferred out of country and Frances sublet his fully furnished flat in Stockholm. Then she hired a cook whose name was Anna, "a splendid cook," as Frances reported in one of her (now available) letters to the family. And

---

[29] Moorhead was the minister. Mr. Crocker was Edward Savage Crocker, II, a career FSO with a great name for the job. So Frances was #2 on the accession list, the list of FSO's qualified to assume acting chief of mission, also called chargé d'affaires. Apparently consuls were not placed on the list at this time, even though everyone was now designated a Foreign Service Officer.

that luxury—at least by late twentieth century standards—allowed Frances latitude for diplomatic entertainment. In fact, for most of her career Frances hired domestics and to a person, they served her well. There always seemed to be an affectionate bond between Frances and her house staff.

Frances had to hustle to find $300 for the first three months rent payment on the flat, as she hadn't been able to save anything in this expensive post. So she asked her mother Belle to sell some of her inherited Anaconda stock and deposit the proceeds in her checking account. Belle did that, reporting an astonishing $190 profit—right in the middle of the depression. Her Uncle George, the family patriarch, was likely behind that stock purchase.

In fact, money had become a major issue in the Foreign Service in 1934. Frances explained the problem in a letter to her mother:

> Congress is supposed to be doing something about our salaries and maybe after July first when the government's new financial year begins we won't be in such a tight fix. So far, I've managed to keep out of debt which is more than most people in the Foreign Service who haven't private incomes can say. You see, in the cash of the country where we are, we are getting just about 50% or less of what we used to before they cut our salaries and the President took the dollar off gold. For a married man it is impossible to live even decently on what he gets from the government.

So that Silver J. Barr caricature in the Foreign Service School play was indeed a poke at the financial vicissitudes of a foreign service career. Silver had become the sole basis for U.S. currency, which devalued the standard of living in foreign posts that remained on the gold standard. Then Frances reported in a later letter:

> Oh, yes I should add that we have had very good news from Washington about our pay, and from now on I'll be getting about 75% of what I was getting in 1932 instead of only 50%. Some of the readjustment is to be retroactive so my next payday I'll get a check I'll be able to see without a microscope.

The Real Business of Diplomacy

Apparently the real business of diplomacy started after the close of business: cocktails, bridge, dinner, theater, supper, then more cocktails, tea and more bridge with the host-country's royalty, elected officials, military and civil servants, along with fellow diplomats from other countries; in short: the resident diplomatic corps.

This game was played every night of the week into the wee hours of the morning —except during mourning when royalty died. So that's why normal mission working hours started at 10 a.m., which allowed a few hours of late sleep. And it was a diplomat's duty to do this—to develop personal relationships with each of these state representatives, just as Hugh Gibson said in Lucile Atcherson's evaluation.

Frances reported this type of diplomatic entertaining in her now-weekly bulletins to the family, usually in great detail. Here is a sample from a series of 1934 bulletins at the end of her tour in Stockholm, starting with her take on the other female diplomat in town, Russian (Bolshevik) Minister Alexandra M. Kollontay:

> Friday afternoon after we got the pouch off, I called by arrangement on Madame Kollontay.[30] I was of course away when we recognized Russia and so didn't call, and shortly after I came back she went away, and then when she came back she invited us to dinner on April 6, so instead of just sending my card I asked if I might call—which I did.
>
> We had a cup of tea together and had a very friendly chat. I still can't make up my mind about her—whether she is diabolically clever (which of course if she were she would conceal) or whether she is just an ordinary mortal who is useful to the Bolsheviks largely because she is a "lady." [She was the daughter of a Czarist general.] That is all I am more or less convinced of about her. I think she is to the "manor-born," or I believe the expression has now been corrupted into "to the manner-born."

---

[30] A diplomatic pouch contains documents, letters, etc. typically sent out to the Department weekly. By international convention it is immune from inspection or tampering by other countries.

Frances continued with the dinner party in a second bulletin.

Friday I dined at the Russian Legation for the first time. Madame
Kollontay is a very gracious hostess, but it was extremely amusing to see
her try to abolish ceremony, such as the "parade" in to dinner, and still
seat the various ministers etc. according to rank. There were place cards
but as we did not parade in we didn't enter in the order of precedence
and she had to show people where to go.

There was an awful lot of gold plate about for it to be the Bolshevik
Legation—and as is the case with everything connected with her there
are several versions as to the origin: one that it belonged to her family,
and another that it is part of the imperial plate confiscated by the new
regime. The gold coffee service had an *A* with a crest over it on each
piece; therefore it might have belonged to one of the Alexanders, but
how should I know?

We had food which would have tickled the palate of any gourmet,
but so much of it that I was almost ill by the time we finished, only to
have a short respite, and then tea at a quarter to eleven! We began with
simply mountains of fresh Russian caviar, which I like. I never did like
the stuff that comes in tins or is salted, and with it we had vodka, which
is certainly potent.

Afterwards we didn't do anything but sit around and talk—I suppose
bridge is too bourgeois a game to be indulged in at the Russian Legation.
I talked for quite a while to the Counselor of the Legation who leaves in
a few days to go to Danzig as Consul General.

I left with Baron and Baroness Ramel (of the Foreign Office) and
de L'Eprevier [French diplomat] about 11:15 and we all lamented the
fact that there had been no bridge. I don't mind talking if people are
interesting or they have something to say but I am afraid the "art" of
conversation is dead, if there ever were one. We were all in the same
frame of mind and at somebody's suggestion the four of us went to the
Ramels, whose flat was the nearest, and proceeded to have quite a game
of bridge.

Madame Alexandra Kollontay's outrageous career was documented in a 1953
newspaper article by Walter Monfried, titled "Uncle Sam's Diplomatic Nieces."

It included write-ups and photos of "Uncle Sam's first six nieces," prefaced by Madame Kollontay:[31]

Unquestionably the most colorful and romantic of all the [modern] women diplomats was the first of them, Alexandra Kollontay. A daughter of the upper classes in czarist Russia, she early joined socialist and pacifist movements and went into exile until the Bolshevik revolution. She was the first woman in the Soviet cabinet.

When Alexandra was a young married woman, and even not so young, it was l'amour toujours l'amour. She advocated the freest of relationships between men and women, she wrote books to that effect, and she followed her own precepts zealously.

Many a gallant countryman gained Alexandra's attention and affection. As a warm blooded lassie of 45 years, she fell violently in love with a Russian naval hero, whose reputation as a Lothario was firmly established. Although the revolution at that time was in a crucial period, the two lovers skipped off to the Crimea for a prolonged vacation.

Members of the top Soviet committee were enraged by this escapade. Some suggested severe punishment, even death, for "desertion in the face of the enemy." Premier Lenin listened carefully to the debate and then spoke: "I fully concur with your view. Death is not adequate for such an offense. So I propose that they not only be censured in strongest terms but be punished in an exemplary manner, to wit: The guilty parties be sentenced to be exclusively faithful to each other for five years." The motion was carried amid laughter, but Alexandra was never overly grateful to Lenin.

Her appointment as trade delegate to Norway in 1923 was hailed as a victory for women's rights. Three years later she was chosen minister

---

[31] The "first six nieces" were:

Ruth Bryan Owen Rohde Minister to Denmark	1933-1936	(P)
Florence Jaffray Harriman Minister to Norway	1937-1940	(P)
Eugenia Helen Anderson Ambassador to Denmark	1949-1953	(P)
Perle Mesta Minister to Luxembourg	1949-1953	(P)
Clare Boothe Luce Ambassador to Italy	1953-1956	(P)
Frances Elizabeth Willis Ambassador to Switzerland	1953-1957	(C)

P = Political appointment; C = Career appointment.

to Mexico. The American government refused to permit her to travel through the United States, and Mexico was hardly more friendly. During her six months in that country, the press was constantly emphasizing her love life, her jewels and Paris wardrobe, and the government treated her so harshly that she requested a transfer.

She then went to Norway. From 1930 to 1945 she was Ambassador to Sweden [where Frances met her], and her efforts towards ending the Russian-Finnish war won her a nomination for the Nobel peace prize. Mme. Kollontay died in 1952, at the age of 80.

To the manner—wealth, liaisons, diplomacy, culminating in a peace prize nomination—born, indeed. Even Clare Boothe Luce should have been impressed.

(Diplomatic) Bridge

Bridge—mostly contract, but with some duplicate and occasionally even auction for the very obsolete dignitaries—was a major activity at these diplomatic corps parties. And it was played with a full set of diplomatic rules, as M. C. Perts shows for junior diplomats: Know your place and lose far more often than you win. Not only that, but always show your game face: no complaining about bad cards, bad partners or bad luck. And never, never any gloating, except in private.

"A Game Loser" from M. C. Perts' 1924 book.

Frances frequently reported her bridge games because she played almost every night. Here are examples, starting with a March 9, 1932, letter to Belle a month after she arrived in Stockholm:

Some how or other the rumor got around Stockholm that I played excellent bridge. I heard about it and Sunday played about the vilest game I've ever been guilty of! Anyway I now take it more seriously and read the Blue Book [a classic bridge book by Ely Culbertson] during spare minutes.

Then in a March 23, 1932, letter to the family:

I had a good game of bridge at the Crockers on Saturday and again on Sunday afternoon, and on Sunday stayed for dinner. On Thursday went from a tea to the Czechoslovakian Legation with Mme. Hurban (wife of the Czech Minister, born in Chicago,) [Folmer] Hansen [a member of the Swedish Foreign Ministry and Frances' competition-bridge partner] and the new French Secretary, de L'Eprevier, for a short game of bridge before dinner, and at 2:45 a.m. we were still there. The Minister had insisted that we stay and have ham and eggs and that we keep on playing. He is in a way the most undiplomatic person I've seen in these parts—I'd call him a typical Bohemian—he has served in Washington and uses perfectly terrible American slang, and wanted to start a crap game when we stopped playing bridge. The C's [Crockers] can't stand him, think he is terribly vulgar, etc. Hansen is very charitable and says you must remember he was wounded or gassed in the war, and therefore isn't quite normal. Anyway he plays the wildest game of bridge and once he gets started hates to stop.

The bridge news went on and on, with this in a later bulletin from Stockholm:

Tuesday Peggy and Bobbie Robbert had a very nice dinner of twenty-two, and afterward I played bridge at the same table with Mrs. S., [Steinhardt, wife of the new American minister] and my partner and I were so lacking in respect for her rank that we set her and her partner six doubled vulnerable, 2,700 points I believe it was.

Wednesday night there was one of the most boring parties I have ever attended and it had to be at the Steinhardts, where I couldn't leave until the last guest had and because the tables for bridge didn't come out even I didn't play and had to sit around and talk to a horrible lot of bores until one o'clock if you please.

Ah, the burden of a junior officer. Clearly Frances was furious over the Steinhardt party because she told the story in one long breath. She did like to play bridge. Although she didn't say, there was no gloating over the Steinhardt 2,700 point set, just a lot of sympathy over "bad luck with those two finesses," precisely as M. C. Perts prescribed in his sketch. Anything else could easily destroy a career on the spot.

But all this was just social bridge. Frances jumped into the big-time competition soon after she arrived in Stockholm as the following photo shows.

The Second World (Duplicate) Bridge Olympic Tournament, held at the Restaurant Gillet, Stockholm, November, 1932.

Team members are from the left: Crocker, Frances, de L'Eprevier and Folmer Hansen. Frances reported this competition in an attachment to her November 6, 1932, letter, starting with a quote from the *Tidningen-Stockholms Dagblad:*

"Also in the seventh group the play had an exciting finish. Mr. and Mrs. Westring had a big lead and it looked as if the international combination of Folmer Hansen-Miss Willis would have to be satisfied with third place (in the group) and consequently be put out of the tournament. However, Miss Willis in the final round gave evidence of extraordinary exhibition nerve, and after brilliant and cold-blooded play she and her partner advanced to second place."

As a matter of actual fact Hansen saved us by a very daring double, which however "came off," and I almost wrecked us by leading a queen of diamonds from an ace-queen tenace [a combination of two nonadjacent high cards of the same suit in one hand], but as a matter of fact we also got two extra tricks by that lead, which Culbertson rates as the worst possible if I remember correctly, in the back of his summary, and put them three down instead of just one—compared with the other table we won over a thousand on that hand.

Frances continued for another page describing the final competition the next weekend. Apparently they didn't win any prizes, but had enough fun to make up for it.

Work

Frances seldom reported work-news in her bulletins because it was often too sensitive or even classified and so couldn't be revealed. Thus much of her "work-data" had to be gleaned from the Annual Efficiency Reports filed in her dossier. Two such reports marked her two and a half-year tour in Stockholm. The first was written August 18, 1932, in longhand by Minister John M. Moorhead, previously a chemist who provided the business foundation for Union Carbide Corp., then Mayor of Rye, New York, and finally a noted philanthropist. Here it is in its entirety.

> *Miss Willis has filled the position of 3rd Secty. & made a very pleasant impression on the members of the Legation staff & on the Diplomatic & Governmental circles in Stockholm.*
> *She is a very well educated woman and has had experience in coding & decoding dispatches & c. [cables]. Is pleasing in appearance & modest in bearing which have made her quite popular in her rather difficult position. She takes her duties seriously & works hard at them. During the absence of Mr. Crocker she is the only secty at this Legation & is discharging the work in a satisfactory manner.*

In sum: "pleasant, pleasing, popular—and satisfactory," not a sterling review. Nor was it the most professional evaluation. But then Moorhead was a political appointee. Probably the best news is that his "quite popular in her rather difficult position" comment suggests that Frances had managed to diffuse some arrival gender bias. That's progress at least for a brief moment.

The coding and decoding work is new. It also required a security clearance at a very high level. That sounds like an impressive credential for a young officer—except that it wasn't. The coding system used before WW II required that the cryptographer manually code or decode each letter of each word in a classified cable, using an ever-changing code of the day contained in a book kept in a safe. The work was incredibly tedious, with brevity being the cardinal guideline for writing cables in those days.

The most important event of Frances' Stockholm tour was documented in two press clippings filed in her dossier. Here is October 13, 1932, *Washington Star* clipping:

WOMAN BECOMES "U.S. MINISTER" FOR FIRST TIME IN HISTORY

Hailing From Illinois, Miss Frances Elizabeth Willis Temporarily Gains Stockholm Post.

For the first time in history a woman, Miss Frances Elizabeth Willis, from the obscure little village of Metropolis, Ill., is the acting American Minister to a foreign country. The news was conveyed to Secretary of State Stimson yesterday in a brief and businesslike cablegram addressed from the American Legation at Stockholm, capital of Sweden. It read, "The Minister left last night. I have assumed charge. (Signed) Willis."

In the midst of grave international problems, Secretary Stimson paused to ponder upon the identity of this "Willis" who is now the temporary chargé d'affaires at an important foreign capital. Inquiries developed she was the third secretary of the legation, one of the two women in the entire Foreign Service of the United States.

For a month, at least, Miss Willis will be clothed with full responsibility to discharge all the duties and functions of the head of the mission in Sweden. Those who know her well say she is perfectly capable of doing it properly. The American Minister, John Motley Moorhead, has just left to return to this country on a payless furlough, and in the absence of others [Crocker was on holiday] at the legation Miss Willis found herself the ranking officer.

Hers was a "break" that comes only about once in the lifetime of an obscure third secretary.

John Moorhead's payless furlough was explained in his November 3, 1932, letter to Frances, first thanking her for orchestrating all his birthday telegrams, which arrived when he was campaigning for Herbert Hoover in New York. Then:

> The campaign is getting quite hot and there is a distinct drift toward Hoover. If the tidal wave catches him before the eighth of November, I think we will elect him, otherwise the situation is quite doubtful.

Well, Moorhead's tidal wave turned out to be a rip tide, with Roosevelt winning handily. While that sealed the fate of Minister Moorhead, Hoover again boosted Frances' career by asking Moorhead to come home and campaign for him, just at the time Edward Savage Crocker was off on holiday.

While these were the only two press clippings covering the event in Frances' dossier, over 100 were in the Hoover Archives, all the way from the *News Democrat* in Paducah, Kentucky to the *Bulletin* in Bend, Oregon. The *Los Angeles Times* ran the story finishing with, "Since then Miss Willis is known as 'Miss American Minister.'" Even Mrs. Moorhead sent Frances a batch with the comment, "No doubt you have enough to fill an entire scrapbook."

All this publicity generated considerable response from the American public. Here are two letters, the first from a former Ambassador to the Vatican, Robert U. Johnson, now at the Hall of Fame, New Your University:

> Dear Miss Willis,
>
> May I offer you my respectful compliments on your new responsibility? Your portraits in the newspapers here inspire one with confidence in your ability and good judgment. I wish you might have been on my staff in Rome in 1920.
>
> I believe you are entitled to the designation of Excellency. I fear there

is no feminine for chargé. The French language would go to pieces if one said <u>chargée</u>! With all good wishes, very sincerely yours.

/s/ *Robert Underwood Johnson*

For contrast, here is one penned by a Southern California evangelical after reading the *Los Angeles Times* article:

"Miss American Minister"
Stockholm, Sweden.
Dear Miss Frances Elizabeth Willis:
*   I congratulate you as being our first Lady Minister from United States of America. I am an Ambassador of the King in Heaven.*
*   Our earthly glory is like a day with our God. Soon the King is coming, to take over this world.*
*   Don't mock me. I will send you each week the Signs of the Times and I pray in time you will be an Ambassador for Christ our King.*

With Love,
Peter

So the first letter was from a former ambassador to the Pope and the second was from a current ambassador to God. That would be enough to convert most heathens. Frances was also invited to become one of a thousand *California Women of Prominence,* complete with biography and photo in a book—a modest, first start to many such honors. (Her major honors and awards are documented in Appendix 2.)

President Roosevelt then replaced Moorhead with Laurence A. Steinhardt in July, 1933. Steinhardt's evaluation of Frances in March, 1934, looked like the work of a career FSO, which he was. It also looked like the ones Carl Deichman produced; the phrases are almost identical:

    ...unusually high degree of intellect ...very observing and penetrating mind ...education and cultural attainments a maximum ...thoroughly dependable ...highest sense of responsibility ...pronounced sense of justice ...unsurpassable devotion to duty ...extremely cooperative ...personal life beyond reproach.

It went on like that for a full page. One critical comment was "limited linguistic attainments." Specifically, Steinhardt was worried that Frances wasn't picking up enough Swedish. And she wasn't, because she didn't have "a pressing need to. We have one clerk here in the Legation who does nothing but translate Swedish newspapers," as she reported in a letter. After that Frances got busy learning Swedish. Steinhardt then added some new, flattering observations about Frances:

> She has a marked ability as respects political, economic and commercial reporting and has the facility of preparing the most excellent and thorough reports on almost any subject assigned to her.
>
> In conclusion I regard Miss Willis' personal qualities and capabilities as far above the average having regard to the post occupied by her and as far above the average man in the service occupying the same post.

No limitations of her sex comment there—in fact just the opposite viewpoint, suggesting another cleaved FSO. And Frances got away with thrashing the minister's wife at the bridge table without recriminations. Very good news all around.

But wait! There is nothing in either of these Stockholm reports about Frances' one-month chargé d'affaires duty in October, 1932. Of course: It happened *after* Moorhead wrote Frances' Annual Efficiency Report. Then Moorhead either forgot to tell Steinhardt about it (likely), or did tell him and Steinhardt forgot about it (possible). So Frances' "once in a lifetime break" fell into a big crack.

Then the first Department-generated Rating Sheet appeared in Frances' dossier. Recall that these sheets were single-paragraph summaries of an FSO's performance over the past two years, prepared by a senior—but anonymous— FSO redactor. The summary was based on memos, letters, press articles and Annual Efficiency Reports that found their way into the FSO's dossier. The redactor would then subjectively assess the data and enter a grade at the end of the paragraph. Most importantly, that sheet served as a critical part of the promotion process. Frances' first entry was for Stockholm, dated January 1, 1933—after the Moorhead report but before the Steinhardt report. It covered her time in Chile as well. Here is exactly what it said:

RATING SHEET

<u>WILLIS, FRANCES E.</u>   STOCKHOLM UNCL—$3000
Entered the Service Aug. 24, 1927   Last Promoted Apr. 17, 1931

<u>Comments</u>: Third Secretary Willis entered the Service in 1927 with
an unusually good educational background and was assigned as
Vice Consul at Valparaiso. Her work in the Consulate General was
entirely satisfactory and her assignment to duty was not particularly restricted, although practically every report on her contains
some such statement as "subject to the limitations of her sex." She
has demonstrated her capacity for hard work. There is, however,
nothing in her record which is outstanding and her career is of
special interest because of her sex and the manner in which she
overcomes her limitations.

January 1, 1933
Rating: SATISFACTORY

The comment, "practically every report on her contains some such statement
as 'subject to the limitations of her sex,'" requires comment. Seven reports for this
period were in her dossier and only three (one each from Deichman, Messersmith
and Bowman) had such statements. So that comment appears to have been a
blatant exaggeration, strongly suggesting that the anonymous redactor had his
Old Guard hat on.

Biased as that was, the real tragedy for this 1933 entry was that it had
nothing about Frances' chargé d'affaires duty, even though two press articles—
with photos—had been filed in her dossier three months earlier. So the redactor
either didn't take the time to find them or elected to ignore them. Furthermore,
he didn't see—or again ignored—one of the entries added to the second page of
Frances' 1927-1928 Foreign Service School Record of Work:

October 11, 1932—In the absence of Minister Moorhead and Mr.
Crocker on leave, Miss Willis, Third Secretary, assumed charge of the
Legation at Stockholm. This places Miss Willis in a unique position,
since it is the first time an American Mission has been left in charge of
a woman.

Well, why should he even look there, because it wasn't in the time frame of the current review? But why it was there and not filed as a chronological entry defies rational explanation—leaving only this demonic speculation: The action memo attached to the report said to file it in Frances' dossier, making the normal assumption that it would be filed according to date. But because it didn't say that explicitly, the filer (an Old Guard clerk or FSO) took the liberty of filing it elsewhere—out of normal sight. Speculation? Yes, but no other rational explanation is apparent.

Consequently, even though the event was documented three times in Frances' dossier, she got no recognition in this new Rating Sheet for her chargé duty, just as she got no recognition for her acting consul general duty in Valparaiso. Thus once again, while Frances momentarily rose through the glass table to sit above the (acting) chief of mission glass ceiling, the Old Guard—in a full dose of perverse gender bias—saw to it that she was immediately returned to her lowly appointed post with no recognition that she was ever permitted up there.

The U.S. Navy

It is time to report another naval event in Frances' life: the one-week visit to Stockholm of the heavy cruiser, USS New Orleans. Here is a photo of the ship with a little of its history.

The USS New Orleans (CA-32) heavy cruiser (courtesy U.S. Navy.)

The New Orleans was a 10,000 ton ship-of-the-line, commissioned 15 February, 1934, the first ship of her class. She carried nine eight-inch guns, three seaplanes and a crew of 1121. She was on her shakedown cruise, and Stockholm was probably her first port of call. So the commanding officer, Capt. Reed, made sure everyone was on his best behavior, and Frances reported they were.

During WW II the New Orleans was at sea when Pearl Harbor was attacked, so survived unscathed. She served with distinction in the Pacific Theater, but was torpedoed during the battle of Tassaforanga at Guadalcanal, which detonated the forward magazine, blowing off the entire bow section up to the second eight-inch gun turret.

During the battle the ammunition hoists failed, so ammunition had to be passed manually. The chaplain on board volunteered to help, calling out, "Praise the Lord and pass the ammunition." The ship did not sink, and managed to put in to Australia, where U.S. Seabees patched her up. She returned to the U.S. for a new bow, and then back into action. They don't build ships like that anymore.

Frances sent a short, hurried letter of May 23, 1934, to her mother:

> Yes, I know it is shocking I didn't get a letter off on Sunday and I haven't yet either. So I'm putting this in the mail so you won't think anything has "happened" and I am not going to write about it now because I've lived through this day promising myself a nap before the Captain's dinner (very exclusive: only 15) on board the USS New Orleans this evening. I left the Steinhardt's dance—a simply marvelous party—at 4 this morning and was at work by 9:30—so you see...
>
> I've had so much work and so much play since the ship arrived I don't have much time even to eat except when it is on board or at a party—of which there have been many. There are several very attractive officers on the ship and Captain Reed is just about perfect. Next week everything will be very flat, so I'll have loads of time to write and I promise I shall.

So the U.S. Navy has just preempted the British Navy for the lady's attention. Her next week's letter was six typewritten pages. Here are excerpts:

> Anchors aweigh my boys![32] For we sail at the break of day! Unfortunately that is practically true, but if they didn't something else

---

[32] Actually Frances wrote "away," and in her next letter—with great distress—corrected the spelling.

unfortunate might happen, so although I hate to admit it, it probably is a good thing. In case I become involved in detail I might say to begin with that the visit of the USS NEW ORLEANS (the newest cruiser afloat) has been a real success—not only from my own personal point of view but from the impression made on the Swedes—from the King on down to the girls who have gone to Tivoli (the amusement park) with the gobs. On the other hand I never even imagined getting through as much work as I have this last week.

The only thing that has cramped my style is that being connected with the Legation I have been surrounded with a certain amount of rank, which at times wasn't as much fun as being able to go it on my own, but fortunately Commander Hersey, the executive officer on the ship, with whom I am often paired off, is—I find difficult to describe—but no end of a good fellow, so when things got dull and too official we have consoled each other.

The ship came in Thursday and the entire day literally was taken up with official visits and returns. I didn't have to go along I am glad to say—and salute. I had told Captain K. [Keppler, the U.S. naval attaché] that I would be glad to have him bring anyone up to my flat for a cocktail at the end of it all if he thought it was a good idea. (The semi-prohibition they have in Sweden and the strictness with which it is enforced we knew was going to be an awful shock to some of them.)

About six o'clock he appeared with Captain Reed and about six others—or more, I don't remember definitely and that phrase you might just apply to the rest of the visit. After two or three cocktails the Captain who had been up since daybreak which means about 2:30 in Sweden now, decided he had better go back to the ship, but the others and I devoted the evening to becoming better acquainted and finding a place to eat in Djurgarden. As we didn't leave my house until almost nine, it was way past some of the boy's "supper-time," and one of them got lost in an art gallery. Altogether it was one of those evenings which if you remember at all you remember a long time.

Friday night the Swedish Navy gave a stag dinner for them so I had my last good night's sleep, which was going to have to do me for some-time. Friday noon I forgot to mention the Steinhardts had the Captain and a few others to luncheon and for the rest of the afternoon I had a couple of Captains, a few odd Commanders and Lt. Hunt, the Captain's aide, hanging around my office while I was trying to dictate a few letters and get a spot of work done.

"Hanging around my office"? United States naval officers? Not unlike the siren attracting sailors in Homer's *Odyssey*—or the men conducting business with her in Valparaiso. Here's what they were hanging around. That velvet gown, which ran along the floor with a two-foot train, would not be too practical for office work or ordinary diplomatic functions— just the haute formal ones.

Frances in formal dress, Stockholm, circa 1934
(Lenkert, Birger, Jarlsgartan, Stockholm.)

Now back to the letter.

Saturday afternoon from four-thirty to six-thirty the Steinhardts had a huge tea for all the officers who could come ashore and at which if I ever saw it, champagne flowed like water. The officers came by motor launch from the ship right to the front door and it was really a thrilling sight to see them coming up the front terrace all in their boat cloaks, frock coats and brass buttons—at least no one could ever accuse me of <u>denying</u> my partiality to the navy.[33] Oh yes, a touching incident I forgot to mention was that on the first afternoon at my flat before we sallied forth in search of food they sang "Anchors Aweigh" for me—with a verse I had never heard before, and several other Navy songs. Imagine my delight.

My job on that Saturday afternoon was to take all the pretty Swedish girls by the hand as they came in and introduce the officers to them—and then leave!— and believe it or not the men had to be ordered back to the ship, and I was busy the last half hour supplying pencils so telephone numbers and addresses could be written down, no trusting to memory at that stage of the game.

There is nothing not to believe about that: She had just let a bunch of roosters into a hen-house; now try to shoo them out. Frances continued:

And even at that I didn't do so badly—both the Executive Officer (Hersey) and the Captain's Aide Hunt got the idea I had said I'd go out for dinner with them afterwards, and it ended in an unholy mess, and finally the three of us, the Steinhardts and Captain Keppler all went to the Operakellaren and had dinner and danced. I was hard, really hard, put to it because I find Hersey much more attractive and amusing than Hunt, but he is not a good dancer, and a little shorter than I, whereas Hunt is very tall and a superb dancer. A situation developed which was rather amusing and I had what turned out to be a very good time, with I might add, a double dose of navy-line.

Frances did not elaborate on "the situation" or "navy-line" but it seems pretty clear what they were up to. The dialogue went on like this for another three pages and four days, with nuggets scattered throughout:

All this last week everywhere I went I was attended by a fleet of

---

[33] For years afterwards, Frances coveted a boat cloak. But they could only be acquired by U.S. naval officers. So when the author was commissioned in 1956, he acquired one and sent it to Frances in Switzerland. She was delighted.

officers. Anna [Frances' "splendid cook"] couldn't quite make it all out having five men call to take me to dinner—it was ridiculous of course but fun, and often easier than singling out one. And they sent me flowers on the slightest provocation.

Monday afternoon not withstanding the holiday, I had to work and about six I had a cocktail party of about twenty-five for some of the lads. Hersey brought me a night-stick or baton, the kind the shore patrol uses so I could get rid of them when I wanted them to go. That so far is my one permanent trophy from the NEW ORLEANS.

Phyllis just fulfilled her prophesy from the Foreign Service School play, "Your girl in every port now furnished by the Government!"

The male-female dynamics in these shenanigans needs clarification. Frances was thirty-five at the time, which was close to many of the senior officers on the New Orleans, including Cdr. Hersey, the executive officer, and department heads such as the gunnery and operations officers. Many of them were married because on the last day Frances reported that she helped them "buy presents to take home to their wives." That left the junior officers in their twenties and more often single, such as Lt. Hunt: available but a bit too young and immature for Frances. So Frances emerged unscathed but totally captivated by the U.S. Navy—as a body.

One other naval officer needs attention, Captain Chester H. J. Keppler, U.S. Naval Attaché to both Germany where he resided and Sweden, which he often visited. "Kep," who was about ten years older than Frances, advised her on many naval issues and in the course of business they became good friends. In fact, Kep became so fond of Frances that during his next tour as Commanding Officer of the USS Minneapolis (CA-36), a sister ship to the New Orleans, he accorded her probably the highest informal honor possible in the U.S. Navy: He assigned one of his officers as her proxy when "crossing the line," thus awarding her the designation "Honorary Shellback."

That term may need an explanation—at least for "landlubbers." All sailors start out as *Pollywogs*. A sailor can only become a *Shellback* when he has crossed the equator <u>and</u> been successfully initiated into *The Solemn Mysteries of the Ancient Order of the Deep*. Thus when a ship crosses the equator all Shellbacks on that ship—officers and enlisted men—hold an initiation ceremony for the Pollywogs, orchestrated by the exalted Shellback dressed as *Neptunus Rex*.

The ceremony lasts the better part of a day and consists of abuses, such as running a gauntlet, then visiting the Royal Barber, the Royal Physician, the Royal Dentist and the Royal Baby. Each station inflicts wretched offenses to the body, such as whacking the butt with cudgels or fire hoses, shaving hair, spraying teeth with purple dye, etc. Then the Pollywog is consigned to the briny deep—blindfolded and heaved overboard, or so he is led to believe. Actually he is thrown into a large pit of breakfast garbage floating in seawater. Then after retrieval the Pollywog becomes a Shellback—if he survived the party. The USN officially banned the physical abuse element of these parties in the 1960's after two men did die. But unofficially, it persists pretty much unchanged.

And the point of all this corporal punishment? Bonding. Such ceremonies, along with shore-leave, bond sailors together. Bonding was—and often still is—needed because life aboard ship, especially small ships with no privacy or air conditioning, was tough. You needed to know your shipmates and tolerate their most basic personal habits—which were literally "in your face"—for weeks and months at sea. And it was easier to do this if you had bonded as a brother through brutal initiation into the Shellback Club.

Furthermore, life aboard any type of ship is dangerous, even in peacetime. So such bonding can generate a level of trust, which in turn can be used for survival. Falling overboard at sea tests this survival maxim. You trust your shipmates' motivation to find and then rescue you, and they are motivated, in a maximum sense, to rescue a bonded brother. Joseph Conrad in his book *Heart of Darkness* called it "the bond of the sea."

Frances and Kep would meet on many subsequent occasions. Even the author, escorted by his father (and Frances' brother), Henry Willis, visited Kep when he was a destroyer squadron commander in San Diego in 1940. Kep and Henry got into a deep discussion about the "Gathering Storm" in Europe, while the six-year-old author got a tour of the destroyer with its massive torpedoes. Sixteen years later the author, now an ensign, was assigned to a similar destroyer in San Diego, serving his "two years before the mast."

8

FRANCES AND HER MEN

Frances and Men in General

FRANCES never married, although she had suitors throughout much of her life, including Paul Daniels her fellow student at the Foreign Service School. When Frances entered the Foreign Service in 1927 marriage was unofficially proscribed for female Foreign Service Officers by the State Department. And she certainly knew that rule, which stood until 1971, as detailed in The Other Women chapter. But beyond that, it appeared that Frances began to make a "nuptial commitment" to the Foreign Service starting in Brussels, which in turn relegated marriage to a back burner. And this dedication to the service, this devotion to duty, virtually defined her life.

Those terms, dedication and devotion, appeared in many of her on-site performance evaluations, and in fact went a long way to break the Foreign Service's aversion to women—that "glass table." Now because of this dedication and devotion, Frances didn't have time for much else. She was a devout Christian, a confirmed Episcopalian, and went to church services every Sunday almost without fail.

What little time that was left, Frances devoted—there's that word again—to family, particularly her mother Belle during the last seven years of her life. Frances brought Belle with her to Berne, her first post as ambassador, and then on to Oslo, where Belle died at eighty-seven. So Frances' life can neatly be summed up by three words: family, church and service.

During her many press interviews, Frances was asked about marriage on three occasions. The first was during an interview with Dorothy McCardle of *The Washington Post and Times Herald* on April 14, 1957:

So comes the question, naturally enough: Why has she never married? She probably answered that one herself when a young Swiss girl wrote her for some advice to the lovelorn. The girl confided that she could not make up her mind about a certain suitor. What would Miss Willis advise her to do? Miss Willis wrote back, as she always writes with careful thought to all the hundreds who plague her by mail: "If you have to ask someone else about a question such as this, then you are not sure in your own mind. And if you are not absolutely sure in your own mind, don't do it." And then added Ambassador Willis in a give-away sentence: "I have always followed this rule myself."

The second was during an interview with Don Shannon in the *Los Angeles Times* June 13, 1968, edition, saying in part:

Frances was also asked why she did not follow the example of earlier Foreign Service women and leave the service to get married. Her answer: "I explained that I got so wrapped up in my work it never occurred to me," the retired ambassador said, her blue eyes twinkling.

The third was in a January 8, 1974, *Riverside Press-Enterprise* interview:

I couldn't see having a husband trail around after me. It just didn't fit in. I enjoyed my life and my work so much that I never missed getting married.

Now all these answers, while different are self-consistent. In fact they can be combined into a virtual statement:

I was so wrapped up in and enjoying my work that I never really thought about it; but when I did, I wasn't absolutely sure; and more to the point, I didn't want to drag a husband around after me.

But just because she didn't marry didn't mean she didn't like men. In fact she preferred the company of gentlemen to ladies certainly in professional gatherings, but also in most social events. That preference for men was driven home in a May 20, 2003, phone conversation with Martha Burns, wife of Findley Burns,

Frances' 1942 Madrid FSO associate. Martha said the first time she met Frances was on a visit with Findley to Berne after Frances had been appointed ambassador in 1953 and just after Martha and Findley were married. Martha said that Frances doted on Findley, leaving the distinct impression that she was just along for the ride.

Martha also said that Findley told her about seeing Frances at a Foreign Service Day gathering in the mid 1970's after Frances' stroke, which caused an ever-increasing memory loss. Frances greeted Findley warmly, and stood by him for much of the session. At one point she put her head on his shoulder, saying that she was glad he was there because she wasn't sure where she was or what she was to do. That was a confession granted to few men inside or outside of her family.

Findley and Frances were extremely close throughout their Foreign Service careers. Frances was eighteen years older than Findley and probably acted as a matriarchal sister during this time. Because Findley was also appointed an ambassador, it is likely that Frances accelerated his career when she sat on various Foreign Service selection boards. Findley appears many more times during Frances' career. Now to her romantic men.

Harry Cook (1891-1918)

Frances first met Harry Cook after the Willis family settled in Redlands in 1916. Apparently it didn't take long for the romance to develop, which soon became a most serious affair. Family lore has it that they became informally engaged (engaged but with no ring display) around 1917 while Frances was attending the University of Redlands.

After the U.S. entered WW I, Harry joined the new Army Air Corps and spent the rest of the war battling the Red Baron, Manfred von Richthofen, in dogfights over France. Here is his U.S. Army commissioning photo, which he probably gave to Frances before leaving for France in 1917.

*Second Lieutenant Harry Cook (courtesy Lucretia (Moore) Irving, daughter of Bill Moore, publisher of the **Redlands Daily Facts**, and grand niece of Harry Cook.)*

The war ended and as Harry was beginning his return trip to the U.S. on a French passenger train, it crashed and he was killed, much to the shock and sorrow both the Cooks and a young lass of nineteen. The Cook and Willis families remained close until Frances died and the Redlands home was closed in 1983.

But when that marriage door slammed shut it allowed a foreign service door to open later in Frances' life. And both couldn't be open at the same time. Maybe the gods find a way to compensate such tragedies.

When Frances was attending the Universite Libre de Bruxelles in 1920 she thought about visiting Harry's grave in France but decided not to. Then during a short holiday visit to France when she was posted to Brussels in 1937, her thoughts again turned to Harry as she said in a letter to Belle:

I did so want to go on to Saumur [in the Loire Valley] and other places Harry had been but had to content myself with spending a Sunday in Tours, as he used to. Since I've been on this trip I can certainly realize how the soldiers felt when they were in France. I've talked to people and understand the language but still I feel so cut-off from the rest of the world. Or at least "my world." I did at times, however, feel that Harry was very near and that meant a great deal. I trust that his influence will never go out of my life no matter how final and complete and physical the separation.

It had been twenty years since Harry was killed in France. The flame never died

Franklin Pierce (1893-1950)

Franklin Pierce was an avid—but intermittent—suitor, who lived in the Wissahickon Inn, just across the street from the family home on West Highland Avenue in Redlands. He was a namesake relative of Franklin Pierce, the fourteenth president. (President Pierce had no male progeny who reached puberty.)

Franklin used to drop by almost every time the family would assemble for Christmas—Frances on home leave from her exotic foreign post, the Vaughans occasionally from Chile, and the Henry Willis family from Salinas, California. He would usually stay for dinner, and the whole family would gush over him afterwards, saying what a polite, elegant, handsome gentleman he was, and from such a fine, noble family. Frances would blush. They were more than friends, writing warm letters to each other in the early part of Frances' career. Then the letters tailed off when Frances began her full commitment to the Foreign Service in Brussels.

One letter survived from Frances to Franklin dated January 19, 1934, following her home leave in Redlands. She wrote it on the Golden State Limited transcontinental passenger train after leaving Redlands on her way back to Stockholm. Here is most of it:

Dear Franklin:

Yes, I am aware of the fact that this is very bad technique: to write to you before I have heard from you, and especially in view of the fact that you asked me for neither my New York nor my S.S. address, so that obviously you have no intention of communicating further until I reach Stockholm. Or maybe it would be better to say you intended to break off diplomatic relations for that period. What care I about all that; I have either got to stop thinking about you or write to you and I can't do the former so it will have to be the latter.

But I can't write to your unrestrainedly as I would talk to you, although I tell myself you are different and this is different. But not believing in divine revelation I have only experience to guide me, and four times in less than six years I have been "gone and forgotten—sic transit gloriae mundi"—we are here today and gone tomorrow—did you ever hear that translation before? Yes, you probably saw the "Show-Off" too [a New York Broadway play, which ran for two years and then was made into a movie in 1926].

Since you are bashful about such things as buying alcohol in Redlands on Saturday night, have you a post box or do you get all your mail at the Wissahickon? If so will Swedish stamps embarrass you? And is L your middle initial, and what does it stand for? And when is your birthday and how did you happen to go to California anyway, and did you graduate in 1916, and there is no end to the things I'd like to know.

I slept fourteen hours last night and wish you were here to keep me awake tonight. Thank you for introducing me to Esquire—it is still with me and so far I have thought it just nicely rough. I've found one word I don't know the meaning of, but Ned [Crocker, her friend and fellow FSO from Brussels] has a wonderful vocabulary so I'll ask him in New York if I can remember.

And darling I shall of course think of you every time I use the cigarette case, which is just the right size—but I'll think of your many, many other times too. You left me wondering about a great many things; you upset some of my axioms, so I have some serious thinking to do. Maybe that is why the tone of this letter is rather heavy, or maybe it's because we're right in the middle of Kansas. Anyway it brings you my love and all that can be transported by a tender little kiss from,

Frances

She was certainly smitten by that boy, obviously intensified by the inevitable loneliness of leaving friends and relatives in Redlands. Then there is this twist: Frances may never have mailed the letter. It was a clean original copy, with only two cross-outs and two word inserts, certainly near her quality-sending-threshold. And there was a partial draft of the letter—but clearly a draft because there were many corrections and cross-outs in it—filed with the quality copy. So she could have read it over and then "chickened out," as guys used to say. In any case, Frances and Franklin never found a way to get to know one another well enough to derail her career.

Here is their status seven years later as reported by Frances in a May 5, 1941, letter to brother Henry in Salinas again after home leave, now from Santa Fe's *The Chief,* "Along about Albuquerque."

> The day and a half in Redlands after our return from Salinas was hectic, but I managed to get away at 1:15 p.m. yesterday on the Chief with Mother and Franklin standing by. It seems that at one time he was contemplating coming to Salinas. I told him he should drive up later— and take Mother—and assured him you would be glad—really glad—to see him anytime he could come.
>
> There is a varied assortment of liquor that I left behind at 503 which won't keep indefinitely, so be sure to use it up next time you are there. What little there was left of the J.W. [Johnnie Walker] after Franklin and I worked on it I brought along.

That had to be the most persistently intermittent relationship in the history of courtship: typically two weeks every two years, which continued right up to Franklin's death in 1950.

Why did Frances kept stringing Franklin along like that? She obviously liked his company—and he, hers—and they were very close friends indeed. But by now Frances was fully wedded to the service. Could it have been in part an unconscious insurance policy for Frances? What if she hit an impenetrable glass ceiling in the Foreign Service, and decided—or had—to retire, as she came close to doing after Spain? If she did, she could come home to Franklin, the loyal, bachelor suitor. And because Frances always liked that type, never mind her service obligations, she could have it both ways: insurance and fun. Apparently, no one in the family talked to Frances about the subject, or if they did, the record is lost. So those questions remained unanswered.

Then it all ended when Franklin died in 1950. His November 29, 1950, obituary was published in the *Redlands Daily Facts*:

> Franklin L. Pierce, 57, orange grower, widely known resident of Redlands, died last night at 522 West Highland Avenue [Wissahickon Inn]. Suffered stroke in September 1949. Born in Milwaukee, came here in the winter season with parents, Mr. and Mrs. Jonathan F. Pierce. Father owned Cliffside Citrus Ranch in East Highland. Attended school

in Redlands, after which he went to Lawrenceville and later to Princeton University. Graduated in 1915. Assumed ownership of Citrus Ranch after graduation. During World War I was a pilot. During the Second World War was active in the Red Cross. Affiliated with All Saints Episcopal Church. Leader of bible class.

Another main man—and another WW I pilot—gone from her life, this one at fifty-seven. Although too late, the obituary reveals some of the things Frances wanted to know, except what that *L* stood for.

Franklin L. Pierce, far right, circa 1945 (courtesy Redlands Smiley Public Library Heritage Room.)

One photo of Franklin was retrieved from the Red Cross files in the Redlands Smiley Library by archivist Don McCue, after he read Franklin's obituary. This is the only available photo of Franklin and may be the only one in existence, since Franklin died a bachelor. Other people in the photo are unidentified.

Frances was posted in London at the time of Franklin's death and was making plans to come to Redlands over the Christmas holidays, as she said in her November 25, 1950, short letter to Belle. She also said, "I do not expect Franklin will be able to make it this year." That was obviously due to the stroke he suffered the previous year. Then two days later Franklin died and Frances wrote another short note to Belle with more Christmas plans, including Christmas dinner guests, and then said:

> With Franklin gone (yes, I had a telegram from Mrs. Goede [possibly his nurse or the Wissahickon Inn manager]) I think it would be especially good to vary the routine a little.

Then in a December 8, 1950, letter, again just to Belle, written on Cunard's *Britannia* en-route to New York she reported how fine her first class cabin and service were—she had been given "a super cabin," one of the best on the ship. She then said,

> There has been a wonderful oblivion which needs no recording. It took me two or three days to get unwound and to realize that no matter how bad the news was there was nothing I could do about it. I have since slept countless hours, read a certain amount, written most of the notes I should, and neither neglected eating nor drinking—although comparatively little of the latter usually just cocktails before dinner or a glass of beer at lunch to make me sleep more soundly during my afternoon nap. No bridge, no dancing, no movies, no horse racing for me so you see I'd done just as I liked.

Clearly this was her mourning period for Franklin, although she didn't say so. In fact only once in all these letters did she refer to him. She likely did it for two reasons: First, she did not want to distress Belle any more than necessary—she was a delicate soul—and second, because that's the way the family operated: "Dead and gone" was a common family mantra, and that meant gone from the world and gone from the mind.

Lieutenant Don Johnson, USN

Frances' social life with men did not fade after she committed to the foreign service cloister. In fact a basic requirement for such work was to socialize with both sexes of all ages. And it wasn't all that bad in Spain during WW II, as Frances summarized in a February 1944, bulletin from Madrid:

Although Lent began Wednesday that does not seem to slow things up much socially in "the most Catholic of all countries." I had four invitations to dinner last night—don't know how much longer my popularity will last as we are getting a lot of American "girls" over here these days and most of them have a pretty good time. Until recently there were several times as many men as women on the Embassy staff, but the balance will be struck soon if the new arrivals continue to pour in as they have been just recently.

Naturally the competition won't affect me so much as others for two reasons, first, because I am older than most, and second, as the Spanish would say I belong to a different category—they don't come right out with the work class, but that is what they mean. I have to go to a lot of dinners, cocktail parties etc, with Spaniards and other diplomats.

That popularity started almost the minute she arrived in Madrid, as she reported in an August 11, 1941, bulletin:

Our young assistant Naval Attaché has apparently decided to give me a big rush. He took me for dinner and dancing to Villa Rosa on Saturday night and Sunday we saw some more of Spain, in my car (he hasn't one over here, came over by clipper and has practically nothing with him.) We made a big circle up to the north through the Guadarrama Mountains and saw some lovely country. For the first time in its life my little Ford just coughed and stopped on the side of a hill. Well, the young Lieutenant opened the hood and took one look. He didn't even touch anything and then he said, "Where are your pliers?" I had literally, I believe, never even taken the tools out of the little sack they come in and when I opened it up there were no pliers. He made a face and went to work with a monkey wrench, and a very clumsy one at that, and fixed a dislocation in the gas line before I had even finished looking around hoping to find a pair of pliers in some unlikely place. And the motor has been running ever since. He was a flying instructor at Pensacola before he came over here, so on the technical side at least he is pretty good.

Certainly a pretty good trade: having to use your car on dates, but having your date keep it running. Frances reported that there was no antifreeze available during the war and she couldn't get a doctor's prescription for alcohol—anything to keep the radiator from freezing. So, likely on Don's suggestion, she bought the cheapest brandy and poured it in. That did the trick.

Commander Lusk, U.S. Naval Attaché and Lieutenant Don Johnson, Assistant Naval Attaché, circa 1941 (courtesy U.S. Navy.)

Don, the good dancer, showed up again in Frances' New Year's Day and January 15, 1942, bulletins:

> There were a few parties last night New Year's Eve, but a long time ago Don Johnson had asked me for a date New Year's Eve—imagine anybody asking me for a date at my age [now forty-two], that is a special date. Well we weren't invited to the same parties and none of them sounded too exciting so we went down town to our favorite restaurant and to a nightclub afterwards.
>
> Sundays, if it is fine and not too cold and I'm not on duty, Don Johnson and I will take a picnic lunch and start off to "see Spain." Week before last we went to Cuenca, over a hundred miles away. It is an extremely picturesque town on a high bluff in a triangle where two small rivers join. Some of the houses literally hang over the river but a hundred or so feet above the stream.

Sounds romantic, even though Don was ten years younger than Frances. Then it ended in an August 1, 1943, bulletin when Frances reported that:

For once there has been something going on this last week, which the censor is likely to let pass. As far as I am concerned it started last Monday night when Don Johnson brought his latest girl (a bee—oo—tiful Peruvian) up to the house to dinner. I knew it was more than usually serious because he asked me if I would have his boss too, Commander Lusk, so I did, and "Cousin Murat" [Murat Willis Williams, but apparently no relation] also an Assistant Naval Attaché. Whereupon it developed that if her sister who had sailed for Peru from Bilbao could get off the boat and come to Madrid and catch the boat again at Cadiz, Don and Isabel were going to be married Saturday.

The rest of the letter was consumed with plans, preparations and politics of the wedding—including the sister's request for an audience with Frances "to tell her all I knew about Don." After the Navy Department gave Don permission to marry "a foreigner," the wedding finally came off, with Frances throwing a huge breakfast for the entire wedding party.

End of the Don Johnson saga—except that nowhere did Frances express any emotion about those sudden turn of events. So Frances, while flattered by all his attention, apparently was not seduced by it. She was now firmly locked in the Foreign Service's embrace. And yet, maybe that's giving her too much steel.

Indeed it was, because in his May, 2003, phone conversation with the author, Findley Burns reported Frances always liked the attention of bachelors, and that Julian Harrington, another FSO in Madrid, told him that Frances was temporarily crushed by the Johnson marriage. So she was human after all; she just wasn't willing to bare her soul to the family. But the bottom line is that, except for the occasional Franklin Pierce encounter, that marked the end of her romantic career, at least as documented in her bulletins.

9

BELGIUM AND THE GERMANS

Return to Brussels

WHAT a break this new post was for Frances. She had already spent a year in Brussels as a graduate student at the Universite Libre de Bruxelles; French was her second language; and her PhD thesis was on the Belgian Parliamentary System. But despite all these incentives, Frances sent the following postcard to friends in Redlands, which then found its way into the family archives:

> *I wanted to go to Peking but I'm going to Brussels. I also like that idea because I had a beautiful time there as a student.*

So Frances' Orient request, first started in Valparaiso in 1930, rose again. Then she specifically requested China on her 1933 Transfer Record "principally for diversification in training." And on the 1936 record she said, "The desire to know China before the changes which are taking place become further advanced." She suspended her requests in 1939 with the comment, "Transfer not desired due to wartime conditions." But the desire never faded; it showed up again on her 1958 record when she was Ambassador to Norway, which finally got her Ceylon.

Although not documented, someone in the Department must have decided that with those glowing reports from a well liberated Sweden, the girl who knew Belgium needed a tougher test in Belgium, where as Hugh Gibson observed, "The Belgians are very old-fashioned and prejudiced against women in public office." So Frances reported for duty July 16, 1934, with an immediate promotion to consul grade VIII, along with a raise from $3000 to $3,500. She also retained her diplomatic rank of third secretary. That was the first Consular Service promotion granted to a woman.

She found an apartment at the Residence Palace on Rue de la Loi for the next five years, 1935-1940, at the rate of $724 per year—not much more than she was paying for her primitive room in Chile. But the accommodations were massively upgraded, including a living room, separate bedroom, private bath, kitchenette, maid's room and service entrance, for a total of about 1600 square feet, not to mention the full restaurant down stairs.

Work With Ambassador Morris

Apparently Frances hit the ground running because just two months later the following back-channel letter appeared in her dossier:

Sept. 5, 1934

Dear Tom,

Since I telegraphed you advising you not to send a woman to Brussels, I feel that in truth and justice I ought to write you that I was completely mistaken in the case of Miss Willis. In the seven weeks she has been associated with me she has fully demonstrated her ability and resourcefulness. She has taken hold very quickly and has pitched in and shown an enthusiasm which one does not often encounter. She has had a splendid education and this shows up very strongly in her work. I am fully convinced that she can do a man's work here!! She is very dignified and every one who has met her here has remarked what a thoroughly nice person she is...

/s/ Louis Sussdorff, Jr.

Tom (M. Wilson) was Chief of the Foreign Service Personnel Division (Code FP) and Louis Sussdorff, Jr. was Counselor and Deputy Chief of Mission in Brussels. Sussdorff was an Old Guard FSO, who—like previous FSO field dogs—changed his mind after Frances disarmed his arrival gender bias by jumping smartly from square zero to square one.

One month later another communiqué appeared in Frances' dossier:

DEPARTMENT OF STATE
DIVISION OF WESTERN
EUROPEAN AFFAIRS
MEMORANDUM

FP: November 2, 1934

I quote a paragraph from a personal letter from Ambassador Morris in Brussels:

"I wish you would tell Tom Wilson that we are all delighted to have Miss Willis with us and that I have no hesitation in saying that she does the work of any two men in the office. Me for the ladies every time! Tell him I am very grateful that he transferred her here and that if he does not have her remain as long as I stay, there will be a murder in Washington which can be readily explained over here in Belgium…"

/s/ *Pierrepont Moffat*

So within a period of three months Frances had cleaved two career FSO's, the ambassador and his deputy from the Old Guard. The bottom line is that all this favorable, back-channel visibility can't hurt a young career, especially because Pierrepont was a son-in-law of Joseph Grew, Frances' future mentor. Furthermore, after Pierrepont's initials, *PM,* started to appear as a reviewer on Frances' Efficiency Ratings, her grades improved significantly.

Frances' boss for the next three years was Ambassador Dave H. Morris, as he signed his name to three of her Annual Efficiency Reports. And they were just as good as the back-channel letters. From the July 20, 1935, report:

Miss Willis' judgment is sound and she is full of common sense. She is forceful, exceedingly just and devoted to the interests of the service …in charge of the Fortnightly Press Review [prepared in part from the Belgium press] she has developed it into an interesting and scholarly chronicle of the main topics of the day along the lines of the Literary Digest. [A magazine, similar to the Atlantic Monthly, published between 1890 and 1938.] She has covered thoroughly the treaties concluded by Belgium. She is thoroughly conversant with problems political, economic and commercial, and has written some good reports. She has had charge of the administrative work in Brussels and has directed it with energy and skill, showing excellent organizing ability. She has won the confidence and cooperation of the male clerks ...has established good contacts with Belgian officials, colleagues, and Americans...

And the rest of the now-standard accolades: "entirely adaptable ...unsparing in time and energy ...working overtime ...neat appearance ...good physical condition, endurance, etc." Morris finished with the following:

> In my opinion, the present post is entirely appropriate for her. Since she has been here only one year and is doing such excellent work, and since the post affords a good test of whether or not an efficient woman can get along in a Latin country I earnestly recommend that Miss Willis be left in Brussels at least two years longer. I recommend her promotion to Class VII.[34]

With that glowing review, Frances took a two-month home leave in Redlands. During home leave, Georgia Oliver interviewed Frances in an article, "Interesting People: Redlands Woman Tells Work as Diplomat," in the March 10, 1935, issue of the *San Bernardino Sun*. Oliver started out:

> "Interview a diplomat? You can't do that," said Miss Willis. "And why not?" she was asked. "Because if he tells you the ordinary things, it doesn't make news; and if he tells you something startling, he is not a diplomat."

That was certainly true, because none of Frances' press interviews (or family bulletins) contained anything startling. Then after recounting her reasons for joining the Foreign Service and her career to date, Frances described what she did at the office:

> "My typical day at the office is devoted to answering correspondence

---

[34] All three of the Morris reports were initialed by Frances. None of her others ever were. It was not until 1952 that the Department directed the reviewer to indicate whether or not he had discussed the report with his subject. And even after that, some of those boxes were left unchecked!

from the home office, from Americans in Belgium who want to know about the country they are in, from Belgian business men wanting to know about American laws and customs.

"We must keep up on all the news of the country in order to report back to the American government anything that may be of interest to it. We must watch the debates in parliament and we must read newspapers controlled by all political parties of Belgium. It would be disastrous [for us] for the home office to learn about some piece of legislation which we had failed to describe to them.

"If there is a banking law pending, I might find it my duty to interview one of the prominent bankers of Brussels, either asking him to my office (if I outrank him)," she adds with a smile, "or calling at his office if he outranks me."

Office hours for Miss Willis begin at 9:30 a.m. "Most Europeans take two hours off for lunch and at our office we work until 4:30 or later, even up to 8 o'clock on evenings when there is an important cable to be sent off to the United States."

Evenings are crammed with social activities, which are a part of the life in every mission. Social events are elaborate and formal according to Miss Willis. While customs of the host country must be observed by visiting delegates, the diplomats at all times try to create a friendly feeling for their own country and, "we must never cease being Americans," she adds. She confesses to having entered more than one bridge Olympic, and reveals her diplomacy again in the fact that she has not yet won a prize.

The only cloud in this sunny sky was one of those pesky, Department-generated Efficiency Ratings, this time with four unknown initials on it for her political work in 1935, around the time of Morris' first report:

Miss Willis has prepared the regular biweekly press despatch [Fortnightly Press Review] from Brussels. Her work has been above the average in this respect, but—perhaps inevitably—displays very little originality. She seems to have a greater flair for social and economic questions than for political matters.

That was certainly different from Ambassador Morris' take on the press despatch. Now the "limitations of her sex" bias has morphed into an "inevitable lack of originality and a limited appreciation for political matters." In short, "Get her back to things girls do best, like woman's wear reporting."

But Morris wasn't swayed by these comments, if he saw them at all. His June 12, 1936, Annual Efficiency Report was even more effusive. Again comments like "absolute sincerity ...wide circle of friends ...very popular ...unlimited time and energy ...absolute unselfishness ...aptitude for all branches of Embassy work ...full of constructive imagination and criticism..."

He also continued his praise for the Fortnightly Press Review:

> From a careful daily reading of the Belgian press extending over a period of nearly two years, Miss Willis has obtained a thorough knowledge of the political and economic situation in Belgium which is very useful. She is careful and accurate in collecting information and her method of presentation is logical and concise.

Morris finished the review with another recommendation for promotion. And eleven months later, May 6, 1937, it was done, this time in both branches of the Foreign Service: second secretary and consul, grade VII, now at $4,000 per annum.

Morris' last review, the day before Frances' promotions became official, continued the tradition with more praise: "even surpassed the high standard described in my last efficiency report ...profound study of conditions in Belgium ...great pleasure for her colleagues to work with her." One new entry in this review finally got her the credit denied her in Stockholm:

> The duties performed by Miss Willis during the past year have covered a wide field. During the absence of the Counselor [and deputy chief of mission] in the United States she discharged the duties of [this] senior career officer, in addition to her own, with dignity and skill.

And to drive home his point, Morris recommended she receive another promotion "as soon as the Statutory Period permits."

Finally, Morris' comments and Frances' reports won over the Department's Efficiency Raters, who were now tasked to add a formal rating at the end:

> Miss Willis appears to have been charged with the major political reporting of the Embassy. Her reports show a keen insight into the reasons motivating the events upon which she reports and good analysis of their portent. She appears to have covered adequately and well all Belgian political events during the year. She may be said to be a very good reporting officer.
>
> Rating: Very Good.

That was a sea change from the last one, which complained about her unoriginal press despatches. The change was likely influenced by Pierrepont Moffat, the earlier (1934) convert to Frances' camp, whose initials appeared at the bottom of the sheet.

This attitude was then reflected in the Rating Sheet entry for January 1, 1937:

> Miss Willis continued to render entirely satisfactory service at the Brussels Embassy during the period under review. Ambassador Morris spoke very favorably of her in two efficiency reports and in the last submitted (June 12, 1936) said, "Miss Willis has shown aptitude for all branches of Embassy work. She is versatile and her judgment is sound. She is full of constructive imagination and criticism. She is a most dependable person, with a high sense of responsibility and an extraordinary devotion to duty. She is both a quick and thorough worker, with remarkable ability for concentration. She has established good contacts."
>
> Rating: Very Good.

So the three planets—Annual Efficiency Report, Efficiency Rating and Rating Sheet—entered syzygy. Not only that, but the Annual Efficiency Report has assumed more influence, with direct quotes appearing in the Rating Sheet. Dave Morris must have carried extra weight around the Department. And for the first time, not a word about sex limitations from anyone. So that problem must be done with. Not even close.

In addition, Frances was enjoying herself.

Frances at an equestrian event with Tom Wailes, 1938.

Tom Wailes was a senior FSO at the embassy from January 1937 to April 1939. During that time he and his wife Cornelia became good friends with Frances. Tom is destined to play a large role in Frances' subsequent professional life.

Ambassador Hugh Gibson and His Crucible

Then a career crucible dropped on Frances: Dave Morris suddenly resigned to tend to his ailing wife and was replaced by Hugh Gibson—the man who did-in Lucile Atcherson when he was Minister to Switzerland back in 1926. Frances reported events in February 24 and July 5, 1937, letters to the family:

> Of course the whole town is agog over the radio announcement of last Thursday and the newspaper story that Mr. Morris is resigning and is to be replaced as Ambassador by Mr. Gibson—who was Mr. Morris's immediate predecessor here and who was sent to Rio at the beginning of the Roosevelt Administration.
>
> The news is at last official and Mr. Gibson is coming here as Ambassador. Mrs. Gibson who is Belgian by birth is at the Belgian seaside at Le Zout for the summer. I have met her at several lunches

and dinners about. She is very good-looking and seems very affable. She is very different from the last Ambassadress and is what I believe is known as a "typical society woman." Mr. Gibson is of course very clever, witty, and almost unanimously rated as one of the best career diplomats we have. Mrs. Gibson told me in no uncertain terms that she did not believe in having women in the service—not that I would have expected her to—but we'll just have to wait and see how it all turns out.

It is clear where Mrs. Gibson got that opinion: straight from Mr. Gibson. It takes the institutional, gender bias to its logical conclusion: Women are so limited that they should not serve. That comment must have been a shock to Frances, coming from the wife of the new ambassador, although she rolled with the punch pretty well. It was also the first time Frances reported any type of gender bias in her bulletins. Not a good way to start with a new chief. Here is a brief resume of the man who will have a massive impact on her career.

Hugh Simons Gibson (1883-1954)

1919	Minister to Poland (at 36)
	Married to Ynes Reyntines (Belgian)
1922	Ambassador-at-large, League of Nations
1924	Minister to Switzerland (mentoring Lucile Atcherson)
1927	Ambassador to Belgium
	Dr. of Law, University Libre de Bruxelles
	(Frances' old party school)
	Dr. of Law, Yale University
1933	Ambassador to Brazil
1937	Ambassador to Belgium (second time)
	+ Minister to Luxembourg
1938	Retired (at 55)
1939	Director of various government commissions, including the Hoover Polish Relief Commission and the Provisional Intergovernmental Commission on Movements of Migrants from Europe (ICEM)
1952	Retired

During his career Gibson authored five books, including *Rio* (1937), *Belgium: The Country and Its Peoples* (1939) and *The Basis of Lasting Peace*, with Herbert Hoover (1945). Here is a photo of Hoover and Gibson when Gibson was on his second Belgium tour. Frances didn't mention Hoover's visit in her bulletins, so the visit was probably off-site. In any case, Frances must have asked Hugh to deliver her best regards, now for a third time.

Herbert Hoover and Hugh Gibson, February 28, 1938
(courtesy U.S. Government.)

One observation before plunging into the crucible. Gibson was a charter member of the Old Guard, with considerable influence on Department doctrine. So why wouldn't the Department send him on his last, short (one-year) assignment to Brussels to check out this Willis girl with-her-shockingly-good-reviews? If she passed that review, then press on; if not, she joins Lucile. Possibly Hugh even suggested it. Both speculative and unknowable, but also feasible and compelling.

Hugh Gibson then assessed this female FSO's work over the following year and filed the following June 11, 1938, Annual Efficiency Report:

> As the Department probably knows, I have always been outspoken in my view that women should not be used in the diplomatic service, on the ground that, regardless of their ability or knowledge and tact, they cannot achieve as good results as men of lesser caliber.

I am obliged to say, however, that Miss Willis has rendered it difficult for me to maintain my objections, except in theory, and I look upon her as one of the most valuable officers we now have in the service. Her position is inherently difficult, as the Belgians are very old-fashioned and prejudiced against women in public office, but in the course of her service she has by her good judgment, dignity and tact completely disarmed criticism, and I have heard nothing but the most friendly and flattering comment about her. She has a position in Brussels that is distinctly useful to the Embassy, and a capacity for winning confidence and securing information such as is possessed by few men.

The only criticism I can make of Miss Willis is that she works too hard, which is tempered by the fact that she undoubtedly enjoys it.

She is very careful and conscientious in her work, is thorough and accurate, and any information she brings in can be accepted as having been carefully weighed and verified. She has excellent ability for office and administrative work, but her intelligence is of a higher order which should be utilized on work of greater importance.

I think the Department should bear Miss Willis in mind for future assignments where she will have greater scope for her undoubted ability. I am confident she can fit into any organization and make herself a useful and comforting member of the team.

That's an excellent report from a normal boss. But coming from Hugh Gibson it's monumental. And what a triumph for Frances: She has emerged from the crucible with tempered sword and armor. Her testing phase must now be over, and she can get on with her career, unimpeded by all gender biases. As before, not even close. But at least she is cracking each glass table as it shows up.

The 1939 Rating Sheet came close to reflecting Gibson's evaluation:

Miss Willis has merited the full praise of Ambassadors Morris and Gibson and her reporting has been rated Very Good by the Department. Both Mr. Morris and Mr. Gibson have reported that Miss Willis fills a most useful position at the Embassy, that notwithstanding her naturally difficult position because of her sex she has, by her dignity and tact, completely disarmed criticism in Brussels and nothing but the most friendly and flattering comment regarding her has been heard. Mr.

Gibson considered that her intelligence is of very high order and may be utilized on work of greater importance. He believed that she can fit into any organization and prove her complete usefulness.

January 1. 1939
Rating: Very Good.

This time the redactor's summary was brief, but what was there was accurate and unbiased. However, the Department's Very Good rating trumped sterling reviews from both Morris and Gibson, thereby keeping her performance rating unchanged from the last review. The home group Old Guard was still functioning.

The 1939 Efficiency Rating—Political Work sheet, accompanied with *PM* initials and another very good rating, signaled the start of Frances' WW II saga:

Miss Willis's reports show a keen insight into the reasons motivating the events upon which she reports and good analyses of their portent…

The "events… and… analysis of their portent" comment refers to German maneuvering in a "Phony War," as it was called, to capture as much territory and strategic advantage as they could before going to all-out war.

Hugh Gibson completed his one-year tour as ambassador and retired from the Foreign Service in 1938. He was replaced, apparently again temporarily, by Ambassador Joseph Davies. And shortly afterwards on April 1, 1939, Frances was promoted to consul class VI at a salary of $4,500. The next-to-last Annual Efficiency Report in her six-year Brussels tour was by Davies in late 1939. It was just like the previous ones:

…extraordinarily able woman …lot of common sense and excellent judgment …high sense of responsibility …no limit to office hours …excellent balance …force of character …patient, tactful and courteous …exceptional work in shouldering the burden…

At various times here, due to conditions which could not be avoided, the staff has been shorthanded, and Miss Willis has done exceptional work in shouldering the burden and doing it exceptionally well. Miss Willis deserves well of the Service and could easily fulfill any post within the scope of the Foreign Service.

Another excellent report and not a word about sex limitations. Now the trend is becoming clear: Bosses who got to know Frances didn't perceive a sex limitation problem. Only those who didn't know her continued their institutional gender bias. And that overseas group was growing—even if some of her achievements kept falling through the crack: This time Frances was appointed chargé for eleven days in October 1938 when Davies took sick leave. That was probably what he meant about "shouldering the burden." But why not say she was chargé? Another major recognition opportunity lost.

Ambassador John Cudahy and the Germans

Then Ambassador Davies left and a new one was announced: John Cudahy. Frances' comment on this turnover: "So now I've polished off another Ambassador." Frances reported his sudden arrival in her January 20, 1940, bulletin:

> What a week and the pouch really is closing in about two jiffies, but when you have a new Ambassador drop from the skies, practically, at one a.m., with about seven hours warning, and at noon of the same day find yourself at the Palais for him to present his credentials (which just between you and me were—well never mind; I'd better not put that on paper) to the King then there has been work to do and plenty—plus putting on all the dog.
>
> It was a record: No Ambassador has ever been received by the King in solemn audience the day of arrival—naturally everyone is talking. I am quite sure the reason it happened that way is because the President and the Ambassador thought Belgium was going to be invaded (they get stirred up in Washington and elsewhere over all the alarmist rumors) and they did not want their new Ambassador to Belgium fox hunting in Ireland (that is one of his favorite pastimes) when it happened. So practically without any notice he descended upon us Wednesday January 17 a little after one a.m. and of course we were all down at the station to greet him—one of the coldest nights I've ever known in Belgium—but no ill effects.
>
> He is as different as day from night from his predecessor. Tall, handsome, blue eyes and fair hair—he is just what Grandmother [Caroline James-Graham] would I am sure have called him "That Irishman." How

able he is or how exacting I have as yet had no occasion to find out, but everybody who has met him so far says "What a charming person." Quite a lady-killer I have no doubt.[35] His wife and two, I imagine grown, sons are in America and as far as I know there are no plans for them to come to Europe. The Ambassador hates cards and does not play golf. Rides, hunts, shoots. He came to dinner at my house last night and we had one of the most informally delightful evenings.

While Frances was quite taken with John, she was also quite nervous about him, as recorded in her next bulletin:

> I don't know why new Ambassadors are such a trial for me but they are, partially I suppose because I never know whether they are going to have me transferred or not, and that means I have to work twice as hard to convince them that I am not utterly useless.

This marks Frances' second report of institutional gender bias, now the arrival type cloaking a new boss when he arrives. She continued by describing an unreasonable request from Cudahy she had to satisfy the next day: Get an automobile through military lines in the north of France, all in two hours notice on Sunday morning. She said that, "If it had not been a new Ambassador I don't think I would have attempted it, but he wasn't here and I could not explain to him," so she just went ahead and used her own car because the Ambassador's hadn't come yet and a diplomatic license plate was essential. She finished with:

> I am afraid this letter is not very flattering to the new Ambassador, but I do like him, and he is infinitely easier to work for than his predecessor. But the first is always difficult for me because I have that hump of prejudice to work against.

There it is again, now cast as "that hump of prejudice"—arrival gender bias—upon first encounter with a new boss. And it wouldn't be the last time she flagged that problem. So while she was aware of it, she simply banished it with good work.

Then Frances came down with the German measles, which put her out of

---

[35] A photo of Cudahy appears in the next chapter.

action for a week.[36] After returning to work Frances discovered she had been made responsible for all official activities under Cudahy, because he brought no American secretary. But it was not all work. Here's how Frances reported fun with her boss:

> Last night the Ambassador had a small dinner (14) for a Polish friend of his who is staying with him here at the Embassy. If you please I sat opposite the Ambassador—first time I have done it for him, although I have done it many times for the others for one reason or other. He had the rug taken up in the big reception room and believe it or not we danced to a Victrola, an electric one that changes the records automatically. I knew the plans in advance so brought with me my wonderful record of the Blue Danube so we had some good waltzing. Everybody had a grand time, and I didn't get home until almost 2 a.m., but that is all right because if I've been dancing it never seems to matter how late I stay up.

Perts showed how the dancing part was done. Even though the genders are reversed, Frances must have had her share of dances with this type. And that's the way it must be in the Foreign Service.

"Cultivating Friendly Relations" from M. C. Perts' 1924 book.

---

[36] But she would agree that having a German *measle* is better than having a German *occupation.*

It is now time for some wartime work, as Frances reported in her April 12, 1940, bulletin:

> One o'clock and a pouch is closing at two so I'll give you at least the high lights of local events. Naturally since the morning [when] we heard the Germans were in Denmark and trying to get into Norway things have seethed. The Ambassador keeps me on the run trying to verify all the wild rumors the newspapermen bring in and then if they aren't true he tells me to find out what is. I suppose I just imagine that he gives me more of that sort of work than the others, but as long as I can get through it I don't mind. It makes doing routine work almost impossible though, but who cares about that when a naval battle of the first order is going on off the coast of Norway.

That naval battle was the "Pursuit of the Bismarck," with the entire British Atlantic Fleet chasing the German battleship Bismarck and two cruisers starting in the North Sea and running across the Atlantic Ocean. The British finally cornered and sank the Bismarck, but not before losing their battle-cruiser Hood on the second salvo from Bismarck, and taking tremendous punishment to their other cruisers and battleships.

Frances' comment on rumor verification also needs clarification. While a few newspapermen might have dropped by the embassy with a rumor or question, they certainly weren't the real source of information. Far better sources were available: the Foreign Ministry, resident attachés, other-country embassy contacts, nationals, the underground and of course the ever-present, deep cover intelligence agents. This was the covert part of Frances' career, which unfortunately will remain covert. And apparently she was good at it, as the scanty clues suggest throughout her career.

Between all this action, diplomatic entertaining continued unabated. Bridge games, large and small dinners at the embassy, daily luncheons, all of which Frances had to attend, as she reported:

> At present there seems to be a large surplus of men in Brussels, so I have to go to practically everything and I am "fed up" in more ways than one.

Then in May, 1940, the action turned personal when the Germans launched a lightning-swift invasion of the low-countries, including Belgium. Frances relayed these events in bulletins to the family in late May and June, 1940. They are augmented by Frances' conversations with her brother Henry during the 1945 Christmas holidays in Washington DC. Frances' May bulletins started the saga:

> As you realize probably even more acutely than we do here, our communications with the outside world have been cut off since May 16, possibly even an earlier date. I have no idea how or when I can send this letter to you, it may have to pass the German and/or French and British censors, but in any case I shall try to set down as coherent an account as possible of some of the happenings of these last sixteen days for you before the picture becomes too blurred.
>
> I had been out to dinner Thursday May 9 and was just going to bed at 12:45 Friday morning May 10, when my telephone rang violently. I answered and it was one of the various newspaper correspondents whose contacts with the Embassy might have been described as "good." [Newspaper correspondent? Not likely.] He apologized profusely for telephoning at that hour but said the news was so bad that he felt he must get in touch with me and let me know that an invasion of Holland was expected at any minute. He has never been one to get excited about rumors and when I finished talking to him, I thought to myself that if there were anything in his story there would surely be someone at the [Belgium] Foreign Office so I called up.
>
> I got in touch with one of the men I know quite well and what he told me was of such a nature that I immediately telephoned the Ambassador, who sounded very sleepy but who never hesitated a minute. He said right away, "I'll have to go to the Foreign Office." His chauffeur does not sleep at the Embassy and I had fortunately left my car outside at the Residence, so I said, "I'll be there in five minutes to take you over." I never dressed so fast in my life, and was at the Embassy by one o'clock but the Ambassador was already downstairs waiting on the sidewalk for me.
>
> We found the news even worse than we anticipated at the F.O. and as soon as we had learned all we could we went back to the Embassy and telephoned for [Military Attaché] Colonel Brown. While the

Ambassador and the Colonel talked by telephone to the White House, I coded a telegram for the Department. The Colonel and I had to take it to the Central Telegraph office and as we drove through the streets we saw lots of activity. I think I got to bed about half past three. A little after four the Ambassador telephoned me after talking to [Consul General] George Weller in Luxemburg, [who said] the Germans had already crossed the frontier there. I had just gone back to sleep when the German planes came over and the show was on.

From May 10 to May 17 we worked night and day…

Frances went on to report rather uneventful, social details for these days, including a dinner party in Brussels on May 14. She didn't report anything at all for May 11, 12, 13 and 15. She also got a short letter off to Mother Belle on May 11:

Dearest Mother,

Mr. and Mrs. Henry Luce (he the editor of Time Life and Fortune and she the author of "Women") have been the Ambassador's guests these last few days and they hope to get away to Paris today, so I am going to ask them to mail this from there as unfortunately our mails are uncertain…

Frances reassured Belle that she was well and everything was under control. The letter was just one page and hastily prepared. She must have been rushed once she found out that the Luces were about to leave.[37]

After the Belgian government fled, the Germans occupied Brussels on May 17, with the still neutral American embassy remaining open. Then when Counselor of the Embassy, Orme Wilson was away, Ambassador Cudahy went to Berlin to contact Washington, because all communications in Brussels had been cut off. So that left the #3 FSO—Frances—running the place, marking the third time she had assumed the duty of chargé d'affaires (once in Sweden and the second time in Belgium.) Frances reported events during this time in her June 9 bulletin:

He [Cudahy] left here Thursday June 6, about three o'clock and a

---

[37] These last two letters loom large in the next chapter, Frances and Clare.

little before six that same day the Germans entered the French Embassy, and what was even worse tore down our certificate of protection—we have French interests here along with those of five other countries.[38] I being Chargé had to go to the Germans and get an apology and an assurance that the necessary steps would be taken to prevent such occurrences in the future. With lots of assistance from Jim [Bonbright, fellow FSO] and Colonel Brown [attaché] I now have obtained a written apology signed by the supreme military authority in Belgium, General von Falkenhausen, and a solemn assurance that orders have been given to prevent similar incidents in the future. Since that excitement things have settled down to the most extreme tranquility imaginable.

Those letters showed up in the massive "Foreign Service Posts of Department of State, Brussels Embassy General Records, 1940" at the National Archives. First Frances' letter of complaint:

Sir,   Brussels, June 7, 1940

I regret to have to bring the following to your attention:

From information which the Embassy received, and which has been confirmed by the 1ˢᵗ Division Police headquarters of Brussels, the premises at No. 42 Boulevard du Régent, forming a part of the French Embassy and under the official protection of the Government of the United States, were entered by force yesterday afternoon by Feldwebel [Staff Sergeant] Habermann.

Without going into details, it is sufficient for me to point out that the entry was made by force in spite of the fact that the certificate testifying that the premises were under the protection of my Government was conspicuously affixed to the wall of the building beside the door. The offense is even more grave because Feldwebel Habermann himself destroyed this certificate.

I feel sure that you will recognize the seriousness of this incident against which I must protest. I must likewise request that appropriate action be taken in regard to those who are responsible for it and that

---

[38] A certificate of protection is a document posted at a foreign mission stating that while the mission is closed, the mission's interests are under the protection of a third party, in this case the neutral United States.

whatever steps are necessary be taken to insure that similar occurrences do not take place in the future.

Please accept, Sir, the expression of my distinguished consideration.

/s/ *Frances E. Willis*
Chargé d'affaires ad interim
of the United States of America
General von Falkenhausen,
Military Governor in
Belgium and Northern France

Then the General's response:

TRANSLATION

The Military Governor in
Belgium and Northern France.   O.U., June 7, 1940

I acknowledge with thanks the receipt of your letter of June 7, and have the honor to inform you, that I strongly condemn the incident related to me and do not hesitate to express to you my deep regret at the error of a low-ranking military person, who greatly overstepped his authority. I especially regret that the military person in question, who acted in ignorance of international diplomatic custom, arbitrarily injured the American seal on the building in question belonging to the French Embassy.

To my satisfaction, however, according to the information I have received, no objects were removed from or damaged in the building. I have at once begun a careful investigation of the matter and can assure you that the guilty person will be called to account. Moreover I have taken steps so that similar incidents will not occur again in the future.

Please accept, Miss Chargé d'affaires, the assurance of my distinguished consideration.

/s/ *Von Falkenhausen...*

Finally Frances' thank you note:

Sir,   Brussels, June 8, 1940

I have received your letter of June 7, 1940, and wish to thank you not only for the position you have taken in connection with the incident which took place at the French Embassy on June 6, 1940, but also for the assurances given by you that the necessary steps have been taken to prevent similar occurrences in the future.

Please accept, Sir, the expression of my distinguished consideration.

/s/ Frances E. Willis…

Clearly, Feldwebel Habermann got a serious talking-to by General Von Falkenhausen:

Next time, sergeant, be more careful how you tear down certificates.

How did Frances find out the miscreant was Feldwebel Habermann? Probably more of that local underground network she cultivated. In any case, Frances can add "Miss Chargé d'affaires" to her previous title of "Miss American Minister." Oh, that all military disputes could be resolved with such "distinguished consideration."

Of course, that's exactly why diplomats were invented: to avoid international incidents. And that was just the way the Germans wanted it. Now all this was the official veneer. Perts revealed what was really going on in his next sketch. Frances and her FSO associates in Brussels must have harbored such a thought amongst all those "distinguished consideration" despatches.

"A Diplomatic Incident" from M. C. Perts' 1924 book.

Then with that crisis defused, Frances snuck off for a quiet weekend with friends to Argenteuil, leaving FSO Jim Bonbright in charge. Argenteuil is a resort town about ten miles northwest of Paris, right on the Seine, and about 150 miles from Brussels. So popping over to Paris for a relaxing weekend—or to deliver the Luce VIPs as she did in the next chapter—was no big deal for her, even with a war roaring about. Frances also introduced the German occupation army in her June 9 bulletin:

> We have seen a lot of the German Army here, and such a powerful machine defies description. In its perfection it is magnificent, but at the same time terrifying. The soldiers on the whole have been extremely well behaved, the discipline is flawless.

That would describe her General Falkenhausen as well. But her frustration at being powerless to do anything on-site finally boiled over:

The heartbreaking part is that there is so little we can do. I see a lot of people at the Embassy every day and in almost every case I have to answer "no." Can you get word through to my family in _____? No. Can you give me a certificate to prevent the Germans from taking my automobile? No. Can you get me gasoline to go to Bruges to see my son who is wounded? No. Can you provide me with an automobile to go to Antwerp to see my brother who is a prisoner there? No. And so it goes on and on...

Frances then drove her car (with a special pass on its windshield and assorted military attaché passengers) up to Dunkerque just after the Allies were evacuated. She elaborated on that 9-hour excursion in a June 23, 1940, bulletin, which had the first part censored. What was left of the bulletin said,

Yesterday I saw almost more of the desolation of war than I could stand. Dunkerque is something beyond words, I literally did not see a house that was intact and most of them had their insides blown out with only part of the walls standing. All of that was ghastly enough but the beach was worse...

She went on to describe the scene, which has been covered in similar detail by most WW II history books. Clearly her trip wasn't planned just for sight-seeing, because all foreign intelligence collection was done by the State and War Departments in those days. It's likely that a pretty shocking report, complete with a count of destroyed and abandoned weapons, went out to Washington at the next opportunity.

Frances' next bulletin reported another trip to Paris, June 24 to 27—suitably sanitized so as not to terrify her mother:

Paris. The Red Cross was so good as to offer me a seat in one of their cars en route for their Paris office, stating that it would go through without disturbance from the German sentries.

But Frances didn't say how she got back to Brussels, because the Red Cross certainly wasn't running a shuttle. Not only that, but Frances said she stopped along the way to inspect ruins and talk to survivors, which wouldn't have happened in a shuttle ride. So it's pretty clear that she drove her own car again. Here's what she saw.

The roadbed of the route had not been disturbed in a single place. Never have the fields and woods of Northern France looked lovelier or more peaceful except, immediately around the highway. Man had recently passed through there and the horror and havoc of what he had wrought was indescribable. In the villages—large ones like Peronne and Roye—here was the stillness of death. Every house was wrecked; not a soul remained.

Past all this destruction creaked and groaned an unending stream of German lorries carrying south or west everything needed to complete the crushing of France and commence that of England.

In the opposite direction, northward in the cloud of dust left by the lorries, crawled the returning stream of miserable humanity—tired and dejected Belgian soldiers, peasants, rich and poor alike, most of them on foot, a few on bicycles, and here and there a couple of families crammed into an automobile drawn by a farm horse. He had come into his own again. There were bicycles partly pulled by dogs, pushcarts with three pulling and two pushing, grandma and the baby perched on top of the clothing.

I found the Paris Embassy as helpless as the one I had left in Brussels, cut off from the outside world. [Ambassador] Bullitt was, however, informing the Germans that, unless he were enabled somehow to communicate with his Government, there might arise retaliation in Washington. Hillenkoetter was holding down the fort for the Navy, and Fuller for the Army, taking a sun-bath behind the coping and balustrade of his office windows. The German military discipline had, as far as Fuller knew, been perfect, with no looting or stealing, which could not at times have been said of French, British or Belgians, when officers were not on hand.

During the 1945 family visit to Frances in Washington DC, Frances told her brother Henry about the German military hospitality in Brussels through July, 1940. Henry recorded it as follows:

From the generals down to the youngest lieutenant and the soldiers who guarded the door of her apartment night and day, their conduct was correct. Whenever the Germans needed to requisition a building or facility, they always paid the price without quibbling and caused the minimum amount of trouble to the Belgians. It was only when the Army moved out and the Gestapo moved in that really serious problems arose.

The German Army will now polish that with a little humanity and good housekeeping on their march across Europe, as Frances reported:

I have been talking to a German Officer directing the repatriation of what he states amounts to about one million Belgians. They have established key centers at ten different points of the arc surrounding Paris, to the west, east and south, so that no refugee enters the city. Similar centers have been established at all the more important heads of likely routes, as far as a line from Tours to Ghent. At all these points, staffs of German nurses, doctors and helpers will receive the Belgians, feed them adequately, wash and house them, give new clothing to all children and finally convey them in monster motor-busses to inside the Belgian frontiers. They are selling Germany, and it is the smartest piece of salesmanship I have ever witnessed.

I asked the officer what had become of all the dead in the region I had passed through coming down here. "Why," he replied, "have you not been shown the cremating machines which accompany the armies? They do away quickly with all sights injurious to the morale of our fighting men!"

Henry also recorded subsequent conversations with Frances—with a few corrections and additions from Frances' bulletin of July 21 and her 123 File in brackets.

About six weeks later [September, 1940] George Kennan, who was in Berlin at the time, brought word to Brussels that Hitler had ordered all Americans out of Belgium including the diplomats, volunteer ambulance drivers and Red Cross workers. They were ordered to drive their own cars, carry all the gasoline needed for the trip and only the clothes they could take in each car. [Frances left all her possessions at a storage company in Brussels.] She really did not expect to see them again, but after the war she found them just as she left them. [Her Madrid FSO associate, Findley Burns, did the retrieving.]

The group of [seven cars with one catching up later] was not allowed to cross northern France, which was occupied by the Germans. Instead they were routed via Cologne, Germany, where they spent the first night of their trip. It so happened that the British made their first air raid on Germany and had selected Cologne as their target. So within less than two months, [Frances] had the dubious pleasure of being bombed first by the Germans in Brussels and then by the British in Cologne. From Cologne, they drove down the west side of Germany.

Frances added that one car lost its clutch so, "We had to go to a garage while that got fixed. Some of us went out and drank beer at a terrible place where a slut of a woman served the drinks and 'Heiled Hitler' two or three times to each guest."

Frances seldom used this type of sarcasm. Clearly her revulsion to that level of national chauvinism again reached the boiling point. Then another car got a flat tire, so the caravan had to stop, "fortunately near a lovely wood," to get that changed. They finally reached Stuttgart after twelve and a half hours on the road. The following morning, after three separate tries with the police and an hour with the Gestapo, "We got going and didn't stop until we got to the frontier about two o'clock." Frances continued:

Then the monkey business at the Swiss frontier getting into a new country—but that was all right because it was a free country. Then Orme [Wilson, the deputy chief of mission] led us to a most heavenly spot (Schaffhausen) on the side of a mountain overlooking the Rhine Falls. About four in the afternoon they gave us one of the best meals I've ever eaten out on the terrace. Then we pressed on to Berne.

Frances and the caravan then rendezvoused with Ambassador Cudahy, who had traveled to Berne by train. She finished her July 21 exodus letter with:

I slept until 9 this morning and when I woke up there was a letter for me from the Ambassador written when he thought he wasn't going to see us before he left. I wish you could read it. The warmth of it and the simplicity are remarkable. I'll hang on to it for a long time. I hate to think I won't be working with him anymore.

That letter is lost, but his September 10, 1940, Efficiency Report must be close:

One has to guard against superlatives in reporting on Miss Willis. For loyalty, alert competence, and devotion to duty, she is, as far as my experience goes, unique in the Foreign Service. She was always first to arrive at the chancery and the last to leave. Her whole interest and career appeared focused on the aims and interest of the service.

During the strain of the bombardment and occupation of Brussels, she demonstrated a cheerful courage and buoyant enthusiasm that was an outstanding example to all and did much to maintain the splendid morale of the organization. She was so unsparing of herself in attending to the innumerable calls and various matters which arose during the two months occupation it was necessary constantly to admonish her against over work.

It is my considered judgment that Miss Willis is the most competent and best all-round [FSO] secretary I have known during my experience in the Foreign Service.

She speaks, reads and writes French with fluency.

High accolades for any FSO, especially a female FSO in time of war. The final report of Frances' Brussels saga is the January, 1941, Rating Sheet entry after she had transferred to Madrid:

MADRID   CLASS VI—$4,500

Entered the Service   Last Promoted
—Aug. 24, 1927   —Apr. 1, 1939

Miss Willis served at the Embassy in Brussels until it was necessary to close the Mission, and she was then transferred, in July 1940, to the Embassy at Madrid where she is now assigned in a dual capacity.

Miss Willis is reported to have performed outstanding work during her Brussels assignment, particularly during the period of the German invasion. Both Ambassadors Davies and Cudahy, in commenting on her cheerful courage and buoyant enthusiasm during the strain of the bombardment of Brussels, stated that she was an outstanding example to all and did a first-class job in adding to the morale of the organization. [*sic*; only Cudahy said those things.] She was unsparing of herself in her devotion to her duty, so much so that admonitions against overwork were constantly necessary. Mr. Cudahy's final comment regarding Miss Willis may be quoted as follows: "It is my considered judgment that Miss Willis is the most competent and best all-round secretary I have known during my experience in the Foreign Service." Mr. Cudahy served as Chief of Mission in Poland, Ireland, and Belgium for a period of about seven years.

The Department is informed that Miss Willis has continued the high quality of her work in her new assignment at Madrid, which is also a difficult one.

January 1, 1941
Rating: EXCELLENT

This time—with nothing about sex limitations and an excellent rating from the redactor—all gender bias issues must be finished. Unfortunately, the previous answer still applies.

One observation before moving on: Frances' performance during the German occupation of Brussels established the *necessary condition* for her selection to flag rank or FSO 2, which is equivalent to one military star under the ranks established by the 1946 Foreign Service Act, Appendix 1.

This assertion obtains in virtually all government, military and civilian deliberations about promotion to such flag or executive ranks. These ranks require operation under great pressure, where decisions affect significant numbers of lives or amounts of money. Thus one question always is asked: "Can he operate with a clear head when confronted with major threats?" In short, "Can he take the heat?" Executives in any profession must have demonstrated this capability before they are chosen to these exalted ranks. And German-occupied Belgium was Frances' demonstration badge—that necessary condition.

Of course, a *sufficient condition* is also required for promotion. Many additional attributes must be established and verified before promotion, such as language proficiency and exceptional performance in the Foreign Service cones, again described in Appendix 1. But without that necessary condition of demonstrated heat-taking, a candidate would seldom make flag rank.

On that high, it's time to hear about Frances' encounter with Clare Boothe Luce.

10

FRANCES AND CLARE

Their Meeting—Frances' Version

FRANCES first met reporter and playwright Clare Boothe Luce on May 10, 1940, just after Clare and her husband Henry Luce, editor of *Time, Life* and *Fortune* magazines, arrived as guests of Ambassador John Cudahy at the embassy in Brussels. Frances reported that meeting in her May 11 letter to her mother Belle in the last chapter. And because the Luces' next stop was Paris, Frances asked them to mail the letter in Paris for her, because "our mails are uncertain" in Brussels. The letter was delivered to Belle shortly afterwards, read and filed away.

All that constitutes the middle of this story. The beginning appeared in the Preface, which related a 1975 evening in Menlo Park, California, with the author when Frances told the story of their meeting and its aftermath. The full story went as follows:

Shortly after the Luces arrived, the Germans invaded Belgium. They bombed Brussels with their Stuka dive-bombers, with some bombs landing near the American Embassy. Those explosions plus other gunfire caused Clare to suffer a nervous breakdown. Then the Belgian government fled and the German army occupied the city.

When it became clear that Clare wasn't going to recover any time soon, Frances volunteered to drive the Luces from Brussels to Paris, with Clare under heavy sedation. Frances dropped the Luces off at a hospital in Paris and returned to Brussels.

Frances later heard that Clare recuperated in Paris until it was about to fall to the German onslaught. She was evacuated on one of the last

planes bound for England, where she finished her recovery and returned
to the U.S..

Frances said that while she had mentioned to a few friends and relatives that
Clare had been "very difficult" during this time, she never said why. She admonished the family not to repeat any details of this story until she and Clare were
dead. Frances died in 1983, Clare in 1987.

Their Meeting—Clare's Version

Ten years later, 1997, Clare's annotated diaries were published in *Rage for
Fame* by Sylvia Morris. Clare's account of these May 1940 events was included:

- May 9: Luces arrive at the American embassy around midnight.
- May 10: German bombing starts, with a bomb dropping just across the
  street. John Cudahy tells Clare that "he has heard at 12:30 AM that the
  Germans were on their way and had telephoned the news to President
  Roosevelt." Clare and Henry have dinner with Ambassador Cudahy
  and ten others. Bombs still dropping.
- May 11: The Luces opt for a car ride to Paris with the wife of a Hoover
  Polish Relief Commission official. Reaching Paris on the afternoon of
  May 12, they find the Ritz as busy as ever. That night they attend a
  dinner party in Versailles.
- May 15: Clare sees Henry off on a train to Lisbon, where he had a seat
  reserved on the Pan Am Clipper back to the U.S.. "Since she was his
  correspondent, he could not argue with her decision to stay behind."
- June 1: Clare leaves Paris on a British plane to Heston, England.
- June 8: Clare flies to Lisbon.
- June 10: Clare arrives in New York via a Pan Am Clipper.

Morris reported that from May 10 to June 1 Clare was interviewing troops,
civilians and refugees, gathering information, sight seeing—including the noto-
rious Sphinx brothel—and sending cables back to *Time-Life* with all this exciting
war reporting. Morris also said that one *Time-Life* editor objected to the quality
of the cables, but John Billings, a senior member of the editorial staff, said to
publish them because they were "absolute perfection."

Clare's cables started in the May 20, 1940, issue of *Life Magazine*: "DER

TAG IN BRUSSELS, American writer, visiting U.S. Embassy, reports on bombings as war again strikes Belgium."

> I was sleeping so soundly I did not hear the alarm at dawn but a maid [from Cudahy's domestic staff] woke me up and said "The Germans are coming again," and she went away quickly. I got up and went to the window and there as I stood I saw a bomb pierce the roof of a three-storied house across the square and gut the home which vomited glass and wood and stone in the little green square. And for a long hour after that there was a terrible noise of the great guns going...

After breakfast—because "not eating would not keep the Germans away"— she saw Cudahy, who said for everyone to go into the *abri* (a makeshift bomb shelter) in the garden. Instead Clare went into the street to watch and talk to the Belgium people and inspect the damage. She was gone for most of the morning and caught a streetcar back to the embassy. Clare continued:

> Now back at the Embassy Miss Willis, second secretary of the Embassy, showed me the abri in the garden, which is a tin tunnel covered with earth, and I said it was very uncomfortable, and she laughed and said, "Don't cast aspersions on our summer home."

Ambassador John Cudahy in the "abri" at the U.S. Embassy, Brussels, May 1940.

The photo was in Frances' effects but with no annotation. Then Clare's description solved that mystery. And Clare is right: It doesn't look particularly comfortable—but still useful in an air raid. After lunch Clare listened to news and music on a radio, and finished the article with, "Two children were killed in that early morning raid but in this brave new world of Hitler's, the sun often sets at dawn."

Five photos accompanied the article: the undamaged U.S. Embassy, the undamaged Brussels North Station, a formal one of Clare and snapshots of Cudahy and Frances taken on site.

It's not clear why Frances appeared in the article. Her clever comment might have rated mention, but certainly not a photo. And those benign photos are a surprise. A distraught looking Belgian would have made for suitable pathos to accompany Clare's closing comments. And why not a photo of the house that "vomited into the little green square?" In any case, Clare's account is fundamentally different from Frances' account: no mention of a nervous breakdown, a different driver on the trip and a different destination in Paris.

Their Meeting—John Cudahy's Version

John Cudahy recorded his version of these events in his short, 1940 book, *The Case for the King of the Belgians*. Only 500 copies were printed. He sent Copy #3 to Frances with the following inscription:

> For Frances Willis, the most distinguished officer in the Foreign Service. From her friend and Ex Chief.
> /s/ John Cudahy
> January 22. 1941.

Cudahy probably kept Copy #1 and sent #2 to the Secretary of State. Starting on page sixteen is his report of the May 10 and 11 events:

> Mr. and Mrs. Henry Luce of New York were at the embassy when I returned. Mrs. Luce is Clare Boothe, the playwright, a very pretty, brilliant, and vividly attractive woman. They had just arrived from The Hague and replied to my inquiry for news by saying that all was quiet on the Dutch horizon. We passed to a more immediately absorbing subject,

American public opinion and the war, and the discussion went on to a late hour.

A little after one the telephone beside my pillow rang. It was Frances Willis, Second Secretary of the Embassy, one of two women officers in the American Foreign Service and for ability, resourcefulness, energy and courage, one of the most distinguished officers with whom I have ever been associated. "Mr. Ambassador," she said, "I have just learned that Spaak [Paul Henri Spaak, the Belgian Foreign Minister] left a dinner party at the Bulgarians and went to the Foreign Office." "I shall go to the Foreign Office," I told Frances Willis.

She was at the Embassy within ten minutes with her Ford and together we went to the Rue de la Loi where we found the Ministry ablaze with lights. Reports of great German troop movements had come in from many sources and at dawn a general attack was expected. It was a little after five o'clock when the Germans came. [One] bomb had struck a house facing the little park, Frere Orban, at a diagonal distance of fifty yards. I looked up and down the Embassy façade to learn what windows had been broken and beheld Henry Luce leaning out of his apartment in the top story, his face ecstatic with the excitement of the born reporter. His only answer to my violent gesture of warning was to wave back to me.

The Luces took the demoralized domestic staff in hand, organized an early morning breakfast in the Embassy, and energetically interested themselves in a variety of matters, as if completely unaware of any danger. I spoke of flying glass and debris, but Mrs. Luce was lost in the dramatic possibilities of the situation and saw no reason at all why she should be forced into the raid shelter.

They were a grand pair, the Luces, gay and very brave, entirely too brave for my peace of mind, and I must say I was relieved when after much insistence they finally left the next day with Mrs. Hugh Gibson, the wife of former Ambassador Gibson, who was going by automobile to Paris.

The first observation is that John indeed had an eye for the ladies, or as Frances said in the last chapter, "That Irishman—quite a lady-killer." But more importantly, his account closely matched Clare's version, which leaves Frances' version seriously compromised, particularly about any nervous breakdown. Furthermore, Cudahy confirmed Clare's version that Mrs. Hugh Gibson, or as Clare said, "wife of a Hoover Polish Relief Commission official," as Gibson was, drove them to Paris on May 11. But Cudahy's comment that "Mrs. Luce was lost in the dramatic possibilities of the situation" was a bit vague and could have stood clarification.

More News from Clare

In subsequent weeks three shorter articles appeared in *Life* under Clare's byline, all in the "From Life's Correspondents" column. The first, titled "Flight from Belgium," detailed Clare's trip from Brussels to Paris, via Ghent, with Mrs. Gibson—and three allied airmen, whom Clare had invited to ride along because they had crashed in Belgium and were trying to return to Allied lines.

Clare described the passing scenes including a stop for tea, the airmen and Mrs. Gibson, along with their conversations during the trip, and the difficulty of getting across the frontier, "because we had no papers for our car." But not to worry, Mrs. Gibson charmed her way across.

Among all these descriptions Clare injected considerable philosophy about the horrors of war. She finished the letter with a description of an air raid following dinner in the *Bois* on the first night in Paris. But her diary said that dinner was at *Versailles*, 20 km from Paris and its Bois. Must have been the fog-of-war clouding her memory.

And nowhere in the article did she say that Henry Luce was in the car. Either there wasn't room for six people and luggage so he was forced to take the next car, or the old man was upstaged by three charming, young pilots and thus totally ignored.

The second article, "Imagine the Worst," was a short report of her week in Paris. It consisted of a quote from an "old, old Frenchwoman," observations of a nurse bathing blistered feet, a Belgian woman discovering that her baby was dead, a girl kissing a young soldier good by, and a short conversation and drink with Vincent Sheehan (author and foreign correspondent) at the Ritz Hotel, rounded out with more horrors-of-war philosophy.

The third article, "Paris Whispers," started with the horrors-of-war mantra and then reported that Paris was calm, but with little news coming from the government. She then opined about how Paris did get their news—the same way a wife intuits how her husband's day went: "And he says: 'My God, how did you know?' And she says: 'Because I know you so well, darling.'"

So Clare did indeed send cables from Paris, just as she said in her *Rage for Fame* diary. But her reports on war-related events were somewhat superficial, and except for that one trip to the Ritz, could have been based on observations in or near a hospital. And there was nothing about interviewing troops as she reported in her diary—unless she counted the three airmen on the Brussels-to-Paris trip.

After Clare arrived in the U.S., she wrote a book about these adventures, *Europe in the Spring*. Chapter 9 covered May and early June, 1940, in fifty pages. Everything from her diary and the four *Life* articles are in the chapter, almost verbatim—plus more details, more quotes, more events, and more observations, including more about Frances starting May 9, the night the Luces arrived in Brussels:

> Although it was late, Ambassador Cudahy had waited up, with the second secretary of the Embassy, Miss Willis, a handsome, clever young woman, to receive me. Miss Willis suggested I go out to Waterloo, if I hadn't ever seen it, in the morning. "It's only an hour's ride," she said. And then Miss Willis said: "Things can't go on like this for ever. Human nervous systems can't stand it," and then she said: "Good-night, my dear."

In this version Clare reported that Frances did meet the Luces when they arrived around midnight. This is the first news of that meeting, along with new and atypical dialogue from Frances. And Clare now remembered that they spent the night in Lille on their way to Paris, arriving at the Ritz on the afternoon of May 12, where she stayed until leaving for England. And that while in Paris, she caught rides with ambulance crews to capture some of the local excitement. Finally, Clare reported that she had nightmares every night from May 10 to June 10 when she reached New York.

Impeachment of Both Parties

Then this January 26, 1941, letter from Frances to her mother Belle impeaches first Clare and then herself:

> I went back to the hotel and went on reading Europe in the Spring.

I am still trying to figure out whom the Ambassador passed off as me the night Clare Booth arrived in Brussels—I definitely was not at the Embassy before midnight that famous night of May ninth to May tenth—that is one of the nights I can give a practically minute by minute account of and I didn't arrive at the Embassy until five minutes past one a.m. the morning of the tenth, and I think you will find the bulletin, if it ever reached you will bear me out.

But anyway, Mother, she was the person who took my first letter to you out and mailed it for me from Paris, and apparently she didn't forget because I remember your saying in one of your letters which reached me months later that you had received it.

First, Frances disputed Clare's May 9 version of arrival events with the powerful argument that she simply wasn't there. If so, Clare must have made up that entire paragraph.[39]

Second, Frances confirmed that the Luces did mail her letter in Paris, which meant that she didn't drive them to Paris. So she fibbed either to her mother in 1941 or to her nephew in 1975 about these events. How could this be resolved?

The Cover-Up Scenario

Frances' passport with an appropriate visa entry could be the key. And sixty years of her passports were filed in the Hoover Archives, including diplomatic passport #1734 covering the month in question, May, 1940. In it was a visa issued by French Immigration dated 15 May, 1940, valid until 15 August, 1940. So she did go to France, not on May 12 but on May 15.

---

[39] Clare was severely criticized for such flights of fantasy by Nora Sayre in her review of *Rage for Fame*, in the 1997 *Columbia Journalism Review*. She wrote that "Boothe kept reinventing herself and her past, showing contempt for facts before she met Henry Luce, whose magazines were also often heedless about reality." Sayre finished with "the biography is engrossing as a chronicle of dishonesties, a lifetime of fabrications." Apparently the second volume of *Rage for Fame* was not published.

To be fair, Clare was not alone in this make-believe writing world. John Steinbeck's 1962 best selling book, *Travels With Charley: in Search of America*, was fact checked by Bill Steigerwald, a former journalist for the Pittsburgh Post-Gazette, in 2010. He found that many of Steinbeck's interviews were conjured up and that many of the dates and places he stayed were bogus, for example sleeping in a swanky motel rather than in his truck. That's ok if the reader is advised that these events are made up. Not ok, otherwise.

Why the three-day discrepancy? And what about Clare's apparent fabrications, the absence of war damage photos and the excessive coverage of Frances in Clare's first article, the superficial reporting in Clare's later articles, her nightmares and Cudahy's comment about her being "lost in the dramatic possibilities of the situation," and then all that adulation heaped on Frances by Cudahy? The data just doesn't add up.

One scenario can answer all these questions: a *cover-up* scenario. Consider the following: Frances fibbed all right, right along with Cudahy and the Luces, about the post-May 11 events. Specifically, Clare did have the breakdown and Frances did drive the Luces to Paris, but on May 15, because Clare was in no condition to go any earlier. And everyone agreed to cover it up, so as not to cause embarrassment to national figures (and good friends) at such a critical time.

The cover-up was hatched by Henry Luce and John Cudahy, with John suggesting that Frances provide the transportation and join the cover-up. Henry agreed, Frances agreed, and it was done. Mrs. Gibson (a Belgian national) was selected as the virtual driver because she had been in the vicinity—even at the embassy—and then left for Paris around May 11, originally planning to take the Luces with her.

John also suggested that to thank Frances for her trouble, Henry might want to give her a little publicity in an appropriate *Life* article—good for the career—and Henry agreed. So he snapped off a photo of Frances and one of John for good measure. But he didn't think to photograph any of the war damage or distraught Belgians because he was too worried about Clare and her "difficult condition," as Frances put it.

So off went the "cover-up gang," Frances and the Luces—sans allied airmen. They arrived at the Paris hospital on May 15. Henry got Clare settled, cabled her May 10 diary notes to *Life,* then took off for the U.S. via Lisbon and the Pan Am Clipper. He arrived just in time to get his photos in the May 20 edition of *Life,* under Clare's byline.

By then Clare had recovered enough to do some writing and take a taxi ride down town. But Henry forgot to tell Clare about details of the cover-up, either that or Clare was in no condition to remember them. In either case, the next cable from Clare probably required some editing by Henry, maybe to add Mrs. Gibson's name and to change the first night's dining spot from Versailles to the Bois.

Henry must have winced a little at being replaced by three airmen on the trip, but decided to let Clare's imagination prevail. Can't do too much editing to a brilliant playwright's prose. Finally, Cudahy was so pleased with these arrangements and their subsequent, flawless execution that he rewarded Frances with kudos in his book, along with some extra praise in his last Efficiency Report.

Now Frances' May 11 letter to her mother makes sense: She first wrote it when she thought the Luces were leaving on May 11 with Mrs. Gibson. Then departure plans were delayed with Frances now driving. But she couldn't say she was in Paris because it would blow the cover-up and probably terrify Belle no end, visualizing her daughter careening all over the countryside dodging German bullets. Because Frances needed an excuse for the French stamps and postmark, her original letter became "just the ticket," but with Frances, herself, mailing it in Paris.

Then to add a little credibility to the cover-up scenario, John Cudahy sent a telegram to SecState reporting that parties of Americans had left Brussels for Paris by automobile on May 13 and another party was planning to leave late in the day of May 14. Because this was the only telegram reporting Americans leaving Brussels by automobile during the invasion, by omission no Americans left between May 10 and May 13—contrary to when Clare and John said the Luces left.

So that May 14 party could have been the cover-up gang. And a late departure would necessitate an overnight stop probably at Lille, France, as Clare reported in one of her later missives. (Lille is close to the border and on a direct route from Ghent to Paris, where Ghent was another waypoint Clare mentioned.) Furthermore, as a result of the late departure and refugee traffic clogging the west-bound Brussels-to-Ghent road, the gang probably crossed the border after midnight, now May 15.

These hypotheses conveniently match Frances' bulletin from the last chapter reporting she had dinner in Brussels on May 14, followed by no entry for May 15, because she was out of town. It also tracks with the May 15 French visa entry in her passport, fitting all the disparate elements into one tidy package.

Unfortunately the scenario is based entirely on circumstantial evidence, including the May 15 French visa entry in Frances' passport, Cudahy's telegram reporting people leaving Brussels only on May 13 and 14, Clare's report of spending the night in Lille, Frances' report of dinner in Brussels on May 14, then nothing on May 15. In fact, the scenario is built around those events—and non-events.[40]

What else could resolve the question? Inspection of the Paris Ritz Hotel registry for Luce entries between May 11 and May 14 would validate the Luce story. But entries after May 14 for Henry (or Henry and Clare if he cleverly signed in that way), would validate Frances' story.

A similar inspection of the embassy guest registry would flag when the Luces left Brussels. But the registry could—and should—have been manipulated to match the official story. And of course, the Luce's passports showing their visa entry to France would resolve everything. But the author's attempts to access these sources were futile. So the direct evidence is missing.[41]

A proper summation of arguments should cite not only evidence but also credibility and motive. For credibility, Frances was guilty of a few fibs, including the Red Cross shuttle ride to Paris, her not-the-whole-truth May 11 letter, compounded by her January 26 letter to Belle. And Clare certainly committed her share, including the May 9 arrival dinner with a phantom Frances, her subsequent conversations with Frances, the three airmen, the lost automobile papers and the tea stop on the trip to Paris. It appears that Frances fibbed so as not to distress her mother, while Clare simply wanted to craft a better story. So credibility marginally favors Frances.

---

[40] No news on May 15 is like Sherlock Holmes' dog-not-barking evidence in *Silver Blaze*.

[41] As the author was pondering these possibilities, the envelope attached to Frances' May 11 letter to Belle flashed in front of him. (Both were filed in the Hoover Archives.) It did not have the stamp on it because Belle had cut off it off to send to her six-year-old grandson (the author) for his nascent stamp collection. If the postmark on (or with) the stamp showed May 11 through May 14, Clare's story would be validated unambiguously. If it showed a date after May 14, that would be a necessary confirmation of Frances' story—but not sufficient, since the Luces could have mailed it a few days after their arrival in Paris.
And that stamp collection was still in existence, stored in the attic of the author's house! So the author inspected all the French stamps pasted into his now very old album. Alas, he had done what all budding philatelists did in those days: steamed the stamp off the paper to paste into the album. And none of the stamps had enough of the postmark left to show a cancellation date.
But there were more loose stamps in the box, both steamed and un-steamed. And five French ones were still attached to part of an envelope, with more of the postmark showing, but still not enough to identify the date. So the author took them to the Hoover Archives to see if any fit that envelope, just like a puzzle piece. Sad result: no match. And the frustrating part is that the *smoking stamp* must be there, steamed to perfection in its singular glory—sans postmark.

For motive, without the cover-up story Clare had everything to loose. In contrast, Frances' reputation was going to be enhanced either way. Not only that, but Frances insisted on total silence until all were dead. Thus Frances gets a significant edge.

Coda

Shortly after a draft of this chapter was completed, Ann Morin's book, *Her Excellency, An Oral History of American Women Ambassadors,* was published. As reported earlier, Frances had died before Ann started her research on the book in 1984, so she wasn't a chapter subject. (And Frances probably would have declined the interview if she were alive.) But Clare Boothe Luce was the second chapter subject, titled "La Signora D'America."

Most of the chapter was an oral transcript of Clare's response to questions posed by Ann in 1986. In fact that was her style for all the chapters. Interspersed with the responses were Ann's annotations, setting a scene or elaborating on a particular event. In all cases, Ann was most genteel in the treatment of her subjects.

And, no surprise, Frances appeared in Clare's chapter. Here are quotes, first from Ann's introduction and then from Clare's comments:

> Mention of friendships led to a recollection about Frances Willis, the distinguished career diplomat.
> The first woman I ever met in the Foreign Service I met under the most extraordinary circumstances, and that was on May 10, 1940. I was coming from Amsterdam and spent the night at Ambassador Cudahy's [in Brussels]; that was the morning the phony war ended. I think she was the consul. At any rate, this remarkable woman became an ambassador. I think she probably was the first Ambassador to Switzerland. She was a regular Foreign Service Officer, a wonderful woman. I thought she was "une femme serieuse" [a reliable woman].
> She was straight and very effective. I'd always thought that the women undergo the same hazard in this occupation—I mean, the ambassadorial career—as they do in federal office.

That was nearly as flattering as Cudahy's comments to Frances at the beginning of this story. Not only that, but Clare's version of events didn't change in any detail over the next half a century, including the date May 10, 1940. But the most important observation is that over that half century Clare kept her part of the bargain—a bargain implied in the cover-up scenario—by heaping adulation on Frances at every opportunity. And that in turn could not have hurt Frances' subsequent career. So that's how diplomacy works.

11

DISASTER IN THE MOST CATHOLIC OF COUNTRIES, SPAIN

Getting to Madrid

AFTER the Germans ejected Frances and her embassy associates from Brussels, they were forced to drive through Germany to Switzerland, dodging British bombs and suffering Nazi salutations in "terrible Biergartens," as Frances reported in the Belgium chapter. She continued her odyssey in Berne and on to Madrid, as reported in an August 4, 1940, bulletin:

> We stayed three days in Bern. Spent one morning in the garage with two of the ambulance drivers pumping our gasoline out of the barrels into small more manageable tins; sounds awful but was really quite fun. Dined twice at the Legation (why I really wouldn't know), had lunch with the Counselor of the French Embassy who used to be in Brussels— he saw me driving down the street, stopped me and invited me. Had tea with Constance Harvey, the other really career feminine secretary.

This was the first—and only—record in Frances' files of the two ladies meeting face-to-face. Of course, Constance was still a vice consul so Frances was being diplomatic. And sadly, that's all there was, with no other details. Frances then described her trip across France with fellow expellees: Orme Wilson, deputy chief of mission, James King, an ambulance driver who had just received the French *Croix de Guerre*, and Dorita, not identified:

The trip across southern France was not as bad as anticipated. The rest in Bern had helped a lot and we didn't try to drive as long each day. Orme took us to see the Roman Arch of Triumph and the Roman theater [at Orange], and as we went through Nimes he took us around by one of the most perfect Roman temples I have ever seen and also by the Coliseum which I believe is still used for bull fights. At Avignon we had lunch in a restaurant on an island in the middle of the river, from where we could see what is left of the old bridge and the Palace of the Popes.

We had a very late lunch at Figueras and then drove along the sea to Barcelona. Dorita, King and I insisted on stopping and going swimming at a nice little beach and the others had tea so didn't mind. We arrived at the Ritz in Barcelona about nine o'clock.

We left Barcelona about three in the afternoon and spent the night at Zaragoza. Got there after ten at night and the last hour I had to drive without lights as mine just wouldn't work, so I went into Madrid that night about nine without lights. It wasn't dark enough to bother me, especially after having driven in the black-out in Brussels, but I was afraid I might get arrested—nice introduction to the Embassy that would have been: "I am in jail, come and get me out."

The trip sounded more like a private tour through the best parts of unoccupied France with Orme as the guide.

Settling in Madrid

Frances arrived in Madrid July 28, 1940, with just the belongings she could pack into her Ford coupe—around the gas tins. She checked in to the Palace Hotel and then assumed her duties as second secretary and consul at the embassy the next day. She reported her reception in that August 4 bulletin:

This beginning has been just like all other arrivals at new posts, and also completely different if you can reconcile the two. There is that same unmistakable misgiving over having a woman on the staff under what I now find a somewhat sticky veneer of cordiality. I shouldn't put it that way because everybody has been more than kind but now I have been through it so many times the symptoms are amusing.

I thought my stay in Chile would prepare me somewhat for the type of life in Madrid but I find it strange beyond words, the more so I suppose because I come directly from war conditions and a regime of German occupation. It is probably a great injustice but with the hours they keep I don't see how they can possibly ever get any great amount of work done.

The Embassy's office hours are a case in point: 10-1 and 5-8. Even if you work two hours overtime until 10 at night you have only done an eight-hour day and then I think of the ten, twelve and even fourteen hour days we put in at Brussels. You would think that you would have a lot of time to yourself, from one to five for example, but I find everyone stays up until so late at night that a siesta is almost obligatory. It has been nearly two or three o'clock before I got to bed four or five of the seven nights I have been here, and for no good reason.

Again, arrival gender bias rises up at a new post. Then as before, good, dedicated work would banish the unpleasantness and she would forget about it. This arrival curse continued to haunt her through her London tour.

Things picked up the next day when Frances' boss, Ambassador Weddell, invited her to meet Mr. Phillips, the U.S. Ambassador to Rome, and Mr. Cudahy, who were arriving at the airport, specifically at Cudahy's request. Frances reported that their arrival was delayed about two hours "while the Spanish customs officials finished their siestas." Then events got rolling:

> That afternoon about five thirty the Weddells had all our Brussels contingent plus some other people for a mint julep (the Weddells are from Virginia) out in the garden and it was very agreeable.
>
> Monday afternoon Mr. Cudahy left on a four o'clock plane for Lisbon and I went out to see him off, and that made me very, very sad. I'll never have another Ambassador like him, and of course he would be the one I'd work with for only six months.

Too bad indeed, because that was the last time she saw him—he died in 1943. But certainly her short time with Cudahy had been a triumph and a huge career boost. So there is this to consider: If they were together another six months, what could she have done for an encore? Almost anything after her German invasion performance would have been an anticlimax, and so noted by Cudahy. Thus Frances, unknowingly, had to sacrifice her attachment to maintain that perfect accolade. Not a bad trade. Frances finished her first bulletin from Spain with:

> As usual I am doing this in the office on Sunday morning and the Ambassador just walked in and asked me to come down and have lunch with them. He and Mrs. Weddell really couldn't be kinder.

Ambassador Weddell (1876-1948) was a career FSO and published raconteur. He was Consul General to Athens in 1922 and Ambassador to Argentina in 1933. The March 2004 *National Geographic* issue on the Olympic Games quoted his 1922 *National Geographic* article titled "The Glory That Was Greece," which praised the Parthenon:

> There are things in this world which we so love or so admire that we are loath to praise them, lest by clumsy or ill-chosen eulogy we should harm or diminish what we are fain to honor.

The 2004 issue finished with, "Happily, the majestic structure survived his prose."

In her next bulletin two weeks later Frances reported even more social progress, along with a rare insight—from her—into significant foreign affairs before WW II:

> People here have continued to be kindness itself—and especially at the British Embassy. Sir Samuel and Lady Maud Hoare invited me to lunch on Friday before I had even met them. I suspect that was a little bit the same thing that produced some of my invitations in Brussels, namely that women around here seem to be extremely scarce, and a single woman is at times a hostess's salvation. That impression was slightly dispelled when I found myself sitting on the Ambassador's right. Whatever the reason, I enjoyed it. It was curious to be talking to a man whose advice had it been followed in 1935 would have prevented Italy from ever becoming an ally of Germany. One of the reasons I could

never trust [British Prime Minister] Baldwin was that he so unctuously let Sir Samuel be made the scapegoat in the whole affair. I had bitter arguments with Louis Sussdorff at the time, my word what ages ago that all was.

Hoare (1880-1959) held many posts in the British government, including Home Secretary, Foreign Secretary, Secretary of State for India, Secretary of State for Air, First Lord of the Admiralty and Lord Privy Seal. One, probably apocryphal story had Hoare resigning a post after WW I, following many trips to Paris. King George V accepted his resignation, saying, "No more coals to Newcastle and no more Hoares to Paris."

Hoare joined Stanley Baldwin's government in the mid-thirties, but was forced to resign because of shenanigans over an India Bill. He then became First Lord of the Admiralty in Neville Chamberlain's government, and when Churchill took over in 1939 he banished—some say—Hoare to Madrid.

That 1935 "Italy ally of Germany" comment by Frances was about Italy threatening to invade Abyssinia, now Ethiopia. Hoare addressed the League of Nations in 1935 about the "Abyssinia Controversy." It was one of those long, elegant, diplomatic speeches with the only message being that England backed the League and all its principles. Italy then invaded Abyssinia in 1936, and the League let Mussolini get away with it. Bottom line according to Frances: Hoare was made the scapegoat and was now in exile for a crime he didn't commit.

Again Louis Sussdorff appears. The first time was as the author of that 1934 letter to Tom Wilson, Chief of the Personnel Division, telling Tom what a good impression Frances had made on her arrival in Brussels—after he said not to send a woman to Brussels. And their contretemps is truly good news: A cleaving (female) FSO doesn't need the same political opinions as the cleaved (male) FSO.

Frances' bridge games continued:

> Last night I had dinner at the Clarks' and he and two men from the Telephone Company (the IT&T) and I played bridge until an unholy hour. But what can you expect, we didn't sit down to dinner until ten or so. I had a siesta yesterday afternoon fortunately.

That late night schedule would quickly wear thin, so she had to curb her bridge addiction. But she didn't have to worry about that hurting her career, because the Weddells didn't play bridge; they played Russian Bank. Not only that, but her Spanish was rusty: "My Spanish is simply hopeless, practically non-existent, so I have a teacher coming Monday at four."

Apparently a three-times-a-week brush-up for the better part of a year fixed that problem when her fluency returned. She finally found a spacious nine-room furnished apartment to rent for $900 per year, including board but not utilities, at 41 Martinez Campos, living there from 1941 to 1944.

Frances was then granted a two-month home leave starting in March, 1941. According to her 123 Files at the National Archives, Frances was scheduled to fly home on the Pan Am Clipper, but was bumped by a more senior FSO, so she had to take a boat, the American Export Line's *Excalibur*. Rank does have its privilege.

After Frances arrived in Redlands she bought a new Ford coupe and drove with Belle to visit her brother Henry and family in Salinas, California. When she returned to Madrid she had to leave the car in Redlands because it didn't qualify for war materiel shipment to the European Theater. But she still had her circa 1934 Ford in Madrid, even though it was getting long in tooth.[42]

Work with Ambassador Weddell

Frances' first Annual Efficiency Report was written (and typed) by Ambassador Weddell on August 8, 1940. It said that she had just arrived, so there was "nothing to be recorded, save the agreeable impression Miss Willis has made upon the reporting officer and staff." That's good news: no arrival gender bias here—at least for the moment. Then on May 1, 1941, Frances was promoted to consul class V, with an annual salary of $5,000, clearly based on her performance in Brussels.

Alas, back to near-square-zero she went. Weddell's next report dated August 6, 1941, showed his true colors:

> Miss Willis is a first class officer, and in the performance of her duties in this Mission no allowance has to be made for her sex. This state-ment is made because the reporting officer admits to a certain prejudice

---

[42] It will be instrumental in bringing her home, as detailed subsequently.

against women in the Service which Miss W's satisfactory record here has done much to weaken. It must be pointed out, however, that the fact of being a woman does militate against her entertaining and thus forming and maintaining valuable contacts.

Miss Willis possesses an adequate educational background, is of high intelligence, well informed, with much common sense. While not thought to possess any special facility in acquiring foreign languages, she has a good working knowledge of Spanish and, it is believed, of French. She is at present the principal executive officer of the Embassy in administrative matters, and the work is being performed with ability. Her ability to establish contacts, save as limited above, is excellent, and her relations with foreigners, officials, and members of the American colony, are entirely agreeable.

Miss Willis is a fairly rounded officer, and would do good work in practically any phase of Foreign Service activities; it is felt, however, that she should in general be assigned to posts with a fairly large staff. She is eminently correct in dress and bearing.

In view of all that is said above no suggestion is made concerning the transfer of Miss Willis.

Intermingled with Weddell's comments, which range from fair to excellent, is a full dose of institutional gender bias, coupled with the recommendation that she only be assigned to large posts. But at least he didn't want her transferred. So after a full year Frances had only partially diminished his bias. In this game, busting through the glass table once doesn't mean women are done with that chore, a chore that can become a lengthy process. And the real irony is that Frances liked the Weddells and thought it was reciprocated. Well, never let friendship interfere with business.

Then Weddell must have had second thoughts about what he said, because he appended this to the report:

This officer is to be commended for her excellent work done at the frontier in the passage of American consular officers and employees and others en route to the United States toward the close of this month. These duties were carried out under somewhat difficult circumstances and their execution was highly satisfactory.

Here's what Frances had to say about her frontier passage duty in two consecutive bulletins to the family in July, 1941:

> Everything has centered around getting our consuls and families and staffs from Germany, the occupied countries and Italy safely across Spain to Lisbon for the journey to the United States on the USS West Point. Everything has been all organized and then completely changed three entire times, with innumerable modifications of the plans literally hourly. I have spent my life in railway offices and all the other offices to try to get transportation for the three hundred and fifty people involved. Other people worked on visas and customs requirements and such, but transportation per se has been my baby.
>
> If the ones from Germany and the occupied countries cross Northern Spain into Portugal tomorrow and Tuesday morning in three special trains as is the plan at this minute, and the ones from Italy arrive in Madrid tomorrow night and leave here for Lisbon Tuesday night I shall probably "escort" the latter party to Lisbon myself.

In her second bulletin Frances reported that she did go to Lisbon and back all in a twenty-six hour period with just a few catnaps on the train and practically nothing to eat. The entire operation went off without a single casualty or straggler—except to her Ford, which had been driven to the border by a young boy. On the return trip it ran out of gas, had a flat tire and continuously needed water for the radiator in the hot weather. But ever the opportunist, while she waited to have the puncture fixed, Frances had a beer with a Spaniard and an Englishman. Then disaster struck: "It was so hot the cake of Hershey's I had brought along had all melted and I couldn't eat it—only time in my life I can remember that's happened to me."[43]

Frances summed up results of the last weeks' action this way:

> The shouting and the tumult has died—or at least has subsided—after the great exodus, and the Ambassador and Mrs. Weddell have gone to the country to rest and relax after the strain. It all seems a bit strange because even until the time I went home on leave, although I had the

---

[43] Chocolate ranked right up there with god, family and country in Frances' life.

feeling I was always welcome at the Embassy I didn't feel "at home" here the way I had in Brussels. But since these last two weeks when I have been here literally at all hours of the day and night I feel almost more at home here than I did there. No, I suppose that would be hardly possible.

She got that one right. Because what Frances didn't know was that Weddell had just given her a less-than-sterling review, but then appended an extra paragraph about her excellent work on the frontier passage duty.

Frances' border duty did not end there. Some jobs were important; some were ludicrous. Here is one in the latter category from an earlier, January 26, 1941, bulletin:

Monday was Inauguration Day and as such was supposed to be a holiday, but as usual there was work to be done and along about eleven Madame Schiaparelli [Italian fashion designer traveling on a U.S. passport] called up; she had had a terrible time at the Portuguese border and been taken off the train because she had stayed a few hours longer than she should and she wanted me to get her a sleeper to Barcelona Monday night.

It being a holiday I didn't want to rout out our Spanish clerk who usually takes care of such things so I did it myself. Went to the Ritz about six or so to see her and found she didn't want to go to Barcelona after all but to Canfranc and as there was only a little time before that train left I went in the pouring rain and got my car and took her to the station and got her tickets changed, which in Spain is more than a major operation and just by a hair's breath got her on the train.

It was a filthy night and I was soaked and cold when it was all over, and couldn't help laughing because some one had just lent me Clare Boothe's "'Europe in the Spring," and I had just read that bit where she asks if Americans ought to die to make the world safe for Schiaparelli— and I was quite sure they shouldn't.

Here is one in the important category, reported in her February 27, 1944, bulletin:

Sweeping statements are always dangerous; nevertheless I'll risk this one, namely that this week has been one of the saddest I've spent since I went into the Foreign Service. Usually when other things go wrong I have at least the thought of work well done to console me (unless that sounds too conceited) but this week it was just that—the job that I both felt and thought should be done wasn't done at all.

Until Monday noon I thought I was going to Irun on the Spanish side of the French-Spanish border to be there when our diplomats from Vichy and consular officers from Southern France, who had been held since November 1942, most of the time in Baden Baden, crossed into Spain [and] out of German-occupied territory. Then I wasn't allowed to go [by the Spanish Foreign Office] and there was no official representative of the United States there. I don't know when anything has depressed me so—it was all wrong, and I am going to say it even if the censor does cut it out.

Constance Harvey will be pleased to read those (fortunately un-censored) comments because, as reported in The Other Women chapter, she was on that train. She and her fellow internees must not have been happy when no Americans met them in Irun. But there is a good chance that when Constance arrived in Madrid she saw Frances, who then explained the situation. They may even have taken the opportunity to celebrate Constance's liberation with a bottle of Frances' Spanish brandy.

Apparently Frances' relationship with Weddell continued to improve, as she commented in her February 1, 1942, bulletin:

> The Ambassador [Weddell] just put his head in my door and asked if I wouldn't come down and have a cup of tea, so I shall go down and join them. He and she are both wonderful people to be with in strenuous times like these. It would be impossible to have a more considerate chief and she is one of the most lovable people I have ever known.

Ambassador Hayes and the Good Beginning

That certainly looked encouraging, except that shortly after Frances wrote those comments, Weddell retired and was replaced by Carlton J. H. Hayes. Hayes •was a former Columbia University history professor with anti-Nazi credentials, whose mission was to keep Franco and his *Falange* from siding with Germany in the war. He wrote Frances' next Annual Evaluation Report in August, 1942, probably with a little departure-coaching from Weddell:

> Miss Frances E. Willis is the wheel-horse of this Embassy. She is the office manager and business administrator, supervising accounts, personnel, the code room, the pouches, and couriers, etc.
>
> She has a high sense of responsibility, a great devotion to duty, immense industry, and inexhaustible patience. She is a stickler for rules and regulations.[44] Miss Willis has an excellent education ...meticulously edits despatches ...converses most intelligently ...is socially popular in Madrid ...well liked by her colleagues ...neat and orderly ...personally attractive, and always sane and reasonable.
>
> She should be promoted to Class IV at the earliest opportunity.

Then Hayes added: "I am a bit surprised that with her background she is not more interested in political reporting." That was probably because her day was filled with other duties, including supervising people and the office, which according to Hayes in a now-declassified memo to the Department, was being greatly expanded. Then there was the diplomatic pouch and pouch couriers to manage, including running courier duty herself. In any case, a much better report than the last one, and not a word about sex limitations. Progress? For the moment.

Speaking about diplomatic pouches and couriers, here is another family story, "The Bombsight Picnic," this time told by Frances over the 1975 Christmas holidays in Menlo Park.

> Whenever an Allied bomber was damaged during bombing raids over France to the point that it couldn't make it back to England, the aircrew would head for a neutral country to land. Spain was the country of choice when the raids were over southern France. The Spanish militia would detain the aircrew and ultimately repatriate them, which was much better than a prison camp. They would also confiscate what was left of the downed aircraft, which with a little material consideration often wound up in Axis hands.

---

[44] Mark the word *stickler* because it will return to bite Frances at the end of this chapter.

So when a very new American B-17 bomber was forced to crash-land near Madrid, the crew was detained and the plane surrounded by militia. The U.S. Embassy's Army Air Corps Attaché was allowed to visit the crew to determine the extent of their injuries and needs. On that visit, the bombardier told the attaché that his new, top secret Norden bombsight was still intact in the airplane. The self-destruct charge had malfunctioned when he triggered it. It must not fall into Axis hands [because it had a new sight glass that used black widow spider webs as the cross hairs.]

Every effort must be made to retrieve the sight glass before the Huns got it. So the embassy requested permission to collect the aircrew's personal effects from the airplane, with Frances and the attaché being chosen for the job. It was such a nice day that Frances packed a picnic and spread it out near the airplane while the attaché collected the effects. The attaché was briefed on how to unbolt the sight glass and camouflage it. He filled his bag with effects, the glass and any small arms he could find, including a knife and two pistols.

The militia inspected the bag, and absolutely would not allow the weapons to pass. Reluctantly, the attaché gave these up, but the innocuous, camouflaged sight glass made it through without a question. That old decoy ruse worked again.

But there were more inspection zones to get through, this time with more perceptive inspectors. So, during the picnic the attaché slipped the sight glass into a false compartment in the bottom of the picnic basket.

Sure enough the basket got re-inspected, which required executing the next line of defense: the distraction ruse. They had packed a second bottle of very good Spanish red in the basket, but left it unopened. The inspector carefully inspected it; what else does an inspector do? Frances said that they didn't need it, and would the inspector like it? Of course, with many thanks—and off they went. The sight glass went out via diplomatic pouch to the U.S. the next day. And we won the war...

In Frances' next Rating Sheet entry of January 1, 1943, Weddell's and Hayes' comments were averaged together by the anonymous redactor:

Miss Willis has rendered highly useful service to the Embassy at

Madrid during the period under review and seems clearly to be entitled to a rating of Very Good.

That was one of the few times the redactor didn't opine about sex limitations. In spite of stepping down a notch to Very Good, she was promoted to first secretary and consul class IV, at $6,000 per year on July 16, 1943. The inertia of that outstanding rating carried her career far up the promotion track.

Social Life in Madrid

Here is an update to the diplomatic social scene starting with Frances' January 15 and April 19, 1942, bulletins:

> There have been the usual number of cocktail parties, lunches, etc. Dinners are rarer than ever and I play very little bridge these days. Played the other night until 3 a.m. after a dinner at Caldwell's. We didn't start until about midnight; that is one reason I don't do it more often because if you play after dinner it means you get precious little sleep. Most of the games begin at five or six in the afternoon and go on until nine or ten, when they stop for dinner, but I can never get away from the office in time for them.
>
> I have to be in the Embassy every morning by nine so like to stop [playing bridge] about half past twelve, but you can never get anybody around here to do it; they consider 1:30 early. No wonder I practically never play any more.

Then Frances found a partial solution to that late hour problem: Play at your place, where you can make the rules, especially with new FSO arrivals, as she reported in a July 26, 1942, bulletin:

> Dinner and a good game of bridge last night at my house, three of the men from the Embassy—one a new comer, Outerbridge Horsey, how is that for a name, individual at least? [45]
>
> Yesterday was a holiday and I discovered that he and [Findley] Burns,

---

[45] A name only chefs, punsters and the Foreign Service could love. And the Foreign Service did, because they appointed him Ambassador to Czechoslovakia in 1962.

another new one, were setting out on foot to visit the Palace. [They] had a special authorization which is necessary, so I gave them a lift and did the palace with them. Also a nearby church I've always meant to see, San Antonio de la Florida with frescoes by Goya which have, however, been so extremely restored or cleaned up that they have almost lost the Goya touch.

Frances' dinner conjured up elegant, formal affairs prepared and served by her domestic staff. Not so. A 1943 bulletin reported that dinner, at least the informal ones, usually consisted of waffles. In any event, Frances and her car were a popular pair around this time, since none of the newly arrived FSO's could bring cars with them. So Frances' Ford became the duty taxi, for example running fellow Episcopalians, Cousin Murat and Findley Burns, to church on Sundays.

Frances didn't have much time for exercise, except for dancing at midnight. She lamented the loss in her April 19, 1942, bulletin:

> I was taught to swim at an early age and it has given me much plea-sure as any one thing… and my lack of knowing how to play tennis has been a constant source of grief. Team sports in school are all right but they are no good to you afterwards. If I played tennis I could get all the exercise I need six months of the year in Madrid in the short time I have available. But as I don't play I have to try to get some exercise by walking down the windy dusty streets. It is not very agreeable so I find I do it less and less.

Out-of-Country Trips

Another new arrival at the embassy was Cristy Bell, a pouch courier. Frances reported in an April, 1942, bulletin that she hadn't seen Cristy since the summer of 1916, when he and his brother came out to visit Harry Cook in Redlands. She didn't elaborate, so his vita and connection with Harry are lost, except that he was now in the Foreign Service. Frances must have viewed their reunion with mixed emotions.

In any case, the arrival of a pouch courier was a relief for Frances and the other staff members, because someone had to carry it out usually weekly. For example Frances reported in her October 30, 1941, bulletin that she had spent five days on courier duty traveling to Tangier.[46] She spent two days and three nights in Tangier, "one pouch down and two back." Then she had to catch up on all her other work when she got home. In fact, Frances reported in her December 17, 1942, bulletin that up to that time she had "worked every day, not a single day away from the Embassy and not many even part-ones." She also said that she did a lot of her letter writing on the night shift. A busy time. So Cristy was a welcomed addition.

On another official trip Frances was driving her own car in Portugal and wound up crashing it. The trip and its accident were detailed in a June 30, 1943, letter from Ambassador Hayes to the Department. He reported that Frances volunteered to take the embassy's official airmail to Lisbon in time to catch the Pan Am Clipper flight scheduled to depart March 28, 1943. Normally, the airmail would have been sent out on Iberia Airlines, but they had suspended service. Furthermore, the official auto that had just arrived at the embassy didn't have the necessary international documents for such a trip. So Frances offered her Ford for transport-service, yet again.

Hayes said that on the return trip the car turned over about fifty miles from the Spanish border. The chauffeur with Frances was unhurt, but Frances' left arm was dragged for some distance along the road and pinned under the car. Then back in Madrid, infection set in and the medical attention, including three operations, was "entirely inadequate." As a result, she has been absent from duty for twenty days.

Hayes' account suggested that the chauffeur should have been driving. In that case, Frances would be sitting in the right seat (of her left-hand drive Ford coupe) and when the car rolled, her right arm would have been the candidate for dragging and pinning. But her left arm was injured.

Because Lisbon is more than 300 miles from Madrid, a two-way trip would require at least sixteen hours on those windy, two-lane roads, an exhausting drive for one person. So Frances was probably spelling the chauffeur. And that's the way it was, as Findley Burns confirmed in his May, 2003, conversation with the author. He also reported that the car rolled because Frances swerved to avoid

---

[46] Tangier was a permanently neutralized and demilitarized zone, carved from Morocco in 1925 by England, France and Spain in their Tangier Agreement. The U.S. Office of Strategic Services (OSS) operated out of Tangier during WW II, and was likely the destination for Frances' pouches. Tangier was finally returned to Morocco in 1956.

hitting a dog and the ten-year-old suspension system could no longer keep the car upright.

It's pretty clear that Hayes letter was written because Frances had used up her allotted sick leave and the Ambassador was requesting more. Otherwise she would be required to dig into her annual leave allotment or worse, take leave without pay. A nice gesture from the chief.

Back to the Beginning

This brings the story back to events detailed in the first chapter, Crisis in Washington. First is the November 9, 1943, letter from F. E. Flaherty of Administration to Joe Erhardt of Personnel, proposing that:

> Miss Willis has long since earned a transfer to some easier post where her arm can be properly taken care of. She is doing a man-sized job at Madrid.

with this note penned in the upper left corner of the letter:

> *JGE*
> *Joe, Secy says Miss Willis OK for night shift. How about it?*

That in turn started Frances' transfer to the Department. Then nothing happened for the next six months. Finally on April 22, 1944, the embassy received the following despatch from SecState Hull:

> Bryan E. Blankinship-unclassified, $2500, Vice Consul at Tijuana, has been designated Third Secretary of Embassy and Vice Consul at Madrid to serve in dual capacity.
>
> Miss Willis is assigned to the Department for duty, and should proceed upon arrival of Blankinship. Travel via any feasible route and means, including air, authorized. Telegraph date departure and submit estimate.

That must have been a small embarrassment to Frances, being relieved by a vice consul and just appointed third secretary out of Tijuana. At least he could speak the language—once he acquired a lisp. Frances reported the news in her May 7, 1944, bulletin:

> I have been transferred to the Department. I should like to leave tomorrow but because of the pressure of work here I am not to leave until some one else arrives. Prolonged farewells and parties are more than I can face, so for the moment I am not saying anything about my transfer. I am, however, nearly consumed with excitement. The prospect of going back to stay for awhile after sixteen years of "exile" is too glorious for words. I have been pleased with all my transfers since I have been in the service, but this is the best yet.

Then Blankinship's arrival was delayed, which generated another round of despatches, ending with a Department telegram of June 7, 1944, directing Frances to proceed anyway. Frances' departure date was then set for July 1, which so energized her that she volunteered to write Joe Erhardt informing him of her plans. That letter is in the first chapter, an emotional outburst from a cool and collected diplomat. And of course they knew about her arm—a major reason they brought her home.

Frances and Findley Burns on her right at her farewell picnic near Madrid, June, 1944. Others are not identified.

Ambassador Hayes and the Bad Ending

The final Madrid entry in Frances' dossier was Carlton Hayes' second Annual Efficiency Report, dated November 4, 1944, after Frances had left Madrid. It was in a new format, which required comments on four specific topics: (a) Nature of duties, with precise details; (b) Professional talents and attainments, promise of development; (c) Post utility; and (d) Summary and appraisal. Furthermore, many of the topics were divided into subtopics; for example, Topic (b) had eleven subtopics, with Linguistic the eleventh, where emphasis was placed on Far Eastern, Near Eastern or Russian languages, a perceptive twist to the diplomatic game in 1944. Frances didn't score too well under Hayes' interpretation of this new format:

> Nature of Duties. Miss Willis was the administrative officer of the Embassy when I arrived in Madrid in May 1942 and discharged the manifold duties of that office with the devotion to detail which I indicated in my Efficiency Report of 1942. As the Embassy expanded, however, her almost excessive attention to detail placed upon her too great a burden. Hence in October 1942 the part of her duties having to do with accounts, Government property, buildings and grounds, and clerical personnel was transferred to Mr. Outerbridge Horsey, and she was left in charge of the code- file- and mail-rooms and of protocol. This arrangement continued until she was transferred to the Department in July 1944. She had been promoted to Class IV in July 1943.

In sum, about half of her duties were stripped away because she couldn't do them all herself, caused by her unwillingness to delegate, a critical-but-fair assessment. So that stubborn family trait finally caught up with Frances in Spain.

In the performance and potential section, Part (b) with its 11 subtopics, Hayes reconfirmed Frances' considerable administrative ability, but then reiterated his concern for her lack of interest in political affairs, and added to the list "no inclination to concern herself with economic matters, and only …some mild interest in cultural relations." He gave her high marks for being a charming hostess and speaking French fluently, with a good command of Spanish. Hayes then finished with his killing comments:

> Miss Willis is now in the Department for what I assume will be a

regular tour of duty. It is best for her at present. She has been too long and too continuously abroad, and has grown a bit stale in using her very real talents. These will come again to the surface, I am sure, in the home environment.

Miss Willis is a very fine person, of good appearance and address, sterling character, thorough devotion to duty, loyal and dependable. She will be, I think, a faithful follower rather than a leader.

As observed in the first chapter, that last sentence can destroy a career. In fact, this review was her nadir, and just after such a fine peak in Brussels. A tough business, especially when you and your boss get crosswise over a minor issue of what to put in the diplomatic pouch. Again Findley Burns was the source of this conflict in his May, 2003, phone conversation with the author, paraphrased as follows:

It seems that Hayes was a staunch Roman Catholic assigned to the most Catholic of countries, Spain. Apparently he intermingled his sacred and secular duties on the job, as it were. Specifically, Archbishop (and currently military chaplain) Spellman was visiting Ambassador and Mrs. Hayes and wanted to send out ecclesiastical material, presumably back to his office in New York. Hayes volunteered the U.S. diplomatic pouch because it would be faster and easier than using the Vatican's Papal Nuncio pouch across town.

Frances, being the embassy's administrative officer, was responsible for these pouches, their contents, their transport and their security. And she disapproved of using official U.S. diplomatic pouches for unofficial business, which included church business. So she blocked the material.

Her meeting with the ambassador notifying him of her decision must not have been pleasant. But Hayes probably didn't get mad—he just got even in her Annual Efficiency Report. And the irony of it was that Hayes was not invoking any type of gender bias; in his view it was simply a critical-but fair evaluation. The problem was that it armed the Old Guard Rating Sheet redactor with all the ammunition he needed to recommend against a promotion, stopping her career dead in its tracks.

Findley also reported that pouches from other U.S. embassies sometimes contained cargo of questionable origin, so the church material might have been allowed at other, more permissive embassies. But not where Frances—ever the sticker for rules—was in charge.

There were no *FEW* initials on this Annual Efficiency Report, such as on the ones written by Dave Morris in Brussels. Nor was there any indication that Hayes had discussed the report with Frances. So she likely didn't know what she had wrought. Even if she did know she wouldn't have regretted it; she would have just chalked it up to the "penalty for principle."

In addition to that major dust-up, it appears that Frances had indeed burned herself out as Hayes reported, especially after her auto accident. What's more, she had her orders and was eager to get home. That made her a "short-timer," as they say in the military. It's awfully hard to stay focused in situations like that.

So on this low (but likely unknown) note, Frances started her trip home. To get there Frances would have to fly over vast stretches of the Atlantic Ocean in a very large, very slow passenger airplane, which is risky business in time of war, especially with fast, agile German fighter aircraft lurking. So the possibly safer alternative would be to take a sea-voyage. That would give Frances time to relax and collect herself under normal conditions, as shown in the next Perts' sketch. While such ship departures were always a festive occasion, Frances would not get that kind of a sendoff because there was a war on. And it's almost never done nowadays with air travel—gone one day and back the next.

"Home for a Responsible Post" from M. C. Perts' 1924 book.

If it were a sea-voyage, she would have to worry about packs of German U-boats roaming around that ocean, ready to torpedo any ship they found, which doesn't make things relaxing at all. So a long, multi-stop air-trip might have been the better bet. And that's what she did—on a Pan Am Clipper, as reported in the first chapter.

Incidentally, a September 6, 1944, telegram in Frances' 123 File detailed her personal effects shipped home: Seventeen boxes plus an eighteenth with her car in it! Plenty of room on those surviving, west-bound Liberty ships.

12

CRISIS RESOLVED

Celebrating in Washington DC

AFTER thirty days of leave in Redlands, Frances reported for duty as a night watch officer at the Department of State headquarters on August 14, 1944. As summarized in the first chapter, she first stayed at the Statler Hotel for a week. Then she moved into an apartment near Dupont Circle for about a year while looking for a house to rent. She finally found a large, four-bedroom home on Fulton Street NW, just off Embassy Row and next to the National Cathedral, two principal icons in her life. Incidentally, Frances said on more than one occasion that in her view Washington DC was one of the two most beautiful cities in the world. Paris, of course, was the other.[47]

Frances' social life kicked into high gear almost immediately, as she reported in an August 27 bulletin to the family. She had dinner with Katherine Fite, "who had been working in the Department for several years." Katherine was the daughter of E. D. Fite, Chairman of Vassar's Political Science Department and the one who talked Frances into the Foreign Service back in 1927. Apparently he was pretty slick at it because he talked his daughter into a similar career. Then in a July, 1945, bulletin Frances reported that

> [She] saw Katherine Fite off to London today. The War Crimes Commission asked specifically for her services and of course everybody is very pleased about it!

---

[47] That was before the 1968 assassination of Martin Luther King and subsequent burning and looting riots, which changed the Washington DC landscape for the next forty years.

That was all the information Frances provided about Katherine. John Q. Barrett filled in more details with his 1999 article, "Katherine B. Fite: The Leading Female Lawyer at London and Nuremburg, 1945:" Katherine graduated from Vassar in 1926 and then from Yale Law School in 1930. After four years of private practice in New York City, she moved to Washington and worked for two years as an attorney with the United States-Mexico General Claims Commission. She then joined the Department of State in 1937, working in the Office of the Legal Adviser. In 1945 she was detailed to Justice Robert H. Jackson's staff at the Nuremberg War Crimes Commission and served there until the Kaplan-Fite case against the Reich Cabinet had been presented to the Nuremburg Court in late 1945.[48]

Barrett reported that because of her gender, Katherine's employment by Justice Jackson was a notable event, which rated an article, "Woman Joins Staff of War Crimes" in the *New York Times*. Justice Jackson and Katherine developed a mutual high regard for each other, which lasted for the rest of Jackson's life. Katherine retired from the State Department in 1962. It's pretty clear why Frances and Katherine hit it off, even beyond the inspirational mentoring of E. D. Fite: They were the vanguard of professional women in public service.

Here is a sample of Frances' social life from that bulletin:

- Church, dinner and dancing with Findley Burns [Madrid FSO], on home leave in Baltimore.
- Dinner with Kep [Capt. Chester H. J. Keppler, former naval attaché to Stockholm] visiting from the Harvard NROTC in Boston.
- Bridge with Graham Stewart [Stanford professor, who gave her his *Tacna-Arica Dispute* book when she first went off to Chile], visiting from Stanford.
- Dinner with Tom Wailes [Belgium FSO, now in Washington and destined to play a large role in her career.]
- Symphony concert at the Watergate with orchestra on a river barge.
- Phone call to Franklin Pierce to give him "a full report on FEW, if not the state of the nation."

---

[48] Not all U.S. jurists were happy about this trial. For example, Supreme Court Chief Justice Harlan Stone called the Nuremberg trials a fraud: "(Chief U.S. prosecutor) Jackson is away conducting his high-grade lynching party in Nuremberg."

Frances urged her mother Belle to visit Washington DC, but it was a tough sell because Belle was not a traveler. Frances also invited the entire Willis family to come for Christmas in 1945 and most of them did. In fact, big sister Caroline and daughters had arrived in August from Chile so that the girls could attend the nearby National Cathedral School. Belle finally agreed to come, traveling in December with the Henry Willis family by train across the U.S. and spending two weeks at Frances' Fulton Street house. And with such a family aggregate, exciting events were bound to occur—and did, as reported later in this chapter.

The Start of Redemption

In between all this socializing and visiting Frances had work to do.[49] She finished her night watch officer duty on December 25, 1944. On January 1 the Selection Board's redactor issued his disastrous Rating Sheet entry for Frances. Then she was appointed Executive Assistant to the new Undersecretary of State, Joseph Grew. All that was detailed in the first chapter, which brings events up to date and to the critical question of her career: Why did Undersecretary Grew pick Frances as his executive assistant?

The simple answer is that Grew had just been appointed undersecretary on December 20, 1944; he obviously needed an executive assistant for his new job and Frances, at the right pay-grade, had just become available. So he picked her. And if anyone had asked that question of Grew or others in the Department, that would have been the official answer. But evidence in Frances' dossier reveals far more than that official answer.

A quick review of Joseph C. Grew's distinguished Foreign Service career will put the answer in perspective. Joseph Clark Grew, 1880-1965, spent more than forty years in the Foreign Service. His first appointment was Deputy Consul in Cairo, Egypt—by Teddy Roosevelt. In 1917 he was appointed Chargé d'affaires to Austria-Hungary. At the age of forty he was appointed Minister to Denmark (1920-1921), then, successively, Minister to Switzerland (1921-1924), Under Secretary of State (1924) where he worked to establish the modern Foreign Service, Ambassador to Turkey (1927-1932), Ambassador to Japan (1932-1942), and into WW II. He and the embassy staff were interned by the Japanese from

---

[49] Actually it was the other way around: Frances squeezed her social life in between her work schedule.

December 8, 1941, to June 25, 1942. But as Grew reported, "It was 'incarceration' not internment."

Heinrichs in his biography of Grew, *American Ambassador*, reported that during his first undersecretary tour, Grew got crosswise with Assistant Secretary Wilber Carr and Secretary of State Kellogg over Grew's attempts to keep the diplomatic branch intact within the Foreign Service. In 1927 and with the help of Congress, Kellogg and Carr won that battle so that all FSO's became fully integrated. Actually, as reported earlier, they were mashed together, with the consuls for the most part, residing under the diplomats.

By then Grew had had enough and in order to shake loose the "dry, dry, dust of the old Department," accepted his new post in Turkey. After Grew left town, Carr was appointed chairman of the Foreign Service Personal Board.

Heinrichs also reported that following repatriation from Japan in 1942, Grew was appointed Special Assistant to Secretary of State Hull, "placing him in effect on detached service to bring the war against Japan home to Americans in any way he saw fit." Grew saw fit to do the job by barnstorming the country, giving 250 speeches in the next year. He was then appointed Director of the Office of Far Eastern Affairs on May 1, 1944, and attended the Dumbarton Oaks Conference as a member of the U.S. delegation.[50]

Then Secretary of State Hull resigned due to poor health and Roosevelt nominated Undersecretary Edward Stettinius for Secretary of State and Grew as Undersecretary. Grew was confirmed on December 19, 1944, and immediately became acting secretary for the time that Stettinius was out-of-town, which was most of the time. Grew resigned from the Foreign Service on August 15, 1945, the day after Japan surrendered and WW II ended.

In sum, Grew was a major player in the Foreign Service and in fact, has been called "Father of the Professional Foreign Service." So Grew pretty much had his pick of the FSO crop—anyone he wanted for an executive assistant. And he picked Frances.

What motivated Grew to pick Frances can be inferred from the following events. First, Grew met Frances in 1927 when she appeared before him for the

---

[50] The Dumbarton Oaks Conference was held in Washington DC between August and October, 1944. The Soviet Union, Great Britain, United States and China met to discuss the possibilities of creating a new international organization for world peace after WW II. (The League of Nations was still in existence.) Out of these meetings emerged the structure and form of the United Nations.

Foreign Service oral examinations. And her comment during the orals that, "if I were ever given a job I could not do I would resign," must have resonated with him because that was precisely his position on women at the time, as Calkin reported in The Other Women chapter.

So Frances and Grew were singing from the same page of the Foreign Service hymnal, right from the start of her career. That must have impressed Grew and, indeed, may have helped Frances over her final Foreign Service School entrance hurdle at the last minute, although there is no record of him directing such action in his 1952 autobiography, *Turbulent Era, A Diplomatic Record of Forty Years, 1904-1945*.

Next, Grew undoubtedly followed Frances' career through reports from, and conversations with, his FSO associates. For example, he certainly was aware of the good impression Frances made upon her 1934 arrival in Brussels, as reported via back-channel communications between Ambassador Morris, Counselor Sussdorff, Personnel Division Chief Wilson, and Western European Division Chief Pierrepont Moffat—Grew's son-in-law.

Grew must also have seen, or heard about, the fine Annual Efficiency Report Hugh Gibson gave Frances in Belgium in 1938 (which signaled the huge change in Gibson's attitude towards women—or at least Frances—in the service) because Grew and Gibson were close colleagues throughout their Foreign Service careers.

Ambassador Cudahy's sterling comments about Frances "being the most competent and best all-round secretary I have known" should have crossed his path. He may also have remembered that Frances received much favorable publicity for assuming chargé duty in Stockholm in 1932. And he certainly saw Stettinius' excellent memo dated at almost the same time the Rating Sheet entry was made. In fact, there is a good chance that Grew drafted the memo as one of the first tasks for his new boss, Stettinius.

Add to these high probability events the following conjectures: Grew likely ran across Frances during her tour as night watch officer, because he was director of the Department's Far Eastern Affairs during that time, and for the last week of her duty he was acting secretary. Unfortunately, Heinrichs reported that Grew stopped keeping his personal diary after leaving Japan, so there is no direct evidence of their conversations or meetings.

Then there was that January 1, 1945, Rating Sheet entry, which could have done nothing but shock him. At this point, Grew should have called for Frances' full dossier to ponder details summarized in the entry. He may have asked Ambassador Hayes and the anonymous redactor to elaborate on their comments, and could even have checked with Frances' previous bosses including Ambassadors Morris, Gibson and Weddell, career FSO's whom he certainly knew well. (Sadly, John Cudahy, one of Frances biggest boosters, had died in 1943.) But the record is again silent on these conjectures.

However the next step is not conjecture: Frances was immediately assigned as Grew's executive assistant. And because of what was subsequently documented in Frances' dossier, Grew obviously decided to take a first-hand look at her and see what she was really made of. Had she faded—reached a plateau of useful-ness—as Hayes reported and the anonymous redactor asserted, or did she still have the energy, dedication and potential that Gibson and Cudahy reported? In short, give her one more chance.

Assisting Joseph Grew

For the next eighteen months Frances was detailed as an Assistant to the Under Secretary of State, first to Joseph Grew and then to Dean Acheson. Both undersecretaries wrote an Annual Efficiency Report, with Grew using the old form (1933 revision) for his August, 1945, report and Acheson using the new form (1943 revision.) for his October, 1946, report. That is important only because the new form required listing "Nature of Duties," as Acheson reported:

> As Assistant to the Under Secretary, Miss Willis had general respon-sibility for facilitating and expediting the work of the office. In addition to regular activities described later, she was subject to special assign-ments covering a variety of activities, which required knowledge of the mechanics of the Department or of the Foreign Service. Specific respon-sibilities were as follows:
>
> 1. Read all incoming correspondence and determine how it should be handled, to whom it should be routed for information or reply and in certain instances prepare the reply.
> 2. Read all incoming telegrams and bring the ones which require the personal attention of the Under Secretary to his notice, together with such background information as needed.
> 3. Receive miscellaneous visitors and telephone calls, usually with a view to helping people who turned to the Under Secretary's Office for information or assistance of various kinds.

4. Draft telegrams, letters and memoranda for the Under Secretary.

5. Expedite Departmental action on matters of concern to the Under Secretary.

6. Review documents of departmental and inter-departmental committees to determine which ones require attention of the Under Secretary.

Now back to Joseph Grew and his Annual Efficiency Report of August 14, 1945, which was going to make or break Frances' career. Grew' evaluation is summarized below, followed by his autographed picture.

I am able to give Miss Frances E. Willis a rating of <u>Excellent</u> in every respect. On my appointment I arranged for Miss Willis' assignment to this office as my Assistant and she has fully justified the wisdom of my selection.

Miss Willis has been of the greatest possible help and effectiveness in following up problems and correspondence throughout the Department as well as occasionally in the White House, and it would appear that she has established relations of confidence both with the higher officials and with the desk officers. She has also drafted much of my correspondence with unusual wisdom and tact and in excellent literary style.

Her judgment, when I have consulted her on current problems, has been both mature and sound. Her thinking is thorough and well balanced.

She has a substantial cultural background and her personality is forceful but at the same time wholly agreeable. I feel certain that in a foreign post her representation of the United States and American interests would be of high quality.

Her dependability, sense of responsibility and devotion to duty are outstanding. Her tolerance and justice, balance and poise, industry, cooperation, initiative, ambition, determination to improve, force and will power are all of high grade.

Miss Willis has high ability to establish contact, including relations of confidence both with foreign officials and with colleagues. Her standing and popularity, temperament and disposition, courtesy, tact and patience are of the best. She has immense energy and endurance.

As to future assignments when she leaves the Department, I believe that the department will be wholly justified in giving her a position of importance and responsibility. I do not believe that her sex would in any way interfere with her efficiency and effectiveness as a Foreign Service Officer in the field.

Joseph C. Grew, 1945 (courtesy State Department.)

Grew's message says, "To Frances E. Willis with highest appreciation of her able and most helpful support through momentous days, from Joseph C. Grew, 1945."

Frances was also promoted to Class III on August 13, one day before Grew signed the review. That promotion was precisely counter to the redactor's January 1 recommendation that "she should not be placed in line for advancement to Class III." Thus it's clear that Grew, himself, rammed the promotion through the system. Even more importantly, Grew's "excellent in every respect" review must have finally ended all gender bias in the Department, especially with his final comment that her sex is not an issue in the field. Read on.

Frances' special promotion triggered its own one-year, out-of-normal-sequence Rating Sheet review. This January, 1946, paragraph entry started with a direct quote from Grew, further noting that he "rated her Excellent, saying that she had fully justified her selection for that post." Then the redactor finished with the following:

> Officers with whom she has been associated in the Department have a high regard for her judgment and administrative talent. The most successful woman officer in the Service to date, Miss Willis has reached Class III after successful consular and diplomatic experience in the field and in the department. The only apparent obstacle to her rising to the top of the Service is her sex which cannot be disregarded in selection assignments for her. That she has done so well despite this is all the more to her credit.
>
> January 1, 1946.
Rating: VERY GOOD

That is simply astonishing on two counts: First, Grew's "Excellent in every respect" was downgraded to "Very Good" by the redactor. The only plausible explanation is that the redactor was prohibited from changing a rating by more than one step per review cycle, in order to smooth out the effect of an odd rating. Because the 1945 report was Satisfactory, this one could not be better than Very Good. In modern-day vernacular, the term *management-challenged system* describes this process.

Second, that sex-limitation incantation was truly institutionalized, just like a broken phonograph record—over and over and over—never mind what Frances' on-site bosses said in their Annual Efficiency Reports. Not only that, the Old Guard kept raising the bar: First, Class IV was quite adequate "until she has demonstrated further fitness." Then when she was promoted to Class III, "her sex cannot be disregarded in selection assignments," which will keep her from "rising to the top of the Service," Class II and above—the flag ranks. In short, the glass table remained firmly in place, with only an occasional glimpse at the glass ceiling.

Extracurricular Events

This ever-present, perverse gender bias is pretty depressing. Battling a hide-bound system always is. So it's time for a little humor that Frances transmitted in her July, 1945, bulletin. At this time James F. Byrnes, another outsider, had replaced Edward Stettinius as Secretary of State. Then Byrnes immediately took off for Europe for the Potsdam and the Tripartite Conferences; then off to England with Truman to meet King George VI. So the new chief hadn't introduced himself much around the office before he left town.

None of this played too well with the kennel dogs. First they were jerked around by one Secretary of State; then they were ignored by his successor. Frances passed along their current angst with the following comment: "The latest diagnosis of what's wrong with the State Department is that it fiddles while Byrnes roams." It's not clear if Frances was the author of that egregious pun-plus-spoonerism, but she was capable of it. In any case she and her fellow dogs must have had a good, sardonic laugh over it.

During the two-week family visit to Washington DC over the 1945 holidays, Frances introduced her family to the Washington establishment via a cocktail and buffet dinner party at her Fulton Street house. She invited friends, local relatives, including Cousin Marion Sanger and her husband, Richard Sanger, a fellow FSO, who lived in Westmorland Hills outside Washington DC, and many Department dignitaries, including Grew and Acheson. The party excitement began that morning, as the next family story, "Cocktails in Washington," relates:

> It had snowed about six inches a few days before the party, so provisioning logistics were complicated by all the snow piled up along the curb, sidewalks, porches, steps and roof-gutters. This last location can become an ice-jam creating large icicles, which menace the house and people walking under them.
>
> On the morning of the party, Frances stepped out on the front porch to retrieve the newspaper and was confronted by a couple of these ice-jam icicles, looking her right in the eye. She called brother Henry and brother-in-law Freddie Vaughan and they conferred for some time, since neither had seen such a phenomenon in sunny California or Chile coasts. The decision was to clear the ice jam by pouring hot water on it—with Frances insisting that she would do the pouring from the top of

a ladder perched precariously against the porch roof. Henry braced the ladder and Freddie handed her pans of hot water provided by shifts of kids racing between the kitchen and porch. The mission took the better part of the morning but was successful. And so the party went off on schedule, with no one injured—at least upon entry.

The party was held in the finished basement, but not all that big and with a fairly low ceiling, especially for twenty guests, the family, a bartender and waiters (kids, pressed into service). All the ladies were dressed to the nines, complete with hats de jour—brims that flipped up, some lined with monkey fur. Everyone was standing, talking, drink in one hand, cigarette in the other. An accurate description of the environment would be "close."

Now Henry's wife and the author's mother, Enid, an accomplished social animal herself, was standing in the center of the room, charming and entertaining as usual. A lady, who must remain anonymous, was standing behind Enid and turned around to either greet someone or accept a fresh drink. It doesn't matter why she turned but as she did, she jammed her cigarette directly into Enid's arm, right at the elbow—the one holding her drink.

Enid's arm and drink shot straight up. The drink contents then came down directly onto Mrs. (Alice Stanley) Acheson, starting with her hat then dribbling onto her dress. Screams and jostling all around. Enid was burned, Alice was soaked and Francis was mortified. This was not the result of an introductory (or career-enhancing) party Frances was after.

But she apparently stepped up to the crisis, handling the fallout and cleanup with grace and humor, salving Enid's burn, drying off Alice and restarting the party. Apparently she did it well enough so that both Grew and Acheson remained fans.

Assisting Dean Acheson

Working for Grew was the first half of her tour as Assistant to the Under Secretary. Grew retired at the end of the war and was replaced by Dean Acheson, who moved up from Assistant Secretary for Economic Warfare. Frances kept one set of papers from this time—obviously papers that she thought worth saving. They deal with the proposed 1946 Foreign Service Act, and start with the following memo:

January 19, 1946

Mr. Acheson:

If you should have time over the week-end to skim through the attached letters of January 11 and January 14 from Mr. Messersmith, I think you would find them interesting, especially the one of January 11... A letter of acknowledgment to Mr. Messersmith, for your signature, is also attached.

FEW

That is the same Messersmith—George S. Messersmith—who, as Consul General to Berlin, was detailed as a Foreign Service Inspector to conduct that long, 1930, American Foreign Service Inspection Report on Frances in Chile. Specifically, he was to check out the new-girl-with-those-good-reviews. While the report was generally flattering, his last comment to keep her locked up in the consular branch "for at least several more years," stopped her diplomatic promotion in its tracks. Frances probably never saw his report, which is a good thing. But she surely remembered him and his interview sixteen years earlier.

So now Messersmith was working on the Foreign Service Bill out of the new Office of Foreign Service and Frances had risen to a level where she could draft correspondence directly to him. That should have given her a momentary charge, especially on such a pressing subject.

As Selden Chapin, Director of that Office, put it in his 1946 address, "The Future of the Foreign Service:" "At the present the Service is undermanned, clogged with deadwood, insufficiently trained, underpaid, inadequately housed and clumsily administered." The 1946 Foreign Service Bill was supposed to fix these problems.

Acheson then penned a typical outsider's note on Frances' memo: *"Please make a summary. I can't read this stuff. DA"*

So Frances did, in a March 20, 1946, "MEMORANDUM FOR MR. ACHESON," starting out:

The attached "Draft of a Foreign Service Bill" has been carefully drawn up under the direction of the Office of Foreign Service; nevertheless I should like to offer comments on the following points: The substitution of seven classes, six numbered classes and one class of career ministers, for the existing eight classes and three unclassified grades...

Well, that had all the earmarks of a short nap for her boss. But Frances kept him awake by suggesting he not worry about that until the actual classes were defined. Ultimately, they were defined and everyone, including Congress, approved. They are shown in the table of Appendix 1. She went on to suggest that:

> The establishment of a recognized class to take care of career ministers, however, is undoubtedly an excellent step as among other things, it should obviate a great deal of administrative fancy work which has been necessary in the past.

That also happened, which served Frances well because she was appointed to that rank nine years later with no administrative fancy work.

Frances continued with her summary, analyzing "The proposed compulsory retirement system, (or the process of 'selection out' as the drafting officers call it)." She argued that selecting out an FSO (via either resignation or retirement) after a given number of years in a class without a promotion was unjust if done later in his career, because he had likely acquired family responsibilities at a time when it would not be easy to find other employment. The solution was to do selection out early in the FSO's career, keeping only the fit for a full service life, whether they rose to the top or not.

Frances then commented about the authors "cloaking old methods in new terminology," the increased costs of these new services, and the need to entirely reorganize the Division of Foreign Service Personnel. She also suggested stripping some rigid provisions out of the bill and leaving them to administrators.

Now her staff work was complete with well-reasoned—and quite altruistic—recommendations for the chief. Incidentally, the Department talked Congress into the selection out retirement system, based on the U.S. Navy's similar "up or out" retention system, which should have mollified Frances' disappointment.

Actually, at this time the system had to be up or out, because the Foreign Service's population, after increasing almost ten-fold during WW II, started to decrease after that war. Specifically, the State Department's Website reported less than 2000 employees in 1930 and 1940, jumping to 16,319 employees in 1950, then decreasing to 13,294 in 1960 and 12,848 in 1970. So WW II dragged the U.S. out of its isolation and into world diplomacy in a big way. That was followed by a peace-time retrenchment as the world crisis abated and more stable relations were established, at least in the free world.

The problem with job tenure in a static or declining system is that all classes (or ranks) soon become clogged with tenured officers, leaving few openings for the bright, young ones just entering the system. That's precisely what happened in the U.S. Army, which tried a variant of the tenured policy after WW II, and wound up with an impenetrable hump of captains and majors—sometimes called the "pig-in-a-python" problem.

Job tenure works well in a dynamic, growing system, which was the case in foreign and military services in the 1940's. Furthermore, in wartime the military uses instant tenure with no luxury of keeping just the fit, as Frances recommended, because replacing casualties overwhelms all other factors. So it's pretty clear that Frances hadn't been in service long enough to fully appreciate the long-term ramifications of her tenure recommendation.

In any case, Acheson was impressed with this good staff work as he reported in the second part of his October 23, 1946, Annual Efficiency Report:

> During the months when Miss Willis was my assistant, I was continuously conscious of and deeply impressed by her ability in all phases of the work which she was called upon to handle. Her routine work was organized with ease and complete attention to detail, and was based on a thorough-going knowledge of the rules and regulations of the Department and the Foreign Service.
>
> All new tasks that were given her were assumed by her with confidence and executed promptly, well and completely. Her reports and memoranda to me were written with clarity and conciseness and an understanding of the important and complicated questions which arose in the Under Secretary's office.
>
> Her knowledge of background material was very full and her judgment and reasoning were excellent. Her record, deservedly, is one of high attainment in the Foreign Service. At the same time that she has assumed fully and executed well the responsibilities brought by her unusual success in the Foreign Service, she has remained a person of poise, balance, and complete modesty as to her record and capabilities. She had the respect, loyalty, and affection of all those who served on my staff with her. In short, I should say that she is an outstanding officer in the Foreign Service.

Next Department Assignment: a Desk Job

Frances' next assignment in the Department was to the Division of Western European Affairs, Code WE, in charge of the Belgium-Luxembourg Desk. She reported for duty in July 1946 with a title of Country Specialist. Here is part of an earlier Western European Country Specialist job description from her dossier:

> Have primary responsibility for the initiation and coordination of policy and action in political, economic, commercial, social and cultural matters involved in the relations of this Government with Switzerland, Belgium. Luxembourg, Liechtenstein ...prepare policy material for use by high officials of this Government toward areas in Western Europe ...work closely with the War and Navy Departments and with appropriate foreign diplomatic missions in Washington ...conduct discussions with members of Congress expressing an interest in matters involving new or revised policy action.

When Frances arrived, Switzerland and Liechtenstein had been split off so she was charged with just Belgium and Luxembourg. In any event, Frances must have been delighted to work closely with the Navy Department, a lasting affection of hers.

About three months later, Frances was invited to speak to her old academic world. The Phi Beta Kappa Chapter of Maryland sent out formal invitations for an "informal reception to recognize the honor students of Goucher College," and to hear "Dr. Frances E. Willis" speak on "The Foreign Service."

Nothing like an academician-turned-diplomat coming home to adulation. This appears to be her first formal speech, although a copy did not survive, as did many of her others. So Frances may have composed it on the fly, possibly on her two-hour drive from Washington DC to Baltimore. In any case, she clearly knew the subject matter, which is a good way to start a speaking career.

The first Annual Efficiency Report for her desk assignment was written by Paul T. Culbertson, Chief, WE on January 20, 1947, and said, in part:

> Miss Willis took charge of the Belgium-Luxembourg desk. In part because of an earlier assignment to Belgium, but more because of her outstanding general ability, she took immediate hold of the numerous

problems, the most outstanding of which was the final settlement of the lend-lease reverse lend-lease account with Belgium.

She has demonstrated here as she has in the past soundness of judgment ...a delightful sense of humor ...industrious and hard working. While Wallner was in Europe last spring she took over, in addition to her own work, the French desk, which is by far the heaviest desk in the Division of Western European Affairs. On the basis of her demonstrated ability and work her rating should be <u>EXCELLENT</u>.

That last EXCELLENT entry is new. While previous reports by Stettinius, Grew and Acheson used those words in the text, this was the first time it appeared at the end and in capital letters—just like an entry in the Rating Sheet. Something new was brewing. In any event that marked her fourth excellent rating in a row.

While Frances was working the Belgium-Luxembourg desk, an old friend, Frank Moore editor of the *Redlands Daily Facts,* dropped by to see her at the "Old" State Department building. They had a long chat about her job, and Frank wrote it up when he returned to Redlands. Here is most of it, dated 1946.

FRANCES WILLIS HANDLING BELGIAN AFFAIRS FOR U.S.

Foreign Service Officer, Redlands Career Woman,
Has Headquarters at State Department

WASHINGTON — Miss Frances Willis, who as a Foreign Service Officer is Redlands' most distinguished career woman, presides at the Belgian desk, Western European Division, Department of State.

To find her you go to Executive Avenue and just across the street from the President's office, enter the old baroque State building. At once you sense you are in no ordinary department, such as Agriculture, where the doors all look alike. Here the corridors are an interior decorator's pastel green and the old high-ceilinged offices are entered through swinging shutter doors.

Miss Willis' desk is situated in one of these stately rooms on the third floor. The top of the desk looks not much different than if an insurance agency were being conducted from it. It is plain to see that she is doing business with papers, reports, bulletins and memoranda and not with tea cups and lady fingers.

Since 1939 the Foreign Service has been the overall coordinator for foreign affairs. So she gets reports not only from the Embassy in Brussels but from Department of Agriculture men reporting on crop conditions, Commerce department agents on business, and so on. "We not only co-ordinate," she says, using the editorial "we," "we also originate."

For example the Belgian Embassy in Washington reported about two months ago that it was in a fix. Before the war Belgian museums, out of generosity, had collected an exhibit of priceless Old Masters and shipped them to America for our people to see. Then came the war and the pictures could not go back. When the Belgians here were ready to send the paintings home they couldn't because their property was frozen by the Foreign Funds Control office of the Treasury Department.

Miss Willis could see readily enough that the Belgians, instead of being shackled, should be thanked for their loan of the pictures and freed from red tape with dispatch. So she "originated" the moves to defrost the Old Masters.

The Treasury Department agreed that the Belgian Ambassador should be permitted to swear out an affidavit that the paintings belonged to certain museums in his country and that would be sufficient proof that they were not touched with enemy interest.

Next the Belgians found that the U.S. Customs would have to open the crates at New York, prior to shipment overseas. If that were done, however, the insurance company wouldn't give coverage because how would they know that someone didn't swipe a picture before the crates were nailed up again? So, the Customs people were convinced that the Belgians weren't trying to smuggle anything out of the country and waived their right of inspection at New York.

That was a fine story about repatriating the Old Masters to Belgium, even though it didn't rate a mention in Frances' last Annual Efficiency Report.

Final Department Assignment:
Assistant WE Chief and Full Redemption

On March 7, 1947, Frances was promoted to Assistant Chief, Division of

Western European Affairs, at the handsome salary of $9200, which was $1000 more than a Civil Service Officer would make in that position.

Six months later H. Freeman Matthews, Director of the Office of European Affairs, EUR, and Culbertson's boss, weighed in with an almost identical Annual Efficiency Report, which was written at the end of Frances' tour in August, 1947. He highlighted the now final settlement of the lend-lease reverse lend-lease work and her temporary handling of the French desk. To this he added "revision of the Civil Affairs Agreement with Belgium and highly confidential relations of a special character" with no further elaboration on the last subject.[51] Matthews finished with the identical rating in the identical format: <u>EXCELLENT</u>. Something definitely had changed. And that was number five in her streak.

It is now time for another two-year entry in the Rating Sheet, with two excellent reports and one outstanding report for the redactor to work with:

> Miss Willis continued to serve in the Department during the period under review until her departure for her new post at London early in September. Under Secretary Acheson said that he was continually conscious of and deeply impressed by her ability in all phases of the work which she was called upon to handle. Her record deservedly was one of high attainment in the Foreign Service, and at the same time she had assumed fully and had executed well the responsibility brought by her success and had remained a person of poise, balance and complete modesty as to her record and capabilities. Mr. Acheson felt that she was an outstanding officer in the Foreign Service.
>
> Mr. Culbertson and Mr. Matthews were generous in their praise of Miss Willis' work in charge of the Belgium-Luxembourg desk because with her outstanding general ability and previous experience in the field, she took immediate hold of the numerous problems which had been current between the United States and Belgium, including final settlement of the reverse Lend Lease account with Belgium, and highly confidential relationships of a special character. She had assisted in handling French relations during the absence of the desk officer with the same competence and in general had demonstrated soundness of

---

[51] Possibilities range from Jewish resettlement in Israel, negotiations for locating NATO headquarters in Brussels, to covert intelligence.

judgment of the highest order and ability to get along with others in a friendly, cooperative manner.

January, 1948.

So here is the rest of the change: The Rating Sheet entry now has no rating! And it wasn't an inadvertent omission, because it was omitted from all subsequent entries. So the Department must have changed the scoring rules, switching the rating requirement from the Rating Sheet redactor to the supervisor preparing the Annual Efficiency Report. In all likelihood, Grew directed the change because he had seen too many inaccurate or contrived Rating Sheet entries—entries that didn't adequately or properly summarize the dossier entries and sometimes added new data and opinions. That was certainly true in Frances' case.

In support of this conjecture, consider the following scenario: Grew read Frances' ugly 1945 Rating Sheet entry, took a personal look at her, decided she was doing excellent work, wrote an excellent Annual Efficiency Report and promoted her on the spot. Then he saw the 1946 less-than-excellent Rating Sheet entry, blew a fuse and abolished the opining job from the redactor.

Equally important, there was nothing in this report about limitations of her sex. That certainly is good news and must signal an end to the gender bias issue. It does for the principal antagonist, the redactor, leaving only minor encounters in London and Helsinki and a perverse parting shot when she left Helsinki from an Old Guard still on the battlefield. And of course, Frances didn't know it was going to end because, except for her encounters upon arrival or acquiring a new boss, she didn't know it had started and had been dogging her throughout her career. In reality, Grew, Acheson and probably a few of their confidants made it end for Frances.

Now off to London to see if Frances—again a field dog—can (a) capitalize on her newfound knowledge of Department workings, (b) continue her good on-site work, and consequently (c) receive more accolades from the kennel dogs.

13

COOL IN LONDON

Arriving in Style

IN September, 1947, Frances sailed to England in first class accommodations on Cunard's Queen Mary, which were truly first class. She reported for duty at the U.S. Embassy in London, September 17, as an FSO-3—changed from Consul Class III by the 1946 Foreign Service act—and First Secretary and Consul in the Political Section. She found a small flat at 60 Park Lane in London, where she lived through 1949.

Almost immediately following her arrival Frances headed for Parliament and reported that excursion in a November 1, 1947, bulletin to the family, with the caveat:

> In view of some of the remarks in this letter I'd rather nobody outside the immediate family saw it [at least while she was posted to London.]
>
> The title of this Chapter should undoubtedly be "Spellbound." Tuesday (Oct 28) I went to the House of Commons to hear Mr. Churchill as leader of the opposition reply to the King's speech on the occasion of the opening of Parliament the week before. He talked for seventy minutes and I have never heard anything that could compare with it, and the extraordinary thing about it is that his delivery is very poor, he fumbles at times and hesitates and looks for a word but when he finds it is worth waiting for. I was one of the fortunate few who had a front row seat for the entire performance opposite the Speaker so that I could hear the Government side and the opposition equally well.
>
> With all the solemnity of the House with the Speaker in his wig and robes and the members having to bow to him every time they

entered or left the chamber, just as we used to have to bow to the Sister [Margaret Clare at Kemper Hall] in the dining room, the manners of the members are unbelievably bad and judged by most standards I should say uncivilized. The interruptions and heckling while a man is speaking certainly adds zest to the whole performance but the thing I wouldn't have believed if I had not seen it with my own eyes was that both the cabinet ministers and the leaders of the opposition, yes including Mr. Churchill and Mr. Eden, put their feet up on the table—and probably the others would too except that only the high moguls have a table in front of them. They don't do it when their own side is speaking but apparently more as a sign of disdain when the opponents have the floor.

Frances enclosed an article, "Impressions of Parliament," from the November 5, 1947, issue of *Punch,* which reported the session:

Tuesday, October 28th.—Mr. Churchill went into action today, moving an amendment [which] roundly criticized the Government for its administrative failures and its lack of a constructive policy.

He also employed figures of speech and metaphors in such profusion and variety that soon the House looked like a coupon-free Government-surplus word store. He said Sir Stafford Cripps had "invited the nation to enter a dark and narrowing tunnel, with no assurance that there would be daylight at the end."

Further that the government "had broken the mainspring with the result that the watch would not go," especially in the "ever-darkening abyss"—also courteously provided by the Government.

But these various metaphors were spread over a speech that was telling and eloquent. There were fiery passages—as when he spoke of the reported bargain inside the Cabinet under which the nationalization of the steel industry was temporarily shelved in return for an immediate attack on the House of Lords.

"This," said Mr. Churchill, in his best form, "is a cheap, paltry, disreputable deal between jarring nonentities in a divided administration!"

Tuscany joined The Rest in nearly roaring its head off in appreciation of this Churchillian thrust. And the whole House, galleries included, shouted with laughter when Mr. Churchill solemnly quoted a speech by

Mr. Hugh Gaitskell, the new Minister of Fuel, in which he advocated fewer baths, to save fuel. "Personally," the Minister was quoted as saying, "I never have a great many baths."

His voice lowered impressively, Mr. Churchill turned towards Mr. Speaker and exclaimed that the Government could not complain, in the circumstances, that it was in increasingly bad odour.

But on the whole the indictment of the government was a stern one: failure in the economic field, failure over India, the cutting of the Defence forces, failure to get out of Palestine. And, finally, unprovoked aggression against the House of Lords to cover up domestic strife in the Cabinet.

To a roar of cheering that lasted for more than a minute Mr. Churchill sat down.

Frances went on about finally unpacking in her small flat, which held a total of eight chairs, and all the people she had to entertain there—hopefully in shifts. But it didn't turn out that way: She wound up with eighteen guests at one time, but nobody seemed to mind. She finished the letter with:

> Life in London is even more fascinating than I thought it would be and there is so much to do. I hope I can stay a long, long time. The work is interesting and so far nothing like the overtime in Washington. Ever since I hit the Queen Mary I've had no trouble sleeping so I don't get so terribly tired as I did that last year in Washington.

Now to Work

The embassy was huge compared to her previous missions. It was so big that it had an ambassador *and* a minister, along with a plethora of first secretaries, even in the Political Section.[52] Now a required duty of newly reporting Foreign Service Officers is to present their credentials to the host country's Foreign Ministry, which in England is done at St. James Court. According to the 1954 article about Frances in *Current Biography,*

---

[52] It was like being transferred from a 2,000-ton destroyer to a 60,000-ton battleship, where you instantly go from 3 to 23 in rank seniority, even with a promotion in between.

When she and Kathleen Molesworth, also of the service, were presented at the Court of St. James in [1948], they were the first women diplomats to have that honor, and the English newspapers commented that it was the first time United States officials had curtsied to the King.

As reported earlier, Kathleen was appointed a Foreign Service Officer in a 1939 lateral transfer from the Department. She retired as an FSO 2 in 1955. Her last assignment was first secretary and consul, again in London. The ceremony must have started this way.

"A Visit to Court" from M. C. Perts' 1924 book.

Just a change in gender and clothing would make the sketch pretty accurate, unless of course the ladies were required to wear top hats, as Hugh Gibson suggested in his 1925 letter to Joseph Grew. Frances reported she solved the top hat problem by wearing a long gown when the affair was black tie and gown with a (lady's) hat when the affair was white tie.

Frances described the presentation in her May 15, 1948, bulletin:

The occasion of this broadcast is my presentation at Court last Thursday, May 13. First time in my life I ever shook hands with royalty with my glove on—but never mind, times have changed and that remark is definitely out of order.

The formal courts have not been resumed since the war but presentations are now combined with Garden Parties at Buckingham Palace. Last year I am told the presentations were actually made in the Garden but people felt cheated because they were only whisked through the corridors of the Palace and out into the Garden without seeing the Throne Room—or anything. So this year the presentations were in what I suppose was the Throne Room and we all "rendezvoused" in a designated room inside the Palace, the Americans believe it or not under a huge portrait of George III—which fact I took great delight in pointing out to Marcus Cheke, the Vice Marshal of the Diplomatic Corps.

The speed with which the whole business was despatched was one of the most remarkable things about the affair. As the members of each Embassy came into the room where the King and Queen [George VI and Elizabeth] were standing, the Marshal of the Diplomatic Corps [announced] the Ambassador and his wife. Next the Ambassador presents the members of his staff and their wives and daughters, if any, individually to Their Majesties.[53]

We were presented to the King first and then to the Queen and were instructed not to speak unless spoken to—and none of us were. The King wore the uniform of an Admiral of the Fleet and the Queen wore an outfit (long dress and hat) and the inevitable feather boa, which makes her look even bigger around than she is.[54]

After we made our curtsies we were hurried along to the Garden where there was a marquee that looked at least a block long. The "tea" was very good considering that there were 2,500 present. I believe they [the King and Queen] did come out in the Garden and circulate for a while but I am afraid I missed them. In addition to the usual tea and orangeade they have very good iced coffee, which unfortunately was served in after dinner coffee cups, sandwiches and an assortment of layer cakes—I took chocolate with chocolate icing, please.

---

[53] For some reason Frances omitted *sons*. But maybe there weren't any sons to present.

[54] That's only the second undiplomatic comment in Frances' correspondence—and a doozy, especially about the dear Queen Mum! Brussels' cleanliness was the first.

In August, 1949, Frances was directed to write an extensive, multi page position description of her job in London. That was a new requirement for her and a direct consequence of the many management reforms that were sweeping the government at the time. It was to be written in accordance with a detailed set of instructions, which mandated nine major topics, each with numerous subtopics. Not only that, but Frances was to estimate the percentage of her time spent on each topic and what would happen if she made a mistake.[55]

To summarize her job, Frances was charged with collecting, analyzing and reporting information about Great Britain and France, along with most other countries in Western Europe, the Council of Europe, the Western Union and matters relating to the United Nations. All this required frequent contact and negotiations with many officials in London's Diplomatic Corps. Receiving visitors and callers and replying to inquiries were also part of her job description. Frances said that her immediate supervisor was Minister Julius Holmes (and earlier, W. J. Gallman), and that when he was absent she saw the Ambassador, but only "on matters of a high level."

Now back to productive business. Frances was promoted to FSO-2—one-star flag rank—in April, 1948, six months after she arrived in London and with no new evaluations in her dossier. Her excellent tour in the Department was serving her well indeed. By the way, her old friend Ned Crocker, the #2 FSO in Stockholm in 1932, was promoted to FSO-1 at the same time. He saw the list first and broke the news to Frances via a letter of congratulations. Those FSO's remained a tight bunch.

Just how tight they were was reported by Frances in a subsequent bulletin. She said she was wined and dined for a few days in Warsaw, Poland "at the invitation of Ned [Crocker] and Findley [Burns], because the Ambassador was away." Ned was stationed in Warsaw at the time and decided a small promotion party was in order. So he invited Frances from London and Findley from Brussels to come and celebrate. Never mind that Warsaw was behind the Iron Curtain—just hop over with those diplomatic passports.

---

[55] These new administrative requirements, including personal introspection, were simply a waste of time and taxpayer's money. Once the war ended some bureaucrats wound up with way too much time on their hands. So they had to think up new and innovative ways to keep their jobs, starting with generating massive amounts of paperwork—far more than Thomas Bowman complained about in his poem sent to Frances in 1932. The government should have held a thorough house-cleaning starting in 1946, and not the kind Stettinius tried and badly botched, as Frances reports later.

While that trip would seem to be frivolous fun and games, there was always the "other agenda" lurking just below the surface: getting to know your adversary better, i.e. intelligence collection. Now while Frances was not doing that sort of thing on her short visit, Ned likely regaled her with local spy stories. That must have whetted Frances' appetite for such things, because she lobbied the Department hard for Budapest, Hungary—also behind the curtain—as her next post. It is reported later in this chapter.

After Frances returned to London she went to a cocktail party at the Crown Equerry's and was first presented to the Duchess of Gloucester by Lady Kavanagh, then to a young (22) Princess Elizabeth.[56] During her introduction to Princess Elizabeth, Lady Kavanagh said Frances had just come back from Poland and Frances reported, "whereupon Princess Elizabeth asked a lot of questions and we had a longish conversation." Unfortunately Frances provided no further details of that conversation. This was the first but not the last time Frances would tease the family with a morsel, and then yank the spoon back. Frank Moore, editor of the *Redlands Daily Facts,* covered the event in his last "With a Grain of Salt" column about Frances, which is in the Redlands Epilogue chapter. He quoted Frances as saying, "Sure, I knew her before she was the queen."

Frances' favorite sport, dancing, bubbled up in her March 29, 1948, bulletin reporting another diplomatic do:

> Last week Sam Reber [member of that 1928 three-bachelor gang in Lima, Peru, including Ellis Briggs and Jack Cabot] had a dinner for the British and French deputies for Austria (he is the U.S. deputy), who are trying to do something about a Treaty for Austria and when I "graciously consented" to be Sam's hostess for the occasion, I didn't know what I was letting myself in for. The French deputy, General Cherriere, was on my right—tremendous six feet two or three—and "il adore la valse." But the only trouble was he doesn't reverse. The second time in the last two weeks I've found myself sitting next to a wonderful dancer who lured me into a marvelous but almost unending [counter-clockwise] twirl.[57]

---

[56] According to Webster's Second Edition: Equerries are officers of a royal English household in the Department of the Master of the Horse. So a Crown Equerry must be such officers in the King's household.

[57] Starting a counter-clockwise twirl requires a guy to step back, pulling the lady towards him. A clockwise twirl requires a guy to step forward, pushing the lady away, with the

Frances' first Annual Efficiency Report in London, dated June 1, 1948, was written by Minister-Counselor W. J. Gallman, and like Grew, he used the old 1933 format. He said, following the standard job description:

Although Miss Willis has been here for only nine months, she has developed very valuable contacts, particularly in the Foreign Office, and many of these contacts are on a high level. Her relations with the Foreign Office are such that she can with ease and promptness get information and expressions of views on the most secret questions. She covers developments in her field with energy, promptness, and accuracy. She brings to her work a very well developed mind, a wide and rich knowledge of contemporary history, and an exhilarating enthusiasm.

Hers is a rich personality as is evidenced by the warm and high esteem shown her by all her colleagues in the Embassy and her large circle of friends outside the Embassy. Her interests are very wide. She has a keen appreciation of music, and the theatre, and her lively interest in her surroundings leads her to attend political rallies of every color, and public meetings of various kinds not necessarily directly connected with her work. It is this lively and broad interest in life in general that make her so very generally popular with all types and classes of people.

She is the most well-trained and responsible officer, and fully equipped for any assignment of extreme delicacy and importance. Miss Willis has a thorough knowledge of French and Spanish, which she speaks fluently.

Rating: EXCELLENT

There it is again, the rating entry now at the end of the report and the sixth excellent score in a row. And once again there is not one word about limitations of her sex.

Those six straight excellent scores must have crossed a Department threshold because Frances was chosen to serve as an alternate member of an FSO Selection Board back in Washington DC. A slot didn't open up so she didn't serve. But just

---

ever-present possibility of stepping on her toes. So after a few embarrassing encounters, most guys only twirl counter-clockwise.

the consideration of such an appointment clearly was significant recognition of her rising status.

Then an old nemesis reappeared in Frances' dossier: a Department-generated Efficiency Rating—Political Work dated July 31, 1948, not just those one-liners of the 1930's, but now cast in paragraphs. Here is the first one.

> The arrival last year at London of a woman First Secretary was, as might be expected, looked upon with some degree of skepticism by the Embassy and the Foreign Office. In a very few weeks, however, Miss Willis, as she has done in the past, soon convinced her colleagues that she was capable of accomplishing her assigned duties as efficiently if not more so than most top-ranking officers in the Service. She has made many friends ...well liked ...highly respected ...good common sense ...cooperativeness ...appreciated in all strata from the Ambassador on down.
>
> In the field of political reporting, she has been covering United Kingdom relations with France and the Benelux countries, and in addition has sent in many useful reports on the movement for Western European Union as observed from London. She thinks well and expresses her thoughts in clear, concise English which greatly facilitates the reading of her reports here in the Department.
>
> Rating: EXCELLENT

This report is significant first, because it marks the last time arrival gender bias appears in her dossier, along with Frances' quick disposal of it; and second, because the author initialed it, with the additional initials *TW* appearing at the bottom right corner. That was her old Brussels friend and FSO associate, Tom Wailes, now at the Office of European Affairs, EUR, who certainly knew about Frances' arrival problems and how she diffused them with good work. In fact, he likely had that second sentence inserted into the rating if it wasn't already there. And that marked the seventh excellent rating in a row. The ranks of the Department's Old Guard were thinning.

Then the final paragraph appeared in Frances' Rating Sheet, dated January, 1949, just a year after the previous entry. It's not clear why they stopped: Either she had run out of people senior enough to evaluate her, or the Department abolished them in favor of reading the real thing, the Annual Evaluation Reports and the just-resurrected Efficiency Ratings.

In any case, this last Rating Sheet entry got most everything right: a good description of her London duties, a comprehensive summary of Gallman's excellent Annual Efficiency Report, a repeat of the excellent rating by EUR in August 1947, and the excellent rating in the newly resurrected Efficiency Rating. The Rating Sheet then said, "Miss Willis has been named an alternate member of one of the 1949 Selection Boards," and finished up with, "Miss Willis is 49 years of age and single."

Finally, this Rating Sheet was penned by an unbiased redactor, unbiased because he objectively summarized the other reports and added no opinions of his own, specifically excluding that institutional gender bias mantra. But why the age and marital status data at the end? Could it be that the redactor was subtly reminding the Selection Board that Frances was not only doing excellent work but was also in her prime of life, unencumbered with other responsibilities and thus ready for bigger things? If so, that would constitute an opinion—but this time biased in Frances' favor.

Well, all those top ratings apparently crossed another threshold, because the Department decided to take another look at the lady, via one of those special Inspector's Efficiency Reports. This one was prepared by Foreign Service Inspector Frederick B. Lyon, dated January 10, 1949. It was much shorter than the first one by Messersmith in Chile, because Lyon used only superlatives, and ran out of them after two paragraphs, followed by an excellent rating. That made eight.

Then a March 15, 1949, letter to Lewis W. Douglas, American Ambassador, London, from H. P. Martin, Director, Office of The Foreign Service appeared in her dossier:

> The Department is pleased to inform you that despatch No. 1968 of September 28, 1948, "Debates in Short Session of Parliament on European Unity," prepared by First Secretary Frances E. Willis, has been rated EXCELLENT.
>
> Miss Willis is commended for the preparation of this outstanding despatch which has been commented on by the Division of British Commonwealth Affairs of the Department of State as follows:
>
> "This is an excellent report of considerable value to this Division in appraising current thinking in Britain on the subject of Western

Union. The writer selects her quotations judiciously and uses them to emphasize the various aspects of the matter. The report is well-organized and well-written, although one must urge the need for the utmost brevity if work of this kind is to be most useful."

This was Frances' first commendation letter coming from the Department to the outback. Although true to the Willis tradition, her despatch was a bit long-winded. It also capped a string of nine excellent reports, beginning with the main man himself, Joseph Grew. How did this sea-change happen? What did Frances do to move to the top of the heap? The three-part answer is straightforward: (1) Frances had always done good, hard work (and at times did too much of it herself.) (2) For the first time in her career she knew what kind of work impressed the Department. (3) Now she was in a prime position—London's Political Section—to do impressive work and she did just that.

Specifically, she discovered that a trenchant political report was more valuable (and visible) than a well-run embassy office, just as the hierarchy of Foreign Service cones says in Appendix 1. So she finally figured out the system and its rules, and then made them work for her, although the process probably was subconscious. It was simply an attempt on her part to do a better job. Sometimes compulsive attempts at self-improvement work out.

The Lettered Lady

All those despatches Frances had been sending to the Department informed both the Department and Frances, to the point that she became an expert on some of her subjects. And like many experts, Frances was subsequently asked to write and speak about them. Her first speech was in response to a June, 1950, invitation from H. Gordon, Esq., in Ashridge, Berkhamsted, Hertfordshire, a few miles outside London. The venue was not recorded but the subject was Anglo-American Relations. And that got her (recorded) speaking career off in good order:

MR. CHAIRMAN, LADIES AND GENTLEMEN:

When I was asked to come and speak to you on Anglo-American relations at first I wondered whether I should give you the usual stereotyped speech about the closeness and the importance of relations between the

United Kingdom and the United States or whether I should tell you what I really believe about [our] relations.

I am at times hesitant to say what I really believe about Anglo-American relations for fear that some people will feel that I assume too much and that I take for granted too broad a basis for the mutual understanding between our two countries. This fear, however, was dispelled in a somewhat unexpected way. I had the great good fortune to be invited to see the Trooping of the Colour on the King's Birthday from one of the windows of the Horse Guards Building. When I heard the massed bands of the Guards play our Souza's "Stars and Stripes Forever" as the King and brigade of Guards left the parade ground I decided that it would be quite all right for me to divulge some of my inner thoughts.

A moment's digression to dispel the myth that Souza stole that tune from the Brits, like Frances Scott Key stole the tune to "The Star-Spangled Banner," which was an old English drinking song, "To Anacreon in Heaven." Not so; he composed it on an 1896 Atlantic crossing to England. So the Guards had sent a warm, heartfelt message to their old Puritan Colony. Frances continued:

> The close cooperation which exists today is sometimes taken for granted but I think we had perhaps better begin by asking ourselves something about the community of interests of the United States and the United Kingdom. We all know that the present close cooperation has not always existed. Although I always maintain that George Washington was one of the greatest Englishmen who ever lived there seemed very little basis for Anglo-American friendship in his generation.
>
> Everybody on both sides of the water knows about our Revolutionary War but it is always surprising to me to find how few people in Great Britain realize that we fought a second war in 1812. As a matter of fact that war is the cause of our having a White House today. When the British troops set fire to the American capital in the course of that war the recently completed stone building in which the President lived was gutted by fire. When it was rebuilt it was found that the surface was so badly marked by the smoke that the whole building was painted white.

Frances then switched from Anglo-American relations to Intra-European relations and the proposed Western Union, which was cited in Frances' letter of commendation. Frances alerted the family to this merger, now called the European Union, in her January 25, 1948, bulletin:

> The highlight of the week was [Prime Minister] Bevin's speech in the House of Commons Jan 22 advocating a Western Union. I stayed to hear Mr. Eden lead off for the opposition—but agreeing with practically everything Mr. B. had said. Then I heard the snake in the grass Zilliacus [apparently a Member of Parliament] tear the Marshall Plan to pieces and attack Mr. B. During Mr. B's speech the two Communists— Gallachon and Piratin—were so obstreperous the speaker had to threaten "to take drastic action" if they didn't stop shouting, interrupting, etc. Mr. Churchill did not speak until the next day so I did not hear him. Even at such close range I think the speech is an historic one as it marks a definite change in British foreign policy.

That triggered a question from her mother Belle, with this reply from Frances:

> Your question, Mother, about what is meant by a Western Union of Europe is well taken. Everybody is talking about it and everybody has a different idea. Some people actually want a political union of some sort of Great Britain and the countries of Western Europe. Others want an economic union with no tariffs and no trade barriers. Others still want a very vague "binding together of those countries which prize western civilization." So you see there is nothing very definite—except a feeling that "in union there is strength."

Finally, fifty years later it happened, which is understandable considering how long European countries had been at each other's throats.

In a second speech to the University of Cambridge four months later and right at the beginning of the Cold War, Frances reported that the U.S. was equally enthusiastic about the Council of Europe. She added:

> Because of the interest of the U.S. Government in the Council of Europe the Department of State sent two unofficial observers to Strasbourg when the first Assembly of the Council met there in August

1949. I was one of them and we did our best not only in following the proceedings in the Assembly but also in finding out the views of the various delegates. At one time there were twelve Foreign Ministers there as well as 102 delegates from twelve countries. Rather a lot for two observers to keep track of, especially when you had to take time to investigate the relative merits of the many excellent restaurants and the various vintages of Alsatian wine.

Frances said nothing about this trip in her bulletins. But it surfaced in now-declassified, confidential telegrams in Frances' 123 File at the National Archives. They show that Secretary of State Acheson selected her for the duty, but that Ambassador Douglas would let her go for only two weeks; then back to work in London. (He was obviously familiar with the Alsatian distractions.)

Frances then got down to the U.S. attitude toward the Western Union:

It is quite true that the Government of the United States does not have a plan for the unification of Europe. It is possible that the Russians have but we don't. There is therefore inevitably a certain vagueness in what I can say to you. I can however clarify one point. We do not urge unity merely for the sake of unity or as the solution in itself of all Europe's problems, but because we are convinced that without unity the job of rehabilitation cannot be done nor can each country of Europe alone stave off aggression.

The phrase, "stave off aggression," needs clarification. The Soviet Union was currently gobbling up Central European countries at a rate equal to Nazi Germany in 1939 and without a unified European response to that aggression, they were about to relive very recent history.

Frances also reported she had worked on the North Atlantic Pact, but with no further elaboration in her bulletins, again because the work was classified. That's a shame because it was almost unprecedented in scope and signaled a formal start to the Cold War, which lasted for the next forty years.

VIP Services

Another part of Frances' London life was tending to Very-Important-Americans-Who-Visit-England. In this case they were Eugene Ormandy and members of his Philadelphia Symphony Orchestra (PSO), performing a series of concerts in England. Two letters tell the story, with the first one, dated July 12, 1949, using official PSO letterhead:

Dear Miss Willis,

We are indeed most grateful for all that you did to help make the orchestra's British Tour a success and it gives me great pleasure to send you the following Resolution, which was unanimously adopted by the Board at its last meeting:

RESOLVE: That the appreciation of the Board of directors of The Philadelphia Orchestra be expressed to Miss Frances Willis for all that she did in helping with the arrangements for the Orchestra's British Tour. The Board realizes that her efforts and guidance were largely responsible for the official acknowledgement given the Orchestra throughout England and that her counsel was of immeasurable assistance to the Manager, and the Board hereby records its gratitude to her.

You were most kind and generous to do so much for our organization.

Sincerely yours,

/s/ *G. Ruhland Rebmann, Jr.*

Secretary.

The key to this accolade was a small name printed to the left of the PSO letterhead: Harl McDonald, Manager. Harl was a relative of the Graham family, old friends of Belle living in Redlands. Harl and Frances in turn became close friends. So when the PSO started planning their tour to England, Harl must have said, "I will call First Secretary Willis, to let her know we are coming."

Frances was in her element: She was senior enough to take complete charge of all planning and execution on the east side of the Atlantic, probably including reservations, transportation, tours, entertainment, embassy receptions and dinners, filling concert hall boxes with royalty—maybe even the King. After all, the PSO was one of the four premier orchestras in the world. Some said it was #1 at that time.

The second letter is the thank you note from Maestro Ormandy, handwritten on elegant Hyde Park Hotel stationary but now typed as written:

June 20-1949
Dear Frances,
    Before I leave may I tell
you how greatly I appreciate every-
thing you did for my colleagues
as well as for myself. Special
thanks for the 'extended 45 mi-
nute' tour of London and for
giving up a beautiful Sunday in
order to drive me around.
Please call me when you get
home at Christmas, and until then,
                    All my best to you!
                    Eugene

Apparently the forty-five-minute tour was just the end of Frances' volunteer chauffeur duties, because she reported in a June 13 letter that she had driven Ormandy out and back from the Harringay Arena by car enough times so that "the doormen out there know my car as 'Mr. Ormandy's car.'" Frances didn't say whether she called him over Christmas, but they reconnected often, as reported in later chapters.

Recognition in Spite of the Bureaucracy

Those Annual Efficiency Reports, which have followed Frances around the world for the last twenty years, first in the 1933 Revision and then in the slightly altered 1943 revision, had morphed into a "new and improved," 1949 Revision, Form Type B, Performance Report, expanded from one to six pages, now in four parts. Frances' August, 1949, review was in this new format. Part I consisted of 31 groups of statements. Here are two typical ones along with their instructions:

The statements, words or phrases below are descriptive of the performance of Foreign Service Officers. They are arranged in blocks of four or five. Considering the phrases in each block, underline the one which is most descriptive of the officer and his job performance, and cross (x) the identifying letter A,B,C,D,E of the one which is least descriptive. A judgment must be made in each group.

A) He will probably not go much further in the Service

B) He demands a high degree of efficiency from those associated with him

C) He is not active in seeking desirable contacts

D) He is imaginative

E) He is probably one of our future Career Ministers

A) He has a good sense of humor

B) He is adaptable

C) He shows little taste in his clothes

D) He is inclined to be pompous

This evaluation process is flawed on three counts. First, the statements in each group are binary—either good or bad, and usually very good or very bad. Example: either a future career minister or not going much further in the service. Very few shades of gray, which will skew the scoring. Second, the statements have very little correlation with each other. Example: What does a sense of humor have to do with taste in clothes? Third, weighing answers between groups is entirely subjective. For example, is "probably one of our future Career Ministers" twice as good as "adaptable"? Four times as good? In any case Frances was scored an *89*, which was handwritten on the first page of her Performance Report.

Apparently enough senior FSO's felt the same way because one year later Form Type B was replaced with Form Type C, which was marginally improved, but with the same fundamental flaws. Still way too much time on the hands of some bureaucrats.

Part II of the Performance Report was mercifully better, starting with a list of 13 factors to be graded in three categories: superior, satisfactory, not up to standard. Factors included "Versatility in variety of knowledges [*sic*] and skills; Accuracy and thoroughness of work done; Productivity; Trustworthiness, reliability; etc." A much better approach, but still a pretty coarse grading system. Frances got five superior and seven satisfactory marks in this section.

Part III was a short section on language, and Part IV was another set of factors on such topics as Political, Economic, Consular, etc. Frances was graded B. Fluent in both French and Spanish, a notch below Bilingual. And she got two A's and three B's in Political Factors, which when aggregated with the other scores gave her about a B+, equivalent to the old Very Good rating.

Now back to Part II, which concluded with a narrative description and recommendations for the officer-under-review, much like the previous Efficiency Reports. It is quoted in its entirety:

Miss Willis has a broad assignment of Western Europe, including the Scandinavian countries, Benelux, France and Spain. In addition she follows matters of a general interest in the United Nations and the North Atlantic Treaty. She is a thoroughly trained and highly competent officer with a penetrating mind and the ability to turn out a large volume of first class work. She has established a large number of extremely useful contacts in many circles in London. Her contacts in the Foreign Office are particularly good, and the fact that she is a woman appears to be no handicap to her whatever, as she is held in high esteem by the officials with whom she deals.

It is appreciated that there is often pressure from women's organizations to appoint women as chiefs of diplomatic missions. It is recommended that consideration be given to meeting this pressure by appointing Miss Willis in that capacity at an early date. It would seem that the desires of women's organizations might well be met by the appointment of a woman who had devoted her life to acquiring a deep knowledge and high competency in the conduct of foreign relations.

This report has not been discussed with Miss Willis.

/s/ Julius C. Holmes,
Minister-Counselor.

I concur.

/s/ L. W. Douglas,
Ambassador.

Then they gave Frances an Excellent rating, defined as "Performance in every important respect was outstanding and there was no weakness in performance in any respect." That's number ten in the string of excellent ratings, but doesn't begin to characterize its importance on four counts:

First, the report appears to have been written by a committee: a senior bureaucrat on the embassy staff marking Part I, the first section of Part II, Parts III and IV, giving Frances an average B+ rating, and the chiefs doing the narrative, giving Frances what can only be called a superb review.

Second, the Old Guard continues to diminish. Frances has systematically won over members as she encountered them, and by now she has been around the block enough times to encounter most of the important ones. The comment "the fact that she is a woman appears to be no handicap to her whatever" is now becoming typical.

Third, and most surprising, is recognition of the growing pressure from "women's organizations" to appoint women as chiefs of mission, and the need for the Department to relieve this pressure. So for a second time they boosted Frances' career—the first being in 1927 when they helped pressure the Department into a last minute commission.

Fourth, Frances had the "right stuff:" right credentials, right experience and right performance—along with being at the right place at the right time—to execute this relief. She was the most senior (and as she said in one bulletin, "oldest living") career woman in the Foreign Service, with nothing but excellent ratings from her last two posts—major posts: Washington and London. She was a natural for relieving the pressure, especially because she was not doing any of the pressuring herself.

Of course they couldn't discuss this Performance Report with Frances, not with stakes that high. That kind of recommendation must be held exceedingly close until it actually happens, to protect both the Department and Frances. Otherwise the press—and women—would jump all over their case if it didn't happen.

And again, while Frances was aware of the women's agenda, she wanted no part of it. Specifically, the fact that she was a woman had nothing to do with her performance as an FSO. But performance and promotions are not always correlated. Outside political pressure is sometimes needed to break hidebound traditions, and this was a specific case in point.

The Leak

Frances' first hint about the chief of mission recommendation was "the leak," which showed up in a June 28, 1949, memo pasted into one of Belle's scrapbooks:

MISS WILLIS
All has been quiet this afternoon. I thought this clipping from today's Evening Standard might amuse you.
mcm

ENVIED WOMAN. — Miss Frances Willis at a USA Embassy cocktail party at the Savoy for the Anglo-USA Press. Envied because of her coolness in the heat wave. Admired because she is First Secretary at the Embassy and on the way to becoming a Minister Plenipotentiary.

Frances wrote on the bottom, "Send it on to Mother, please. It will amuse her too." So that's how it got into Belle's scrapbook.

The initials *mcm* are for Miss Montgomery, "my theatrical, smart and efficient secretary," as Frances reported in an earlier bulletin. Now Frances always tolerated the heat well, so that is no surprise. But strange that the last sentence should appear in the British press just as Frances' last Performance Report was being prepared—the one recommending her for chief of mission.

A simple scenario can explain these events: Both Ambassador Douglas and Minister-Counselor Holmes likely attended the USA Embassy cocktail party. One of them—probably Holmes—was casually talking to an Evening Standard reporter, who remarked that Miss Willis certainly was handling the heat wave well, she appeared so cool.[58] Holmes responded something like, "Of course, present and future ministers must remain cool under all circumstances."

Then the reporter—probably a woman because they notice things like that—excused herself for a moment to record that conversation privately on her pocket notepad. (Never do to whip it out in front of the source, especially because he might then decide it was off-the-record, please.) It is likely that Frances got a momentary surge of excitement when she read the memo, and then just brushed it off.

As good as the Morris, Gibson, Cudahy, Grew and Acheson performance reviews were, this represents the pinnacle because it was the first to say publicly the words, "Minister Plenipotentiary." And those words finally shattered the glass ceiling.

More Recognition

The last Performance Report was followed closely by another annual Efficiency Rating dated August 30, 1949, with the now-standard comments "wide circle of

---

[58] Air conditioners were rare-to-nonexistent in England then. And they aren't all that common even today.

friends ...highly regarded ... concise and direct reporting ...valuable part of the reporting staff," along with the eleventh consecutive EXCELLENT rating.

The accolades kept rolling in, now with a second commendation letter from SecState, via Richard P. Butrick, Director General of the Foreign Service, dated June 21, 1950. This time she was a contributor to "British Attitude Towards Economic Integration of Western Europe," authored by First Secretaries Samuel D. Berger, William C. Trimble and Frances. The Department of Commerce provided the following comments on the report:

> This report is immensely useful. It presents a carefully prepared statement by informed people on a problem about which there is much confusion. This report pulls together certain historical facts which are not widely known and provides a lucid explanation of the British motivation in regard to current proposals.

This subject was virtually the same as her European Unity report, which also received a commendation almost two years earlier. So this was the most successful part of her work in London, in the sense of getting the most favorable response from the Department—a critical requirement for further flag rank promotions.

The next annual review (August 31, 1949 to August 31, 1950) was by Interim Chief of Mission J. C. Holmes, using the newly revised, expanded, marginally improved and renamed (back to the past) "Efficiency Report, Form Type C," now increased to five parts. Holmes wrote the narrative Part V, Summary Comments and Recommendations, which ran to almost two pages, and scored her just like the previous ones: excellent. His new comments included:

> Fine example of the highest type of American woman ...great experience and social poise which permit her, as a single woman, to entertain in a most effective manner. The fact that she is a woman working largely with men is no handicap ...factual and analytical approach to problems plus a wisdom which, in another setting and other activities, might be called woman's intuition. However in her case, more the stamp of wisdom than that of intuition.

> She is now under orders to transfer to Helsinki where, it is understood, she will be assigned as Deputy Chief of Mission. Although she will be a great loss to this post, it is appropriate that she be assigned as

Deputy Chief of Mission. This next post should serve as an interim step for her to be assigned as Chief of Mission. It is strongly recommended that she be promoted to Class I. Although Ambassador Douglas did not see this report before his departure, he specifically stated that he concurred in the rating and instructed the Rating Officer to add that he personally strongly recommended that Miss Willis be promoted to Class I.

No personal or family problems intervene to influence Miss Willis' assignment to any post beyond the fact that as she is a woman there are perhaps certain places where this factor would provide sufficient handicap to reduce her usefulness.

Helsinki, Sorry Not Budapest

Holmes' last comment summarized the Department's side of a long dialogue between Frances and the Department in September, 1950, about her next assignment.[59] It started with a September 12, 1950, confidential letter—now declassified—from Frances to Arthur G. Stevens, Executive Director, Bureau of European Affairs:

Dear Art:

I did not see Tom Wailes when he passed through here on his way to Belfast as I was away that week-end, and I thought I would wait until he returned to ask him what the news about my transfer is. Julius, however, tells me he talked to Tom on the telephone and learned that the Department is still considering sending me to Helsinki. Realizing that the timing in such matters is often important I decided I had better write immediately to you as I understand there is an alternative to Helsinki which I should greatly prefer, namely Budapest.

When you were here in the spring you mentioned Helsinki as a possibility then but as it was decided I was to remain in London until the end of the year I thought the Helsinki assignment would go to someone else. Sometime later I learned it was still under consideration for me, and accordingly when I had a letter about a month ago from Pen

[59] Even though the Holmes review was for the period August, 1949 to August, 1950, he didn't submit it until December 18, 1950. So he had the benefit of hindsight.

Davis saying he would like to have me go to Budapest as Counselor, I welcomed the suggestion as an alternative. As Tom Wailes was leaving for Washington the day the letter arrived I asked him to act as my emissary and to let you and Durbie know that of the two assignments I greatly preferred Budapest.

I await with interest an indication of what my fate is to be and am sure that as you and Durbie (to whom I am sending a copy of this letter) are at the controls all will be well.

Tom Wailes, from the Office of European Affairs, appears yet again. Julius Holmes, chargé in London, was her immediate boss and mentor. Pen Davis was Ambassador to Hungary. Finally, Durbie was Elbridge Durbrow, Chief, Foreign Service Personnel, a 1927 Stanford graduate and a second secretary in Rome when WW II broke out. Like Frances, Durbie got more than a thousand Americans out of France, through Spain, then to Portugal and home on a troopship. And he had as much trouble moving the people through Spain and Portugal as Frances did.

Frances' attraction to Budapest is a surprise. It certainly wasn't locale, government or the natives. Budapest was right in the middle of the Evil Empire, complete with a heavy dose of press censorship, mind control and poverty. In contrast, while Finland was heavily influenced by the USSR ever since they lost the Russo-Finnish War in 1939, the Finns were not part of the Soviet Union and ran a democracy under a free-market economy. And they were a robust bunch— in spite of their long winters and too much *Koskenkorva viina* (Finnish vodka). It should have been no contest, except for one thing: foreign intelligence.

During WW II foreign intelligence collection had been transferred from the State Department to the OSS and then to the CIA after WW II. (The intelligence analysis function was split between the military and the CIA.) But foreign intelligence collectors often worked out of the Foreign Service missions and consulates, and the smart ones relied on direct help from FSO's assigned there, especially the ones who "knew the neighborhood and everyone in it." And that was one of Frances' strong suits.

There are only a few hints that Frances was involved in foreign intelligence collection during her career. And that is exactly as it should be, because virtually everything, including the fact of collecting intelligence in the first place, is highly classified.

The first hint of this kind of work was a 1939 letter in Frances' dossier from Grant Mason of the FAA, thanking her for helping his American Delegation to the Fourth International Conference on Private Air Law. That had to be a cover, because with hot winds of war howling in 1939 no one was really interested in Private Air Law.

Then there were her special contacts in Brussels who tipped her off about the German invasion of Belgium, and her two—and probably more—trips just after the invasion of France to Dunkerque and Paris. Those were just the tip of the iceberg, with the rest unknowable probably forever. So that was the kind of excitement Frances was after. Art Stevens responded in an unclassified September 18, 1950, letter:

Dear Miss Willis,

Durbie and I have talked over the matter of your next assignment at some length and we are both of the opinion that the Helsinki assignment is the right one. Mr. Cabot was most enthusiastic about it when he was through here.

Julius wrote me last week about your interest in the assignment at Budapest. As you know, an assignment of this sort is fraught with so many uncertainties that after considering all of the factors it is our belief that by being assigned to Helsinki as Counselor you will be able to make a larger positive contribution than if you were sent to Budapest. Aside from the value of Helsinki as a listening post we are planning a rather large expansion in the Information Service, which will need a strong guiding hand to keep it on even keel.

Durbie added more arguments in his September 26 letter:

Dear Frances:

As you know, the Moscow boys have almost completely sewed us up in Budapest so that the possibilities of doing any constructive work there are very limited. On the other hand, Helsinki is comparatively "free" and I sincerely believe, on the basis of my own experience in Eastern European areas, that you cannot only do much useful work at Helsinki but you can learn more about the Soviet machinations there than you can in any real Curtain capital. Incidentally, you should be very flattered because not only has Pen Davis asked for you but Jack Cabot called on me recently and made a personal plea that you be sent to Helsinki as his Counselor. Such popularity must be deserved!

Art Stevens' phrase, "fraught with uncertainties," can be read as "fraught with dangers, certainly not to be faced by a woman." Durbie's phrase "almost completely sewed us up" means just that: The Moscow boys knew who the Western intelligence gatherers (spies) were, and wouldn't let them out of sight—both visual and weapon—when they went out on the town.

Thus the Department's policy change was clear: While Frances was on her way to a chief of mission appointment, she must sit in the lounge and not belly-up to the bar with the big bad boys. Much too dangerous for a lady there. Why you never know when a gunfight might break out.

And that was literally the truth. Budapest and most other Communist capitols were judged too dangerous for a lady intelligence agent or FSO. In any case, they did like the woman, even if they didn't think she *should do* everything a man does. And that was quite a change from *could do*. This attitude can be characterized as a quite rational, "protective gender bias," the last of the gender biases Frances would encounter.

Good reports capped the last six months of Frances' tour in London. Another excellent (the thirteenth) annual Efficiency Rating for Political Reporting dated October 1, 1950, said in part,

> Miss Willis is an energetic and capable officer and enjoys excellent relations with British official circles. Members of the Embassy have frequently expressed their high regard for her work in London.

Then amazingly, another Inspector's Efficiency Report, now dated November 29, 1950, not two years after the last one. And this one was done by none other than Edward (Tom) Wailes! The Department certainly didn't leave any stone unturned before they committed to a mission assignment for Frances. It was almost identical to the previous ones, for the fourteenth excellent rating in a row. As an aside, Frances stayed in touch with both Tom Wailes and Julius Holmes and made every effort to visit them in retirement. They certainly were her fans, even though she probably never saw their reports.

Finally, another Woman

In his Inspector's Efficiency Report Tom Wailes said this about Frances:

She has also been particularly helpful to newly arrived members of the staff in seeing that they meet people and in helping them to become established.

Ambassador Margaret Joy Tibbetts amplified on that comment in Chapter 4, "Trail Blazer," of Ann Morin's book, *Her Excellency*:

I don't think that many things have ever been difficult for me being a woman, and maybe it's because I was fortunate enough to land in the heart of the department. When I went to London, I went from EUR to the political section in London. And I was always helped by the fact Frances Willis, who had been the great establishment woman, was a very good, close friend of mine when I hit London. She was very wary at first, but when she saw that I wasn't going to do the sort of thing that she didn't think was right, she let me go pretty much on my own.

When I first went to London and Frances Willis invited me out to tea, she asked me if I was much interested in the women's issue, which, in 1949, was not very burning.[60] I said no. I'd never paid much attention to it, because I'd always been too interested in getting ahead on what I was doing, and when I was in college at Bryn Mawr, everyone was a woman. I mean, the question never would arise. She said it had been her experience that you did most for women by becoming a competent officer. Well, that's what I was interested in anyway.

"Becoming a competent officer" also paid off for Margaret: She was appointed Ambassador to Norway in 1964, the year Frances retired. She then talked about her appointment as the third female chief of mission to Norway:

Mrs. Harriman, of course, had been a novelty. She was back in the dark ages.[61] Frances Willis had been extremely good, and this was a great

---

[60] Not burning but certainly smoking, as Julius Holmes observed earlier.

[61] Harriman was the second woman minister, politically appointed to Norway in 1937.

asset to me, because when I arrived, Trygve Lie [Norwegian cabinet minister and former U.N. Secretary-General] said to me, "You know, it came up in the cabinet, another woman," and Lie said, "Look, the last one was better than most of the men." And that was absolutely true. But they all liked the fact I was a professional.

Ann Morin then compared Margaret's and Frances' careers:

Luck, of course, played a part in her success, particularly the luck of being mentored by the highly successful Frances Willis, the first career woman to be an ambassador.

In at least one respect, however, the customs of the times limited her. After her return from Norway, when she was a deputy assistant secretary of EUR, she felt obliged to return to Bethel [Maine] to care for her elderly mother. Subsequently, she became a college professor.[62] Had she been a man with such high rank—she was a career minister—she probably would have been given a leave of absence without pay. Instead, her resignation was accepted. Even 15 years later more than one senior man declared it regrettable that Tibbetts' talents had been lost to State when she was only 52 and at the height of her abilities. If the service had accorded her the consideration her reputation merited, she might well have outdistanced the redoubtable Frances Willis. Both women held doctorates and were very able, with comparable qualifications, although it was said Tibbetts brought "more steel" to the job.

The similarity in their overlapping careers is striking. Virtually the only difference is that Frances was able to persuade her mother to come with her to help run the embassy residence, and Margaret didn't—or couldn't. Thus Frances was able to care for her mother on site right up to her death, and Margaret had to leave the service to do it. Most unfortunate.

Morin's statement about bringing more steel to the job requires comment. Frances was first up the Foreign Service ladder and on her way up had to practice patience, fortitude and resolve, along with good work, to show a skeptical establishment that she was a capable team player. But once she did that—cleared

---

[62] Tibbetts earned a PhD in History and never married. Her avocations included reading, bird watching and skiing.

the way, so to speak—succeeding women could climb more aggressively and fear-lessly. In short, they could now carry a tougher, steelier attitude to the job. And Margaret did just that, with a little help from Frances.

14

MARKING TIME IN FINLAND

Top of the Ladder and the Press

FRANCES arrived in Helsinki April 7, 1951, following her February reassignment orders. Her official job title was Deputy Chief of Mission and Counselor, with Political Officer thrown in for good measure. She was still disappointed over the assignment, but like a good sailor, saluted and sailed off smartly to her new post with her old, 1928 Chile-Peru friend, Minister John M. Cabot at the helm.

That stoic attitude paid off because less than a month after she arrived she was nominated for FSO-1, equivalent to two stars in the military service and top of the FSO ladder. Then just a month later she was appointed FSO-1. Only the ultimate rank of career minister awaited her under the 1946 Foreign Service Act, Appendix 1.

That promotion got a spot on the radio program, *Women in the News,* hosted by Helen Thomas, *Washington DC Bureau of UP Radio* in January, 1952. And just after her nomination, Carlisle H. Humelsine, Deputy Under Secretary of State for Administration, issued a glowing press release, calling attention

...to the increased opportunities for American women in the field of Foreign Affairs. Noting that the number of women in the Foreign Service has increased nearly ten-fold since just before the last war [WW II], Mr. Humelsine declared that opportunities for promotion have grown accordingly.

As an example, he cited Miss Frances Willis, nominated a few days ago to be Foreign Service Officer Class 1, the first woman in American history to reach the top of the career Foreign Service ladder.

Humelsine then cited numbers to make his case, starting with the grand total of over 2400 American women in 294 missions overseas. He then broke out that number as follows:

- 810 staff officers (translators, interviewers, librarians, etc.)
- 1500 clerical and stenographic workers
- 21 reserve officers (specialists appointed for two-year terms)
- 21 career officers (eligible to be chief of mission)

So less than one percent of the women in overseas missions were career FSO's. Furthermore, Humelsine was a bit high with his "nearly ten-fold" estimate for the career FSO class: Their numbers went from 4 to 21, a 5.25-fold increase. The press release continued:

Mr. Humelsine added that the women who served in the Foreign Service can be justly proud of their achievements during recent years. He noted that duty in many of the Department's outposts was difficult and dangerous but that the women of the Foreign Service have demonstrated their courage and patriotism countless times.

Well, FSO women faced danger during wartime (WW II) on just three occasions: Constance Harvey's internment in France by the Germans, Frances' time in Brussels during the German occupation and Minister Florence Harriman's brief time during the German invasion of Norway. (Following the invasion the Norwegian government left Oslo April 9, 1940; Harriman left Oslo April 22, but the embassy stayed open until July 15 under a male chargé d'affaires.) So in order of danger, Constance faced invasion, occupation and interment, Frances faced invasion and occupation and Florence faced invasion. And that covered all women FSO's posted to enemy or enemy-controlled territory during WWII.[63]

---

[63] Kathleen Molesworth, who was in the Foreign Service during WWII, served in Guatemala from 1940 to 1944. She was transferred to Algiers in late 1944 after it was liberated from the Germans and then posted to London in 1946, where she served with Frances.

Consequently, Humelsine's claim that women FSO's have faced danger countless times appears a bit extravagant—unless he used a different definition of danger. For example he might have included Algiers after it was liberated or better yet, London during the German blitz. By that token, all English women staying in London would have faced equal danger—and demonstrated equal courage and patriotism—hardy a unique attribute under that definition.

It is pretty clear that Humelsine was touting opportunities for American women in the Foreign Service in an attempt to pacify the ever-expanding "Women's Organizations." They were becoming a major force after WW II and targeting the Department's Old Guard—getting on their case. So this was the Department's response, with Frances as Exhibit A.

But the Department wasn't done; at exactly the same time, April 1951, they enlisted Exhibit A for more flackery: Frances, herself. Specifically, Frances gave a talk to the National Council of Women of Finland, titled "Women of the United States." She first paid tribute to humanitarian Eleanor Roosevelt, always a good way to ease into the subject. She then cited some of Humelsine's numbers and added first-hand comments about discrimination, among them:

> I can say to you with complete honesty that since the day when I entered the Foreign Service I have been given equal treatment with the men in the Service. I have heard it said, of course, that there is discrimination against women who wish to enter the Service. All I can say is that my personal experience does not bear this out.

Frances' first statement about equal treatment is precisely what Joseph Grew established back in 1924 and what the Department exercised for the next twenty-five years, as detailed in The Other Women chapter. So that was a statement of official policy.

Her next statement about discrimination upon entry to the Foreign Service is another story. It was finally told by Calkin in his 1978 book, *Women in the Department of State*—published twenty-seven years after Frances' comment—documenting the disparity of a 20% acceptance rate for men versus a 2.8% acceptance rate for women between 1920 and 1941. And even if Humelsine were aware of those figures, he wasn't about to cite them in his press release.

Finally, Frances statement that she wasn't aware of any discrimination when she applied to the Foreign Service was accurate, as recounted in the Foreign

Service School chapter. While she might have wondered if the long delay in admitting her to the school after she had passed the examinations was because she was a woman, she never said so. And the available data indicate otherwise: The delay was caused by her just-passing score, which placed her near the bottom of the list of eligible candidates. So she had to wait until those on the list above her decided what they wanted to do before she would be given a chance. And that took time.

So Frances' comments were accurate—except for what she didn't cover: discrimination *after* entry. Whether she purposefully omitted it or simply forgot about it, arrival discrimination—having to start at square zero to show she could do a man's work—certainly plagued the first twenty years of her career. And Frances documented these events in her bulletins, either upon her arrival at a new post or at a change-of-command. But that was only the tip of the iceberg: Institutional and perverse gender bias hammered her early career—and she was never aware of them.

Then later in her career Frances would generalize her comments, dropping the "on entry" phrase, and declare simply that "sex has nothing to do with it." And that was quite a stretch, as the data in this biography attempt to show. In any case, the equal treatment viewpoint would become her mantra, indeed her life.

Work as a Deputy Chief

Both the revised on-site Efficiency Reports and the resurrected Department Efficiency Ratings, along with an occasional Inspector's Efficiency Report continued to enter Frances' dossier. And without exception, all used similar superlatives and reported excellent performance. Not only that, but they were now signed and except for repeating the Julius Holmes-initiated worry about assigning women to dangerous outposts, none of the authors used the institutional phrase "limitations of her sex," or variants thereof, in the dialogue. It would have been hard to justify such use when the subject was now at the top of the ladder. So except for that one perverse parting shot covered later, the Old Guard's campaign against Frances was finished. Frances "did 'em in," as her mother Belle would say.[64]

---

[64] But not for other women in—or entering into—the Foreign Service. It was not until 1971 that the Department lifted its last restriction on women.

What remains of the story is how Frances fared in her new management role, first as deputy chief of mission and then as chief of mission. In retrospect, she was clearly up to the job of running a mission, equivalent to that of a chief operating officer in the business world, because the Department gave her three such jobs: Switzerland, Norway and Ceylon. And if she botched the first one, she wouldn't have been given any more. Then she turned sixty-five and had to retire.

So the question becomes, How'd she do it? How did she transition from worker to manager? The answer should be cast in terms of what she was supposed to do, starting as deputy chief, which incidentally is functionally equivalent to an executive officer on a USN ship.

John Cabot, chief of mission, succinctly listed Frances' duties as deputy chief in his first (abbreviated) Efficiency Report of August, 1951:

> <u>Duties of Position</u>: Supervises running of office. Acts for me when I am absent. Carries important representational burden. Often takes initiative in suggesting desirable action, reports, etc. Drafts many major telegrams, reports, etc. Visits Foreign Office to discuss all matters we consider it appropriate to discuss at that level. Maintains contacts with Finns and diplomatic corps.

Clean, crisp and to the point. Frances should have been comfortable with these duties because she had done all of them in the past. For example she ran the office in Madrid; she acted a chargé d'affaires in Stockholm and twice again in Brussels; she drafted documents and suggested action for Grew and Acheson in Washington DC; and visited, contacted and talked with the diplomatic corps in virtually all her posts. But now of course, she must do them more often and even better.

Cabot then added two new comments:

> <u>Judgment</u>: Excellent. Analyzes coolly and perceptively. Is not fooled by superficial deceptiveness nor by attractive but shallow suggestions. Does not get rattled or go off on tangents. A sound and shrewd judge of men, words and events.

Summary Comments: I consider Miss Willis one of the outstanding officers now in the service. I do not give her high marks on the way she
dresses, but her clothes are adequate and suitable.

Cabot's comments in the Judgment factor seem a bit out of the ordinary,
suggesting that some kind of testing was going on. It's not clear who the testers
were; members of the legation staff, Finnish Foreign Ministry or Cabot himself.
In any case, Frances passed.

Cabot may also have explained why those two never hit it off in South
America: John didn't like the way Frances dressed. Obviously he never saw Frances
wearing that full-length velvet gown that capsized the U.S. Navy in Stockholm.
But in truth, Frances' basic sartorial model was her mother, Belle, who mostly
wore mourning-black after the 1905 divorce (or death) of first husband Gilbert
Willis and then the death of her second husband Bayard Cairns in 1934. Frances
must have received Cabot's message because her formal wardrobe lightened up,
as shown subsequently.

Frances expanded on some of these duties in answers to new questions
appearing in an Inspector's Efficiency Report, just five months after she arrived:

> For which (one or more) of the Foreign Service duties do you consider
> that you have the greatest aptitude? …the greatest interest?
> I grew up in the age when FSO's were expected to be versatile—so
> I have done a great variety of tasks. Modesty or conceit prevents my
> saying for which I have the greatest aptitude. I enjoy negotiations as
> much as anything.

> What is your ultimate goal in the Foreign Service, expressed in terms
> of assignment and type of work?
> I'll try anything the Department asks me to do.

> Are there any other remarks that you wish to make concerning your
> status and future in the Foreign Service, for the benefit of the Inspector
> and the Department?
> I truly hope the future may be as satisfactory as the past—and I do
> not say that in the sense of the diplomats who used to say, "You
> should have known Vienna when…"

> Are there any constructive suggestions you would like to make?
> I hope to make some contribution to the solution of problems facing our young Americans stationed here. To date I have been occupied trying to get on top of my job and trying to establish myself in a new apartment and have done very little in this connection.

Frances didn't elaborate on the problems facing young Americans stationed here, but it probably was similar to hers: finding an affordable apartment, which when found was very small and very expensive. So the young Americans were probably doubled and tripled up in an apartment half the size of hers.

The Department's next act was to appoint Frances to the FSO Promotion Panel. So they didn't forget her after all. The panel was to start deliberations on November 1, 1951, in Washington DC and run for sixty days. In fact it took about seventy-five days for the panel to finish, apparently with a week off for the holidays. During that week Frances flew home to Redlands for a family reunion.

Apparently the deliberations were quite stressful, as she reported in a series of six letters to Belle during the first two weeks of 1952. For example, Frances wrote:

> Jan 4 Until we finish Class 4, the one we are working on now, none of us will have a spare minute literally. I turned down two or three invitations to dinner but there was no help for it.
>
> Jan 7 We are winding up another class and it is a full time operation.
>
> Jan 10 I really think we'll finish by next week. I have to stay on for a few days to get the records in shape.
>
> Jan 14 I think we really are almost through and is about time! We have been working almost steadily but I did not know it would be so bad after last Tuesday, so accepted dinner invitations for every night last week—and twice had to go back afterwards.

Frances reported that Tom Wailes and his wife, "evermore good friends," were among the dinner hosts. Frances reciprocated by inviting them to dinner at the Sulgrave Club, where she always stayed when in Washington DC. Frances also reported in her January 10 letter:

The Philadelphia Orchestra gave a wonderful all Tschaikowsky (or however you spell it) program here Tuesday night. I just managed to get there—without any dinner, so Harl [McDonald] and Ormandy took me out and fed me after the concert.

That had to be a coup: walking out of Constitution Hall with the PSO Conductor and entourage on the way to a late-night supper, probably in Georgetown. Impressive as that was, it was overwhelmed by an event just a year earlier when Frances reported another PSO encounter in Washington DC, again sitting in Ormandy's box followed by dinner. But this time her box-mates were the retired Joseph Grews!

Grew must have been impressed seeing his old assistant included in such lofty social company. And because Grew was soon to play a major role in Frances' ambassadorial nomination, this chance encounter must have persuaded him she had the right social stuff to go with the right work stuff he knew about. And that's the way good things happen in the foreign service world. Now back to work.

Frances had a chance to elaborate on her duties in a stultifying long, seven-page Position Description, Form FS-418, for her position as Counselor and Deputy Chief of Mission, dated April 18, 1952, which was filed in her dossier. The first page listed names, titles, units and three levels of certification signatures. It also listed each topic to be addressed, then added two pages of single-spaced, 1000-word instructions on what to include in each topic, including the percentage of time (to 5% precision) the subject spent on each topic. The pseudo-science of personnel administration continued to grow at a fearsome rate after the war.

Fortunately, pages 2 through 5 were written by Frances, while the last two pages were written by Cabot. Here is a sample of Frances' part:

Because of the weakness of the administrative section at this Legation prior to the arrival of the new administrative officer, and of his subsequent absence on sick leave, I have performed the functions of an administrative officer during a large part of the eight months I have been on duty here. When [I was] not actually doing the work the section has required detailed supervision. The work of the economic, political and consular sections and the USIS has likewise been followed closely by me in order to see that it is kept up-to-date, that there is no unnecessary overlapping, and that the work of all the sections is properly integrated.

As a result, Frances had to add acting administrator officer to her normal duties, which is surprising because the position is usually filled by the next most senior member of that section. So there must not have been anyone capable enough or experienced enough to do the job and, as Frances said, fix the weaknesses. While Frances didn't elaborate on the weaknesses, they likely included inadequate and delinquent reports, incomplete book-keeping and other consular jobs—jobs Frances had mastered long ago. So she went to work squaring away that ship, to borrow another nautical phrase. Then when the new administrator, John Crawford, did return he must have done a fine job because he followed her to her next post in Switzerland.

Frances' next Annual Efficiency report, again by John Cabot, was in a new format that did away with those silly Part I multiple-choice boxes, replacing them with a list of assignments such as Political, Reporting, Negotiating, etc. Each required a numerical grade from 1 (lowest) to 6 (highest) with the majority of officers expected by be rated 3 or 4 on most items. Boxes were added to indicate whether a review panel was used, and whether or not the report was discussed with the officer rated. Finally, some rational progress.

Cabot's review was an odd mixture of praise and criticism. Cabot gave Frances thirty 6's, eleven 5's and a "not observed" in Ability in Field of Intelligence. Frances couldn't have been happy about that, because intelligence action was what she was after. Cabot then gave her the best possible Overall Rating: "Performance in every respect is outstanding and there is no weakness in any respect." So Excellent has now been replaced by Outstanding.

However, Cabot's Summary Comments and Recommendations section was another story:

> Miss Willis is invariably conscientious in her work almost to the point of a fault. She is, however, somewhat inclined to take too many duties upon herself and to be unable to delegate work to others—a minor fault, since the work gets done. While I have seen her annoyed on quite a few occasions, I have never seen her when I thought there was the slightest possibility that she would lose control of herself. Miss Willis has exceptionally few of those weaknesses with which even the best officers

are occasionally afflicted. On two or three occasions I have noted orders
on her part which were unquestionably correct and perhaps necessary,
but which seemed not altogether to take into account the human factors
involved. I mention these trifles as much to show how trifling the faults
she has are, as to criticize her for them.

There's that Willis failure-to-delegate flaw once again. But more importantly,
Cabot worried about Frances issuing orders, but then becoming annoyed when
they weren't executed to her satisfaction. And that in turn affected morale, or
as Cabot said "human factors." It's also clear that some—probably most—of
the orders were issued to square away her administrative section. Usually such
measures can be effective when administered with a uniform, fair hand. But
Frances, in her usual drive for perfection, appears to have pushed that envelope a
bit too zealously. Cabot continued:

> Miss Willis' executive ability is on the whole good. Miss Willis suffers
> from the inevitable handicap that any woman has in her representational
> and contact work but within this limitation she does an outstanding
> job. Miss Willis' work has been circumscribed by the fact that this is a
> relatively small post where the problems, while sometimes difficult and
> annoying, are seldom serious.

There's a variation of that Holmes' worry again. But Cabot balanced things
out with the following comments:

> I am delighted to have Miss Willis as my Counselor, and from a
> personal viewpoint hope that she stays here as long as I do. She handles
> her representational work with dignity, grace and skill, despite the fact
> that she is somewhat handicapped by the small apartment she had to
> take in this overcrowded city [and most importantly] I feel that, as I
> have already said, Miss Willis has earned her mission.

Then Cabot weaseled out of showing Frances this report with the following
entry:

In discussing other reports with Miss Willis, I mentioned that there was really nothing in the way of a criticism in my report on her. She laughed and said: "Under those circumstances we could consider the discussion of it finished."

And he left the "Discussed with officer rated" box empty. Could it be that Cabot unconsciously set the bar higher for Frances once he had recommended her for chief of mission, and then ducked out of her review session once he realized how many "trifling faults" he dropped on her? A more cynical assessment says he was creating a *CYA* (Cover-Your-Arse) report, so that if Frances botched her future assignment Cabot could then say, "I told you so; look at my last Efficiency Report." Either looks plausible.

Cabot's comment about Frances' small apartment leads to the next story, the only insane thing Frances ever did in her life: She invited five teenagers to come to Helsinki, stay in her apartment and watch the Olympic Games over a period of three weeks in July, 1952: Bob and Bill McAfee from Redlands; Bill Trimble, Jr., son of First Secretary Bill Trimble in London; Frances Vaughan, her namesake and second-born daughter of big sister Caroline; and the author. The apartment had only two bedrooms, which were occupied by the two Franceses. The guys slept in the garage.

Fortunately, the five teenagers were well behaved because they were so busy attending social engagements and using the plethora of extra Olympic Game tickets at the legation: a full day's worth each day for each of them. Simply unheard of nowadays; the cost alone would be prohibitive.

So much for John Cabot. He was transferred to Pakistan, leaving Frances to run the store as chargé d'affaires for about six weeks. Then Jack K. McFall showed up, and Frances reverted back to her old job of counselor, with the added task of breaking in a new boss. Such is life in the Foreign Service—up one day and down the next.

Minister Jack McFall and staff at his credential presentation ceremony,
November 15, 1952 (courtesy State Department.)

Deputy Frances, at Jack's right hand, is now wearing an adequate—and quite suitable—outfit. Other members are unidentified.

Then the Climax

Frances spent the next two months getting to know—and breaking in—the new minister when she received the following letter from her old Brussels boss, Hugh Gibson:

30 April 1953

My dear Ambassador,

I suppose the congratulations are pouring in on the strength of the newspaper stories and don't want to lag too far behind. I hope the stupid publicity has not slowed things up any and that you will soon be our near and welcome neighbor. I have a story to tell you about the nomination which I think will amuse you, but I shall save it until you get here. Please let me know when you are coming. I want to get you down here and have some worthwhile people in to meet you.

For a good many years I have felt this recognition was overdue, but now it has come. I think I take as much satisfaction in it as anybody.

With all wishes for success and happiness, I am
Yours always...[65]

Recall that Gibson was a harsh critic of all women in the service, but made
an exception for Frances after he vetted her in Brussels in 1937. His wife Ynes
died in 1950, but he was still active in retirement. Frances' responded:

American Legation
Helsinki, Finland,
May 19, 1953

Dear Mr. Ambassador,

Your letter of April 30, 1953 brought me great pleasure and was also
reassuring. Even in this remote but most interesting corner I have heard
some strange stories about the rumored appointment (I have no official
word yet and that is one reason for my delay in writing) and it is most
reassuring to know that the idea originated with you, Mr. Grew and Mr.
Armour. It is encouraging to have the confidence of such a triumvirate
and you can be assured that I shall continue to try to merit the trust
which you have placed in me.

I look forward to seeing you again and hearing what you think about
many things. Your views always made sense to me and I hope we could
see each other from time to time and discuss some of the problems that
are besetting the world. We should not lack material.

Again with many thanks for your letter and the kind things you
wrote...

As ever,

/s/ *Frances E. Willis*
The Honorable
Hugh Gibson
Director of the Intergovernmental
Committee for
European Migration,
63, rue des Paquis,
Geneva.

---

[65] This and subsequent letters from Gibson were unsigned because they were carbon copies.

Unfortunately, that amusing nomination story that Hugh was going to tell Frances is lost. It probably had to do with tactics cooked up by Gibson, Grew and Armour to get Frances' name in front of the Secretary and then the President. Gibson and Grew are of course familiar names, but Armour needs an introduction.

According to Heinrichs in his biography of Joseph Grew, Norman Armour (1889-1982) started his Foreign Service career as a private secretary to Grew one summer when he was attending Princeton, around 1910. He then became a career Foreign Service Officer, who from 1932 through 1954 was chief of mission to seven countries: Haiti, Canada, Chile, Argentina, Spain, Venezuela and Guatemala. His appointment to Spain started in 1944, shortly after Frances left.

In between these chief of mission posts, Armour was appointed to the newly created post of Assistant Secretary of State for Political Affairs in 1947, when Frances was in London. So for about a year Armour likely received condensed versions of political despatches from the outback, including some pretty good ones from Frances. It's not clear what Armour did between 1948 and the start of his tour in Venezuela in 1950. He may have remained in one of those new assistant secretary slots, reading more of Frances' despatches. Armour retired in 1954 just before the career ambassador rank was established in 1955.

There was nothing in Frances' dossier about nomination deliberations. In fact it would have been most unusual if there had been any such records. Those deliberations—what the issues, worries and risks were, and who was for and against it, for example—are never revealed. The successful candidate just hears the outcome with congratulations and all best wishes.[66] But what is clear is that both Grew and Gibson came out of retirement and supported Armour in the crusade.

This appointment represents the climax of Frances' career. Even though she rose to higher ranks, this one marked the hardest climb—the climb that met continuous resistance from the Old Guard. Once she reached this peak the rest would be a *cake-walk* by comparison.

In response to the author's letter of congratulations, Frances said that both

---

[66] A cryptic March 10, 1953, entry on one of Frances' *Name Index* cards at the National Archives identified a standard—but quite unnerving—request for the FBI to conduct a "full field investigation on [FEW], whom the President is considering as a Chief of Mission." Results were not included.

Grew and Gibson had sent letters. Unfortunately Joseph Grew's letter is not in any of the archives. Frances then said:

> But it is difficult to accept congratulations when the dear old Department hasn't told me anything about the story that made the front page! And you certainly cannot depend on newspapers.

In between all this action, Jack McFall wrote an Efficiency Report in June, 1953, covering the previous year. This report matched—maybe even exceeded—those of Grew, Gibson and Holmes. It went beyond excellent or outstanding; McFall said it was the best one he ever wrote. McFall started out with twenty-nine 6's and fourteen 5's, including one in the intelligence box. So Frances finally must have found someone with secrets that were worth reporting. While that wasn't as good as Cabot's score, McFall put it in proper context:

> This is the first time during my career in the Foreign Service that I have ever given a "6" rating to any officer.

And he gave her twenty-nine of them. He scored Frances a 3 (Limited) in Swedish, a 4 (Useful) in Spanish and a 5 (Fluent) in French, and checked the outstanding box, as did Cabot. But his narrative soared to new heights when he addressed Adverse Factors:

> Miss Willis as a Foreign Service officer is as well rounded in all phases of capabilities called for in this field as any officer I have ever observed. The fact that she is a woman essentially imposes some few limitations on the character of contact responsibilities that one would call upon her to handle, but this limitation in no way affects the true measure of her usefulness to the Service. Furthermore, she shies from no responsibility, and will tackle any chore with consummate vim and vigor. I have found no weakness, in any respect, in this officer's performance. The analysis resolves itself, therefore, into a question of the relative measure of her various strengths.

There's that protection gender bias again, but now minimized. McFall continued:

Not alone should I be willing, but enthusiastically pleased, to have this officer serve with me at any post at any time. Miss Willis' willingness to tackle any chore, her long years of fruitful service, her adaptability and her alertness in keeping abreast of changed methods and techniques of operation and administration of the Service, eminently qualify her, in my opinion, for consideration as appointment as Chief of Mission.

The measure of her work as Chief of Mission should, of course, be the determining factor in subsequently considering her for designation as a Career Minister.

McFall's Summary Comments rained even more accolades, including that ever given a 6 comment, along with "superb grasp of the Foreign Service regulations, most effective method of address, fluent pen, etc." He finished with:

She has the charm of the woman in the drawing room but need give no quarter to men in any phases of office management or business or political judgment. During a six week hiatus between the departure of my predecessor and my arrival at this post, Miss Willis served as Chargé d'affaires. All responsibilities incident to that charge were promptly and effectively discharged.

I consider Miss Willis a real credit to the Foreign Service and 'Exhibit A' of what a woman can accomplish given academic background, perseverance, dexterity, ability and charm.

McFall checked "Yes" in the discussed with the officer rated box. He also marked "Career Minister" in the box asking if the evaluator would "urge his promotion in the next higher grade as soon as he is eligible." That was significant because a chief of mission must serve with some distinction before he is recommended for that three-star rank. While some might call those comments gratuitous because Frances was already in the nomination queue, they were a nice touch—certainly in stark contrast to Cabot's *CYA* report.

The last official evaluation document from her Helsinki tour was a new Department form called an Annual End-User Summary Report, prepared by Andreas G. Ronhovde, Officer in Charge, Northern European Affairs. It was highly complimentary of her political and economic reporting and of her relationship with the legation staff and the Finns. He finished with a comment that her new appointment "was a well merited recognition of her faithful and outstanding service in Helsinki and previous assignments."

While these words in Ronhovde's Evaluation Section were flattering, Frances was rated only a 5, even though she had just been appointed ambassador. An explanation appeared on the back of the form, which gave the scope and definition of the rating scale. The scope was limited to "reports or other work products submitted to the Department." And under this constraint the two highest rating levels were defined as follows:

5 - The work product or performance was so exceptionally well done as to leave no recognizable room for improvement in any significant respect.

6 - The work product or performance was superior in every respect, denoting the highest degree of resourcefulness and initiative with no recognizable room for possible improvement.

Under these evaluation criteria even God would have failed to get a 6 and probably not even a 5 rating in the world-creation category. Lots of room for Homo Sapiens' improvement as a start.

Then more letters from Hugh Gibson, this time with Hugh writing to "The Hon. Frances Willis, American Embassy, Berne" even before she had been appointed ambassador:

14 July 1953

Dear Ambassador,

At last I see in the Times the news that your nomination has been sent to the Senate, so things are apparently happening.

I want to tell you that within the last few days I have moved into a nice house overlooking the lake, which you will kindly make use of as your headquarters when it is convenient to you.

I don't want to pester you, but Geneva is bound to be a secondary field of activity for you and when you have got through the first rush in Berne I hope you will pay me a visit and I'll invite in some of the people who should know you (in conference with Ed Ward, our very able Consul General). I don't want you to commit yourself now, but just want you to have this thought in mind.

                              With congratulations and all good wishes...

Frances was nominated by President Eisenhower on July 11 and confirmed by the Senate on July 20 to be "Ambassador Extraordinary and Plenipotentiary of the United States of America to Switzerland."[67] She succeeded Richard G. Patterson, Jr., whose resignation as Minister to Switzerland was effective May 30, 1953. Elevation of the mission from legation to embassy occurred on the date Frances presented her credentials.

By this time Frances' appointment hit the newspapers. Oddly, only one article was filed in her dossier—and none were in her effects at the Hoover Archives. But more than fifty were in Belle's scrapbooks in the Redlands Archives. So Belle must have directed all her friends, relatives—and Frances—to send them to her; she was going to be the repository of this great event.

The articles came from everywhere; some newspapers had multiple articles: *Los Angeles Times (4); New York Times (3); Metropolis (Illinois) News (3); Christian Science Monitor (2)*. At least one appeared in *The Economist, Hauburger Abendblat, New York Herald Tribune, Reuters, UPI, AP, Philadelphia Enquirer, Philadelphia Evening Bulletin,*[68] *Washington Post, Washington Star, Memphis Press, Hartford Courant, Detroit Free Press, St. Louis Post Despatch, St. Louis Globe-Democrat,* and all the local papers: *Redlands, Riverside, San Bernardino and Salinas.*

The *Armed Forces Daily* got into the act with an August 12 article worrying about spelling "Madam" as in "Madam Ambassador." They decided that it must be with an *e*, as in "Call her Madame." (That spelling was also used by Life magazine.)

Then in an attempt to claim their own, headlines in the July 21, Illinois *Daily Republican Times* said, "Illinois Woman OK'd as Envoy to Switzerland." Frances hadn't lived in Illinois since 1912. At least the July 7 *Milwaukee Journal* was willing to share the glory: "Illinois Girl, Wisconsin Schooled..."

Probably the worst article of the lot was the only one in Frances' dossier: "Miss Willis, New Envoy to Swiss, Is Veteran in Diplomatic Service," by Elizabeth Ford of the Society Section, *Washington DC Times-Herald*, July 23, 1953. It was

---

[67] Plenipotentiary means invested with full power to transact business.

[68] Sent to her by Eugene Ormandy.

full of typos and factual errors and was written in the breeziest journalistic style. Here is a sample:

> In the blue-book group (the State Department has its own social register, based on top-rank posts) are 26 women who are classified as career foreign service officers. Come the day, one or all of them may merit a class one F.S.O. and a good hearty "yea" from the Senate.
>
> There are 23 more who are rated as foreign service reserve officers. They are appointed for two-year terms as specialists in various fields, and in this group are cultural officers, information officers, social welfare attaches and economic officers. All keeping house for Uncle Sam.
>
> The others from the distaf [*sic*] side work as translators, interviewers and librarians and there are some 1,500 who can dive into any steno-grafic [*sic*] pool and come thru like speed boats…

Factual errors included the claim that Constance Harvey served longer than Frances, that there was a new career program for women FSO's in the 1930's and that Frances often cooked. None true. Why that was the only article in Frances' dossier when, for example, there were far better ones to pick from the *Los Angeles Times* or the *New York Times* remains a mystery.

Or maybe not. One cynical explanation goes back to the first newspaper article filed in Frances' dossier: a grossly distorted and poorly edited 1929 *San Francisco Examiner* article when Frances went off to Chile. It was the worst of that lot and also the only one filed in her dossier. Simply too much of a coincidence to ignore. It appears that selective culling—along with selective redacting and selective filing—were the stealthy weapons in the Old Guard's arsenal, or what little was left of it at this point. Mercifully, that was their parting shot, which finally ended perverse sex bias in the Department—at least for Frances.

So Frances was off to Washington DC to accept her appointment.

Frances, escorted by Minister Jack McFall, departing Finland,
July 1953 (courtesy State Department.)

Someone must have complemented Frances, who is reacting with embarrassment: hand to chest and head tilted back. That pose will appear often in the next twelve years.

After arriving in Washington DC, Frances responded to Gibson's letter:

August 6, 1953

Dear Mr. Ambassador,

Thank you for your letter of July 14, 1953, which was waiting for me here in the Department when I arrived from Helsinki August 4. I am to be here until August 18, then go to California for three weeks, I hope, as I have had only fifteen days leave in the two and a half years since I have been in Finland. With two or three days here en route to Switzerland I should arrive there about the middle of September. At least that is my best estimate at the present time.

I am looking forward to seeing you as soon as possible after my arrival and am depending on you to give me guidance on innumerable matters...

Three more letters appeared after Frances arrived in Switzerland. The first was from Frances, dated October 29, 1953, now ensconced at the embassy in Bern with Belle (who was to stay with Frances for the last seven years of her life). Frances was still attempting to rendezvous with Hugh:

> I am afraid that it will be impossible for me to come to Geneva on November 1 or 2, but I am planning to come on November 20 when the Swiss-American Society for Cultural Relations has arranged a meeting, and again on December 17 when I believe the American Club is arranging a luncheon meeting at which I am to speak. There are also tentative plans for short trips to Zurich, Basel and St. Gall. It is all keeping me very busy in addition to my official calls. If, however, you can ever spare the time to come to Bern not just to call on me but for a quiet visit, please let me know as I am greatly looking forward to seeing you...

Apparently none of these plans worked out because the next letter was also from Frances, dated February 18, 1954:

> When are you going to pay me your long promised visit in Bern? I had hoped that life for me would become a little less strenuous and I was waiting for some leisurely interval before extending a definite invitation to you. The schedule, however, seems to become fuller and fuller as the weeks roll by and I therefore do not want to wait any longer.
>
> There are some people coming to lunch on Monday, March 1, including the Papal Nuncio. It occurred to me that you might be able to get away on Sunday and come to Bern and stay over until after lunch on Monday. Does that idea appeal to you?

That drew the following reply the next day from Hugh:

> My favorite Ambassador,
>
> There is no invitation I would rather accept than the one which reached me this morning for March 1st. Unfortunately that clashed

with the arrival of Senator and Mrs. Styles Bridges who are coming to stay with me for a few days. They have insisted that everything be kept frightfully secret, but it has been published confidentially in the Herald Tribune. I imagine they will be with me only a few days and when they are gone I shall call up and suggest a trip to Berne at some time convenient for you.

That was the last available correspondence between Frances and Hugh. So it's not clear whether they did meet, but there seemed to be significant affection between them, almost like an admiring niece—doting uncle relationship. And they had less than ten months left to meet because Hugh died in Geneva December 12, 1954, at the age of 70.

Those last, bittersweet pages are hardly the way to cap such a peak in Frances' career. So here is Frances relaxing in Redlands following her swearing-in ceremony.

Frances in her rose garden, September 14, 1953.

15

WATCHES AND ONIONS
IN SWITZERLAND

The Appointment and its Reaction

BEFORE reporting to Bern (German spelling) or Berne (French spelling, which the Department—except for Frances—usually preferred because they had been at war with Germany twice in twenty-five years), Frances visited the Department for three weeks in August, 1953, with a full schedule of appointments, including swearing in and a Finland debrief and then meetings with Undersecretary Matthews, Secretary Dulles and finally the President.

Frances and President Eisenhower, August 22, 1953 (courtesy U.S. Government.)

Ike has just greeted Frances as his new Ambassador to Switzerland and asked her a question that required a detailed answer, accompanied by appropriate gesticulation, typical of someone fluent in French.

Frances' appointment received mixed reviews from the European diplomatic community, as summarized in her biography appearing in the January, 1954, issue of *Current Biography:*

> The appointment of Dr. Willis to the post of Ambassador in Switzerland aroused speculation as to the suitability of the choice, inasmuch as Swiss women do not have the right to vote. According to the New York Times of April 15, 1953, foreign diplomats in Berne, though not Swiss themselves, predicted "unfavorable repercussions in Switzerland because of the country's opposition to women's participation in politics;" however, the New York Times stated that "the business-like attitude of the Swiss" was "likely to ignore such reasoning." In the New York Times of the following day, a dispatch from Geneva quoted a spokesman for the Swiss Federal Government as saying that "he had no reason to believe that the fact that Dr. Willis was a woman would influence the Federal Council's decision" in accepting the appointment.

Two despatches in Frances' 123 File, from Howard Donovan, Consul General in Zurich, to the Department in August, 1953, identified a more mixed Swiss reaction to her appointment:

> In the issue of August 7, 1953, the weekly paper published by the MIGROS organization for distribution to its customers and members (but not for sale to the public) published an article about Ambassador Willis which is reproduced in translation from the German below:

THE DISTURBING MISS WILLIS

> The Swiss men are worried. The reason is a woman! This is nothing unusual in itself and is said to happen fairly often, especially if it is a woman who is closely connected and personally well known. The strange thing is, however, that up to now no Swiss man knows this disturbing woman except from her photographs. And this shows an open, intelligent

and very matter-of-fact woman's face of the type known to Swiss men as "ordinary" (because not dolled up) and therefore highly appreciated.

No, it is not this woman personally who worries the Swiss, but her function: Miss Willis has, after much discussion, been appointed by President Eisenhower as "Ambassador" to Bern. He is sending his first career woman diplomat to Switzerland! As if the USA had not enough male ambassadors: since the new wave of economy there must be lots of prospective ambassadors walking around without work in Washington. As if it were not sufficiently known that Switzerland is, in this respect, a "special case!"

Why then a woman? ask the Swiss men, what does the President of the USA mean by it? A broad hint? Does he want to demonstrate with a living example that women are as good as men, by sending the cleverest of them from his Foreign Office to Switzerland, or does he consider our country as so unimportant as to be worth "only" a woman?

These are the thoughts of an average Swiss man. The open-minded, world-wise man who is in favor of woman suffrage (and I am glad to say that there are many such in our country) is looking forward with sympathy towards the arrival of the new Ambassador and, at most, remarks: "I hope Miss Willis is a pleasant woman, and nice to look at, one that one can get along with not only objectively but also as a human being." Reports from Washington are, in this respect, very reassuring: Miss Willis is said to have the gift of inspiring confidence in men, of meeting them without restraint, "to put them at their ease" is the actual expression used in the information received.[69]

The Swiss men in the Bundeshaus show no signs of anxiety; in fact they assure us so positively that a female ambassador cannot shake their calm, that this is a little unsettling. In short, one is well pleased for the present in the Bundeshaus with President Eisenhower's choice, especially as one prefers a capable career diplomat, even though a woman, to a politician who has been rewarded with an ambassadorial post for other services. Officially nobody sees any sign of a hint in this appointment from the USA to Swiss politicians as to how women should be treated

---

[69] That un-attributed quote is new, but clearly promulgated by the Department, maybe even by Secretary Dulles.

in a modern state because, so they say with pride and quite rightly, we brook no outside interference in this respect.

And what is the Swiss woman's reaction to this diplomatic event? "If having more women at the head of political life will mean less chances of war, then we are all for it," say some; "do not make such a fuss about this woman," said an acquaintance of mine who mixes in diplomatic circles, "who was more liked in Bern than the former USA woman Press Attaché?"

"I'm glad," said another with a malicious smile, "let the men learn from an Ambassadress that women are just as clever as they are." Miss Willis herself will be much too intelligent and, in political matters, much too experienced to provoke anything in [suffrage and equal rights.] After all, it is not her task; she must work not for Swiss women but for her own country.

Obviously Miss Willis' position will not be easy solely in regard to etiquette, wardrobe and questions of representation. Even before her first public appearance, even before she has crossed our frontier, she will be examined with critical attention. But precisely because she can stand such close scrutiny was she appointed to our country by President Eisenhower, and for no other reason.

Donovan then added his own take on the situation:

In Zurich, after the announcement of the appointment, those who favor woman suffrage expressed approval. Those who are strongly opposed—less numerous but perhaps more influential than the other group—expressed the view that the appointment was a mistake. In other words, there is evident a considerable degree of prejudgment of the new Ambassador prior to her arrival based on established individual convictions. Also, it is clear that the fact of the appointment is being used for internal Swiss political purposes.

So, like Belgium in 1934, Frances was confronted by host-country gender bias. And, like Belgium, she would quickly disarm it. Frances weighed in on the Swiss woman suffrage issue in a fifteen-minute, CBS radio broadcast from Los Angeles during home leave on December 17, 1954:

When I went to Switzerland in October 1953, it was my first assignment as an Ambassador and for the Swiss it was the first time they had ever received a woman Ambassador. Some people have asked me if the United States Government deliberately chose to send me to Switzerland because women in that country do not have the vote. As far as I have been able to learn, there was no connection between the political state of women in Switzerland and my assignment. There were those who prophesied that the fact that women do not vote there might make it difficult for me. I can assure you that this has not been the case. The Swiss are among the most practical people in the world, and they are more interested in getting on with the job than in the size, shape or sex of the person with whom they are conducting the business.

Naturally reporters tried to induce me to express my views on the subject of Swiss women not having the vote, but I have not been in the Foreign Service for 27 years for nothing. I began by saying that I wanted to stay in Switzerland a long time—and I do, because it would be difficult to find a more agreeable place to work. Then I said that the quickest way for a diplomat to bring about his or her recall was to get mixed up in the internal politics of the country. Obviously, as I did not want to be sent away, I had no intention of getting involved in the domestic political questions of votes for women in Switzerland.

As the *MIGROS* article predicted, Frances was much too experienced to provoke anything like that. But what *was* behind the rather odd decision to post a woman to Switzerland in the first place? The answer, like all such deliberations, is buried in confidential Department files, which would never be released.

Whatever the deliberations, Frances probably asked that question when she was consulting with the Department, something like, "Are you sending me there as a not-so-subtle signal to the Swiss to join the modern world?" Of course the answer is even more elusive than the question, but hindsight suggests the following:

Good grief, no! On the contrary, we need someone of your vast experience and capability to handle diplomatic problems, which seem to be brewing there, like tariffs we are about to drop on their watches, because they are so much better than ours, which as a result aren't selling well enough here.

But what was not said to Frances is even more suggestive:

Of course we are, by showing them that a woman can do the job as well as any of our career men—never mind that we, ourselves, have just come to that (tentative) conclusion. So after the Swiss see that you can, they should want to try it and that will give us reason to remove the "tentative" part so you can continue your ambassadorial career.

Good chance that was part of the Department's motive for sending Frances to Switzerland—their hidden agenda, and certainly hidden from Frances. Such a scenario requires a confluence of disparate agendas: the Old Guard's desire for a final test of the lady's mettle and the suffragist's desire to send a strong signal to Switzerland. Both agendas were present in the Department at this time and were likely aired in deliberations of the selection committee.

Homer L Calkin in his book *Women in the Department of State,* covered both Frances' and Clare Boothe Luce's near simultaneous appointments:

President Dwight D. Eisenhower appointed two women ambassadors in 1953, one a political appointee to Italy and the other a career officer to Switzerland.

Clare Boothe Luce (and her husband, Henry Luce) had made significant contributions to President Eisenhower's presidential campaign, and she expected substantial recognition of this. American aid to Italy [was] of continuing concern to Clare Boothe Luce. She was also concerned with the continuing problem of Italian Communism.

When a mysterious case of arsenic poisoning terminated Luce's appointment in 1956, President Eisenhower congratulated her for "a job superbly done." Unquestionably, she had shown that women chiefs of mission could be effective.

President Eisenhower nominated Luce as Ambassador to Brazil in 1959. The Senate approved by a vote of 79 to 11. Senator William Fulbright of Arkansas complained that partisan considerations caused the President "to hand out ambassadorships as rewards for political services."

He criticized the Luce nomination, and Senator Wayne Morse of Oregon also attacked it with violence. As a result, Luce decided to decline the appointment.

That Luce nomination to Brazil rippled through the career FSO ranks, as the following 1961 letter from Ellis O. Briggs, U.S. Ambassador to Greece, to Frances in Washington DC—then on her way to Ceylon—demonstrates.

American Embassy
Athens, Greece
March 2, 1961

Dear Frances,

You do get around, and I hope the move to Ceylon is as pleasant as I should think it would be. The fact that you have a Lady in Charge [Madame Bandaranaike] reminds me of a story, possibly apocryphal, that before La Luce tossed me out of Brazil she had really wanted London, advancing the theory that since England has a Queen, Grosvenor Square [site of the U.S. embassy] should have one too.

Should you be flying east via Athens, please be sure to let us know. Otherwise Lucy and I may see you in Washington in mid-April, when we turn up beside the Potomac to help chaperone the visit of the Greek Prime Minister.

We join in sending you our very best wishes.

Sincerely yours,
/s/ *Ellis*

As reported earlier, Ellis was one of the three bachelors posted to Lima, Peru; the other two were John Cabot and Sam Reber. All made ambassador. In fact, Ellis (1899-1976) was ambassador to eight countries between 1944 and 1962, including the Dominican Republic, Uruguay, Czechoslovakia, Korea, Peru, Brazil (1956-1959), Greece and finally Spain. He was also appointed a career ambassador in the set before Frances. Not only that but his son, Everett Ellis Briggs (b. 1934) followed in his footsteps with ambassadorships to Panama, Honduras and Portugal in the 1980's.[70]

---

[70] Incidentally, a lady friend of the author's family reported that she was assigned to Ellis Briggs' staff in Brazil just after graduating from college. She said he was an impressive boss

So apparently Ike turned down Clare's request for London, offering her Brazil instead. Then he moved one of those peripatetic FSO's out to make room for her there, in this case, Ellis from Brazil to Greece. But only that latter part happened.

Frances answered Ellis' letter, hoping to see them in Washington DC, but sorry, she was going to Ceylon the other way round, so wouldn't see them in Greece.

Calkin then spent equal time describing Frances' career, starting with "the first woman Chargé d'affaires ad interim in American history." Finally, recognition by the Department! He then added kudos from her old chiefs:

> In 1944 Hugh Gibson, former Minister and Ambassador, had written of her that she had received "greater distinction in performance than in recognition," and should by then have been recognized by appointment as Chief of Mission.
>
> When Willis was nominated in 1953 as Ambassador to Switzerland, her old chief, Ambassador Joseph Grew, said that "nobody could do a better job." She had been an able, quiet, and hard-working officer who thought "you must take your work seriously but never yourself."

That's probably close to Grew's letter of congratulations to Frances. Note that Calkin identified Grew as a former chief, but not Gibson. He probably wasn't aware that Gibson was her chief for that critical, career-changing year in Brussels.

Frances then took a California vacation, starting in Redlands for a family reunion and celebration. On that visit Frances persuaded her mother Belle to come help her with the massive entertainment workload at the embassy in Switzerland. At first Belle was reluctant but with family pressure finally accepted. Actually Frances took a leaf out of Constance Harvey's career with a second objective: to care for her aging mother, because in Frances' case other family members were in no position to do so. And it worked out well, allowing Belle to stay with Frances for the last seven years of her life. Frances reported in a 1974

---

who used a cane. The staff suspected it had nothing to do with helping him walk, but was used for enhancement and convenience—enhancement of image and convenience for a handy nip, right from a small flask hollowed out in handle.

Redlands Daily Press interview that "Mother was an absolutely perfect assistant." Frances covered all of Belle's expenses for those seven years—no surprise there.

Arrival in Berne

Frances reported her "Arrival and Presentation of Credentials" events in Despatch #326 dated October 12, 1953, from her 123 File. This is the first despatch from "Ambassador Willis," and provides a detailed, two-page summary during a change-of-command ceremony, extracted as follows:

> Upon my arrival by rail at Bern at 4:57 p.m. October 4, 1953,[71] I was met at the station by Dr. Robert MAURICE, Chief of Protocol of the Swiss Federal Political Department, who welcomed me in the name of the Swiss Government. After the Chargé d'affaires a.i., Mr. REAMS, introduced about a dozen members of the staff of the legation to me, Dr. Maurice conducted me to the residence in an official car of the Swiss Government...
>
> In accordance with arrangements made by the Federal Political Department, I was received by Dr. Philipp ETTER, President of the Swiss Confederation, and Monsieur Max PETITPIERRE, the Foreign Minister, at 11:30 on October 9, 1953, in the Federal Palace. The ceremony of the presentation of [my] credentials was extremely simple.
>
> There followed a conversation lasting about ten minutes in which only the President, the Foreign Minister and I participated as we were seated somewhat apart from the other members of the staff. This conversation, which was in French as neither the President nor Monsieur Petitpierre converses in English, was confined to non-political subjects. The tone of it, however, was extremely friendly as was every aspect of the welcome given to me to date.
>
> As a number of newspaper correspondents had telephoned to the Legation before the presentation of my credentials and requested individual interviews, it was decided after consultation with Mr. Charles DUBOIS, the Chief of the Press Section of the Foreign Office, that [instead, I would] hold a press conference.
>
> Accordingly, at 5:00 p.m. on October 9 about thirty representatives

---

[71] Ever the precise and punctual diplomat, she.

of the press and newsreel photographers arrived at the Embassy Chancery. The camera men were first allowed to take pictures and I then made a statement containing about one-half of the text of my remarks to the President. Mr. Dubois then introduced the correspondents to me individually. He was attending the press conference at his own suggestion and it is believed that this is the first time that the Federal Political Department has assisted a Chief of Mission in holding a press conference. I [then] said that in the future I would be very happy to receive any one of them individually should he or she so desire.

The correspondents remained for about 45 minutes [and] all of the questions were extremely friendly in tone and comparatively easy to answer in generalities. Contrary to expectations, no question was asked about my views concerning the fact that Swiss women do not have the vote.

Cartoon welcoming Frances to Switzerland, October 29, 1953 (unknown source.)

Two artifacts from the Redlands Smiley Public Library illustrate these arrival events: a cartoon and a poem. The cartoon was published in a local, but unknown, newspaper. Professor Jacolyn Harmer of the Monterey Institute of International Studies translated the Swiss-German language caption and provided the interpretation: *Dr. Frances Willis, America's new diplomat in Switzerland. Welcome in the living room, Miss Willis!* (Make yourself at home, Miss Willis.)

The poem was written by the embassy staff, which by now should not be surprising because diplomats possess an affinity for foreign languages and poetry is just another foreign language. Here are excerpts.

THE WELCOME MAT IS OUT

A Lyric Epic in One Canto

Welcome Frances Willis to the valley of the Aare—
    To golfing on the Gurten, where 68 is par.
To a very pleasant residence, most pleasantly terr-aced—
    Where Mrs. Vincent's chickens fell afoul of Shelley's taste.
We feel that we should warn you, though it may not be quite nice—
    That your Counsellor of Embassy's a demon with the dice.
That Robert Bean, your Counsellor and Economic Czar—
    Is smugly enigmatic as he drives his limey car.
That Francis Lowell Coolidge has a fund of Concord wit—
    He's dreaming up a riot as these very lines are writ.
On Mr. Merrill Blevins you should keep a baleful eye—
    His martinis and his honor are unconscionably dry.
Your assistant Henry Pleasants is considered autocratic—
    Disregard his firm opinions, they're appallingly dogmatic.
Of youthful Mr. Woodward our knowledge is much less—
    What lies behind that big moustache is anybody's guess.
Peter Paddock's waistline may strike you as excessive—
    You should have seen his predecessor's; the trend is retrogressive!
We should like to add a word about your service attaches—
    We seldom get to see them for they go their service ways.
But we know that Colonel Hoska, who heads the aggregation—
    Suggests a genial pastor, greeting all his congregation.
Elder Patteson's not elder, the chance is most remote—
    For the average Air Force Colonel's hardly old enough to vote.

This could go on for ever or at least right through the list—
    But no matter where we stopped, there'd be someone we missed.
So we leave you with this sample, a cross section of your staff—
    And hope you'll get acquainted before it's cut again in half!

While the poem was not signed, most of the staff surely had a hand in its creation. Note that Counsellor is spelled with the archaic double "*l*." The last line of the poem is telling: It marked a major downsizing of the State Department by the new Eisenhower administration in an attempt to return to a peacetime manning level.

As reported earlier, the number of overseas FSO's increased from 840 in pre-war 1940 to 7710 in post-war 1950, then decreased to 5865 by 1970. But these cuts were not nearly as draconian as those made following WW I when the isolationists captured Congress and prevented the U.S. from joining the League of Nations. Then the overseas FSO level fell by half—from 1043 in 1910 to 514 in 1920.

Getting to Know the Place

As is the diplomatic custom, Frances was greeted with a host of welcoming parties, each requiring "glad to meet you and to be here" remarks from the new arrival. Apparently a long tradition for U.S. envoys is to give their first public remarks to the *Swiss Friends of the USA* in Zurich, which Frances did to an audience of over 300 in a not-so-short speech titled, "The Foreign Policy of the United States." The seven-page, single-spaced speech was extensively reworked by Frances, which should be no surprise because it was also her first speech as an ambassador.

She started with the standard greetings, and then described common bonds and differences between the two countries. She said she must get to know the people and country, and when she did she was sure to find the following common bond, which can be expressed by the following relationship, where the colon is translated "are to" and the equal sign is translated "as."

Cantons : Swiss = Texas : Texans

She said the U.S. had no quarrel with Swiss neutrality versus the recent open U.S. policy, because the U.S. was "looking for united strength to counter imperialistic communism." In fact that "threat to freedom" was the big theme of her speech. She also said that the U.S. wanted to remove impediments to free trade and currencies, a comment that would return to haunt her when a year later the U.S. dropped huge tariffs on Swiss watches, as described shortly. She finished with this rather tortured sentence:

> I am sure that we shall find many ways in which our two countries can work together and in which to continue the harmonious relations which have always existed between us.

Many of her hundred or so speeches in the Hoover Archives were written with this rigorous formality, at least the ones in English. Not only that, but the majority of them were serious dissertations on serious foreign policy subjects, which in sum can be quite intimidating, even off-putting.

Then a review of photos and reports of Frances giving a speech cracked the code: Her writing and speaking styles were quite different. She would write out her speech in the most formal syntax, revise it many times and then memorize it by mentally translating it into a normal conversation, complete with idioms, metaphors and extemporaneous humor. She usually took a copy of the speech with her but seldom referred to it. Sometimes she would use cue cards with general topics on them. And she often rehearsed her new speeches in front of her mother Belle—a high school graduate rehearsing a PhD! But speech-making requires rehearsal and Mother Belle was a ready audience and proctor.

Frances reported reaction to her neutrality comments in a November 17 despatch:

> Following the delivery of my speech in Zurich there were a number of Swiss who commented on the fact that I had spoken as I had on the subject of neutrality, but none appeared to resent the fact that I had. A number of Chiefs of Mission in Bern, while congratulating me on my speech, have likewise expressed surprise, in mild tones, that I should have "gone so far" on the subject of neutrality. Several persons who have mentioned the speech to members of the Embassy staff or to me have indicated that it is not a bad thing to have the Swiss roused from time to time into taking another look at various aspects of their neutrality.
>
> No government official has spoken to me about the speech and no

press comment on the subject has come to the attention of the Embassy except two articles published in the German and French language organs of the Swiss Workers' Party (Communist): the Vorwaerts and Voix Ouvriére. The articles were not identical but followed closely parallel lines and differed only in detail.

Voix Ouvriére wrote that statements were made about Switzerland and its policy "which no citizen who is concerned about the real independence and freedom of our country could accept."

Vorwaerts added the following: "The talkative Ambassador has to be watched closely and, at the first opportunity, the people must express their opinion regarding neutrality so that the Federal Council cannot keep silent. The flow of words from the Ambassador of the United States of America will also cease."

Possibly no better proof than these articles in the Communist press could be found to indicate that the point of the carefully worded passages about Swiss neutrality and Switzerland's contribution to the defense of the free world had not been missed.

So Frances again hit the ground running, as she had in Brussels. But this time it was "running and gunning—gunning for the bad guys," apparently with the Department's full approval.

Frances reported a subsequent speech to the America Club of Geneva titled, "What Has Been Accomplished 1945-1954," which again contained free world defense arguments. And it was again critiqued by *Vorwaerts:*

Seldom has an official representative of a foreign country in Switzerland delivered such a propaganda speech, praising a policy that runs counter to important interest of our country. And seldom have official representatives rallied in such numbers in order to applaud such a speech.

Of course, the *Vorwarts* editor intended his second sentence as a call to vote those traitorous, applauding representatives out of office, but it doesn't read that way: The representatives liked what she said and told her about it with applause. So Frances forced the cold war onto the Swiss stage of neutrality with surprisingly good reactions.

Frances provided a perspective on her job in a 1954 CBS radio broadcast from Los Angeles. It started out, "This is your Ambassador to Switzerland reporting to you." That should have grabbed some attention, because a woman was talking, and there were only two such ambassadors around, Frances and Clare. At the outset, Frances noted the passage of "another outstanding diplomat, the Honorable Hugh Gibson, who was born in Los Angeles and died in Geneva the previous week." That was a heartfelt gesture. She then described the Swiss government, Swiss commerce, and getting to know the place:

> It is not enough for an Ambassador to sit in the capitol of Bern. It is necessary to get out and know the different sections of the country and the people who live in them.

There it is again: "Know the country and the people in it." Mark those words because they are precisely the instructions Jack Kennedy would relay to all his ambassadors, including Frances after her appointment to Ceylon in 1961. Not only that but it was a hallmark of her success as an ambassador for the next twelve years. To illustrate that point, here are photos of Frances getting to know the place—intimately.

Left: Frances inspecting a Swiss watch, no date (unknown source.)

Right: Frances inspecting the Thun Swiss Cheese Union, August 4, 1954
(unknown source.)

The Department picked up on this theme as part of their press release announcing Frances' Career Service Award in 1962:

> Miss Willis traveled through every canton in Switzerland, getting to know the people of the country. Her friendliness, straight-forward manner and dedication to her job soon earned her the liking and respect of the Swiss nation.

The Swiss Watch Tariff Dispute

Frances introduced the 1954 Swiss watch tariff dispute at the end of her 1954 CBS radio broadcast, then updated it in a 1955 TV interview with Edward R. Murrow. Subsequently, she recapitulated it in a 1970 letter to the Department in reply to their Questionnaire on the Stimulation of Creativity, and in a 1971 talk recorded in the *Stanford Alumni Association* magazine. These sources are combined to yield a full story, starting with a tidy summary from that 1954 CBS radio talk, right in the middle of the dispute:

> I scarcely need to report to you that when our President announced on July 28, 1954, that under the escape clause on our trade agreement with Switzerland he was increasing by 50% the duties on watches with from 7 to 17 jewels, this action was unpopular [with the Swiss] and I believe misunderstood.
>
> The escape clause in our trade agreements may be invoked and duties raised only if injury to the domestic industry has been proved. In extensive testimony before the Tariff Commission earlier this year, the American watch manufacturers had indicated that Swiss watches were being imported into the United States in such quantities that the domestic producers were having difficulty competing.[72] It was brought out that the number of workers employed in the jeweled watch industry in this country had dropped in six years from more than 10,000 to just over 4,000.[73]
>
> The President followed the recommendation of the Tariff Commission

---

[72] By 1953 the Swiss had captured about 85% of the U.S. market for jeweled movements.

[73] In contrast, the Swiss employed over 60,000 workers, making it the second largest industry in Switzerland.

and increased the duties by half again what they had previously been. In announcing his decision, the President pointed out that [based on an earlier Office of Defense Mobilization study] it would give us, in times of national emergency, the mobilization base required in an essential sector of American production, that is the watch industry.

[The watch industry was essential] because watch makers must be highly skilled, and I am told it takes years to become a really skilled watchmaker. Once trained, they have a skill, which is not equaled in any other industry.

I am not very mechanically minded and I admit I have difficulty comprehending it when I am told that in making the very fine watches they work to tolerances of a thousandth of an inch. I can, however, understand the story about the order that was sent by a firm needing some tiny screws to a watch manufacturer. The firm asked if the watch-maker could supply 10,000 screws like the sample enclosed and sent along six screws. The watch manufacturer replied that he could produce the screws but before undertaking the job would have to know which of the six screws the firm wanted copied.

My job obviously was to explain the background of the President's action to the Swiss.

Frances went on to report her efforts to date, including the national security argument and how that would help withstand Communism; not really abandoning a foremost principle of our foreign economic policy; taking occasional exception to the liberalization of trade, such as the Swiss did in protecting their agriculture; and the need to maintain good will between countries. She hoped that the Swiss would understand, especially because they would "still be selling 70 to 75 percent of all watches in the United States [15 to 16 million]." Then Frances said she was going to eat her Christmas turkey with her family in Redlands and return to Switzerland.

Now what Frances did not say just jumps out of the talk: U.S. watchmakers like Bulova and Elgin were getting clobbered by Swiss watchmakers, because Swiss watches were much better—not cheaper but better. So they needed relief from that competition and went to the government for help. And they got it in the tariff guise of national security, which would make Swiss watches more expensive.

But the U.S. watchmakers weren't done; now they wanted quotas added to the tariffs because people would still pay more for the better product. And this is where Frances stepped in to say, "Enough is enough," as she reported in her Stanford talk:

> There is one more function I performed as ambassador to which I attached great importance. That was not only keeping my government informed about what was going on in the country but also consulting on what I thought we ought or ought not to do. To illustrate: We increased the duty on watches by 50 percent in 1954. Obviously, this evoked bitter reactions in Switzerland. On the other hand, there was pressure from the U.S. watch industry for action to curtail the importation of watches. I came back to Washington and spent hours consulting on the subject, not only with those in the Department of State but in the Tariff Commission in the Department of Commerce and the Treasury, and in the White House. Those of us who were opposed to any further restrictions, such as a quota, won out, and I went back to Switzerland to convince the Swiss that the increase in duty on watches was not going to reduce the importation into the United States of Swiss watches—and it did not.

Frances provided more details in her Department letter:

> In 1954 after the U.S. raised the duty on watches I argued strongly against the imposition of a quota on the importation of Swiss watches. With the support of the appropriate officers in the Department, including the Swiss desk officer, and of Nelson Rockefeller, who was an adviser of President Eisenhower at that time, the idea was dropped.

So Frances was proficient at marshalling resources to get the job done. "Give a little, get a little," as the old aphorism goes. And that assuaged the Swiss, as the following September 18, 1955, *Los Angeles Times* article, "Ambassador Willis is Popular with Swiss," subtitled "Redlands Envoy Praised for Watch Tariff Work," by Elvira Marquise reported:

> It had also been learned that the Swiss Foreign Office had voiced

appreciation of the ambassador's attitude relative to their side of the problem, and had publicly stated that "Ambassador Willis has judiciously discharged the function of a diplomat to act as a shock absorber," in this case.

However, the American watchmakers did not give up the fight, as Frances' following letter shows:

December 9, 1955

Dear Mr. and Mrs. Bulova:

This is a very difficult letter for me to write, but write it I must.

First, let me say that I am most appreciative of the warm hospitality which you have extended to me during my stay here in New York.[74] My only regret is that because I am overloaded with extra assignments this last week I am unable to visit the plant as I had hoped. Will you please let me do so on my next trip to the United States?

Now for the difficult part of this letter. As you know my Mother, Mr. Bulova, you can understand how I was brought up. Even before I went into the Service the rule was no presents except flowers, books or candy. In returning a gift one always runs the risk of offending the giver but I do hope that you both will understand and I believe you will. One exception always leads to another and therefore since I have been in the Service I have been even stricter than before about observance of the long-established rule. I should love to have the Carlos Primero brandy but cannot bring myself to depart from the precepts which have guided me all these years. You have shown me such great kindness in so many ways and I am counting on your indulgence in this instance to understand.

With renewed good wishes to you both, I am,

Sincerely yours,

/s/ *Frances E. Willis*

Mr. and Mrs. Arde Bulova,
Pierre Hotel,
5th Avenue and 61st Street,
New York, New York

---

[74] Frances was detailed as an advisor to the U.N. at the time, as reported later in this chapter.

Arde Bulova, of course, was president of the Bulova Watch Co., headquartered in New York City. Now Bulova first popped in to meet—and lobby—Frances the day after her ambassadorial appointment in Washington DC. He then visited Switzerland to check out his competition and of course called on the ambassador. Frances in her inimitable entertainment style feted him at the embassy. He probably stayed there, met Belle and was charmed by her.

The watch dispute—likely instigated by Bulova himself—quickly got him the first part of his agenda, tariffs. But the second part, quotas, got rejected by the U.S. Government. Undeterred, he kept fighting, including more lobbying of Frances when she was detailed to the U.N. in New York: inviting her to a factory tour, entertaining her in his Fifth Avenue apartment and then sending her a present of very expensive brandy. And of course, Frances, the straightest of straight arrows, shut that ploy down.

End of that story, except for the following question: Then what happened? Specifically, did those tariffs do any good; did they help save the U.S. watch industry? One answer lies on the Bulova Website, called "Bulova Accutron History." Here is a summary.

In 1952 watchmakers Elgin and Lip introduced battery powered watches, the kind that never needed winding. Bulova was caught with his pants down on that one, and asked his Swedish engineer Max Hetzel, who lived in Biel, Switzerland, to check out these revolutionary things. Max did, and reported that while they didn't have to be wound they weren't any more accurate because they still used the balance-wheel movement. But keep an eye on those new battery powered transistors coupled to a tuning fork oscillator, which could be a lot more accurate.

Bulova—not to be caught sitting again—did, and had Hetzel begin developing a battery powered, oscillator watch in 1952. He made the first prototype in Switzerland in 1955 and completed development in New York in 1959. Bulova then introduced the *Accutron 214* to the public in 1961, and the rest is glorious history. It became a bestseller and the first wristwatch certified for railroad personnel; NASA used it in all their space flights; and President Lyndon Johnson declared it the official *Gift of State*.

In sum, that tariff respite gave Bulova enough breathing room to exploit a totally new technology to counter the Swiss quality edge and get back into the market with the far more accurate Accutron 214. And if he had been given quotas to go with the tariff, he—and the rest of the U.S. watchmakers—probably would have sat back, taken their profits, postponed or even ignored this new technology and gone out of business. Some ultimately did go out of business when U.S. production costs for these watches were undercut first by Japan, then Korea, Taiwan and China. But that's another story.

Department's Reaction

What did the Department think of Frances' work on the Swiss watch dispute—in fact her work to date? Excerpts from a November 14, 1954, despatch in Frances' 123 File from Samuel C. Waugh, Assistant Secretary E (Economic Affairs) to SecState Dulles begins the answer:

> Last Saturday, November 13, I had a 5-hour visit, including a delightful lunch at the residence, with Ambassador Willis. I went to Bern from Geneva at her invitation to talk about the Swiss watch case.
>
> It is extremely difficult to conceive, without first-hand observation, the concern in the political and business circles in Switzerland over the tariff case, followed so closely by the anti-trust suit filed by the Department of Justice [signaling the start of the quota action].
>
> Following the luncheon [we] visited with four Swiss guests: Messers. Hans Schaffner, Head of the Division of Commerce; Jolles, Division of Commerce; de Graffenried, number 3 man in the Political Department; and Dupont, head of Financial Section, Political Department.
>
> The purpose of this memorandum, Sir, is to tell you that, in my estimation, Miss Willis is an Ambassador par excellence. She has knowledge, courage, poise and charm. From many reports received during my week in Switzerland it can be reported that she has represented our government under particularly trying circumstances with distinction.

That was followed a few months later by this March 11, 1955, despatch to SecState Dulles from Counsel General Gowen in Geneva:

> Ambassador Willis' visit to Geneva was an outstanding success. She was welcomed most cordially by her very many Swiss and American friends. When at the huge official luncheon preceding the opening of the international automobile show she took her seat at the right of

the president of Switzerland and received the most enthusiastic and prolonged applause. Again when Ambassador Willis arrived at the international automobile show for the official inauguration by the President of Switzerland she was very warmly applauded by the public and the attending officials.

These despatches lead directly to the last Efficiency Report in Frances' dossier, dated June 13, 1955. It was written by William B. Dunham, Officer-in-Charge, Swiss-Benelux Affairs and reviewed by William R. Tyler, Deputy Director, Office of Western European Affairs. In fact, this report is the last of all the personnel evaluation reports—Annual Efficiency, Inspector's Efficiency, Efficiency Rating and that ominous Rating Sheet—in her dossier.

Well, Dunham's report was one notch shy of perfect. He gave her the usual overall rating of Outstanding, and the usual language marks. And then he gave her thirty 6's and one 5 in the Duties Performed and Factor Analysis Sections. The 5 was for Sense of Humor!

While the box checking exercise is important, the Summary Comments and Recommendations Section is always the heart of the matter, which is summarized as follows:

This report is based on continuous and close knowledge in the Department of Ambassador Willis' work in Bern, as well as on personal acquaintance with her, and is limited only to the extent that there has been no opportunity for direct observation of her performance at her post.

Miss Willis is the most outstanding of the career women in the Foreign Service and one of the Service's most highly-regarded officers. Although the appointment of a woman as U.S. Ambassador caused some misgivings in Switzerland, Miss Willis' outstanding professional and personal qualities quickly won the respect and admiration of the Swiss officials and public alike.

Ambassador Willis' performance and her contribution to U.S.–Swiss relations must be judged against the background of the serious difficulties relating to the watch industry which began with the events leading up to the raising of the U.S. tariff on watches in 1954 and which have continued up to the present time. These difficulties, in addition to being complex, have caused highly emotional public reactions in the U.S., Switzerland and elsewhere and have placed the heaviest strain on U.S.-Swiss relations since the end of the war. In this delicate situation, much greater damage to U.S.-Swiss relations could have resulted from less competent handling of the many complexities involved and is a tribute to Miss Willis' skill that such damage as occurred was held to the barest minimum. She has represented U.S. policies and interest vigorously and ably, but at the same time, she has succeeded in retaining for the United States and herself an enviable reputation with the Swiss, which consistently bring her, as the U.S. Ambassador, unusually warm and friendly acclaim on her frequent public appearances.

The second paragraph marks the end of all gender bias events in Frances' career. Then the usual accolades followed: wide experience ...highly skilled ...unusually perceptive ...marked energy, initiative and resourcefulness ...thorough knowledge and understanding of all matters ...conscientious, hard worker, meticulous craftsman ...[but] seems occasionally to do too much herself. Dunham's review finished with:

> The effective manner in which she has worked with officials at the highest level both here and in Switzerland, particularly with respect to the complex legal, economic, business and policy aspects of the various U.S.-Swiss watch problems, is symptomatic of the outstanding personal and professional qualities which have made her performance as an Ambassador a credit not only to herself, but also to the women of the Foreign Service, whom she represents, and to the Service itself.

Gowen's applause kudos was translated by Dunham into his "unusually warm and friendly acclaim" comment at the end of the third paragraph, while Waugh, who was about two levels up the Foreign Service ladder from Dunham, rated a full paragraph for his Swiss watch comments. Thus Dunham had plenty of incentive—and ammunition—to write his near perfect report. But the sense of humor mark is a surprise.

Frances provided the reason in a rare bulletin to the family dated July 10, 1955, rare because she often relied on Belle to send news:

Life is wonderful, only I have far too much to do. It is all very well to say that an ambassador should pass on the unimportant things to others to do and concentrate on the important things. I remember that but in an office when little things are done badly on a big scale, that can easily counteract some of the effectiveness of work in the important fields. In other words I wish I could run my office as easily as I run my house.

The household staff came through the past week or ten days with flying colors: two cocktail parties of seventy to a hundred, plus over five hundred for the Fourth of July, plus three sets of house guests who overlapped, and two of them were there on the Fourth and that meant having a sit down dinner served in place. There were of course several small dinners and luncheons of from six to twelve all the time the guests were there.

This weekend I simply signed off and said I would not have house guests no matter who turned up. The man who stayed a week is the Chief of the Swiss Benelux Division in the Department of State so he required special attention.

But before the Dunham markdown is resolved, Perts will illustrate Frances travails. Frances certainly didn't keep a ladder in her office, but her engagement schedule was probably as long.

"Quo Vadis?" from M. C. Perts' 1924 book.

Now to Dunham. That one-week visitor around July 4 was of course William B. Dunham, who wrote that last Efficiency Report on Frances. The following postulated scenario might sort things out: Dunham submitted a perfect report on Frances—with all 6's—to the astonishment of his boss, William Tyler, who then must have said,

How can you give her a perfect review when you have not observed her performance in situ? If you insist on sticking with those numbers, get your butt over there and see if she is all that good.

So Dunham did, arriving just a few weeks after he had submitted his perfect report. Frances didn't know that he was there to justify the report, because Dunham checked "No" in the box asking if the report was discussed with the officer rated. And, of course, he couldn't tell her why he was there. That would have been exceedingly awkward. But Dunham likely did change the report: He reduced the rating for Sense of Humor because Frances decided that Dunham was overstaying his visit and got a bit short with him. It sounded like that from her letter.

Dunham picked up the "do-it-myself" family trait, just as Frances had in her July letter. "There's just no helping it," as Frances and Belle would say. H. Freeman Matthews, Jr. made a similar—but more positive—observation about this obsession in a 1993 oral interview with Charles Kennedy:[75]

As far as Frances Willis was concerned, any piece of paper that came to us from the Embassy in Bern even if it was a letter having to do with visas (because Bern didn't issue any visas, and we did), Frances Willis would have seen it. She kept very close track of everything.

Matthews was Frances' boss' boss (EUR) during the last part of her tour in Washington DC and wrote one of her excellent Efficiency Reports. He also appeared in a photo with Roosevelt, Stettinius, Hopkins and four others on the cruiser USS Quincy in Egypt at the 1945 Yalta Conference, which puts him at the top of the FSO heap.

So the small stuff does count—as long as it doesn't consume you. It will fully

---

[75] Enclosed by Marilyn Bentley from the ADST-DACOR Office when she provided their publication, *A Brief History of United States Diplomacy*, with the author's thanks.

play out in the Frances and Julia chapter. But the bottom line is clear: There's no need for further evaluations after this one.

Onions and Speeches

Next comes the onion caper. Vic Pollard, a *Redlands Daily Facts* reporter, triggered the story in his well researched, March 31, 1965, article, "Frances Willis comes home to the Redlands she loves:"

> Her first ambassadorial assignment, to Switzerland in 1953, was a difficult one. Despite the unconventionality of her position, reports indicated she conquered the hearts of the conservative, conventional Swiss.
>
> A Swiss friend once told an American reporter that Miss Willis won the affection of the people of Berne when she appeared in the market place alongside Swiss housewives to buy a supply of onions for her household.

Yet again, Belle provided the onion details from an article and photo pasted in her scrapbook. The press article was written by Richard S. Simons of *The Indianapolis Star Magazine*, no date but circa 1953. Simons was visiting "Berne," Switzerland, from Berne, Indiana—a "Hoosier Bernese" as he called himself. He was being given a private walking tour of the outdoor vegetable, flower and meat markets on the Bundesgasse by Walter H. Rubli, manager of the Swiss Official Enquiry Office. Simons quoted Rubli:

> "On the last Monday in November we have an onion market. There are onions everywhere—baskets of onions, strings of onions, onion bread, onion cakes, roast sausage with onions, onion salad." He lifted his arms in mock despair. "The whole town smells terrible."
>
> Originally the onion market gave the Bernese a last chance to lay in a winter's supply of vegetables. But today it is a festival, the Berne version of the Marti Gras, complete with amusements, parades and show booths.
>
> Rubli's assistant, O. Fetzer, described his shock at first seeing the onion market spread out in front of the [Swiss Federal] Palace.
>
> "It would be like selling vegetables in front of your White House," he explained. "But when I asked about it the Bernese told me that the

onion market had been there for 500 years but the Palace had been there only since 1848, so they could see no reason [to stop]."

Berne's 500-year-old onion market has become a festival occasion. Shopper is American Ambassador Frances Willis.

Frances caught shopping at the Berne onion festival, circa 1953 (unknown source.)

The photo had no credit or date. It was probably this photo published in one of the Berne newspapers that caused an affectionate stir among the Swiss. Clearly, little gestures count in this business. Pollard also quoted that anonymous "at ease" comment again:

> It was this warm direct style, which made her a success wherever she went. One of her men colleagues once said, "Miss Willis can put a roomful of men at ease the minute she starts to talk."

Speaking of speeches, Consul General Howard Donovan in Zurich sent the following despatch to the Department: "Lecture by Ambassador Willis at Zurich," dated July 8, 1955, now in her 123 File:

> The Swiss Institute of International Studies of Zurich, in coopera- tion with the Swiss-British Society and the Swiss-American Society for

Cultural Relations arranged for a series of six lectures to be given at the University of Zurich during the summer term, 1955. The subject of each lecture was "The Way of Life of the English-Speaking Nations."

I have attended only two of the lectures, the one delivered by Ambassador Willis and the other by the British Ambassador, Sir Lionel Henry Lamb. The Department will be interested to know that the American Ambassador's lecture had twice as large an audience as did that of the British Ambassador. While I did not attend the lectures on Scotland and the South African Union, I am advised by friends who did attend that the same situation obtained with respect to the size of the audience.

The American Ambassador's speech has attracted a great deal of favorable comment in Zurich. The Swiss Friends of the USA, a Zurich organization which is well known to the Department, requested 450 copies through the Consulate General in order that each member of SFUSA would have the opportunity of reading it. The Union Bank of Switzerland also requested several copies and various Swiss residents of Zurich have commented on the speech to me.

I do not recall any public address made in Zurich by an Ambassador of any country which has received so much favorable publicity and comment.

The lecture, also in her 123 File, was a long, entertaining look at life in America, which should please the Chamber of Commerce. Here is a summary.

Frances began by saying that most Europeans have a very limited perspective of America because those who visit only stay a short time—not nearly enough time to appreciate the vastness, diversity and beauty of the place. So they return home to report only the highlights, such as New York City skyscrapers, Washington DC monuments and museums and maybe San Francisco hills and cable cars.

Other Europeans settle in America, which gives them enough time to develop the full perspective. But they seldom return to their homeland to relay that perspective because intercontinental travel is expensive. Then Frances described what the European tourists missed, things like the vast interior of America with it millions of acres of agriculture, its interlocking roads, and massive coal, textile, steel, automobile and airplane factories. Not only that, but this extended enterprise was developed and manned by immigrants and children of immigrants, mostly from Europe. She added a description of the spectacular scenery to be had along the way, including Yellowstone, Yosemite and the Grand Canyon.

She also described the cultural, political and religious diversity existing in most communities, especially the larger ones. That is a two-edged sword, which could cause tension and animosity within a community, but with proper laws and education could engender tolerance, which would lead to great social and intellectual progress.

Conference Work

In May, 1954, Secretary of State John Foster Dulles visited Geneva to attend a Foreign Minister's Conference. Of course, Frances was there to assist him diplomatically and logistically, as the next photo suggests.

Frances with Mr. and Mrs. Dulles, Geneva, May 28, 1954 (unknown source.)

This press photo was taken near the end of the Geneva conference showing intense conversation, with Secret Service agents lurking directly behind. The vigorous walker on the right is not identified, but appears to be an agent on his way up to shoo away the photographer. There seems to be a special bond developing between Dulles and Frances.

The conference was described in a U.S. Information Service (USIS) press release that found its way into a family scrapbook.

The conference on Asiatic questions opened at the Palais des Nations, Geneva, on April 26, 1954. It had been convened by the Foreign Ministers of the United States [Dulles], Great Britain [Eden], France [Bidault] and the Soviet Union [probably Molotov].

During the first part of the conference sixteen allied and three Communist countries confronted each other in an effort to find a solution to the Korean problem. The second phase of the conference got under way on May 8 with discussions on Indo-China at which the four powers, the three Associated States, Communist China and the Communist Vietminh regime are taking part.[76]

Then in July, 1955, Frances stepped into the limelight as the only woman diplomat invited to the Big 4 Summit Conference in Geneva. The *Los Angeles Times* picked up the story from the *NY Herald Tribune News Service*, extracted as follows:

ONLY ONE WOMAN AT BIG PARTY

GENEVA — Miss Frances E. Willis, American envoy to Switzerland was the only woman present at the most formal and glittering dinner party of the summit conference. The quiet-spoken ambassador circulated among some 40 men at Geneva's beautiful Eynard Palace, at one of the most impressive diplomatic banquets in modern history...

Then when President Eisenhower landed at Geneva's airport last Saturday, Miss Willis was the first person to [greet him]. This was a matter of diplomatic protocol in order to introduce him to his Swiss host...

From the airport, she drove with the President to show him the villa that was arranged for him on the shores of Lake Geneva. The next morning she sat in the Presidential pew at the American Church and then returned to Bern, the Swiss capital. She came back to Geneva this

---

[76] With the final result: a Korean cease-fire and the French quitting Vietnam. But the U.S. couldn't stand the vacuum, so filled Vietnam with 55,000 dead soldiers starting ten years later.

afternoon for the gala dinner and will remain here until the President
leaves this weekend.

Frances and the Chief at his villa on Lake Geneva (courtesy U.S. Government.)

*Frances with Swiss President Petitpierre and President Eisenhower at the "gala
dinner" (courtesy US Government.)*

Frances is translating (complete with gesticulations) since Petitpierre's English was non-existent and Ike's French wasn't much better. Frances reported more details in her July 31 letter:

> As I was not a member of our delegation at the Geneva Conference I did not stay down all the time—had work to do here [Berne]. The only dinner which all four delegations attended simultaneously was the one given by the Swiss government. The representatives of the four countries in Switzerland were also invited and that was how I got in. I sat next to Marshal Zoukov—or Zukov. Interpreters sat behind each of the Russians and the one behind the Marshal was a Swiss who did a beautiful job interpreting very smoothly and rapidly. The Marshal and I had an animated conversation but nothing political.
>
> The next day the Eisenhowers had a lunch at the "Geneva White House" for President and Mme. Petitpierre and I worked hard at that, because Mrs. E. speaks no French and President P. understands not one word of English and I was on the other side of him.
>
> Saturday July 23 was a hectic day but finally I made it about 4:30 to the Palais des Nations where the meetings took place. Mr. Dulles was planning to leave at 5:30 and I was to drive to the airport with him. Well he didn't as they had another session at 6:30—the winder-upper—and I just went in with our delegation and sat with our advisers. All very interesting. We made a dash for it as soon as the meeting was over, as the Secretary had to get off before the President. Then I stayed at the airport to see the President off. Came back to Bern the same night.

And that was that—yet again. Here was a perfect opportunity for Frances to report on one of the principal antagonists of the Cold War, and all she said was "animated conversation but nothing political," followed by "All very interesting."

Fortunately, Selwa Roosevelt of the *Washington DC Evening Star* (and wife of Archie Roosevelt, Jr., grandson of Teddy Roosevelt) provided more details in a September 14, 1955, interview with Frances in her "Diplomatically Speaking" column:

> The next day the Swiss papers reported that [Frances] spent the evening teaching the Russian how to speak French. "That's not what

happened at all," she laughed. "It was just like any other dinner conversation. We discussed such things as Marshall Zhukov's daughters. He asked me if I liked to ride horseback. He was a very direct, forthright person, with a good sense of humor and the simplicity of a great man."

Both Ike and Dulles must have liked what they saw during the conference, because on July 20, 1955, Frances was promoted to the class of career minister, following her nomination a week earlier. A feature story, "Career Ambassadors," by Donna Miles on the State Department's Website, February-March, 2000, gives a brief description of the selection process for a career minister:

> Career Minister board proceedings are closely guarded, and findings and recommendations are submitted to the Secretary for nomination to the President. Nominations require confirmation by the Senate and must be attested by the President.

Miles didn't say what the selection criteria were or how often the selection boards met, but in Frances' case the process was probably initiated by Dulles. However it happened, her selection came pretty quickly: four years after she made FSO-1, and just two years after appointment as ambassador. She was clearly on a roll and making her mark with good, dedicated work. The selection criteria for career ambassador were spelled out in much greater detail in this article, which will be covered in the Ceylon chapter.

Running the Embassy

Frances, in an April 24, 1956, response to a letter from Loy Henderson, Deputy Undersecretary for Administration, reported how she ran the embassy:[77]

Dear Loy:
Your letter of April 13, 1956 concerning the responsibilities of Chiefs

---

[77] This letter is the first known communication between Frances and Loy Henderson, who subsequently became good friends. Loy was appointed to the post in 1955 after chief of mission assignments to Iraq, India, Nepal and Iran. He was the first FSO (in a group of four) to be appointed career ambassador, three weeks after he wrote his letter to Frances.

of Mission for coordinating the total U.S. effort at the country level has been given careful attention.

Here in Switzerland, we have one of the few small American Embassies which still exist. At the present time, the total officer staff in Bern consists of 11 Foreign Service Officers, 3 Attachés with FSS [Foreign Service Staff] ratings, 2 Army officers, and 3 Air officers. The Information Program is conducted by a single Foreign Service Officer. There are no peripheral activities connected with the Embassy. There is no Mutual Security Program, no MAAG, and no technical assistance program. Switzerland does not belong to the United Nations or the Council of Europe.

Under the circumstances our problems of coordination are relatively simple. We have weekly staff meetings attended by the heads of all segments of the Embassy, non-Department of State as well as Department of State. Furthermore with such a small group it is possible to work together on a daily basis. Any officer of the Embassy can discuss his work or any other problems with me any day of the week.

Obviously I try to leave the supervision of the day to day operations of the Embassy to the Counselor, with whom I am in contact many times a day. The work is not only coordinated, it is integrated. Different segments of the Embassy cooperate in obtaining information and preparing reports. There is no duplication except insofar as the end-users in Washington desire it.

With our small staff our problem is more often to make sure that nothing useful is left undone and that we do stretch our activities to cover all essential fields and developments. We cannot afford the luxury of overlapping reports and we must pool our resources in order to meet requirements.

The coordination of the work in the three constituent posts in Switzerland is primarily the task of the Counselor of Embassy under my immediate supervision. In the case of Consulate General in Zurich and the Consulate in Basel, this supervision presents no great problem. The combined office of the Resident Delegation to International Organizations and the Consulate General in Geneva is a far more complex matter.

Frances then wrestled with this complex administrative matter using her two available officers, and concluded they just couldn't do it; so Geneva should become administratively independent. And she understood that as soon as funds and personnel were made available it would be. Then she got to the issue of bureaucracy:

> Foreign Service Circular No. 171 of March 26, 1956 called for a resubmission by Foreign Service Officers of personal history data on a new form. It is this continuous encroachment on the time of officers to deal with administrative matters that makes the accomplishment of all substantive tasks increasingly difficult. In February of this year, Principal Officers at consular posts were called upon to submit extensive descriptions of their positions, thus duplicating and adding to information already on file in the Department in the position descriptions of these officers. There appears to be no end to the administrative paper work. This may not be the place at which this administrative encroachment should be pointed out. If, however, Chiefs of Mission are expected to be the interpreters of American foreign policy to the government and to the people of the country where they are stationed and to carry out the representational functions imposed upon them, not only with relation to the people of the country and their diplomatic colleagues but to American travelers as well, some relief from the administrative burden should be sought.
>
> Sincerely yours,
FEW

In short, we've got more important things to do, so please call off your pack of administrators. This is a first in the annals of Frances' career: a formal criticism of her beloved Foreign Service, and an unsolicited one at that. But that sort of license comes with the turf, and if used sparingly is an effective method of cleaning a clearly cluttered command.[78]

---

[78] Frances' comments motivated the author to critique the near-useless personnel description and evaluation forms that popped up after WW II.

Nieces and Nephews

Frances, now ensconced in her lofty position, began to entertain family visitors, starting in July, 1955, when the author showed up at the embassy—unannounced. He was on special leave from his senior midshipman cruise on the USS Wisconsin, an Iowa-class battleship, which had put in to Edinburgh for a one-week port call. He was warmly received by both Frances and Belle and royally entertained for five days. Besides the company, he found the greatest contrast between battleship and embassy living was room, board, privacy and leisure. And that pretty much covered the waterfront, as the U.S. Navy says.

Frances must have also enjoyed that visit, because a few months later she invited her niece and namesake Frances Vaughan, who had graduated from Stanford University in December, 1956, to be her social secretary for about a year. Frances Vaughan reported highlights of that year, which are extracted as follows, with "Frances" = Frances Willis and "I" = Frances Vaughan.

When I first arrived Frances gave me several books about Switzerland to read and engaged a French tutor to polish my French. I became fairly fluent, at least enough to carry on a polite conversation at diplomatic receptions. These receptions were rather a chore, as it meant standing in a reception line, being formally introduced to everyone as the ambassador's niece, and then cut loose to find my way around for conversation with people whose names and positions I was supposed to have memorized. I remember one conversation in French with a Russian diplomat and since neither of us was very fluent, it was rather tedious. I also remember being quizzed by a young Indian diplomat on what I had learned at the university [Stanford]. It seemed clear that he thought my education was greatly inferior to the one he had received at Oxford.

Although I was somewhat familiar with diplomatic life from growing up in Chile when my father, Freddie Vaughan, was attached to the British Embassy, I still had a lot to learn about the nuances and subtleties of life at the top. My job was essentially that of social secretary. I sometimes helped with such tasks as stuffing and addressing envelopes and invitations and writing thank you notes, but much of my time was spent as a tour guide with the endless stream of visiting dignitaries who expected to be treated royally, forgetting that Frances had work do at the office every day. In some ways I filled the role of "ambassador's wife." I was given an allowance, but I was not paid a salary.

Frances certainly went out of her way to train me and to keep me busy. Sometimes I was included in invitations to formal dinners at other embassies. One of the highlights was a wonderful dinner at the Indian Embassy where the tables were all outdoors in a beautiful garden setting and the food was superb.

Frances also took me on trips to Germany, Austria, Italy and Yugoslavia. These were sometimes vacations, sometimes combined with business, and always a delight. I also traveled to Italy with friends from California and to Spain with a woman friend from the embassy staff. I have wonderful memories of the cruise that Frances and I took from Venice to Dubrovnik and the beautiful place we stayed on the Adriatic.

Sometime in May I finally met a young man I really liked, who was not intimidated by the embassy. He was a German prince who came to Switzerland on business, and invited me to visit him in Germany. To my surprise, Frances let me go and even lent me one of her hats to wear on the train, which she thought was appropriate. Before I went, however, she made me read about his ancestors and his family in the encyclopedia. I had a wonderful time and the relationship made me long to be out from under weight of all the formalities of embassy life. We would see each other from time to time and always had fun.

The year I spent in Switzerland with Frances was a wonderful experience. I developed a long lasting fondness for the country and the people. I could not have asked for a more thorough educational experience. One thing I learned is that no matter what their station or title, people may be kind, compassionate and fun loving or cold and difficult. What seems glamorous from a distance becomes ordinary when you get close.

My overall impression of Frances was that she was a person of impeccable integrity, always conscientious and duty bound. She lived her ideal of service to her country with extraordinary grace and talent. She earned the respect of those who worked with her and the admiration of those who knew her. I don't think she could have done what she did if she had married. Although she had good friends and was widely held in high regard, I think she paid a price in not being married. I never heard her talk about feelings, only about what should be done and her willingness to do it. She expected no less of others, and she ran a tight ship. What she did, she did very well.

United Nations Duty

Then another first in Frances' career: this time a letter from the Department asking—not commanding—Frances to do something. The letter is dated August 10, 1955, and marked *OFFICIAL—INFORMAL—PERSONAL* from her immediate boss, Walworth Barbour, Deputy Assistant Secretary for European (EUR) Affairs and later Ambassador to Israel for twelve years:

Dear Frances,

We have been asked to provide a top level officer of ambassadorial rank to serve as adviser on the U.S. delegation to the Tenth U.N. General Assembly session which opens in New York in September, and I am writing to seek to persuade you to accept the assignment.

The job is principally one of general liaison with other delegations on one of the seven major working committees and will necessarily also involve political work within the delegation on the many questions on the agenda that particularly involve European countries or affect our relations with them...

Since the questions on the 70-odd item agenda range from disarmament to New Guinea, from east-west trade to South Africa's apartheid policy, I'm sure you would find the assignment challenging and interesting. It is, needless to say, the universal opinion around here that you would be ideal for it...

The letter is signed *Wally*, with the following handwritten PS:

I sincerely hope you can take this on. It is of considerable importance to EUR and I would be much relieved to know it will be in your capable hands.

So Frances accepted the U.N. Adviser assignment in New York. The session closed sometime in December; then Belle flew to New York and with Frances on to Redlands for Christmas and a reunion with the family. Secretary Dulles wrote Frances a nice note of "appreciation for your outstanding service as a senior advisor" but didn't say what her service was. And neither did Frances in her now infrequent bulletins. So her contributions are lost.

Incidentally, Henry Cabot Lodge, Jr. was U.S. Ambassador to the U.N. at the time, so Henry probably reported her good work to Dulles. But working with Lodge, Jr. should have been stressing for Frances because she didn't much like his grand-daddy, ever since Lodge-the-first trashed her hero, President Wilson, who was orchestrating U.S. entry into the League of Nations back in 1919. (Lodge won that battle of course.)

But Frances harbored no grudges, as Henry's March 2, 1956, letter from Paris shows:

> My dear Miss Willis,
>
> You are very kind to write to me to suggest that I stop in Bern during my all too short visit to Switzerland. I would have very much enjoyed doing so, but, unfortunately, the exigencies of my tour did not permit it. I am sorry because I am much interested in Switzerland, and, in particular, it would have given my wife and me great pleasure to see you again.
>
> It was kind of you to say what you did about enjoying your work in New York. Let me say in reply that you were a real tower of strength and that your sound judgment and willingness to take responsibility were a great help to me.
>
> Very sincerely yours,
> /s/ Henry Cabot Lodge, Jr.

Clearly, nothing will stand between old wounds and the diplomatic work-at-hand with those warriors. In fact Henry, Jr. likely never knew that Frances had a problem with Lodge-the-first. Frances certainly wouldn't have told him—just not done in these diplomatic circles.

More VIP Services

Throughout her tour in Switzerland Frances reported people visiting the embassy but with few details. This section fills in some of those details. First is an excerpt from Chief Justice Earl Warren's hand-written letter accepting Frances' invitation to stay at the embassy.

SUPREME COURT OF THE UNITED STATES
WASHINGTON 25, D. C.

CHAMBERS OF
THE CHIEF JUSTICE
July 14, 1956

Dear Miss Willis:

It was generous of you to invite us to the Embassy for the night of July twenty fourth. We are happy to accept and we look forward with pleasure to the occasion. It will also be a pleasure to see something of the Capital City of this lovely country...

We will all look forward to our visit with you and will be happy to meet the President of Switzerland and his wife.

This is a delightful spot and we are enjoying it immensely.

Sincerely,
/s/ Earl Warren

Warren must have misplaced Frances' letter telling him the president's name and didn't have his executive assistant nearby to find out. But he did manage to bring his official letterhead along.

Earl Warren was the fourteenth Chief Justice of the U.S. Supreme Court, appointed by Eisenhower in 1953, retiring in 1969. His reign established the liberal court legacy that conservative politicians have been trying to undo for the last forty years, starting with the 1954 Brown vs. Topeka board of Education school desegregation decision. And the irony of it is that Warren was a Republican all his life—just one of those centrist types who acted too much like a liberal. Unfortunately, Belle, an unreconstructed Southerner, chose to remain in her room for his visit.

Now to the other end of the celebrity spectrum with the next photo, which suggests that Frances' job wasn't all work: She is greeting Mr. and Mrs. Louis Armstrong. Louie has just given her a gift, which she is holding in her left hand. Frances told her brother Henry that she had invited the entire Armstrong orchestra for dinner and when they arrived, Louie told Frances this was the first time he and his orchestra had ever visited an American embassy. And Bell, true to her Southern convictions (reject the race; accept the individual), joined them for dinner.

*Frances with Mr. and Mrs. Louis Armstrong in Switzerland,
no date (unknown source.)*

At about this time another musician, pianist Arthur Rubenstein, considered the greatest Chopin interpreter of his time and fluent in eight languages, visited the embassy on one of his tours in Europe after WW II. Belle, a casual pianist, attended his reception and after the formal introductions, said to the maestro, "Oh, Mr. Rubenstein, would you play us a tune on the piano?" And before Frances could intervene, Belle slipped her arm into his and, as only a *Memphis Belle* can do, guided him over to the grand piano.

What was the poor guy to do? Play, of course. So he did: waltzes and marches for about five minutes, which just delighted the quickly gathering audience and Belle in particular. After acknowledging the applause, he took Frances aside and said, "Madam Ambassador, your piano needs tuning." Belle was "a live wire," as she liked to say.

A July 18, 1954, article from the Travel Section of the *San Francisco Examiner* titled, "A Teenager in Switzerland," completes the spectrum of visitors.

(Editor's Note: This is the last in a series of articles by thirteen year-old Francie Huffman, a Canton, Ohio school girl who toured eleven European countries. In this article she tells of her experience in Switzerland.)

By Francie Huffman
Written for International News Service

I made a wonderful new friend in Switzerland with the same two first names as I have—she's the American Ambassador. Her name is Frances Elizabeth Willis.

I had lunch at her home in Berne. A butler and a maid [Alberto and Livia Gay] greeted us and took our coats. They led us into the living room. Great windows looked out on flowerbeds that were in bloom. In the distance were the snow-topped mountains. A fire burned in the fireplace. The room was soft and comfortable.

Then Miss Willis walked quietly into the living room. She is tall, slender, graceful, dresses plainly with very little makeup, has her long hair done up neatly, and her face is friendly and sincere.

The lady ambassador's mother was there too. She is eighty years old with sparkling eyes. She joked and talked with us like we were next-door neighbors over for a visit.

Just an hour before our visit to Miss Willis a Berne tourist guide said to us" "You know it's remarkable that in a country where women can't vote, we have a lady American ambassador."

Daddy said: "How do the Swiss people feel about this?" The guide answered, "At first we weren't sure. Now that we know her, she can stay as long as she likes. She's a real lady. She is intelligent. We love her."

When we told Miss Willis what the guide said, she laughed and blushed.

There were four other guests, including the new counselor at the American Embassy in Berne, and his wife.

We sat down to lunch, with Miss Willis at the head of the table. The maid came around with the dishes and we served ourselves. I kept watching Miss Willis to make sure I used the correct silver.

The plates were plain white with a band of gold stars around the edge and the United States government seal set in the band.

Looking from the band to Miss Willis, I was proud to be an American. She was dignified but not stuck-up. Her home was lovely but modest. She was both a good talker and a good listener. She made us feel at home even though she is accustomed to talking with presidents and kings and has a PhD degree.

After dinner Miss Willis took me for a walk in her garden. It was just like she was an older sister or an aunt.

I think I liked my visit with Miss Willis even better than the mountains, although the Alps are very impressive…

Francie continued her article with a description of those mountains and the Swiss trains. She finished with: "I liked Switzerland, but the best part of the visit was meeting an American lady."

Departure Kudos

Following her nomination as Ambassador to Norway on April 9, 1957, Frances started making departure preparations. Her Swiss farewell luncheon was held on April 26 and was reported in a May 6, 1957, despatch titled, "Federal Council's Farewell Luncheon for Ambassador," authored by Anthony Clinton Swezey, Chargé d'affaires a.i., part of which follows.

It is customary for the [Swiss] Federal Council to honor a departing Chief of Mission at a farewell luncheon but in this case the presence of six of the seven Federal Counsellors may be interpreted both as a personal tribute to the Ambassador and as a gesture of courtesy and friendship to the United States.

The cordial tone of the President's remarks, the frankness with which he recognized the existence of occasional differences of view between the United States and Switzerland, and the warmth with which he referred to the community of interest of both countries in the preservation of peace and freedom created an atmosphere of unusual dignity and sincerity on this occasion.

It is believed that the expressions of mutual friendship between the United States and Switzerland voiced on the occasion of the Ambassador's departure go considerably beyond the formal exchange of courtesies at such times and will therefore be of interest to the Department.

16

NORWAY WITH
GUTS AND GRACE

Stateside Action

BEFORE traveling to Oslo in June, 1957, Frances spent the now obligatory time in Washington DC for swearing-in, Department consulting, press
interviews and public appearances.

Secretary of State John Foster Dulles congratulating Frances
(courtesy Department of State.)

For one of the few times in Frances' photo-career Frances is listening, not
talking. Henry Stimson, Secretary of State from 1929 to 1933, is looking over

Dulles' shoulder. Dulles, speaking to the Girls Nation at the State Department auditorium a few weeks later, said:

> Frances Willis is the first woman in this country, and as far as I know, the first woman in any foreign service, to reach the grade of ambassador through working her way up the regular foreign service.

Frances was nominated on April 9 and confirmed on May 20, 1957, following Ike's reelection. Frances' first remarks following her appointment describe a diplomat at work:

> Although this is the second occasion on which I have taken my oath as American Ambassador, I am looking forward to taking up my new duties in Norway with the same eager anticipation I had before going to my first post. Every assignment is a new adventure, but I must say that the privilege of serving as American Ambassador in Oslo is something which exceeded my greatest hopes.
>
> The brief glimpse I had of Norway a few years ago when I was there on a short visit was enough to convince me that I am extremely fortunate. I made my previous visit to Norway because I wanted to make the trip by railroad from Bergen to Oslo which I had heard was one of the most beautiful in the world. I was not disappointed and I look forward to making many more trips throughout Norway by land and sea.[79] My mother and I are planning to sail from New York on the [Norwegian] Bergensfjord on June 7, arriving in Oslo on June 17, just at that most beautiful time of the year. We come with great anticipation of what we are sure <u>will be</u> a most interesting and rewarding life.

Mark those underlined words, because Frances will scold Jack Kubisch, one of her new Ceylon staff members, when he substituted "should be" for "will be" in a similar statement just before both went to Ceylon in 1961. While diplomatic-speak is usually riddled with nuances, there are times when absolute certainty is demanded, and this was one of them.

---

[79] Frances then wrote in, "and possibly by air," probably at the suggestion of someone on the Department's Norway Desk who told her they now have airplanes and more than one airport.

Frances was then invited to be a guest on the TV show, *What's My Line*. Her appearance was reported by Frank and Bill Moore in their June 3, 1957, *Redlands Daily Facts* column, "With a Grain of Salt," extracted as follows:

> By inviting Miss Frances E. Willis of Redlands to appear on "What's My Line?" last evening, the TV program producer succeeded in outwitting the panelists.
>
> The quartette of occupation guessers, in spite of their shrewdness, did not discover that she was the U.S. Ambassador to Norway. They had to be told after they had exhausted their quota of questions.
>
> And no wonder. If you are going to guess what a person's profession may happen to be, you have to have an active awareness that such a profession does exist.
>
> Sure, everyone knows that Clare Boothe Luce was Ambassador to Italy. But they regard that as an exception that proves the rule—the rule that ambassadors are men.
>
> The association of "ambassador" and "women" is not a spontaneous one. That Miss Willis might hold such a position never crossed the minds of the occupation guessers last evening...
>
> The producer accomplished what he set out to do—to choose a person in a profession so rare for a woman that it would baffle the experts.
>
> "I enjoyed it tremendously," Miss Willis said. And so did her many friends back in Redlands, California, who had been watching.

Getting Started in Norway

Just after she arrived in Oslo, Frances was invited to the Eisenhower/Nixon Inaugural Ball in January. She didn't go because the acceptance letter was still with the invitation. In any case, she probably didn't vote for Ike because he ran against one of her heroes, Adlai Stevenson, who among other things had a hand in drawing up the U.N. charter in 1945.

Speaking about Adlai, he popped in to visit Frances on one of his many world trips after failed runs at the presidency. He then wrote Frances a thank you note from Stockholm on July 8, 1957:

My dear Miss Willis:

I am distressed that I went "over the side" so hurriedly that I had no chance to say good-by. Someone seemed to be prodding me to get ashore before we missed our airplane. So, I got ashore—and then waited for a half hour for the others!

I don't feel that I could have told you properly how much we enjoyed the evening at your house and what a warm and friendly atmosphere we found in your Embassy. Moreover, I heard the same feeling expressed in many ways more than once while I was in Norway.

I think, having traveled so much, I know something of the imposition of visitors and I am perhaps the foremost offender. But I never imposed with less anguish than I did on you! You were most kind to us, and Mrs. Field and the young people share my gratitude.

I hope you will pay my most affectionate respects to your Mother. If I had a disappointment that evening, it was that I had so little time to talk to that enchanting "senior citizen," as the sociologists say.

With my esteem, thanks and warm regards,

Cordially yours,

/s/ Adlai E. Stevenson

"Mrs. Field and the young people" remain unidentified, but it appears that he was escorting the group, probably from Illinois because he was its governor before running for president. Except for the tortured salutation—not quite familiar enough for "Frances," yet too familiar for "Ambassador"—that was a "personal letter," as his sociologist would also say. His writing style matched his speaking style, which has been classed in a league with Winston Churchill.[80] John Kennedy appointed Adlai Ambassador to the U.N. in 1961. Frances did duty at the U.N. at the end of her Norway tour in 1960, so just missed serving with him. Then he died of a heart attack on the steps of the U.N. in 1965.

After settling in Oslo, Frances began her now typical visits to other cities, starting with Bergen. She gave one formal and four informal speeches, which were reported by William R. Auman, U.S. Embassy Public Affairs Officer, to be well received by officials, citizens and the press. Her formal speech was similar to

---

[80] Probably the best Stevenson story happened during one of his stem-winding campaign speeches. Someone in the crowd shouted out, "You have the vote of all thinking Americans!" Stevenson shot back, "Not enough; I need a majority."

one she had used in Switzerland with good effect. As a result, she gave it many times after she discovered it captured the audience's attention. Not only that but she had it refined and fully memorized by now.

Foreign Languages and the Ugly American

About this time Frances' foreign language skills came under intense scrutiny by the Department via four intimidating language proficiency forms. In fact, eleven such forms populated her dossier, spanning the period 1956 to 1962, along with a telegram and a letter. The telegram of February 20, 1958, requires special attention, because Frances sent it "PRIORITY" directly to SecState:

> Arrived Oslo June 1957 with no knowledge of Norwegian language but have taken lessons regularly. Conducted conversation February 11 on subject of visit to Minnesota with Prime Minister, who speaks no English, in Norwegian with some help from interpreter. Reading knowledge of Norwegian fair. I write and speak fluent French and have good command of Spanish although I lack practice since last assignment to Spanish speaking country which ended 1944.
> WILLIS

A *PRIORITY* stamp means that the despatch is important, and must be sent before all routine and deferred traffic. It's also clear that Frances' telegram was in response to a Department directive to all missions that at least the ambassador report his language proficiency—and quickly.

The trigger to this exercise must have been the 1958 novel, *The Ugly American* by William J. Lederer and Eugene Burdick, which detailed why American diplomacy was failing in Southeast Asia and why Communism was succeeding. As a fall-out, both the U.S. press and Congress put great pressure on the Department to show that their FSO's in the field were better than that ugly archetype. Consequently SecState wanted to know "right now" which foreign languages, particularly in-country foreign languages, chiefs of mission could speak. Thus Frances' emphasis was on Norwegian, and her answer must have helped their case.

At this point, Graham Stewart, Frances' old Stanford political science professor, reentered her world. He took exception to the book in his article,

"Stanford's Fair American," in the June/July, 1959 *Stanford Review*, with Frances as Exhibit A for the defense. Stewart started out:

> One of the authors is Eugene Burdick, a Stanford man and former student of mine. Some of the incidents related in this work of fiction are drawn from actual happenings. But the average reader, who has little knowledge of the Foreign Service or its functions, is apt to fall into two traps. He is likely to think that The Ugly American is typical rather than a carefully drawn picture of the worst that happens; and he is likely to hold State responsible for all mistakes when in fact there are other independent public and private agencies in the field. (Most of the actual cases Burdick used were the doing of these agencies, over which State has no control.)[81]

Then Stewart spent the rest of his article on Frances, the "Fair American," and her accomplishments at each post in her career, including stumping the *What's My Line* panel. The only problem was that he recited some events from memory, which tends to embellish facts with age. For example, Graham said Frances "had passed the French and German examinations for her doctorate." The French part was correct, but Frances audited just three German courses at Stanford. She did claim a reading knowledge of German on her Foreign Service application and that almost cost her a passing grade on the oral exams as reported in Foreign Service School chapter.

Stewart then said Frances "made a valiant attempt to learn Finnish, but she was not to have enough time to gain complete mastery." Frances was advised not to learn Finnish—and she didn't, as she will report shortly. Finally Stewart claimed Frances "was a prominent figure in the Summit Conference at Geneva in July of 1955." He then cited the photo of Eisenhower, Petitpierre and Frances, claiming that Frances was introducing the two. Frances was not a member of the U.S. delegation to the conference and she was translating not introducing.

But Stewart did provide the most concise (and engaging) quote on why Frances joined the Foreign Service: "[Frances] wanted to be an actor rather than

---

[81] And that is precisely why President Kennedy wrote his masterful instructions to all ambassadors in 1961 (as quoted in the Ceylon chapter): From now on, the Ambassador will be in control of all mission functions—to prevent such ugly incidents.

a critic." That must have been from a private conversation between Frances and Graham because it never appeared elsewhere. Altogether, an entertaining apocrypha from a big fan.

The eleven language proficiency forms in Frances' dossier assessed how well she could speak and write foreign tongues. All of her scores, both self-appraised and tested, over the six-year period 1956 to 1962 were almost identical, not surprising coming from a straight-arrow lady. Scoring ranged as follows for both spoken and written skills:

0 no practical knowledge
1 sufficient for routine travel requirements
2 routine social and limited office discussions
3 professional discussions
4 fluent on all levels
5 equivalent to that of English

Frances' scores for spoken / written are as follows (where a + meant that the person had greater proficiency at an earlier time):

French 4 / 4+ Finnish 0 / 1
Spanish 3+ / 4+ Norwegian 2 / 3
Swedish 1+ / 3 Sinhala 1 / 0

Frances added the following comments in her 1956 self-appraisal report:

My experience in interpreting has been extremely limited. At all of my posts, however, for the past twenty-two years I have carried on my conversations at the Foreign Office in the language of the country in which I was stationed, except in the case of Finland.

Frances explained why Finnish was the only language she didn't try to learn in her 1962 letter to Herman Pollack, Acting Assistant Secretary for Administration, when she was in Ceylon:

Your letter of January 5, 1962, on the subject of language proficiency of Chiefs of Mission has presented me with a good opportunity to review my own efforts in this respect.

Shortly after my arrival I began taking private lessons in Sinhala during the lunch hour two days a week and I have kept it up as regularly as my official duties would permit with only a few brief interruptions. I am still pegging away but there has not been much progress. I keep at it because I have learned to speak (after a fashion) the language in every country in which I have served with the exception of Finland. I was there just over two years and my Finnish friends advised me not to devote my time to learning a language which would do me no good once I left Finland. In Finland also there were newspapers in the Swedish language which I was able to read. Also I could do my shopping in many places in Swedish.

It is not only because speaking the vernacular is useful from the professional point of view that I have struggled with as many languages as I have. I know from my own experience that unless you speak the language of a country you cannot understand or appreciate it to the full. There was a special reason here [Colombo] for trying to learn something of the language in that I found not one single American in the Embassy who spoke or read the language. That circumstance I consider deplorable. We should not be completely dependent on locals for translations.

That point was driven home in an August 14, 1958, article by Irene C. Kuhn titled "The Way Things Are" published by the *General Features Corporation,* New York:

Miss Willis began studying the Norwegian language as soon as she arrived in Oslo in 1957. The first big, important occasion for her to speak publicly was a day in April when she'd been in her post just a few months.

This was kranselag, the word the Norwegians have for the ceremony of putting a small evergreen tree atop the construction of a new building as soon as the roof is on. The word covers all the festivities that accompany the successful completion of the roof and the exterior of the building.

When word was brought to Miss Willis that the roof would be

finished on the new American Embassy in Oslo in mid-April, she realized she was not yet sufficiently proficient in Norwegian to speak extemporaneously. It never occurred to her to speak in English to her Norwegian friends. She solved the problem in characteristic fashion. She wrote her speech and had it translated by the best man in the Embassy. Then she studied the pronunciation carefully, rehearsed often and, when the day came, read the speech through in excellent Norwegian.

The Oslo workmen on the embassy building, all present at the <u>kran-selag</u>, got up from the tables and cheered and clapped the American woman until it seemed they'd bring down the new roof they'd just put on.

That distinguishes a career diplomat from the rest.

Guts and Grace

Now back to Frances' Norwegian trips. On August 8, 1959, she traveled to Harstad for an exposition and then on to the branch USIA office in Tromso, both above the Arctic Circle where the midnight sun lives. Capt. Leo R. Jensen, the naval attaché, flew the party up in his amphibian airplane, but they had to turn back because the hydraulics failed an hour into the flight. So they caught connecting commercial flights, while Capt. Jensen stayed behind to fix the plane. Frances continued the saga:

> We made it in quite stormy weather to Harstad a little after nine. We got off the [commercial] plane onto the three-masted barque, the Statsrad Lemkuhl, a Norwegian training ship. The municipality had arranged a big reception, cruise and dinner on board, but the hoped for glimpse of the midnight sun was denied us so we came back early at 1:30 a.m. Anyway I got piped over the side with both national anthems and a guard of honor.

Then on the way home, again on Capt. Jensen's now-repaired aircraft, Frances reported:

> Friday morning we took off and were having one of the most beautiful flights down the coast you could possibly imagine. A little south of

Tromso the sun came out but even so in our seaplane we stayed low so we could see everything. Then about an hour north of Trondheim the left motor began to leak oil so the Captain flew into Trondheim and landed with one motor.

Naturally, I have not told Mother about all the trouble with the plane, but the first thing I did Monday morning was to telephone Capt. Jensen and ask what I could do to help him get a new plane. He said it was all taken care of and a new plane for the attachés here was being delivered. As it is the only American seaplane anywhere around it is just as well to have one that is in good order.

Obviously, what swung Capt. Jensen's request was his report that the Ambassador was aboard both times, with the implication that her life was endangered twice on the trip. Jensen, himself, was probably chewing a few fingernails.

That was—and probably still is—perilous country even on the ground, as events from an earlier trip will demonstrate. This trip occurred on March 19, 1958, when Frances was visiting Alesund on the northwest coast of Norway, which is the closest point between continental Europe and Iceland. On her way to an official lunch she fell on the ice and broke her femur. But despite the pain and with some help, she took part in the lunch and even spoke to the attendees.

Frances was then sedated and flown via Bergen to Oslo, where she was hospitalized for two weeks, followed by about a month of home recuperation. Then she was up and around using elbow-length crutches for the next six months. John Foster Dulles wrote her a fine get well note—just after he was told he had terminal cancer. He died a year later at the age of 71. Another main man gone from Frances' career.

Frances' Alesund performance also impressed the Norwegians. The following poem was published in the March 31, 1958, edition of the *Morgenposten* newspaper and translated by Ella McGeorge, who worked in the Embassy's Air Attaché Office. She finished her letter enclosing the translation with, "May I wish you a pleasant convalescence and a very speedy recovery."

MISS AMBASSADOR

The American Ambassador to Norway, Miss
Frances Willis, fell on the ice in Alesund
And broke a thigh bone.

But she partook, nevertheless, in a
Breakfast at the mayor's home.
In Alesund—as everywhere
There can be ice when it is cold.
And ice most oft' is where
One doesn't 'spect it to be there.
So learned our Miss Ambassador
Who follows quite a cautious track.
She stepped out wrong and slid—alors!
She noticed quite an awful crack,
But she was brave and full of verve
So laughed away her downward swerve.
For duty called; she kept her word
And went to the city's breakfast board.
    (It stood on her program
     set up by Uncle Sam.)
But alas, that she should ever try
To sit down there with broken thigh.
Jest eating smorbrod and some salad
With aching break that was no ballad.

——

Now here's the moral at the end:
Does't matter if a bone was broke?
'Twas better far, we are so proud,
A promise made was kept.

The poem said breakfast whereas other reports said lunch, a trivial difference. Now Frances' comment about not telling her mother about all the trouble with the naval attaché's plane makes sense, because there was no way of hiding the broken leg from her mother, who was living with Frances at the embassy residence.

Naval Action

Apparently Frances' first visit to Bergen was a success because she was invited back on January 16, 1960, to christen a new ship, the MS Siranger, built by the Bergens Mekaniske Verksteder for the Westfal-Larsen Steamship Company.

Because Frances knew "the custom of Norwegian shipbuilders [making] a handsome present to the sponsor of a ship," as she said in a January 18 despatch to the Department, she persuaded Bergens to contribute 12,000 Norwegian crowns to the Foreign Service Association Scholarship Fund. It then wound up funding a year's student-fellowship at Stanford University.

No photos of the christening survived, but she must have been delighted to launch that ship with the familiar champagne bottle surrounded by a full complement of naval brass. That was just one of her many naval events—both Norwegian and U.S.—in this seagoing country, and it was one of her fondest official duties. So it is again time to document some of them.

First are two official U.S. Navy photos aboard the USS Intrepid (CVA-11), an aircraft carrier making a port call to Oslo in July, 1958, about four months after Frances broke her leg. As is the naval custom, Frances was invited for an official visit soon after the carrier anchored in the bay. But a broken leg didn't stop her, as shown in the next photos.

Frances being piped aboard the USS Intrepid (CVA-11),
July 10, 1958 (courtesy U.S. Navy.)

Frances has just climbed up the "accommodation ladder" (a temporary, light stairway) to the quarterdeck, using her crutches. She is now walking through the honor guard while being piped aboard by the boatswain's mate, the sailor on the left piping with his right hand and saluting with his left. The admiral's barge with crew manning the rails, which brought Frances to the ship, is "laying off" waiting for her return trip.

The significance of this photo is that the accommodation ladder is both tall and steep, owing to the aircraft carrier's very high freeboard, i.e., tall hull. So to get to the quarterdeck she must either climb that ladder or be hoisted aboard in a boatswain's chair. But that would have been most undignified. So Frances chose to climb. Then she inspected the Marine Detachment on the carrier's hanger deck.

Frances inspecting the marine detachment aboard the USS Intrepid,
July 10, 1958 (courtesy U.S. Navy.)

That was probably the first time this detachment—or any marine detachment—had been inspected by a woman on crutches. Frances reciprocated by inviting the Intrepid's officers and midshipmen to the embassy residence four days later.

*Party and dance for the officers and midshipmen of the USS Intrepid
(Jack Engeman, Baltimore.)*

The party was held in the embassy residence's garden with many fetching Norwegian lasses attending. Frances and Belle lived in the embassy residence, or as Frances called it, "the big house."

According to a September 14, 1960, *Christian Science Monitor* article, it was built by Alfred Nobel's brother for his daughter when she married. Later it was rented by L. S. Swenson, U.S. Minister to Norway, who then persuaded the U.S. Government to buy it in 1924. The article quoted Frances as saying, "she has been grateful many times for that man's good judgment." The U.S. Navy would seem to agree.

While Frances didn't report this particular party in her bulletins she did report a similar one a year later, on July 12, 1959:

> Thursday the dance floor in the garden was put up and on Friday we had a dance for 250 of the cadets from the Training Ship Empire State; 424 present in addition to the 125 very pretty girls—I rang in a few extra. No whisky, but 888 bottles of beer, 696 coca cola plus 120 Jaffa, a Norwegian soft drink.

Shades of Stockholm 1934! Did Frances again furnish pencils and paper for the inevitable address and phone number requests after the dance? The record is silent.

The next photo completes the USN saga in Norway: a visit by the Chief of Naval Operations, Admiral Arleigh Burke, "31-knot Burke" of WW II fame. During that war Burke was Commodore of Destroyer Squadron 23 in the South Pacific. The squadron was ordered by the task force commander to proceed at maximum speed of 30 knots (34 mph) to engage enemy ships at Bougainville. Haste was paramount. Burke radioed back, "Proceeding at 31 knots." He did, won the battle and his squadron won a Presidential Unit Citation. He was so renowned that the USN named a new class of destroyers after him.

Frances greeting Admiral Arleigh Burke, Chief of Naval Operations, in Oslo, May 9, 1960 (courtesy Department of State.)

Admiral Burke was in town to assist Norway modernize their navy. This photo is classic because of what the admiral is doing: He is carrying his gloves in his left hand so that he can return salutes or shake hands with his right, as prescribed for all USN officers. Because Frances doesn't salute he is shaking her hand. Now observe his left hand: He is tipping his hat to the lady! That was exactly how gentlemen were trained to greet ladies up through the mid-twentieth century. But because Arleigh outranked Frances, four stars to three at the time, he didn't have to be so solicitous. He was just being a gentleman.

Press Interviews

Responding to requests for a press interview has always been an ambassadorial obligation, and probably more so for Frances who was the female FSO vanguard. One request came from Lenore Brundige, *Pittsburgh Press* fashion writer, on August 12, 1959, followed by one from Mary V. R. Thayer, *Washington Post* reporter, on November 15, 1959. They both reported extensively on the new U.S. embassy, a rather startling structure, as Brundige described it:

> ...one of the most modern buildings—a triangular shaped structure designed by the Finnish-born American Eero Saarinen. Americans gape at it in dismay, but a taxi driver described it as "a good looking building, once you get used to it."

Unfortunately, it was built directly across the street from the nineteenth century Royal Norwegian Palace. Both reporters met with Frances in her embassy office for surprisingly informative interviews. First from Brundige:

> Miss Willis met me in her triangular-shaped office and her handshake was as firm as the steel that had gone into this new building. Her smile was as bright as her sleek office furniture. Her manner was friendly and exuded competence.
>
> Miss Willis "really runs the Embassy," as a spokesman in the information office said, "and there is no mistake as to who is boss." But the girls in the outer office will tell you "Miss Willis is easy to meet; she likes informality."
>
> That is the way she entertains, too, mostly at informal teas or dinners

in "the big house" as she calls her official residence. And that is the way she greets official callers at the Embassy.

Instead of sitting behind her imposing desk, flanked by the American and Norwegian flags, she prefers to conduct interviews at the little conversational grouping of furniture opposite her desk. She sat on a long blue sofa; I on a comfortable upholstered chair with a low coffee table between us.

"My job is a seven-day-a-week one," she began. "Five days I devote to appointments and official duties. Saturday I catch up on all loose ends. Sunday is when I run the house. Mother is 87 years old and doesn't take over as hostess [any more.] So I plan the week's menus, outline all my entertaining, make out guest lists and do all the things anyone must do to run a home."

The social side of an ambassador's life is "tremendous," she points out. "The more people you know, the better you can fulfill your primary task of reporting back to Washington."

As a result, she entertains people from all walks of life—bankers, artists, local people as well as those in government positions. "You can't restrict social activities to those in government only. It's my job to know the people of the country in general."

Then from Thayer:

Funny angle to the complications of embassy life, adds the Ambassador, is that when only Norwegian-speaking-Norwegians tele-phone, she has to take the call. Why? Well, domestics are hard to come by in Norway and her staff, brought from a previous post, are Germans and Italians who, so far, have picked up nary a word of the local language.

Handsome, trim, cozy to be with, Frances Willis has no time for sports or hobbies but likes the theater, symphony concerts and bridge. Oddly, for so well contained a person, she has an inexplicable weakness for picnics.

For many years a lone woman among many masculine colleagues, Miss Willis is having herself a ball in Oslo with two other feminine ambassadors, Finland's Mme. Leivo-Larsson and [Austria's] Mme. Monschein.

When she returns from home leave after the Christmas holiday, Ambassador Willis hopes to attempt Norway's national sport, skiing. Its hazards will scarcely dismay her for she's broken a leg already. How? "Just slipping on the ice."

Finally from Brundige:

This streak of [Norwegian] self-reliance and independence, asking no favors from anyone, is also reflected in Miss Willis. It was also mirrored in her reply to the subject of Dior's latest fashion news about hobble skirts up knee high. "Isn't that ridiculous? Other women can wear them if they wish. I never shall."

With that, the friendly ambassador stood up, looked at her watch, smoothed the pleated skirt of her gray suit and gave a firm, warm handshake indicating the interview had ended. "I always try to keep appointments on time. It's part of my job, you know. Next time you visit Norway, let me know and we'll have tea in the big house."

Frances did not report any attempts at skiing and it is not likely that she did, given the recent memory of breaking her leg on ice.

Thayer's comment about three lady ambassadors in Oslo is illustrated in the following photo from Oslo's *Verdens Gang,* newspaper on April 18, 1959. A partial translation of the caption is: "Three lady diplomats are placing fingers on their respective homelands on the globe." Mme. Leivo-Larsson's finger is obscured but probably pointed at Finland, which is below the horizon at this camera angle. Frances' right finger is on the U.S. and her left finger is on Austria, assisting Mme. Monschein, who has just found her reading glasses after rummaging through her purse.

Three lady ambassadors posted to Oslo: Frances, Mme. Leivo-Larsson from Finland, and Mme. Monschein from Austria (courtesy Verdens Gang.)

The Thayer quote of Frances going on home leave for the Christmas holidays was Frances' first in two and a half years. It was coupled with a full, three-month tour at the U.N.'s Fifteenth General Assembly in New York. Belle, who had recently fallen and broken her hip, was too frail to travel.

Frances first stopped in Washington DC for consultations and took time out for a reception at the Women's National Press Club honoring the diplomatic corps. An article by *Washington Star* staff writer Frances Lide titled, "Norway Called a 'Glorious Country' by Ambassador Frances Willis," included the following:

> Mrs. J. Borden Harriman, former United States Minister to Norway, was among the guests and she and Miss Willis greeted each other warmly. This wasn't their first meeting, however. "Mrs. Harriman still has a great many warm friends in Norway and I brought back many messages for her," Ambassador Willis said.

Apparently their other meetings weren't recorded. Frances would have many similar visits with a successor lady ambassador to Norway, Margaret Tibbetts, whom Frances first mentored in London.

Consulting and Corresponding

Frances' consultation with the Department had always remained obscure: whom she saw and what they talked about. The following confidential but now declassified memorandum from her 123 File provides a barely legible clue through all the stamps, notes, marks, slashes and initials.

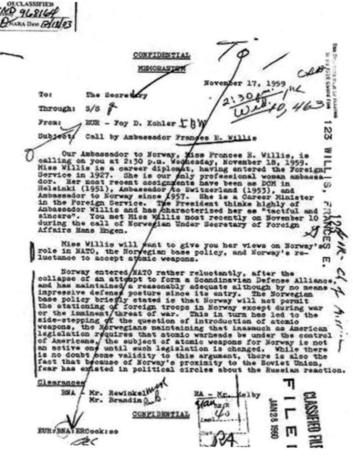

Memo to SecState Herter from Foy D. Kohler, European Affairs
(courtesy National Archives.)

The memo reveals that Frances was doing serious consulting on Norwegian defense subjects. And it's clear why the memo was classified: It opined about a less-than-impressive Norwegian defense posture, which would have interested the Soviet Union. But even more importantly, it would have insulted the Norwegians and that would never do.

Frances continued these consultations throughout her tour in Norway, but no other declassified details are available. Here is an April 5, 1961, thank you note from the Department written after her tour in Norway.

My dear Madam Ambassador:

The debriefing which you gave to the members of the Intelligence Community on March 28, was excellent, and I want to thank you for giving us your time. The officers who attended the conference now have a clearer picture of the situation in Norway. They welcomed the opportunity of meeting with you.

If we can be of any service to you, please call us.

Sincerely yours,
/s/ *Donald B. McCue*
Director, Executive Staff,
Bureau of Intelligence
and Research

Because the note was not classified it couldn't say what she talked about. But the "intel crowd" was clearly impressed. That was the covert phase of her career—and except for an occasional peek, hidden forever.

The now-typical set of letters and thank you notes were also in Frances' dossier; most were genuine and complementary—and now familiar; others were ludicrous, entertaining or poignant. Here is a ludicrous "form job" to SecState from Lt. Gen. Hershey, Director of the U.S. Selective Service:

December 27, 1957

Dear Mr. Secretary:

I am appreciative for the courtesies extended to me and the means provided for the procurement of information concerning manpower by the United States Ambassador to _____ on my visit to _____ in September.

Sincerely,

/s/ *Lewis B. Hershey*

Lt. General, USA

Hershey must have said to his secretary, "Here is a list of the countries I visited; insert each country name into this draft and I'll sign them when ready." Frances got the one with Norway inserted. Hershey then received a thank you note in return from A. S. Brown, Deputy Director of Personnel, saying:

> It was thoughtful of you to take the trouble to write, and I assure you that commendations such as this are always greatly appreciated.

Brown listed the nine countries Hershey had visited, so at least he was able to condense everything into one note.

Here's an entertaining one from Clarence J. O'Brien of The Pallotine Fathers, Milwaukee, Wisconsin, to Henry C. Boudreau, First Secretary in Oslo:

June 19, 1958

Dear Mr. Boudreau,

In your letter of November 4, 1957, to Mr. Ted Winnicki you advised that our present Ambassador was going to forward a small parcel for the International Booth at St. Anthony of Padua Church Festival. The Festival was held and I was fortunate in receiving the Norwegian mittens.

The sending of these mittens was very commendable on the part of our Ambassador and indeed very much appreciated.

I am enclosing a news article on the auction. I am sorry there is no mention of the mittens in the news article but I assure you it was one of the better articles that was auctioned that day.

Very truly yours,

/s/ *Clarence J. O'Brien*

And that letter found its way into Frances' dossier—even without O'Brien knowing the name of "our present Ambassador." Winnicki and O'Brien probably chewed up more salary in their communications with Oslo than the mittens fetched at auction.

Here are two poignant ones, the first a letter from Belle to her son Henry:

October 5, 1959

My precious Children,

On the night of October 2, I saw the King! He and Princes Astrid came to our supper after the Bernstein Concert [with the New York Philharmonic Orchestra] in Oslo. The Embassy and all its attributes were in perfect order—red carpet and all. I was dressed and frizzled and waiting in the Big Drawing Room, which was a mass of flowers and lights.

As soon as the Concert was over they came—Frances just a moment or two before the King. Everything timed just right. I had my speech to him learned by heart, and just as I was about to use it, a young, agile woman appeared before him and made a charming curtsy. I said, "Make one for me, please." He was standing near and heard me and turned and said, "Sit still." I did and so he won my heart.

He is taller than I was led to believe and very pleasing in every way. Not a stuffed shirt at all—human!—with simple sweet manners. I didn't have eyes for Astrid at all, I was so busy looking at the King—trying not to stare.

Belle went on to describe the gowns, food, flowers and silver service. She finished with:

Never have I seen such a magnificent display. With extra help the service was perfect, with Alberto [the butler] directing it. Astrid sat opposite the King. I was at one end of the table. The King didn't make a move to go 'till after 1 a.m., so I know he had a good time.

Frances inserted a comment that it was really over at 9:30 p.m. Belle's live wire was still sparking.

The second is a letter nine months later from Loy W. Henderson, still Deputy Undersecretary for Administration, in response to a letter from Frances telling him "Mother passed away yesterday morning, and I am happy to say the end was very peaceful." Frances went on to say that she wanted to return to the U.S. for the funeral services and that she could stop by the Department for consultations afterwards:

July 26, 1960

Dear Frances:

I have just received your letter of July 22 informing me that your mother passed away on July 21 and hasten to extend my sympathy and those of your other friends in the Department to you. We were quite aware that your mother had been suffering for a long time and that her end came as no surprise. Nevertheless, we can understand how much grief this has caused you.

I think the suggestions contained in your letter, with respect to the timing of the funeral service and of your trip to Washington via California, are excellent. I am taking steps at once to bring about their implementation. You will probably be hearing from us by telegram within a few days. Our telegram will also let you know what day you should be in the Department in order to be briefed.

With kindest personal regard,

Sincerely,

/s/ *Loy*

The essence of diplomacy. No surprise there, because it was written by the Department's first Career Ambassador.

And while on the subject of private people in Frances' life, her butler Alberto Gay and his wife Livia provided virtually perfect service to Frances during her twelve years in Berne, Oslo and Colombo. They signed on as Frances' personal staff early in her Berne tour and continued on until Frances retired. Frank Moore captured this service in his July 14, 1976, "With a Grain of Salt" article:

Alberto was born just south of the Swiss border in Italy and in addition to his native language spoke English and fluent French. Upon arrival in Oslo, Frances was told by the wife of the former ambassador, that 44 people could be seated at the embassy dinner table. Alberto, however, cast an experienced eye over the table and the space available around it for serving the guests and set the maximum at 38. Frances never planned a dinner for more than 38.

Although Madame Ambassador paid careful attention to the guest list and the seating plan for dinner, Alberto would take it from there. Oh, he would consult on the menu and Frances might make a single change, but he did not bother her with details. He knew how many extra people he would have to hire and where he would get them.

They continued the service even after the birth of their daughter, Adriana, everyone living in the embassy residence as a family. Frances then requested visas for them to continue service when she retired to Redlands, but it was not to be. Frances would go out of her way to see them on her subsequent trips overseas. Surprisingly, there are no photos of the Gays in Frances' effects. Because they were old school personal staff—to be neither seen nor heard—they clearly preferred to have it that way.

Important communiqués occasionally appeared in Frances' 123 File. Here is a "Priority Telegram" from Frances to SecState, dated June 26, 1960, and marked "limited official use." U.S. embassies in Moscow and London got copies. It was written in caps, just like all US Navy messages, probably using a teletypewriter operating with the navy's old, cap-only, Remote Information Exchange Terminal (RIXT) protocol. The navy is finally phasing RIXT out in favor of mixed-case text.

AT 4:50 P.M. SUNDAY AFTERNOON DAILY SKETCH TELEPHONED FROM LONDON AND ASKED IF I WOULD COMMENT ON STORY IN SUNDAY PEOPLE ON "PRIZE BLUNDER" COMMITTED BY ME AT OPENING OF SOVIET EXHIBITION OSLO YESTERDAY. WHEN I SAID I KNEW NOTHING WHATEVER ABOUT IT CORRESPONDENT READ ME STATEMENT TO EFFECT THAT MISS WILLIS SHOOK HANDS WITH ALL DIGNITARIES IN FRONT ROW BUT WHEN SHE CAME TO MIKOYAN SHE DREW BACK HER HAND AND TURNED ON HER HEEL. I MERELY REPLIED THAT STATEMENT WAS CONTRARY TO FACT AS IN FACT IT WAS.

FOR DEPARTMENT'S INFORMATION WHAT HAPPENED

WAS THAT AS BALLENTINE, SYVRUD AND I WERE BEING SHOWN TO OUR SEATS WE HAD TO WALK BETWEEN FRONT ROW AND STAGE. AS WE WENT ALONG I NODDED TO SEVERAL CABINET MEMBERS AND WIVES BUT PRIME MINISTER GERHARDSEN IN THIRD SEAT FROM CENTER AISLE (MIKOYAN IN AISLE SEAT AND INTERPRETER IN SECOND SEAT) ROSE TO GREET ME SO I SHOOK HANDS WITH HIM AS NORWEGIAN POLITENESS DEMANDS, THEN WITH MRS. GERHARDSEN WHO WAS SEATED ON HIS RIGHT (AWAY FROM MIKOYAN) AND THEN WITH FOREIGN MINISTER WHO WAS ON MRS. GERHARDSEN'S RIGHT AND WHO ALSO ROSE TO GREET ME. I INTRODUCED BALLENTINE OUR NEW ECONOMIC COUNSELOR AND WE PROCEEDED ON TO OUR SEATS AT EXTREME FAR END OF FRONT ROW, ESCORTED BY ASSISTANT CHIEF OF PROTOCOL [SYVRUD.] NO ONE PRESENTED MIKOYAN TO ME OR ME TO HIM AND HE REMAINED SEATED.

OUR PRESS ATTACHE HAS JUST INFORMED ME MORGENBLADET IS INQUIRING ABOUT AP AND UP DISPATCH TO EFFECT THAT "US AMBASSADOR OSLO SNUBS MIKOYAN."

I SUGGESTED THAT PRESS ATTACHE MERELY SAY THERE WAS NO SNUB AND ENOUGH EYEWITNESSES TO KNOW THERE WAS NONE.

WILLIS

There was nothing further in the 123 File about this alleged snub, so the Department must have decided to let the matter fade with Frances' simple denial.

The man Frances allegedly snubbed was Anastas Ivanovich Mikoyan, first deputy chairman of the Council of Ministers, the Soviet Union's #3 man under Khrushchev and later (1964) chairman of the new Supreme Soviet Presidium, the #2 man under Brezhnev. Earlier he had been the Soviet trade minister. And because he knew the trade ropes, he was in Oslo for the Soviet exhibition.

But despite the denials, an inadvertent snub did get delivered—not by Frances but by the Norwegians. After her warm greeting from the Norwegians there was no way Frances could steal more of the limelight by then addressing

Mikoyan. That greeting had to be done by Prime Minister Gerhardsen, who started the whole thing. But he didn't. So Frances and entourage moved on, allowing Mikoyan to see how much his Norwegian friends liked Americans right in front of him at his show. Consequently, an indirect message was sent by the Norwegians and inaccurately read by the press.

More Action at Home

At the end of her tour in Oslo Frances was appointed one of five Alternate U.S. Representatives to the Fifteenth Session of the United Nations in New York. Calkin reported in his 1978 book, *Women in the Department of State,* that Frances was the first career woman FSO to serve in that capacity.

Frances first flew to Redlands for a ten day vacation, then on to Washington DC for a few days of consulting with the Department and finally to New York for duty with the U.S. Delegation between September 18 and December 18, 1960. During this time she popped back to Washington DC for further consultations, including one with officials of the Norwegian Embassy—her "opposite number."

Her boss at the U.N. was Ambassador James J. Wadsworth, a non-career appointee for just four months, September 1960 through January 1961. Wadsworth had previously been deputy to the permanent representative, Henry Cabot Lodge, and was acting as a gap-filler after Lodge left. That's too bad because the next U.S. Ambassador for four and a half years was Adlai E. Stevenson, who appeared earlier in this chapter.

In his thank you letter to Frances Secretary of State Herter summarized Frances' efforts during the three months, including work on the Special Political Committee and "your cheery willingness to assist in Plenary and the First Committee." He finished with

> I would like to make special mention of your skillful handling of the difficult question of the South Tyrol and your work with Austrian and Italian Delegations on this issue.

.

The "difficult question of the South Tyrol" began when the Allied Forces defeated Austria and Germany in 1918 (WW I) and Italy was ceded part of Austria's Tyrol—up to the Brenner Pass. The ethnic Germans living in this South Tyrol region weren't happy about these events. Things got worse when Mussolini's

Fascists took over in Rome a few years later, and *Il Duce* began to systematically purge his country of all foreign impurities, including the Germans in South Tyrol. Not only that, he started populating South Tyrol with industries manned by "thoroughbred Italian employees," along with renaming everything in Italian. The Website *Initaly* reported that

> Even the very word Sudtirol was outlawed and transformed into "Alto Adige," referring to the northern reaches of an Italian river.

At the end of WW II, the Treaty of Paris granted South Tyrol autonomy, but with protection from both Italian and Austrian armies. *Initaly* then got to the 1960 problem:

> To make matters demographically worse, most of those [ethnic Germans] who had remained were isolated rural farmers. The cities and large towns were populated by Mussolini's factory workers and their offspring. Fearing that they would be eradicated altogether, the ethnic Germans asked first Rome, then Vienna, to safeguard their heritage. Austria pleaded their case before the United Nations, which ordered the two countries to come to some sort of negotiated agreement.

That was likely Frances' contribution. However, the agreement did not go smoothly: Bombing attacks took nineteen lives and injured countless others until 1969, when legislation was passed to protect the German minority. And even the term minority was misused, because two-thirds of the province was still German! *Initaly* reports that nowadays there is a strong separatist movement, especially in Trentino-Alto Adige. In any case, contrary to what the American tourist industry says, South Tyrol is not part of Tuscany.

Frances also gave a series of speeches and TV interviews and served on a University of Rochester academic panel during her U.N. tour.

University of Rochester's first All-University Convocation panel discussion, "Communications and the Cause of Peace," October 13-15, 1960 (courtesy Melissa S. Mead, Rochester Collection Librarian)

Panelists are, from left to right: Dr. Joseph E. Johnson, President of the Carnegie Endowment for International Peace, and moderator; Frances E. Willis, U.S. Ambassador to Norway and U.S. delegate to the United Nations' Fifteenth Assembly; Dr. George B. Kistiakowsky, President Eisenhower's Special Assistant for Science and Technology; and Edward R. Murrow, radio-television commentator and analyst.

The theme of this convocation was "Perspectives on Peace—as seen by distinguished authorities in the fields of government banking, communications, foreign affairs, business and education." The transcript is not available, so it's not clear they identified a path to peace. But this sort of process should have helped because the U.S. never went to war with the Soviet Union. In any case, the University must have liked what she said because they awarded her a Doctor of Humane Letters degree.

Then Frances went solo as a guest of the WCBS-TV program, *New York Forum*, moderated by Dallas Townsend and accompanied by a panel of three members of the New York City Bar. Here are excerpts from the Forum transcript.

MODERATOR TOWNSEND: Today's guest is the U.S. Ambassador to Norway. She has been described as perhaps the most successful woman in government today. She is the first woman Foreign Service Officer. Here to answer questions on the Fifteenth General Assembly is Frances Willis. Ambassador Willis, welcome to New York Forum.

QUESTION: Ambassador Willis, during the past few weeks you have been witness to one of the extraordinary events in the history of international diplomacy. From your vantage point how would you assess the reaction of the newly admitted African nations to the activities and policies of the Soviet Union?

DR. WILLIS: In my observation they are intensely proud to be members of the United Nations.

QUESTION: Have they been impressed with Mr. Khrushchev?

DR. WILLIS: Who hasn't?

QUESTION: Seriously, I agree with you, but have they felt that he has demonstrated a kind of power which they feel they must bow to or go along with or do they consider him to be a threat?

DR. WILLIS: I think that they are very eager to get on with their own affairs [and] to cooperate with the rest of the world—but they want to be left out of the cold war. I don't think they are intimidated.

QUESTION: Ambassador Willis, when you say that, do you mean that these newly admitted nations of Africa consciously intend to become part of a neutral bloc between East and West?

DR. WILLIS: No, I don't think they want to become members of any bloc because if you [do] you surrender some of your independence.

QUESTION: Ambassador Willis, we are all very conscious of the arrival of these new nations and it makes a difference in arithmetic. Now, Khrushchev made a real bid for leadership in which he would pay off, in effect, the neutralist bloc, with one of the three secretariats, which he proposed to have in his newly formed organization.[82] Now, my question is, what happens when the votes start to tilt against us on issues which are crucial to the United States?

DR. WILLIS: I don't think that appeals to them. I think that the neutralist nations realize that you are not going to strengthen the United Nations by having a triumvirate instead of a single Secretary-General and introducing into the executive branch of the United Nations the veto. If he [Khrushchev] expected that to appeal to them I think he has made a mistake...

---

[82] The U.N. had—and still has—just one Secretary-General. Khrushchev wanted to dilute the leadership, among other changes, so that the Soviet bloc and the neutral bloc could control U.N. action with both a majority vote and the veto. It never happened.

MODERATOR TOWNSEND: Excuse me, Ambassador Willis. I am afraid we have time for just one more quick question. It goes without saying the Foreign Service has been a superior field for you. How would you assess it right now as a career for young women?

DR. WILLIS: My answer to that question is always it is not a question of sex; it is a question of whether the individual, whether a man or a woman, has the special qualification… [and at this point, the rest is well known.]

MODERATOR TOWNSEND: Well, you obviously do. Ambassador Willis, thank you very much for being with us here today.

Following the WCBS-TV program Frances was interviewed on October 24, 1960, by Mary Frances Harvey, U.N. Correspondent of the *Patriot Ledger*, who then wrote an article, "'Determination To Make It Work' Cause of U.N.'s Growth in Strength."[83] Harvey drew more out of Frances on Khrushchev's attack on the U.N.:

I had lunched with her [Frances] the day the Soviet leader arrived, and interviewed her again on the afternoon of his departure. Like many other diplomats who hoped for a while that Khrushchev might conduct himself in a constructive way while at the U.N., Ambassador Willis, after listening to his sputnik speeches and watching him brandish his shoe around, seemed disappointed on this score. But summing up her impressions just after Khrushchev waddled out of the Assembly, she said:

"I've had the feeling that the U.N. has really reached the point where it's strong enough to withstand attacks and attempts to undermine it. And it isn't just because it's bigger, but because there's a greater determination to make it work—to make it effective.

"This is not only on the part of the older members but also of the newer members. Whenever there's been an attack on the Secretary-General or the President of the Assembly, the reaction has been that everybody wants to defend the organization."

She said she "still believes" constructive work can come out of this year's Assembly. Even in the field of disarmament, where Khrushchev

---

[83] The article was kindly provided by Goucher College.

"ultimatums" were so depressing, Miss Willis hoped some success could be registered by the General Assembly in a "step by step approach." She flashed her bright blue eyes and said, "You know, I'm an optimist."

Before Khrushchev arrived to launch his attack on the U.N., Miss Willis saw "unlimited possibilities" for progress at this session. "I don't think anyone can see just what will happen," she said. As for what Khrushchev would do, she said "Well, he's playing his game," and remarked that he was a very clever man who'd risen to Soviet chief "in a very tough game."

She expects no large-scale reorganization in the wake of Khrushchev's demands. "Perhaps the U.N. isn't perfect but it's workable, and when it is under attack the reaction is to be careful to keep what we already have."

Miss Willis has all the dignity of an ambassador. But dignity aside, Miss Willis has about her a light-hearted quality, a quick wit—which can be most useful in diplomacy—and a warm-hearted, completely unassuming charm.

A Middle East diplomat who had made her acquaintance in Geneva said with great respect, as she passed by in the delegates' lounge, "Ah, there is a very clever woman."

That's certainly disconcerting. Maybe it's possible to attach a different interpretation to Frances being a "very clever woman" than to Khrushchev being a "very clever man." Harvey drew further comments from Frances:

Asked whether, as a woman, she had ever experienced discrimination in government service, she waved her hand and replied, "Oh, I wouldn't bother with anything like that. If there is any, I don't even see it."

Asked whether she would someday write a book about her life in the Foreign Service—she holds top seniority among women Foreign Service Officers—she said, almost with exasperation, "That's the one thing I'm NOT going to do."

Eligible now for retirement if she wants it (she doesn't seem to), she says someday she wants to go back to teaching, "to see how much I can get across to the students."

She stresses [among other attributes] dedication—"to represent your government faithfully all the time, not just when you think it's doing the right thing. It has to be, always, your country right or wrong."

A few comments on her comments. Discrimination: Frances certainly wouldn't experience any discrimination at this stage of her career. Memoirs: She did consider writing her memoirs in retirement but decided not to, as detailed in the Redlands Epilogue chapter. Teaching: She decided not to return to teaching, as detailed in the Ceylon chapter. Government support: She subsequently added an escape clause in a 1967 interview about Vietnam in the Redlands Epilogue chapter: "If you can't rationalize your government's action on a major issue you must resign."

Following her U.N. assignment, Frances stopped again at the Department for three days, flew to Santiago, Chile for Christmas with Freddie and Caroline Vaughan, then returned to Oslo. Then it was back to the U.S. and off to Ceylon. But first, a report of Frances' encounter with Julia Child.

17

FRANCES AND JULIA

The Child Career Change

IN May, 1959, towards the end of Frances' tour in Norway, Paul Child was assigned as the U.S. Information Agency's Cultural Attaché to the Embassy. He would have arrived sooner but was granted a six-month delay so that he could learn Norwegian. Paul was also accompanied by his wife, better known to the world as Julia Child.

According to Noel Fitch in his book, *Appetite for life: the Biography of Julia Child*, the Childs first met in Washington DC during WW II when both were serving in the Office of Strategic Services (OSS.) Then both were posted to the Far East. After the war Julia (McWilliams) left government service but Paul pursued her in Pasadena, California, where they were married. Then Paul's OSS Presentation Unit was transferred to the State Department in September, 1946, and Paul began his Foreign Service career, including a tour in France where Julia learned the "Art of French Cooking."

Fitch reported that after arriving in Oslo, the Childs found the Norwegian food just awful—except for the salmon. He ascribed much of this problem to the dominant religion in Norway: Evangelical Lutheran, with their Puritan approach to food and drink. The Childs also had to adjust to the Norwegian's life style, which has been described as rectitude, fresh air and early nights.[84]

---

[84] L.M.Boyd reported in his "Facts & Fancy" newspaper column that the Norwegians and Fins have long exchanged jokes, with the Fins telling this one: "When Norwegians come to Finland, they have to set their watches ahead an hour. When they go home, they have to set them back 20 years." That changed when oil was extracted from the Norwegian Sea in 1969, transforming Norway's economy. Their unemployment rate in 2011 was 3.4%; Gross Domestic Product per capita was $94,000, twice that of the U.S.; and their sovereign wealth fund was $525 billion, growing a year later to $681 billion—the world's largest.

Then Fitch got to the essence of this Frances and Julia story:

But it was not until she attended her first embassy luncheon and sampled the tasteless fare that Julia made plans to resume giving cooking lessons. When the canned shredded chicken in what Julia called a "droopy, soupy sauce" was passed to her, she looked across the room to Debra Howe, [a member of the embassy staff] who gave her an apologetic, knowing look. Years later she [Julia] would recall the phallic-shaped aspic filled with grapes and cut-up mushrooms: "It was sitting on a little piece of lettuce so you could not hide what you didn't eat. I didn't think anything like that still existed!" When the coconut frosted cake-mix cake, molded lime Jell-O salad, and artificial key lime pie were served, Julia glanced wide-eyed at Debra. "I knew how bad the food was," Debra Howe said in 1994, "and I knew what Julia would feel about it." The entire meal was appalling, thought Julia; everything was sweet, and sickening.

Julia determined that no such embassy meal would ever be served to her again and made plans to offer cooking classes for those who wanted them. Few did, but her Norwegian friends were enthusiastic. She began two practices here in Norway that continued for several years: she would cook a meal in the kitchen of a family and she would offer small classes for six to eight women. Debra, who thought [Julia] "was a good sport, especially with diplomatic wives," cared nothing about learning to cook herself, for she had two young children and planned functions for the Ambassador, Frances Willis, whom Julia admired.

So the Embassy fare wasn't up to Julia's standard; in fact not even close. In Frances' defense, while she certainly had a taste for good food, and expected it from her embassy chefs, she apparently was stuck with this one. And even her right hand man, Alberto, couldn't fix the problem. That, plus Julia's empyreal standards of cuisine, doomed that luncheon before the first bite.

Then a June 5, 1961, letter from Frances to Fisher Howe, Counselor and Deputy Chief of Mission in Oslo, wrapping up administrative loose ends from her tour in Oslo, mitigates Frances' culinary deficiencies. Frances talked about social events and finished with: "I hope the [Clifford] Whartons can find a better chef." So at least she knew she had the problem. (Clifford Wharton relieved Frances as ambassador and is profiled in The Other Woman chapter.)

Fitch then reported that about eighteen months after the Childs arrived, and shortly after Frances departed Oslo, Paul submitted his resignation from the Foreign Service, citing a very slow promotion track. Because it is virtually certain that Frances either wrote or approved Paul's Annual Efficiency Reports, now the cardinal element in awarding a promotion, she contributed to Paul's decision to resign.

According to Fitch, the Childs almost regretted their decision to leave early because the new ambassador Clifford Wharton and his wife Leonie were good friends from Marseilles. But the Childs didn't change their decision, and the rest is culinary history.

To again quote Alexander Graham Bell, "When one door closes another door opens." [85] Certainly, walking through that second door was an excellent choice for the Childs—and world cuisine. And Frances influenced that event twice: first, by motivating Julia to start cooking classes and second, by discouraging Paul from continuing in the Foreign Service.

Julia's Report

But this story is not over, because Julia will reveal solutions to Frances' twin problems of working too much and culinary deficiency: delegation and education. They are reported by Frank Moore in his July 13, 1976, "With a Grain of Salt" column:

> French Chef' Julia Child was explaining hospitality at the White House Wednesday evening in a television dialog when a recollection of Ambassador Frances Willis of Redlands bubbled to the top of her mind. The enthusiastic members of the Frances Willis Fan Club—an organization which I have just invented—sped to their telephones to talk to each other, to put a bug in my ear and to felicitate Frances.
>
> In the latter endeavor they were frustrated for the evening since Frances—a Johnston College Overseer—had gone with Chancellor Bill Thomas to have dinner with Japanese students on a Japanese ship at

---

[85] That quote was also applied when Harry Cook was killed in 1918, thus opening the Foreign Service door for Frances in 1927.

Los Angeles Harbor. I promised fellow members of the Fan Club that I would not let her slip away—not completely—and so I now have a report.

Channel 28 was covering the State Dinner for Queen Elizabeth II on Wednesday evening. Robert MacNeil, host of the show, was trying to give the audience some feel for entertaining at the White House—how the menu is chosen, how the food is served, how guests are made to feel at home, and so on. Julia Child, as an interviewee, was helping him.

"The Fords are informal and relaxed people," MacNeil said. "I would think that this would express itself in their manner of entertaining, that they would make people feel at ease." Julia returned his serve with one quick stroke: "I imagine that they do." Then she diverged immediately in this way:

"In the White House there are all kinds of meeters and greeters and mixers—all part of the staff—so nobody who is invited will ever feel alone or as if nobody is paying any attention to them. You are standing there and you don't have anyone to talk to and someone immediately comes up. That does give an air of informality. Very nice!

"We were in the embassy service for awhile. I remember we had an ambassador in Norway, Frances Willis. Wonderful! When we had a big entertainment she would say to all of us wives, 'You are here to work. You (Mrs. Jones) are to take people from the reception line down to the bottom of the garden. You (Mrs. Brown) are to mix. You (Mrs. Johnson) are to do this and that.' It is very hard work. By the time you are through (with your duties) you are ready to go home."

"Yes, that is all true," Frances told me. "I used to tell embassy people that they were not coming to a party just to have a good time themselves but also to see that the guests did, too."

At dinner parties she would personally decide who was to sit by whom, for two reasons. In Oslo, for example she would match Norwegian guests and American dinner partners, from the same fields—politics, economics, culture—to seek mutuality of interest and congeniality. But as an ambassador an important part of her job was to help members of her staff get to know their Norwegian counterparts so they could carry out their governmental work.

Frances was fond of the couple, personally, and didn't mind a bit when Julia would occasionally send her some delicacy that she had prepared. Frances has a memento of that friendship which she wore for my amusement, a bit of laughter I wish all members of the Fan Club could have shared. This item is a kitchen apron, made of cloth similar in appearance to a bed pillow without the cover. (It has ingenious drawstrings which lower or raise the apron, according to tightness or looseness.) On the front is a large, orange-red patch on which the scroll lettering is stitched—bold and black. The message is:

Thank You
Julia Child

The merriment surrounding the origins of the apron have escaped Frances' recollections, but whatever they were, she laughs as she models the gift now, after a lapse of some fifteen years.

Sadly, the apron was discarded in the 1983 Redlands house closing, its historical importance unappreciated at the time. And it's not surprising that Frances didn't remember its significance, because by 1976 her memory was fast fading due to a stroke.

It's not clear who gave the apron to Frances, but its use was obvious: whenever Julia would send over a delicacy for Frances to sample, Frances would don the apron, sample the offering and then loosen the drawstring, lowering the apron and exposing the message.

It's not likely that Julia gave Frances the apron; that would be somewhat gratuitous from the chef, herself. But Julia's friend Debra Howe might be the instigator. Debra was a member of Frances' staff, knew what Julia thought of the embassy's fare and could see how Julia was subtly trying to improve it. So why not add a little fun to the education process? Unfortunately, neither the Department nor DACOR could track Debra down to verify the speculation.

There is a sequel to this story from the author's sister Elaine (Willis) Mannon:

Frances liked to visit her many relatives in California when on home leave. And when in San Francisco, she would visit Elaine and Joe Mannon.

On such a trip in 1963 the Mannons invited Frances to dinner at their flat on Twin Peaks. And because Joe was a gourmet cook, they planned a sumptuous feast—right out of Julia Child's *Mastering the Art of French Cooking, First Ed.* That's the one that uses every pot, pan and bowl in the house, just to cook up the sauce.

Precisely at the appointed hour, Frances arrived by taxi and was ushered into the drawing room by Elaine. Following the usual greetings and health inquiries, Elaine said that Joe would be out shortly, just as soon as he came to a break point in the dinner preparation. She added that everything was being done from scratch, exactly according to Julia Child, and that the entree was to be coq au vin. Frances clapped her hands together and said, "How wonderful; I haven't had coq au vin since Julia served it to me in Oslo!"

Frances didn't say where Julia served the coq au vin. It certainly could have been one of those samples she sent over to Frances, which likely initiated a pull on the apron drawstring. Or it could have been in a more formal setting if the Childs had Frances to dinner at their apartment as a normal part of diplomatic entertaining. In any event, Frances—ever the diplomat—said Joe's was as good as Julia's.[86]

Frances' Fix

Frances finally revealed the solution to her lack-of-delegation problem. Julia flagged it in the Moore article with her comments about "meeters and greeters and mixers." Precise details are in Frances' June 28, 1960, memorandum to her staff, "Subject: Request for Your Assistance at the Fourth of July Reception at the Embassy Residence, 4:00 to 6:00 p.m.," which is summarized as follows:

The Fourth of July Reception offers everyone on the staff of the Embassy and MAAG an opportunity to do an extremely useful public relations job. Many of the guests present at the Residence on that day may never have been in an Embassy before, and may never be again. It is therefore up to us to give the thousand attending a good time and to

---

[86] The author wrote to Julia in 2002 asking if she remembered Frances and further details of these encounters. She responded: "I didn't know Frances intimately, but I did admire her very much. She was one of our most distinguished and attractive members of the Foreign Service. I always wish I had known her better, but she was rather shy and of course rather busy." That's the first time Frances has been called shy, but who's to argue when it comes from a fellow maven?

send them away with the best possible impression of how their representatives abroad function. It is to this end that I ask your assistance...

During the periods when not on duty at specific posts, you are requested in so far as possible to help in seeing that all the guests have someone to talk to and something to eat and drink if desired...

Details of the procedure to be followed at the Residence and specific assignments are set forth below:

INTRODUCERS

The function of the Introducers is to stand in the front hall and greet the guests, direct the ladies to the coat room (upstairs in the case of bad weather), ask the names of the guests as they approach the head of the receiving line and announce the name of each guest to me, saying the name distinctly. In addition to the duties mentioned above the Introducers are requested to see that commercial or press photographers are courteously turned away and that any attempt by a person unknown to the Ambassador to leave a gift for the Ambassador is prevented without giving offense...

THE RECEIVING LINE

The following persons are invited to stand in the receiving line with me during the periods indicated... Those who receive with me are requested when not in line to circulate and draw guests to the lower end of the garden if the weather is good, and if the weather is bad, to the dining room, Ritz Room, library and covered terrace, if usable.

THE CONDUCTORS

The function of the Conductors is to take people from the end of the receiving line as quickly as possible in order to prevent congestion and to see them established at a point as far away from the line as conveniently possible. If the guest is obviously ill at ease, shy or handicapped in any visible way the Conductor whose turn it is to escort the guest from the end of the line is requested not to leave the guest until a Mixer has taken over.

THE MIXERS

The persons assigned to fixed stations other than those indicated above are designated Mixers, they are requested to remain in a given area during a given period to assure that all guests in that area are properly and hospitably taken care of. The main duty of the Mixers is to see that every guest in his or her area has someone to talk to and has something to eat and drink.

That's less than half the memo. The other part included names of the staff who were assigned to each helper unit, detailed instructions of operation and location in the event of good or bad weather, along with eligibility rules for invitees and procedures for rejecting undesirables. Frances finished with:

It is important to have the wheels turn so quietly and so smoothly that no one is aware that there is any organization. An appearance of regimentation or rigidity is to be avoided, and intelligence and tact are to be used at all times in applying these directions, or if necessary in disregarding them for good and sufficient reasons.

This was her solution to the criticism that she did too much work herself, and did not delegate enough to her staff. So she delegated—delegated in micro-detail, to the point that a ballet choreographer would have been impressed.

A similar but even more detailed version of the memo appeared in the Ceylon archives, and an earlier but less detailed version in the Switzerland archives, titled "Invitation List for Reception July 4, 1956." In that memo Frances defined the role of "Announcers and Conductors." She must have had second thoughts about "Announcers," because she changed it to "Introducers" in the Norway memo. Possibly it sounded too much like running a prizefight, which had become popular on U.S. television about then. In any case, the concept evolved into a fine-tuned process over her twelve years as ambassador.

18

FINALLY THE FAR EAST: CEYLON

Pre-Ceylon Action

FRANCES was nominated Ambassador to Ceylon—now Sri Lanka—on March 8, 1961, then confirmed by the Senate and attested by President Kennedy on March 15, 1961. After he administered the oath Secretary of State Rusk said, "That she is [a] 'she' is really irrelevant because she is one of our great diplomats and we are intensely proud to have her going to one of our posts."

Frances reported for duty in Colombo, Ceylon on May 9, 1961, following consultation literally all over the world: two days in London, two weeks at the Department (including her Norway debrief), then one day each in Tokyo, Hong Kong and Bangkok—with two weeks for a Redlands vacation sandwiched in between.

While in Washington DC, Frances met Jack Kubisch, who had just been appointed Assistant Director of U.S. Operations (now AID) at the embassy. Jack, now a retired ambassador and living near Frances' old Madrid FSO associate, Findley Burns, in North Carolina, said in a May, 2003, phone conversation with the author that after ten years in industry, he reentered the Foreign Service in 1961. His meeting with Frances went well enough until he commented, "Ceylon should be an interesting place." Frances coolly responded, "Mr. Kubisch, all countries are interesting." As Frances implied at the outset of the Norway chapter, some diplomatic topics require absolute pronouncements and this was one of them.

Jack also reported that for the first six months or so Frances' relations with her embassy staff were quite formal, with Frances addressing her FSO's by their last name and having them call her "Madam Ambassador." But once Frances got to know the staff, she began using first names. (They continued addressing her as before.) Then after Frances retired and Jack was appointed Assistant Secretary for Inter-American Affairs they became close friends, with Jack and his wife Connie dining with Frances at the Sulgrave Club or other spots around Washington DC once or twice a year. Jack last saw Frances in 1974 when he was appointed Ambassador to Greece.

While in Redlands, Frances was interviewed by old friend Frank Moore, editor of the *Redlands Daily Facts* on April 17, 1961:

> For Frances E. Willis, America's top-ranking woman career diplomat, the Foreign Service has provided a series of experiences of unending fascination. Now she has been sworn in as U.S. Ambassador to Ceylon and is at home, 503 West Highland Avenue, until April 28.
>
> "I am almost as excited as I was on April 13, 1928, when I sailed from New Orleans on my first assignment," she exclaimed. That was as [acting] vice consul at Valparaiso, Chile.
>
> "In this assignment, there is allure, novelty, fascination. For one thing," she laughed, "I've never been west of Catalina. But seriously—it presents a whole new world for me.
>
> "The civilization is old and yet politically it is very new. From the ancient times there are temples, many yet to be excavated, an archeologist's paradise. Then the Portuguese, the Dutch and the British were there for about 150 years each. They have been running their own affairs for only a few years."
>
> Miss Willis saw President Kennedy for the first time when she called on him at the White House last Thursday.
>
> "He is impressive for the grasp he has on the subjects he talks about," she said. "When I talked, he would get to the point before I was half way through my sentences. He listens with remarkable concentration."
>
> Since she is transferring from a cold climate to a tropical one, the first question people ask her is: "Can you stand the heat?" She replies: "The Washington summers [without air conditioning] never bothered me." And then, with a merry laugh, she exclaims, "I won't be able to wear a thing I had in Norway. I will have to buy a whole new wardrobe, practically starting from scratch."

She also finds it a striking fact of geography that her new post is just half the way around the world from California. From here she will fly the Pacific—Tokyo, Hong Kong, Bangkok [with the then obligatory stop in Hawaii.]

None of her en-route stops were ordinary travel stops. More likely, representatives from the resident U.S. mission showed up to greet and then fete Frances when she landed. The Tokyo stop certainly did, as the following April 20, 1961, telegram from "Tokyo to SecState, FOR AMBASSADOR WILLIS FROM AMBASSADOR REISCHAUER" shows:

> Very pleased you are able stop over Tokyo May 4-5. My wife and I hope you will stay with us Embassy residence unless you prefer nearby hotel at which reservations confirmed per reference telegram. In any event, we would like give luncheon for you May 4. Regards.

"Reischauer" was Edwin Oldfather Reischauer, Ambassador to Japan from 1961 to 1966, with one of those old-school-diplomat names, even though he was a non-career appointee. Not only that, but he wrote his telegram the old fashioned way, without superfluous words. Frances didn't talk about any of these stops in her bulletins, so events must have been low key, just as she liked them.

Critical Courtesy Calls in Colombo

After she arrived in Colombo Frances started her official round of introductions and speeches, all similar to her earlier ones: "Greetings, best wishes from my country, glad to be here, all share basic ideals, hope to strengthen ties, etc." Then a subsequent, confidential—and now declassified—despatch of June 2, 1961, reported courtesy calls to Ceylon government dignitaries, starting with Frances' summary:

> Courtesy calls have been paid on all but one of the Cabinet Ministers. All were cordial in their reception but there was little discussion of any substantive matters in the course of these calls [including her call on Prime Minister Mrs. Bandaranaike.] A few of the remarks worthy of recording are reported in the body of this despatch. [I have concluded]

that considerable effort will have to be made before any kind of effective working relationship can be established.

Then Frances got into specifics:

> The Minister of Education and Broadcasting spoke at some length about the underlying philosophy of the takeover of the schools. One was the desire for a truly national education in the national language [now mandated to be Sinhala.] Second, the national education system was to be so organized as to make the best use of the resources available. Third, every child would be instructed in every school in the religion which was the choice of the parents. He continued to say that under the old system the private schools had created a dangerous group of agnostics and atheists. The Christian schools would not teach anything but Christianity and a great many students would not accept Christianity and they had become agnostics and it was from among this group educated in the missionary schools that you found the leaders of the communists.

So that's how communism evolved in Ceylon: not imported but as a reaction to Christian missionary schools. This school-takeover was one of many such nationalization acts the Sinhalese-controlled, socialist government had executed after they declared a state of emergency. Frances continued:

> The Minister of Finance, Mr. Felix Dias Bandaranaike [among other titles he held as the prime minister's nephew] intimated without making a flat statement that possibly modern democracy was not easy to graft on to Ceylonese society. He speculated that possibly it might be better to build on Ceylonese tradition and the way of life which prevailed in the Island when authority was concentrated in the hands of the few. He said it might be easier under such conditions to deal with some of Ceylon's problems. Almost as if he suddenly realized where his line of reasoning was leading him he added that even good dictatorships did not last. The discussion took a completely philosophical and abstract turn at that point with speculation on the eternal search for a balance between the authority of the state and the rights of the individual.
> Mr. Bandaranaike's remarks could not fail to call to mind a speech

made in Parliament on May 17 by Mr. J. R. Jayewardene, UNP [United National Party, the opposition party], in connection with the extension of the state of emergency regulations. There Mr. Jayewardene said, inter alia: "We know—I have heard it on good authority—that the Hon. Minister for Finance has ideas that he can be a pocket Napoleon. That he stitched himself a siren suit like Mr. Winston Churchill and wears the military costume in front of mirrors that surround the (radio) control room at Temple Trees (the official residence of the Prime Minister)."

Whether Mr. Bandaranaike does in fact harbor secret dictatorial aspirations it is generally conceded that he is a very ambitious young man (he is just thirty). Furthermore, as is often the case in newly established or independent countries there is a struggle going on for the consolidation of power, even if not for its seizure.

Frances' despatch generated some alarm in the Department because less than two weeks later Frances received a letter from Assistant Secretary Phillips Talbot offering his help in coping with this apparent Ceylonese turmoil. While his letter was not in the archives, Frances' "confidential, official-informal"—now declassified—June 30, 1961, response was in her 123 File:

Thank you for your letter of June 13, 1961. Although we here at the Embassy have a multitude of problems at the present time, I do not believe that there is any particular one which I need to bring to your special attention. It is good, however, to know that the lines of communication are open and I appreciated your letter very much.

One of the most vivid first impressions is that the government is continuously increasing the scope of its activities. In the economic field, if this continues, there will be very little left for the private sector. The economic development of the country will inevitably be dependent in a large measure on the ability, foresight, integrity, and energy of the government. Since the present government came into power in July 1960, however, it gives the appearance of having devoted most of its time to measures which are having an extremely divisive effect, such as the implementation of the law making Sinhala the only legal language, the take-over of the schools, the establishment of the oil corporation, to name only a few of the most notable measures.

Add to her list: nationalization of the bus companies, the life insurance companies and the Port of Colombo. But nationalization of the oil industry through establishment of the Oil Corporation will soon capture everyone's attention. It will put Frances to a diplomatic test she hadn't taken since the watch dispute in Switzerland.

The Kennedy Missive

On May 29, 1961, President Kennedy sent a confidential—now declassified—letter to each of his ambassadors, including Frances. Frances quoted some of hers, along with reasons why it was written, in her a January, 1971, talk titled, "When the Russian Ambassador Couldn't Speak Norwegian and the American Could—And Other Recollections of a Career Diplomat," to the Stanford Alumni Association and then printed in the *Alumni Almanac*.

In that talk Frances' was describing the massive expansion of the Foreign Service between 1927 and 1971 (which mirrors that of Anthony CE Quainton, as quoted in Appendix 1.) Frances then described the difficulties these changes created:

> This tremendous proliferation of U.S. activities abroad obviously put a much greater burden on an ambassador and expanded his role. Inevitably he had a much larger office to run. But a far greater problem was the coordination of the activities of all the representatives of different agencies of the U.S. government operating in the country. Sometimes it was even difficult to find out what all the different agents were doing. They received their instructions from their head office in Washington, but the ambassador was responsible for assuring coordination of projects or programs.

> Probably there is no better way to give you authentic information on what was expected of me when I was Ambassador to Ceylon than to [provide] a few brief excerpts from President Kennedy's instructions to me in a letter dated May 29, 1961, [expanded to include more of the letter.]:

Dear Madam Ambassador:

We are living in a critical moment in history. Powerful destructive forces are challenging the universal values which, for centuries, have inspired men of good will in all parts of the world.

If we are to make progress toward a prosperous community of nations in a world of peace, the United States must exercise the most affirmative and responsible leadership. Beyond our shores, this leadership, in large measure, must be provided by our ambassadors and their staffs.

I have asked you to represent our Government in Ceylon because I am confident that you have the ability, dedication, and experience. The purpose of this letter is to define guidelines which I hope may be helpful to you.

The practice of modern diplomacy requires a close understanding not only of governments but also of people, their cultures, and institutions. Therefore, I hope that you will plan your work so that you may have the time to travel extensively outside the nation's capital. Only in this way can you develop the close, personal associations that go beyond official diplomatic circles and maintain a sympathetic and accurate understanding of all segments of the country.

Moreover, the improved understanding which is so essential to a more peaceful and rational world is a two-way street. It is our task not only to understand what motivates others, but to give them a better understanding of what motivates us.

Many persons in Ceylon who have never visited the United States, receive their principal impressions of our nation through their contact with Americans who come to their country either as private citizens or as government employees.

Therefore, the manner in which you and your staff personally conduct yourselves is of the utmost importance. This applies to the way in which you carry out your official duties and to the attitudes you and they bring to day-to-day contacts and associations.

It is an essential part of your task to create a climate of dignified, dedicated understanding, cooperation, and service in and around the Embassy.

In regard to your personal authority and responsibility, I shall count on you to oversee and coordinate all the activities of the United States Government in Ceylon.

You are in charge of the entire United States Diplomatic Mission, and I shall expect you to supervise all of its operations. The Mission includes not only the personnel of the Department of State and the Foreign Service, but also the representatives of all other United States agencies, which have programs or activities in Ceylon. I shall give you my full support and backing in carrying out your assignment...

Let me close with an expression of confidence in you personally and the earnest hope that your efforts may help strengthen our relations with both the Government and the people of Ceylon.

Sincerely,

/s/ *John Kennedy*

Of course, Frances had been doing precisely that stuff for the last eight years. Frances' confidential—now declassified—response was in her 123 File.

Colombo, July 21, 1961

Dear Mr. President:

I had hoped to be able to submit to you a substantive report evaluating the impact of American foreign policy on Ceylon. This I find too ambitious a project after having been here only two months. The people of Ceylon were given their independence as a nation only in 1948, and they are still very much in the stage of asserting not only their political and economic independence but also their spiritual independence.

This has led to a zealous movement of Buddhist nationalism on the part of the Sinhalese majority. It has also served to sharpen the divisions in this community of approximately ten million, rather than to unify the country. There are over two million Tamils whose religion is not Buddhism and whose language is not Sinhala [presaging an ugly civil war with the Tamil Tigers starting in 1983.] There are nearly a million Christians and possibly 700,000 Muslims. The struggle for power, which I presume characterizes most newly independent countries, is in full spate here, even between the various factions of the ruling party, the Sri Lanka Freedom Party. All in all, it is a very complicated society and our efforts to help them help themselves and to help them to safeguard their independence are not made easier by the extreme complexity of the society and the divisive forces at work.

Although I have been in the Foreign Service for nearly thirty-four years, I have never had an assignment which was quite as challenging as this one...

Faithfully yours,   /s/ Frances E. Willis

And she had faced some daunting ones, including the 1940 German invasion and occupation of Brussels and the 1954 Swiss watch dispute. While Frances didn't "evaluate the impact of American foreign policy on Ceylon," she did give a tidy summary of their problems, which is the first step in such a process.

The Summit

On March 9, 1962, Frances flew back to the Department for ten days of "official consultation." That trip was preceded by this telegram from Frances to SecState:

> News of [Counselor of Embassy] Cameron's unexpected transfer has already caused some stir. If Cameron's departure delayed and I am ordered to Washington we should be able to give explanation to government and diplomatic colleagues in attempt to keep to minimum possible distortion these developments [would cause] in this rumor ridden city.

It's not surprising that Colombo was a city of rumors, because the country was under a state of emergency with the entire commercial sector up for grabs. But the top two embassy officers departing simultaneously should cause a stir almost anywhere—as it did when Frances assumed chargé duties in Sweden way back in 1932. Hence the telegram.

Although her telegram didn't say why she was going, Frances had just won a prestigious career service award, which would be given in a Washington DC ceremony on March 13, 1962. "So, Miss Willis, please attend even though you must travel half way around the world for this two-hour ceremony," or words to that effect. That must have tweaked Frances' curiosity.

Well, the real reason was in this "official use only" telegram of March 1, 1962:

FOR AMBASSADOR ONLY FROM SECRETARY

President has today signed papers for transmission to Senate nominating you for promotion to Career Ambassador. My heartiest congratulations to you on this well-deserved recognition. Expect White House announcement shortly but in meanwhile your promotion should be kept confidential.

With warm personal regards,

/s/ Rusk

That is a much better reason for going half way around the world. Now Rusk couldn't have told Frances he was just submitting her name along with two others to the President in February, and that if chosen she must come to Washington DC.[87] What a let down if she weren't chosen. So he found a clever way to finesse a reason for the trip and give her enough time to plan it.

A February 25, 1962, article in the *New York Times* reported the career service award dinner, which was attended by about a thousand people at the Sheraton Park Hotel and addressed by Senator Henry Jackson of Washington. Co-awardees were Dr. W. C. Grover, Archivist of the U.S., W. H. Godel, Deputy Director of the Defense Advanced Research Projects Agency, and D. V. Auld, Director of Sanitary Engineering for the District of Columbia. So they pretty much covered the waterfront, as the U.S. Navy likes to say. After receiving her award Frances stopped by the Oval Office to visit the President.

---

[87] The others were W. Walton Butterworth, Ambassador to Belgium, and Walter C. Dowling, Ambassador to Germany.

Frances consulting with President Kennedy in the Oval Office,
March 1962 (courtesy U.S. Government.)

That is indeed JFK's special rocking chair, which he used to ease his chronic back pain. And as usual, the cameraman caught Frances doing the talking, complete with (modest) gesticulation. And they had plenty to talk about because Frances had enough time to get her story together about the "impact of American foreign policy on Ceylon." It is also clear that JFK is listening intently, just as Frances reported earlier: "He listens with remarkable concentration."

To finish the saga, Frances spent five days in Redlands and returned to Colombo on March 29, after a forty-five hour trip, including a seven-hour layover in Hong Kong as Frances reported in an April 1 bulletin to the family:

> I do believe old age is creeping up on me as the trip back was almost more than I bargained for. I did go in town to a hotel, where I arrived about 2:30 a.m. Hong Kong time. I had just gotten to sleep when my telephone rang and the operator said, "Sorry, it is a mistake."

This wasn't the only time such false alarms would occur in Frances' Ceylon tour. But the other times were self-inflicted, as Frances reported in her 1967 "Your Representative Abroad" speech:

There is one aspect of this modern communication which can be trying to an ambassador, as I found out in Ceylon. An ambassador must be available to the White House and to the Department of State 24 hours of every day. That means you must be sure the telephone is answered at any hour of the night. Rather than depend on a member of my domestic staff to make sure that my telephone would be answered at night, I had the telephone on my bedside table. But in Colombo, unfortunately the telephone number of the Residence was just one digit off the number of the de Sayso Maternity Hospital. It was not surprising that a frantic husband would sometimes dial the wrong number between three and four in the morning.

Frances said she could go for weeks without a false alarm, but never said she changed the arrangement. So she probably had her bell rung once a month for four years running. Nowadays there are private hot-lines for such things.

Frances also reported in that April 1 bulletin that she was very busy answering the mail, both the official mail that arrived in her absence and personal letters of congratulations, including one from Admiral Arleigh Burke, Chief of Naval Operations, which must have greatly pleased her. A post-promotion telegram to Frances from SecState Rusk said:

> Warmest personal congratulations on your promotion to Career Ambassador. It was a great privilege for me as an amateur to forward to the President your name as a real professional.

Then this one jumped out of the stack:

> American Consulate,
> Strasbourg, France,
> March 20, 1962.

Dear Frances:

No one can possibly understand more than I, your long-time traveling companion, how much it means to the Service for you to be named Career Ambassador. I was simply delighted when I read this in the Bulletin this morning. My thoughts are with you very often. I spent

Christmas in London with the Summerscales and we spoke of you with much affection and admiration.

In Switzerland you are still mentioned with great nostalgia!

Sincerely,

Constance

Constance R. Harvey

American Consul General

Frances' official reply was not in any of the archives, but she penned part of her draft on the bottom of Constance's letter:

Dear Constance:

Last para: Your assignment to Strasbourg is one I almost envy. If you ever see the French Representative to the Council of Europe, Luc, do give him and his wife my warm regards. My best to you.

Always sincerely,

This was the only correspondence between Frances and Constance in any of the archives, with the Summerscales establishing a singular link. Surprisingly, they don't appear in any of Frances' letters.

The career ambassador selection process was detailed in a 2000 article, "Career Ambassadors," by Donna Miles on the State Department's web site, which said in part:

Congress established the personal rank of career ambassador in 1955 to recognize career members of the Senior Foreign Service who had "rendered exceptionally distinguished service to the government" over a long period through a wide range of challenging assignments. The enabling legislation specified that a Foreign Service officer must serve at least 15 years with the federal government, including at least three years as a career minister, to be considered. Until 1980, appointments were made solely at the discretion of the President.[88]

[Then] the 1980 Foreign Service Act established the rank of career ambassador under the Foreign Service promotion system. That transition

---

[88] As detailed in SecState Rusk's March 1, 1962 telegram to Frances, the appointment must also be ratified by the Senate.

made career ambassadorial appointments less political and more performance based, as are Foreign Service promotions.

But the career ambassador designations are not promotions, at least in the standard sense, rather a designation for the Secretary to acknowledge unusually long and distinguished Foreign Service careers [rewarding] people who have demonstrated through a wide variety of assignments that they have what it takes to tackle the toughest foreign affairs challenges.

The appointment comes with no pay raise and no special benefits. Career ambassadors receive only a certificate acknowledging their status and a white lapel pin with a gold star.

The Miles article then provided a list and short biography of career ambassadors appointed up to 1998. Initially, they were appointed in groups. The first group of four was appointed March 7, 1956, just after the rank was established. It included H. Freeman Matthews, one of Frances' admiring bosses at the Department in 1947, and Loy W. Henderson, another mentor who wrote that fine letter of condolence when Belle died in 1960. The second group of seven was appointed June 24, 1960. The third group of three—Frances' group—was appointed March 20, 1962.

Two more groups were appointed in 1964 and 1969, then no more until 1981, when the new selection board appointment system started. Then they came out in smaller groups—as a percentage of career ministers—every other year or so, including such notables as Douglas MacArthur II, Lawrence S. Eagleburger, Thomas R. Pickering, and Mary Ryan, the second woman and last appointment reported by Miles in 1998. She was nominated by Secretary of State Madeleine Albright.

Because the selection process at the time consisted of a Secretary of State nomination (then President and Senate approval), the key player must have been Secretary Rusk. Consequently a principal clue for her nomination lies in the phrase from his telegram: "a real professional," implying that Frances had met all guidelines outlined in the Kennedy missive. She would interpret those guidelines as:

Learn the language. Meet the people. Make contacts. Know the country. Report important events. Know the regulations. Interpret policies. Negotiate diplomatically. Sell American ideals. Throw good parties. Run a taut ship. Then work hard doing all these things sincerely and tactfully.

At this juncture, the career of another FSO woman, Rozanne Lejeanne Ridgway, must be reviewed. In her book *Her Excellency*, Ann Morin reported that Rozanne got off to a slow start after entering the Foreign Service in 1957, but with advice and counsel from mentor George Vest, her career took off. She wound up as ambassador to Finland and then the German Democratic Republic. She was the first woman to head a geographic bureau, as Assistant Secretary of State for European and Canadian Affairs.

On her way up the ladder Rozanne worked as Class 4 Political Officer for Ambassador Margaret Tibbetts in Norway, starting in 1967. And of course Margaret Tibbetts worked for Frances as a Political Officer in London—a continuous mentoring chain of women FSO's. That's the good news. Morin then detailed the bad news:

> Given the high office she held in [George] Shultz's State Department, Ridgway's many admirers hoped she would achieve the personal rank of career ambassador. Only Frances Willis, the first career woman to make ambassador, had been elevated to that high rank, and Willis's assignments had been much less important than Ridgway's. The number of career ambassadors is limited to a percentage of career ministers, and the single opening that occurred in this period went to Ridgway's friend, George Vest, in 1987. By the time more slots opened up, nemesis, in the guise of a change in administration, had overtaken Ridgway. George Bush became president and placed his friend James Baker as secretary of state. Once again, several high-ranking careerists were shunted aside.
>
> Constance Harvey, at age 84, had driven herself the 180 miles from Lexington, Virginia, to attend Foreign Service Day, always held the first Friday in May. There, for the first time, she saw and heard Rozanne Ridgway, whom she deemed by far the best speaker of the day. (James Baker's speech was "not much.") She thought it was a great loss Ridgway was leaving the service because she was "far and away the best."

That was a tough one, especially to be beat out by your mentor. Certainly, current regulations and politics played against her, especially that quota system for appointments, which wasn't operative in Frances' time. But as argued earlier, Frances' contribution was to clear the way on the Foreign Service ladder, allowing succeeding women to climb more aggressively and fearlessly. And Ridgway, like Margaret Tibbetts, did just that.

The Oil Expropriation Dispute

The Ceylonese government started expropriating foreign oil resources and operations on April 28, 1962, when according to a July 8, 1962, lead article in the *Ceylon Observer*:

A total of 176 filling and service stations were taken over by the Government and put into service of the [Ceylon Petroleum] Corporation on April 28. Esso lost 40 petrol stations and 29 kerosene depots. Caltex lost its port bunkering facilities, 43 petrol stations and 27 kerosene depots. Shell lost 96 petrol stations, 42 kerosene depots.

The article also reported that:

Miss Frances Willis, U.S. Ambassador to Ceylon, has dropped a "gentle hint" to the government that if compensation is not paid early to Esso and Caltex for the filling stations installations and other property taken over, the flow of American aid to Ceylon may be halted.

These events were reported in the July, 1962, issue of *Time* magazine titled "Ceylon: Miss Willis Regrets." It started:

Ceylon which is famed for such exotic birds as the grey-headed babbler, red-faced malkoha and Legge's flowerpecker, also boasts two even rarer Aves: the world's only female Prime Minister and the only female U.S. Ambassador currently on duty... Their relations instead have been as cool as Ceylon's breeze-swept uplands. Miss Willis, a cordial onetime (1924-1927) Vassar assistant professor in political science, believes that the "basis of diplomacy is to be tactful and sincere at the same time." Mrs. Bandaranaike, who confides that Ceylon's fortunes are in the hands of "angels and my late husband," has vigorously assisted the heavenly host by nationalizing Roman Catholic schools, the Bank of Ceylon, transport services, life insurance and the Port of Colombo... [and seizing] almost 200 gas stations and oil depots owned by a trio of U.S. and British firms...

The article reported that Frances reminded Ceylon's Finance Minister—also Mrs. Bandaranaike's nephew—about the aid suspension. The article finished with:

The Prime Minister's response was to draft a waspish letter to the ambassador, retorting that "the best form of foreign aid the U.S. can give to small countries is to abstain from interfering in their affairs."

The letter was also leaked to Ceylon's tightly controlled press; though on reflection a government ministry later denied that the letter had ever been written. Tactful and sincere at the same time, Miss Willis last week pointedly said nothing. Mere men agreed that such a display of patience in quick-tempered Ceylon was as rare as a yellow-eared bulbul—or, for that matter, a lady Prime Minister.

Frances calling on Ceylon's Prime Minister Bandaranaike in Colombo
(courtesy Department of State.)

A similar photo accompanied the *Time* article, with the caption, "What is so rare as the yellow-eared bulbul?"

As soon as Madame B. got wind of the *Time* article, she seized all copies of the magazine and had the article cut out before going on sale! Of course, boot-legged articles immediately started circulating around Colombo and one ended up with Frances. Not only that but one of the not-so-tightly-controlled papers grabbed one and printed it in a local edition.

Frances commented in her August 5, 1962, bulletin to the family that, "the Article in Time is cockeyed. The P.M. never wrote me any such letter. (Personal and private information only)." And of course, the last paragraph in *Time* flagged exactly that point. It probably was a little spin by Ceylon's government to test the diplomatic waters. In that same vein, other short articles in the Ceylon press had Madam B. trashing Frances, calling her a lackey and other pejoratives. But forewarned by the foregoing, Frances ignored them.

Frances then reported "most hectic negotiations" in a letter to the family, which were summarized in a December 28, 1962, lead article in the (closely-state-controlled) *Ceylon Observer* by an "Observer" reporter, with a full banner headline, "Warning on U.S. aid to Ceylon: MISS WILLIS GETS TOUGH," Along with a photo of Frances. The article said in part:

> The frail-looking Miss Frances Willis, U.S. Ambassador in Ceylon, has been giving the Ministry of Trade and Commerce straight from the shoulder tough-talking on the question of oil compensation for the oil companies.
>
> Miss Willis, in effect, told the Ministry that the United States will not be bound by any compensation paid for the assets of Standard Vacuum and Caltex take over for the Ceylon Petroleum Corporation if the payment is not fair and equitable and in keeping with the standard of international law.
>
> She suggested an alternative—that the companies be consulted before notification of Section 44 of the Act [authorizing the take over] in order to explore any other possible methods instead of following in every detail of procedure set out in the Act.

The Ceylon Observer got one thing right: Frail-looking ladies can indeed be tough—not only tough but diplomatic. That alternative suggestion was vintage Frances.

Frances gave her version of the dispute in her 1971 *Stanford Alumni Almanac* article:

> In July or August of 1962 the Congress of the United States added what was called the Hickenlooper Amendment to the Foreign Aid Act. It provided that when a foreign country expropriated American property, aid to that country had to be suspended unless within six months the country took steps to make appropriate payment for the property expropriated.
>
> The properties in Ceylon belonging to U.S. and British oil companies had been taken over by the government of Ceylon shortly before the Hickenlooper Amendment was adopted. As I remember it, we at the Embassy made 35 approaches, at all levels, to the government of Ceylon to get them to negotiate an acceptable settlement. The Ceylonese government maintained it planned to make a suitable payment, but took practically no action. So in February 1963 U.S. aid [$3 million] to Ceylon was suspended.[89]
>
> The outcry was terrific. The U.S. government was stridently denounced. I spent a great deal of time explaining that when the Congress of the U.S. passed a law the executive had to carry it out.
>
> To me, the most interesting result of the U.S. action was that it brought about a reconciliation between the three Communist parties of Ceylon (the three were a regular Moscow-aligned party, a Trotsky party, and a Nationalist Marxist party). They had been at odds with each other for years, but when U.S. aid was suspended the leaders got together and made speeches throughout the country saying that, thanks to Miss Willis, the forces of progress would get together. They even had a great rally and burned me in effigy on the Galle Face Green, not far from the Embassy, and had a Buddhist Monk dump the remains into the sea.[90] The three parties also went so far as to sign an agreement to cooperate,

---

[89] The *Ceylon Observer's* "Miss Willis Gets Tough" article was written about a month earlier, so at that point negotiations had just about ended.

[90] Frances' brother Henry reported in his 1983 Chronicle that the sign over Frances' effigy said, "Go Home Aunty Frances and Uncle Sam."

which was something they had never done before. But within a few
months there were five Communist factions instead of three in Ceylon.
China had invaded India, and the Maoists and Leninists began to fall
apart.

We at the Embassy persuaded the U.S. government, although aid
was suspended, not to cut off the funds for the exchange of professors and students. Before the expiration in 1964 of the agreement on
this subject we negotiated a new one. It was signed not by the Prime
Minister [Bandaranaike], who was also the Minister for Foreign Affairs,
but by the Minister of Finance [N. M. Perera], who had for years been
head of the Trotsky Party. Even before he became Finance Minister I had
established good relations with him just to keep informed about what
his party was up to.

That's where the impasse stood when Frances left Ceylon in 1964—and as far as
Frances went in the article.

The end of this story is documented in a series of *New York Times* articles,
summarized as follows: Ceylon's problems of inflation, crop failures and unemployment, along with strikes by the Marxists, continued to grow, apparently
exacerbated by the U.S. aid cutoff. So Finance Minister Perera came up with a
compensation offer of 47.5 million rupees in the fall of 1964, which was rejected
by the oil companies as too little.

Then Ceylon's economic problems got worse. Consequently Bandaranaike's
Leftist Party and her Communist supporters were voted out of office in March
1965. The new, conservative, pro-Western, United National Party, led by Prime
Minister Dudley S. Senanayake, immediately upped the ante to 60 million rupees
($12.6 million) and that settled the matter. U.S. aid was resumed in February,
1966, at $7.5 million per year—two and a half times the earlier amount, and
over half the one-time compensation payment.

That looked like a pretty good deal for Ceylon. Then Ceylon recovered
economically, now in camp of the West. So a rare battle was won by the good-
guys. But these stakes were pretty small compared to the hundreds of billions of
dollars being thrown around each year by the military during the Cold War. On
the other hand, Ceylon's vote counts just as much as the U.S. vote in the U.N.
General Assembly and it's even better to have friends as temporary members on
the Security Council. So it had a worthwhile cost-benefit trade-off.

Embassy Busyness

Frances reported in a December 29, 1963, bulletin that she played bridge with the Lutkins (her counselor) over the Christmas holidays, and that it was the first time in two and a half years in Ceylon. So that was the penalty for her dedication to embassy busyness, including disputes. The following photos document this dedication.

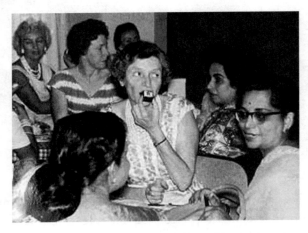

*Frances at a 1961 Christmas party hosted by the American
Women's Club (unknown source.)*

The significance of this photo is that Frances is eating the bottom of the cake—where the chocolate is. She probably didn't eat the sugar icing. Other women in photo are not identified.

*Ambassador Willis inspecting the USMC barracks—and everything in it
(courtesy Department of State.)*

There she goes again, up close and personal, right into the marine's skivvies. Note that the marine being inspected is at full attention, braced and expressionless. But the barracks sergeant has an ever-so-slight grin on his face. This is probably the first time they've been inspected by a woman, especially one taking such a personal interest.

Frances also managed to take some extended vacations. During her California vacation Mildred Schroeder of the *San Francisco Examiner* tracked her down for a May 3, 1963, interview, titled "It's Always Ladies [*sic*] Day" in Ceylon:

> Californian Frances E. Willis arrived in Ceylon just two years ago and immediately made friends by correctly pronouncing and spelling the name of the country's leader, Madame Bandaranaike. She also apparently wiped out the memory of that deficiency in an earlier foot-in-the-mouth U.S. representative.
>
> The tall graying "Madame Ambassador"—always being asked "How can you be Miss Willis and Madame Ambassador"—has had 36 quietly successful years in foreign service. When her Ceylon assignment was announced, Norwegian newspapers wrote editorials protesting "taking her away."

She spent one weekend last year in her own home in Redlands but managed 18 days this trip, which will take her on to Washington, D.C., for official reports to President Kennedy.

In Colombo, Ceylon, she lives in the Embassy, "a lovely tropical house with air-conditioned bedrooms, a beautiful garden filled with exotic birds and an occasional monkey."

Well, a little horn-tooting from the old gal with those "foot-in-the-mouth" and "taking her away" comments. And why not, she was absolutely untouchable now: the senior woman in the Foreign Service, in the most exalted rank and approaching retirement.

But that "official reports to President Kennedy" comment is pretty cheeky. Frances must have mentioned that she had seen Kennedy a few times on her Ceylon assignment, which certainly would impress most American woman. But reporter Schroeder probably got confused in her note taking, and wrote that Frances was on her way back to brief Kennedy. In fact, Frances was on her way to the Department for consultations and might have popped in to see Secretary Rusk at the end of her visit. But no foul, no harm, except that either way she would not see Kennedy again. He was assassinated six months later.

The Lengthy Process of Retiring

Soon after Frances returned to Colombo she hit the big "65," which is the mandatory retirement age for career ambassadors. Now birthdays of that gravity require massive foreign service celebrations, as Frances reported in a May 24, 1964, bulletin:

Thank you all for your birthday good wishes. And what a birthday it turned out to be. Weeks ago the American Women's Association asked me if I would have lunch with them on the twentieth [Frances' birthday] and it turned out to be a joint luncheon given by both the Men's Association and the Women's, and they presented me with a very fine framed batik by a talented young Ceylonese artist. It (the batik, not the artist) is now hanging in the drawing room in grand style.

That evening when I got home there were about a dozen beautiful lots of flowers arrayed in the front hall. There was one mass of thirty or forty orchids of at least a dozen different varieties and colors, the like of which I have never seen before and probably never shall again, from a Ceylonese couple. In fact most of the flowers were from Ceylonese, only two lots from other diplomats—and how they knew it was my birthday I'll never know.[91]

Then the retirement process began, announced by Frances in a June 14, 1964, "information-only" letter to the family:

> The time has come—to let you know that I am retiring from the Foreign Service. My intention to retire after I reached 65 has been in the back of my mind for sometime but now the time for action has come. Details as to timing have to be worked out with Washington, of course, and once that the fact that I am retiring gets into the vast machinery then the "news" may "leak" but I want you to hear about from me first.
>
> If I can manage it I should like to return to the U.S. by ship via Australia and New Zealand…
>
> I have had one or two offers of jobs from colleges, which took note of the fact that my sixty-fifth birthday was in May. But I am planning not to tie myself down to anything for six months or a year.

Frances didn't say which colleges made offers in this or subsequent letters, and those retirement avenues never resurfaced. The basic problem was that, except for the University of Redlands, taking a full or even part time professorship would mean living away from her home in Redlands. And that wasn't going to happen for a while. Then after "that while," Frances had committed to so many civic duties in Redlands and vicinity that she became pretty booked up. Frances did get involved with the University of Redlands' Johnston College trying to sort out their dysfunctional administration, and that ate up the rest of her time. Then she suffered a stroke, which began to curtail all her activities.

Then the deed was done in her July 5, 1964, (confidential) bulletin to the family:

> The Fourth of July reception has come and gone once again—and it

---

[91] She certainly did know. Frances had been plotting those kinds of celebrations for her chiefs of mission all her career and now she was trying to be modest when it was her turn.

is my last one as Ambassador. I have indicated to the Department that I intend to retire and the wheels have begun to grind.

I told the Department I wanted to withdraw as gracefully as possible. I never want to be in the position of being regarded as a hanger on, and although they say "few die and none retire," here is one that is going to.

Frances said there had been no slackening in her duties as a result. In fact it was just the opposite, including 500 guests for the Fourth of July reception. She then described what can only be called a boring chore:

> As soon as I finish the [American Community speech] I have to start that hour and a quarter trek out to the airport to be on hand to say goodbye to the Prime Minister when she leaves for London for the Commonwealth Prime Ministers' Conference. We (all the diplomats) have to stand around out there for about an hour, then the hour and a quarter journey back.

Frances reported that the PM's plane was over an hour late, so she spent close to five hours on that chore. On top of that, she probably had to do it all over again when the PM came back! What a painful ritual, which calls up this Perts sketch.

"Duty before Pleasure" from M.C. Perts' 1924 book.

This is not quite the same scenario that Frances was reporting, but close enough. Certainly the pain's the same. And again, one of Hugh Gibson's top hats probably was not required for the event.

Her next, July 25, 1964, bulletin reported more progress on the retirement front:

> The White House did in fact announce that I was retiring and that Cecil Lyon [another son-in-law of Joseph Grew—still a small diplomatic world] is to succeed me as Ambassador here. From now until the time I leave I dread. Leaving each post has got progressively worse—what with the house, the office and all the farewell calls, parties, etc. I'll have my hands more than full. At least there will by the consolation that I'll never have to do it again.
>
> This afternoon maybe I can get a little done on that horrible job of sorting. Yesterday I gave a few clothes away, but it is the papers that really pose the tough job. Obviously I do not take any official papers with me—but do I or do I not keep copies of speeches? Just to cite one example.[92]

Then retirement documentation started to appear in Frances' dossier, not just one form, such as DS-1031, Request for Personnel Action, which would seem to do the job, but roughly two dozen forms, letters and telegrams, including a flurry of Operations Memoranda worrying about retirement dates and travel authorizations "Upon the Departure of Chief of Mission."

On August 27 a Request for Personnel Action form in Frances' dossier set the date of November 9, 1964, including a note that "Ambassador Willis became eligible for retirement on May 20, 1964." Good to know that sort of thing, even if it was three months late. Then more telegrams authorizing household effects shipments and ten days consultation at the Department, followed by even more telegrams fussing over excess baggage and unaccompanied air-freight weight limits, along with final salary payment, which of course is important to the retiree.

Frances went on to document details of her final schedule, including signing

---

[92] Frances did take most of her speeches. They subsequently found their way into the Hoover Archives.

a new Fulbright Agreement, which had been under negotiation for the last two years, and the usual lunches, dinners, parties and plays. Frances added,

> About two weeks ago I began refusing invitations because I'll never last if I do not stay at home one or two nights and go to bed early. This last week nearly finished me because Thursday night at about eleven thirty I was about to say good night at a party for me and the host said, "Oh no, we are just going to show films of —," and we were stuck for another hour.

So that kind of punishment happens even in high diplomatic circles.

Frances elaborated on the departure chaos in her next letter written on the RMS Oronsay, bound for Australia, Saturday, September 26, 1964:

> After what must have been just about the most hectic four weeks in my life, I sailed away from Colombo on Sunday, September 20. Why was it so hectic? One reason was that I was trying very hard to leave everything in as good order as possible and write "finis" to as much as I could for this was my last post—and I wanted to leave nothing undone that I possibly could do. It was doubly hard because until two weeks before my departure the Counselor [Larrie Lutkins] was absent and until a few days before my departure the head of USIS was away, recovering from a serious illness.
>
> Then another reason was that the Ceylonese must be among the most hospitable people in the world. It was hard work from early morning until the last minute with a lunch and a dinner almost every day. I tried to save out a few but then the Governor General and the Prime Minister both asked for dates and of course I had to give them dates. The G.G. I could only give a luncheon date.
>
> A third reason was the size to which my farewell reception grew, [and it] is a custom for a departing ambassador in Ceylon to give a farewell reception. As the Fourth of July reception has to be largely official this last time I decided to invite a minimum of officials and try to get in as many friends as possible. It did not rain and there was plenty of room in the garden by the drawing room. The verandah and the part of

the garden under the temporary roof were absolutely packed with 547 people.

There is nothing surprising about Frances getting everything right before she left; that went with her territory. So Frances transitioned from total stress to total relaxation on her sea voyage home, just like that last Pert sketch in the Spain chapter. Well, not quite: She had to pen over one hundred thank you notes to letters of congratulations.

Here is a letter from her old Madrid FSO associate, Findley Burns, who knew her the longest in the Foreign Service. It is the only one from Findley in her archives:

> American Embassy, London
> September 4, 1964
>
> Dear Frances,
>
> Your letter of August 15 arrived just as I was about to write you. I wanted to learn when you would be leaving Ceylon, and to express the hope that your return journey would take you through London. I also wanted to say how grateful I shall always be to you for the training and assistance you gave me at my first post, and for the help you have been ever ready to extend to me thereafter.
>
> Since receiving your letter of August 15 I know that you will not be traveling via London. I hope, however, that you may decide to make a trip to London from Redlands in the not too distant future…
>
> I note by the State Department NEWSLETTER that you have been attending Buddhist ordination ceremonies—all the more reason you should pay a visit to London so that I can take you to a proper ordination performed by a bishop in the apostolic succession.
>
> With affectionate regards from Martha and me.
>
> Sincerely,
> /s/ *Findley*

Findley, a fellow Episcopalian, was referring to Henry VIII's Church of England. But their services hadn't diverged much after 1776. The second one is from Clifton Wharton, her "Norway relief," another U.S. Navy term:

American Embassy, Oslo
July 25, 1964

Dear Ambassador Willis:

In this morning's news file I read the announcement of your impending retirement and the appointment of Cecil Lyon to Ceylon. Leonie and I thought of you, your many kindnesses in helping us to get started here, and want to send you our warm good wishes for the future, as well as our regrets that we cannot remain together in the Service longer.

As you are aware I also reached mandatory retirement age in May and will be succeeded by Margaret Joy Tibbetts. [Frances' biographical clone] A unique position I have had in replacing you and then being replaced by another career lady officer.

Even though we have not had the pleasure of seeing you again since the delightful evening we spent with you in Washington in March 1961, it has been a constant source of satisfaction to feel that we had made another good friend in the Service. I know that you must derive a great deal of well-justified satisfaction as you think of your mission at Colombo and Oslo, and other earlier accomplishments in such a long and distinguished career as you have had.

Leonie and I wish that you may have many long years ahead of interest and happiness in your retirement.

Sincerely yours,
/s/ *Clif*

Finally, a 24 September, 1964, press release from the President of the Colombo Plan Council, Mr. Tilak E. Gooneratne:

We miss very much the presence of a very familiar and outstanding figure of our Sessions. Miss Willis was very deeply interested in the aims and objectives of the Colombo Plan and she had such an intimate knowledge of its working, its plans, its procedures that we were always impressed by the intimate grasp she brought to the Council's discussions on any matters right up to the minutest detail.

I was always full of admiration for her very clear and precise analysis of any situation and the masterly presentation of any issue which made such a valuable contribution to the Sessions of the Council and made the President's duties a comparatively light one. I am sure I endorse the views of the members of the Council when I say that we were very fortunate in having in her such an able and distinguished colleague who brought with her such a friendly and warm personality that helped us always to maintain the cherished ambitions, aims and objectives of the Colombo Plan.

On behalf of the Council, I should like to record our appreciation of the invaluable contribution she made to the Council and to request the distinguished delegate of the United States to convey to her on behalf of the Council and myself our appreciation of the services she rendered.

A bit heavy but heartfelt. The Colombo Plan began in January, 1950, in Colombo; hence the name. It is still in operation, now with a "Plan for Co-operative Economic and Social Development in Asia and the Pacific." That plan provides education, health, training, loans, food, equipment and technical aid to lesser-developed Asian countries, including a drug reduction program to Afghanistan.

After a ten-day cruise, Frances debarked in Australia, flew to Los Angeles, spent the night and then flew on the Washington DC for her final briefings/debriefings and the official retirement ceremony.

The action now shifts to a letter from Secretary of State Dean Rusk in Frances' dossier.

November 3, 1964

Dear Miss Willis:

Upon your retirement from the Foreign Service, I wish to express my own appreciation and that of the Department for your many years of distinguished public service.

Yours has been a career of many firsts—the first woman to act as Charge d'affaires, the first to be appointed Career Minister and later Career Ambassador, and finally the first to serve as Ambassador to three countries. Your record exemplifies true professional excellence and I want you to know that I personally hold in high esteem your talents of which you gave so unstintingly during your years in the Foreign Service.

You have earned our gratitude and that of your country which you served so well.

With warm regards and best wishes for health and happiness in the days ahead.

Sincerely,

/s/ *Dean Rusk*

*Dean Rusk congratulating Frances upon retirement
(courtesy Department of State.)*

The inscription on the bottom of the picture said: "With high esteem and warm good wishes to Frances Willis. Dean Rusk." Frances, clearly flattered and pleased, is doing her head tilt again.

Whoever penned that letter for Rusk did his homework finding the trees. But he totally missed the forest. The forest was the Foreign Service ladder. Specifically, Frances was the *first woman up the Foreign Service ladder—all the way to the top as FSO-1.* That accomplishment overwhelmed everything else.

Her first chargé assignment happened because she was at the right place at the right time: a small legation with only two officers senior to her, who had to travel at the same time. And while that event hit the newspapers, it was completely omitted from her two-year Performance Rating Sheet and had little or no effect on her career. What was important was that Frances had achieved a qualified rank to assume chargé duties, due to her recent promotion—the first for a woman in the Foreign Service.

Further, her appointments as career minister, career ambassador and at her last two posts as head of mission were caused by momentum—Frances-generated momentum. She was "on a roll" with sterling performance in Switzerland, so nothing could stop her. A far more significant milestone in her career was positioning herself at the top of ladder for that first appointment as an ambassador.

Finally, her appointment as Ambassador to Switzerland was in large part a political decision. Such an appointment was being vigorously pursued by the women's movement, while continuing to face resistance from the Department's Old Guard. So when they finally caved, they picked the woman with the right stuff, again in the right place at the right time: Frances, who also happened to be the most senior (and "oldest living," as she said many times with a twinkle in her eye) woman in the Foreign Service.

But getting through all the Foreign Service promotion wickets, year after year, to reach that most senior—and eligible-for-appointment—position had to be Frances' major accomplishment. In short, she had to break through all those glass tables before she even got to the glass ceiling. That was Frances' legacy, which of course allowed more women to follow.

That said, Frances had company on her trail-blazing journey: Constance Harvey, who retired as a consul general also in 1964. Constance hung in there with Frances, working her way through those same wickets, along with a two-year internment by the Germans. Then her Medal of Freedom award—while still a vice consul—finally got the Department's attention; so they rushed her to top of the consul ladder. The U.S. Navy has an accolade for this kind of performance: *Bravo Zulu* (Well Done) to both ladies.

Frances' Foreign Service career officially ended on November 9, 1964, with the following Notification of Personnel Action entry in her jacket:

RESIGNATION AS AMBASSADOR TO THE REPUBLIC OF CEYLON AND RETIREMENT FROM THE FOREIGN SERVICE UNDER THE PROVISIONS OF SECTION 631 OF THE FOREIGN SERVICE ACT OT [*sic*] 1946, AS AMENDED, EFFECTIVE CLOSE OF BUSINESS NOVEMBER 9, 1964. LUMP SUM PAYMENT TO BE AUTHORIZED UPON RECEIPT OF LEAVE INFORMATION...

ADDRESS CORRESPONDENCE: 503 WEST HIGHLAND AVENUE, REDLANDS, CALIFORNIA.

19

REDLANDS EPILOGUE

Transition Time

FOLLOWING her 1964 retirement ceremonies in Washington DC, Frances returned to the family home in Redlands via a relaxing railroad trip. As expected, it had been neglected, especially over the last ten years, because Frances and Belle returned to it for only a week or so every few years. A gardener kept the roses and orange grove alive but not much else. So Frances pressed on with essential house repairs, including rotted siding replacement, furnace replacement (from coal to gas), long-overdue painting and—finally—a bedroom air-conditioner. Frances, along with her new gardener Jesus, began renovating the garden. Frances also reported in a letter to the family that she planned to "sort her treasures from other lands" in a small den she had built off the living room. And big sister Caroline, who with her husband Freddie had retired from Chile to the Redlands home in 1962, made sure that the den was large enough to accommodate a card table and four chairs—for bridge games, of course.

Frances and her sister-in-law Enid—the author's mother—started a biweekly letter correspondence that lasted for the next fifteen years. Frances saved all of Enid's letters, which were attached to the draft of her response. These letters provide a substantial resource for this chapter. A recurring theme through these letters was Caroline's declining health mainly due to emphysema. Enid also developed it. Both were caused by smoking and both ladies died in their seventies. So a good part of Frances' early retirement life was devoted (that word again) to caring for Caroline when she was not doing other things—which started almost immediately.

Back to Foreign Service Work

Frances' official retirement didn't last long because just a few months later the Department tracked her down with a request to do a second tour as an alternate representative to the U.N.'s Twentieth General Assembly in New York from September, 1965 to January, 1966. This assignment now required nomination by the President (Johnson) and approval by the Senate.

Frances with Arthur Goldberg, U.S. Ambassador to the U.N.,
*September 21, 1965 (courtesy, **Redlands Daily Facts**.)*

The caption said, "MISS WILLIS AT U.N.—Retired career diplomat Miss Frances E. Willis of Redlands is congratulated by U.S. Ambassador to the United Nations Arthur Goldberg during swearing-in of the U.S. delegation today at opening of the U.N. General Assembly. Miss Willis was called to New York last weekend to join the 10-member U.S. delegation as an alternate."

In an expansive 1967 interview with Maryan Foster, a *Riverside Press-Enterprise* newspaper staff writer, Frances summarized her U.N. tour:

"In the U.N. I sit on the Third Committee, popularly known as The Women's Committee. There is a membership of 112 women, with perhaps one-fourth of them representing new nations eager to get on.

"Our primary concern is with the conventional elimination of racial discrimination and a man, a Ghanaian lawyer named Lampe, was moderator. He is moderate in his views and being an African could get his country-women to listen. One session lasted 11 weeks.

"In our discussions there is some compromise, but great care is taken to insure that nothing is passed that will be in opposition to our constitution, that we do not let newly-independent nations' agitation sway us and that the first amendment to the U.S. Constitution (Freedom of Speech) is not breached."

Miss Willis points out that there is a great change in the status of women world-wide. Newly independent countries she says want to appear very advanced in their viewpoints.

Frances found time to have lunch with Margaret Tibbetts, current Ambassador to Norway, protégé and biographical clone of Frances, and to attend a concert and visit with her old friend, Eugene Ormandy, both of whom were in town.

A New Civic Service Career

Frances did not neglect Redlands, where she joined all sorts of local organizations: Redlands Council of Community Services as a VP, Redlands Book Club, Redlands Trinity Episcopal Church, World Affairs Council of Southern California, the Stanford University Alumni Association, Redlands University's Johnston College Board of Overseers and the Johnston College Long Range Planning Committee, as Chairman (and Frances called herself "Chairman.")

Frances would devote considerable time to the newly established Johnston College, which sported a liberal—even radical—curriculum quite different from the conservative curriculum used by its overseer, Redlands University. And like many college students of the day, Johnson College students protested the war in Vietnam. Frank Moore detailed these problems and solutions in his 1987 book, *Redlands—Our Town*. Solutions included revamping curriculum, redirecting policy, returning Johnston to the fold, and restoring community confidence. Oh, yes, and rebuffing Communist threats to the college. And who better to do that than a retired career ambassador who practiced the art of diplomacy, was a stalwart member of the Redlands community and knew the Commies first hand?

Johnston College did survive this turmoil. As of 2011, approximately two hundred students—about the same number that enrolled in 1969—live and learn together in the Johnston complex, which includes two residence halls and five faculty offices. Students design their own majors in consultation with faculty and write contracts for their courses, for which they receive narrative evaluations in lieu of traditional grades.

Frances also received invitations to speak at local organizations and clubs, such as Rotary, Kiwanis, AARP, Contemporary, Soroptimist (a worldwide service organization for women), Highlands Woman's and Lions. Maryan Foster captured the essence of Frances' now fully developed speaking style in her 1967 *Press-Enterprise* interview cited earlier:

> Miss Willis, whose well modulated voice makes listening such a plea-sure, swears she will never be tempted to write anything "that is not obligatory," writes the texts of her speeches in advance and then does not refer to notes when on the podium. She may, or may not adjust her topics in keeping with the climate of the audience.
>
> "With some groups I find it all worthwhile because of their rapt attention, their interest in every word. Others are deadpan and obvi-ously not too concerned about the world. They are the ones I can't get away from fast enough."

Writing out and then memorizing her speeches was a process Frances honed over her career. She clearly had the capacity for such recall, given that she could converse in five languages. As reported earlier, Frances saved more than one-hundred of her mostly typewritten speeches, which found their way into the Hoover Archives. As one would expect, some were better than others. The not-so-good ones were usually dry and noncommittal. Frances acknowledged that problem in the 1966 *San Bernardino Sun-Telegram* article:

> When I first started in this business, I spoke to a Rotary Club meeting. I was very cautious about what I said and after the meeting concluded, one member said, "I never heard nothing said so gracefully." I will never forget.

More Foreign Service Work

Interleaved with this civic service duty was more Foreign Service action, as Frances reported in her September 23, 1966, letter:

> The day after Labor Day one of the Assistant Secretaries called me up in Redlands and asked if I would be available to go to Geneva in October as the head of the U.S. Delegation to the Fifteenth Session of the Economic Commission for Europe's Committee on the Development of Trade [also known as the Kennedy Round of Tariffs]. The meeting of the Committee starts Monday October 17 and lasts a week or ten days. I do not have to return directly to Washington. I may therefore be able to drop down to Oslo and London before going back to Washington.

That was all from Frances, but an October 10, 1966, *Redlands Daily Facts* article provided a summary of the Geneva meeting:

> The Committee was established by the United Nations Economic Commission for Europe and first became active in 1964. One of the main purposes of the Committee is to seek improvement of trade relations between countries with different economic systems. In ordinary language this means suggesting ways of removing obstacles to peaceful trade between communist and free enterprise countries.

The *Facts* reporter—most likely editor Frank Moore—finally got wise to diplomatic-speak, and said, "Frances, tell me what that means in ordinary language." And to her credit, she did.

Frances did manage to squeeze the London and Oslo excursions in between Geneva meetings, including another visit with Margaret Tibbetts. Those connections were a most important part of her life. But it was not always good news in the FSO world, as Frances' July 7, 1967, letter reported:

> On June 26 I had terrible news from Washington. Cornelia [Wailes] let me know Tom Wailes had dropped dead in N.Y. the day before. Soon I won't want to go back to Washington any more. A year ago Julius [Holmes, Minister-Counselor in London who was the first to

recommend Frances for chief of mission] died and now Tom is gone. Two of my very dearest friends. Very depressing news.

Finally, Some Opinions

Another *Riverside Press-Enterprise* staff writer, Gloria Greer, caught up with Frances in Palm Springs, California for a May 8, 1966, interview. Her article started with the usual events of Frances' career and her now-familiar aphorisms: "Sex has nothing to do ...must be able to pull up roots" etc. In fact the article was titled, "Frances Willis relates 'musts.'" Greer briefly covered why Frances was in Palm Springs with this entry:

> Lecture tours throughout the United States have found her in six cities in just as many days. Her visit to Palm Springs was under the auspices of the United Nations Organization.

She then abandoned details of the Palm Springs lecture to cover Frances' diplomatic opinions:

> "Those who come to the diplomatic corps with illusions of a social and glamorous world don't last long. When an ambassador goes to a party it is to do a job, not to have fun. You are representing your country at all times and are on call long hours seven days a week."
>
> She described the essential operations of a diplomat as having wide and reliable contacts in the country. She said he [*sic*] must know and have contact with as wide a number of the segments as possible—particularly those who influence. Miss Willis described editors, journalists, youth leaders and those in agriculture as the most influential people in each country.
>
> "The only way to build these relationships, which are the tools of the trade, is to build them on a personal basis. The more informally you know the people, the better you are able to establish a two-way communication."

Agriculture is more influential than industry, politics, military? How could that be? Well, her brother Henry was in agriculture—the produce business—and for the last forty years spent the winter months just south of Palm Springs in the

Imperial Valley growing and shipping lettuce. And Frances visited Henry and Enid there almost every year after her retirement, where she made many good friends. Probably some of those friends came to her Palm Springs lecture, and Frances—ever the diplomat—wanted to do some local stroking, including her little brother, whom she greatly admired. Gloria continued the interview:

Asked whether she had found evidence of "The Ugly American" in her travels abroad, she replied, "In my opinion, The Ugly American is one of the greatest misrepresentations of our country and people that has ever been put on paper. The authors took isolated instances and made those instances appear to be the general rule—contrary to fact."

Miss Willis took issue with the impression that foreign diplomats make a study of the country's language while our diplomats do not. "I have never known a Russian ambassador who spoke the country's (where they were stationed) language," she said firmly. "I don't say that there aren't Soviet ambassadors who do converse in the language of the country in which they serve, but I have never known one who did in the three countries where I have been ambassador."

"It is not enough," according to Miss Willis, "to understand the present when a diplomat is sent to a foreign country. You must know the history—and not just political, military and religious history—but the culture of the country so that, as much as possible, you can understand the psychology of the people."

She is often asked her opinion on the issue of seating Red China in the United Nations. "In my estimation, the United Nations was established for certain purposes. The qualifications for membership were laid down clearly in the United Nations charter. Red China has never given an indication that it is prepared or willing to live up to those qualities. I sincerely hope some day Red China will be willing to abide by the charter, but in my opinion, if the U.N. is to be effective you can't throw the charter out of the window." [93]

She feels it is unfortunate that critics of the United Nations ignore the fact that 95 per cent of the U.N. business concerns economic and social development programs, rather than political aspects.

And she is outspoken in her personal criticism for critics of the

---

[93] Five years later (1971) Red China was admitted to the U.N. and Taiwan was booted out.

administration's policy in Vietnam. As she put it, "In the second half of the twentieth century, if a country that is free and wants to be free isn't qualified for assistance —who is?"

Frances expanded on Vietnam in the 1967 Maryan Foster interview:

When asked if reports that our national prestige was at its lowest ebb in history as some of our own Congressmen charge, Miss Willis stated: "It is not true that our prestige in other nations is low. Many factors are shaping today's history. There is dissension here at home for one thing. Our European allies can once more stand on their own feet. They have rebuilt their industries and have become more independent of us.

"France was on its knees at the end of World War II and President De Gaulle remembers it and deplores that memory. He's an extraordinary personality who has done a great deal for France. Frenchmen are too individualistic for France to be an easy country to govern."

Germans, she said are concerned about our foreign policies, as are Latin Americans. The concern, she believes, is natural. We are paying less attention to them and devoting our main efforts to where the problems are and Vietnam is our No. 1 problem today.

"Our alliances in Europe and Asia are going extremely well. The stronger our allies get, the less they need us. That's as it should be. Whether or not peace marchers are hurting our image abroad is debatable. Liberal Americans don't believe they are and conservatives do. If Hanoi chooses to think they (peace marchers) will change our policy toward Vietnam, it is indulging in wishful thinking." [94]

Members of Congress today either back our current policy or attack it, but Miss Willis said the situation is nowhere near as virulent as the attack Sen. Henry Cabot Lodge (grandfather of the former U.S. Ambassador to Vietnam) laid on President Woodrow Wilson in 1919 [as described in the Switzerland chapter.] "This situation is mild compared to the 1919 one."

An ever-loyal administration spokesman. In fact Frances once commented in

---

[94] Unfortunately, it was "our policy toward Vietnam" that was the wishful thinking.

a 1967 *Claremont Courier* article that if you disagreed with U.S. foreign policy, "You'd better resign." Later in the article she elaborated:

> "The President and the Secretary of State make the decisions. They must consider the entire picture of the United States in world history. Usually their decisions are, on the whole, wise. But there's a line (with yourself) beyond which you cannot go. Ambassadors have resigned."

Then Frances began to record second thoughts about Vietnam, first in a 1968 "after-action" report to SecState from her seventeen-day speaking trip to Japan celebrating Human Rights Year:[95]

> If we are to have the necessary cooperation between our two countries we must explain to a wider audience 1) our aims in Vietnam, 2) our defense requirements in the Pacific area, 3) our policies on the liberalization of trade, and 4) on foreign aid.

That gentle nudge about Vietnam was a new pronouncement from Frances. Then a year later in her May 11, 1969, *Los Angeles Times* interview with Ursula Vils, she said,

> The United States is so powerful that we have seen some of the results in terms of limitations [when using such power.] In the world today, military and economic power cannot accomplish whatever a strong nation wants. We must follow policies to win voluntary cooperation from other nations.

Those comments were capped by this statement at the end of a talk she gave to the Stanford Alumni Association in 1971:[96]

> No nation, not the United States nor any other nation, can

---

[95] Frances spoke on women's role in human rights and in government. Her new title for this assignment was "American Specialist in Japan." She gave nine speeches and attended "countless social gatherings" during her tour.

[96] Frances was Stanford's first "Alumnus(a) in Residence." She also spoke to classes about her life as an ambassador, visited with students and was honored at a faculty reception.

concentrate on the solution of domestic problems if it is engaged in war. Because of the mega transformation of our world I believe that never before has it been so essential to find peaceful solutions of conflict between nations. As I see it, it is a key test of man's intelligence to devise and operate an organization which can cope effectively and peacefully with world problems.

Those are pretty strong—but of course indirect—words from a diplomat, especially on current foreign events. Because Vietnam was the principal U.S. foreign event during this period, it's no stretch to infer that Frances was pointing directly to the floundering war in Vietnam and the increasingly ugly fallout. So she was gently but firmly nudging the administration to both face unpleasant facts and change their ways—and doing it publicly.

In February 1970 Frances crashed her automobile in Redlands, breaking her ankle in two places and sustaining whiplash. The ankle needed multiple operations, followed by a multiple year recovery on and off crutches. (She was still using crutches in March, 1973.) The whiplash was severe and apparently began to affect her memory.

That accident slowed her down for the better part of a year, which gave her a chance to answer the mail, specifically two requests for her opinions on current State Department problems.

The first request was a March 16, 1970, letter from the Department, describing an internal study to reform and revitalize itself. It then asked Frances for her opinion on "obstacles to creative thinking in the Department," cast as answers to questions in an enclosure to the letter. The first question and Frances' answer is, in part:

Question: From your knowledge of the Department did the top leadership encourage or create a climate conducive to creativity?

Answer: The role of the Department of State and of the Foreign Service, their functions, and their size have expanded since World War II to such an extent that comparisons of creativity in the pre- and post-war periods are not likely to be helpful. One observation, however, is important: The vastness of the present organization is a serious obstacle, if not barrier, to "creativity" on the part of almost all except those in high level positions.

Each time a new level is introduced in the chain of command the effectiveness of creativity at the lower levels is inevitably reduced. Progressively, therefore, with the population explosion in the Department of State and the Foreign Service the "climate conducive to creativity" has deteriorated.

A great obstacle to effective creativity on the part of lower ranking officers was introduced when Mr. Stettinius became Secretary of State and for the first time in the history of the Department established a prolific Executive Secretariat. The effect was not immediately obvious because during his tour of duty, which lasted only a few months, he was absent a great deal of the time, in Yalta, in San Francisco, etc. and the Honorable Joseph C. Grew was Acting Secretary. Mr. Grew had been in the Foreign Service for forty years and he worked directly and in close contact with the officers, no matter how junior, who were handling a problem which required top level decision. Since Mr. Grew's time this has never been so to my knowledge.

Then in response to the last question about "recommendations for the future," Frances wrote:

My recommendation is for a considerable reduction in the size of the establishment. The Department has far too many "layers" in it and it is "over structured." The necessary work could be done by a much smaller number of persons if less time was spent in meetings, at all levels.

Here was another first for Frances: a direct shot first at her old boss Secretary of State Stettinius and then at the Department's bulk and resulting bureaucracy. Well, they asked for some candor and they got it. Her comments also confirm that Grew was her hero as well as mentor.

The second letter was from Miss Shirley Newhall, editor of the *Foreign Service Journal*, who asked Frances to respond to seven questions that were troubling the Department—triggered by George Kennan's interview in the *August 1970 Journal.*[97] Frances responded in September, 1971, with apologies for the delay, including her "antipathy to writing:"

---

[97] The Kennan interview was conducted about the time of the first Department request. So

One of the greatest joys of retirement was the release from the obligation to write. I have never liked to write and I seldom like what I have written.

Again, that aversion surfaces but now in an even stronger statement. Then the last piece of this puzzle fell into place: Frances had been trained in formal writing all her life. It started during her early school years and continued with the Kemper Hall sisters, who probably would have used Latin if they could have snuck it by the Wisconsin School Board. All her Stanford theses were written in this formalism, which of course was the prescribed style of the times. And certainly her Foreign Service despatches and reports had to be written that way.

In contrast, Frances' bulletins and letters to the family were both conversational and witty. But this informal style was certainly not appropriate for official correspondence. So if she were going to write serious things like letters to the Department—or her biography—it must be in the formal, tortured syntax. And that's what she was talking about: She didn't like to write that way.

But Frances did suffer through the *Journal* request, which is fortunate because her answers capture many of her convictions formed over thirty-seven— now forty-four—years of service.

Question: Miss Willis, George Kennan said that he would not recommend that a very ambitious competitive and bright young person enter the Foreign Service at the bottom. Would you agree with this after your distinguished career?

Answer: Service of our country should, in my view, be the dominant concern of a Foreign Service officer, not personal advancement, wealth, power or prestige. Personal gain should not be the goal but service linked with a lifetime of incomparable and rich experience. I would, therefore, encourage any young woman or man who has the desire and ability to serve at any time in any place, and in any capacity, to try to enter the Foreign Service.

Question: We know that you have been reading The Task Force reports. Do you think the Foreign Service is capable of reform from within?

---

the two requests were either coordinated or in reaction to one another. In any case, reformation was afoot, likely instigated by George Kennan.

Answer: I am sure that the only effective change that can be made and prevail in the Service must be "reform from within." Whenever outsiders who have no first-hand knowledge or experience in the Foreign Service take over, [again read Edward Stettinius] the long-term results are likely to be detrimental. This conclusion is well substantiated by the happenings during my thirty-seven years in the Service.

Although I am not prepared to comment on the Task Force recommendations, I would like to offer comments on three current issues. First, I oppose the joining or establishment of a trade union by Foreign Service officers. If there is conflict of interest, the structure should be altered to restore the essential unity. Second, service persons should not be retired because their promotion is not rapid. Third, the retirement of Career Ministers at the age of sixty instead of sixty-five is irrational and detrimental to the Service.[98]

Question: Do you agree with George Kennan and Ellis Briggs [her 1927 FSO bachelor friend from Peru] that the Department is overstaffed?

Answer: I fully agree. I also agree with George Kennan 1) on the futility of most committee meetings; 2) on the need to integrate policy making and administrative functions; 3) on the desirability of a reduction in the volume of reporting of facts and an increase in evaluation and judgment; and 4) on the wisdom of an increase rather than a decrease in the number of U.S. Consulates since every Foreign Service officer really needs the experience of serving as a consular officer.

Question: It has been charged that the National Security Council has become so powerful (and important in the mind of the President) that it tends to downgrade the Department. What do you think of this?

Answer: The modern excess of bureaucracy is harmful whether it is connected with the President's staff, the National Security Council, the Foreign Service, the Department of State, the Department of Defense or any other government agency. The relationship between the President and the Secretary of State is always a matter of crucial importance in the formulation of foreign policy.

Question: In this jet age, some say that the importance of an

---

[98] Frances argued that second issue to Dean Acheson back in 1946, but lost to the USN's up-or-out promotion system. Obviously she never became a convert. But she ultimately won the first and third issues.

ambassador has decreased since the Secretary or other high-ranking officers can reach a trouble spot so quickly.

Answer: In our changing world the role of an ambassador as well
as a great deal else has changed. [One of her favorite speaking themes.]
The functions of an ambassador have not decreased but escalated almost
immeasurably since World War II.

Surprisingly, Frances didn't present arguments or examples supporting this
last assertion, so she and her fellow ambassadors lost that one. But her answers to
both the Department and the Journal questionnaires were incisive: Stettinius did
a bad thing; service is paramount, the bureaucracy is much too big and ambassadors are still important. And with the exception of their answers to the Foreign
Service entry question, Frances and George Kennan were again singing from the
same page in the Foreign Service hymnal.

George Frost Kennan, 1904-2005, is best known as the chief architect of
Soviet containment policy during the Cold War (1947-1989), starting with
his anonymous 1947 article in the *Foreign Affairs* journal, popularly called the
"X-Article." He also played a key role in the Marshall Plan and the rebuilding of
Japan after WW II.

He was then assigned as the first Director of the Policy Planning Staff for
the State Department, then becoming Counselor to the Secretary of State in
1949. It is now called Undersecretary for Global Affairs. Kennan left the State
Department to join the Institute of Advanced Studies at Princeton, New Jersey,
for writing and instruction in U.S. foreign policy.

That didn't last long because Eisenhower recalled him to become Ambassador
to the Soviet Union, 1952-1960. That was followed by a Kennedy appointment
as Ambassador to Yugoslavia in 1961. Kennan had a significant role in launching
CIA's covert operations, which he later said was "the greatest mistake I ever
made."[99] He then returned to Princeton as a Professor Emeritus to continue his
prolific writing. He died in 2005 at the age of 101.

Kennan published six books and many reports and articles, and gave
numerous interviews, lectures and opinions throughout the twentieth and into
the twenty-first century. Consider, for example, this spot-on prediction he made
in Jane Meyer's "The Talk of the Town" column from the October 14, 2002, *New
Yorker* titled, "A Doctrine Passes:"

---

[99] Because they were so bad at it.

The apparently imminent use of American armed forces to drive Saddam Hussein from power, from what I know of our government's state of preparedness for such an involvement, seems to me well out of proportion to the dangers involved. I have seen no evidence that we have any realistic plans for dealing with the great state of confusion in [Iraqi] affairs which would presently follow even after the successful elimination of the dictator. I, of course, am not well informed. But I fear that any attempt on our part to confront that latent situation by military means alone could easily serve to aggravate it rather than alleviate it.

When that prediction came to pass, it was followed by Kennan's 2004 pronouncement that U.S. foreign policy "suffers from confusion, ignorance, narcissism, escapism and irresponsibility." Clearly, the lesson from these observations is to pay attention to the old guys, especially those who have been around every block in town.

Autobiographical Agony

The final Kennan contribution to this biography is his March 14, 1973, letter to Frances' brother Henry, in response to Henry's letter asking Kennan how he crafted his memoirs and how to proceed with the one Frances was considering. (Excerpts are reproduced in the Introduction.) Henry then forwarded Kennan's letter to Frances, reporting that all agreed she should write it herself and that "you should let your hair down, bare your soul, as Kennan did." Henry and Enid, along with Graham Stuart the retired Stanford Political Science professor, offered to help in organizing the material she kept after retirement. Frances responded to her brother:

> Needless to say since the arrival of your letter of March 27, with a copy of George Kennan's letter to you, I have been cogitating almost continuously about the contents. I agree wholeheartedly that George's principles of "preliminary clarity as to what one wants to say and then much care on the saying of it" are essential.
> But there are two factors which I fear would in my case make it difficult to achieve "preliminary clarity." The first is that I never retained any written record of what I did officially. I never took away from any

post a copy of any official document, a telegram, letter, despatch, note to a foreign government, memorandum of a conversation, and I never kept a diary. The really well constructed autobiographies or memoirs, such as those by George Kennan, Joseph Grew and Kenneth Galbraith, are firmly based on the written records which they had kept, and from which they quoted. I have none. (I said "well constructed autobiographies and memoirs," not "good ones" because I could not call Galbraith's "good" because he published things that in my opinion he should not have.) [100]

The second factor which would also impair "preliminary clarity" in my case is that my capacity for "complete recall" is now dubious. As you know, particularly since this last accident, my memory is agonizingly weak.

If my mental and moral recuperation catches up with my physical healing our attack in May on the superficial material stored in the attic and the basement may help us decide what, if anything, is worth doing, even if "preliminary clarity" is difficult to attain.

I have commented on a number of occasions about what I consider my unsatisfactory style of writing. It follows that "much care in saying" what one wants to say might not produce results of which I would approve.

Do not let these dismal comments discourage you because I still hope we can accomplish something acceptable, even if not entirely satisfactory...

While those "dismal comments" were daunting, a critical element of her biography was missing: her struggle up the Foreign Service ladder. That element was documented only in her dossier, which she did not have. And not once did Frances say she should request it from the State Department archives. She either forgot about it, or if she did think about it, decided there was nothing useful in it.

Enid and Henry did visit Frances in Redlands in May, 1973, but there is no record of them sorting or documenting anything. Thus the result of these letters, phone calls and visits was nothing. It remained so until the Redlands home was

---

[100] Galbraith and Frances knew each other when he was Ambassador to India and Frances was Ambassador to Ceylon; they would meet again a year from the date of this letter.

closed ten years later in 1983 and Frances' effects were sent to the Hoover and Redlands Smiley Libraries, where they were sorted and cataloged—with the author's eternal gratitude.

Frances finally recovered enough to cast off her crutches and get back to work, this time as a Consultant-Public Member of the U.S. Information Agency Selection Panel, held for a month starting January 7, 1974, in Washington DC. Frances was worried about this new assignment, as she told the *Riverside Press* in a January 8, 1974, interview:

> "I just hope I can do a good job for them," she says, not once, but several times. She is "after all, getting old. It makes me so mad when I have to struggle to come up with a word, a word I know so well. It just makes me mad."

There's that memory lapse again, now really beginning to bother Frances, along with the family. Frances did not report how she did on this job.

Frances also got back into local events, entertaining her old ambassador-in-arms John Kenneth Galbraith, with cocktails at her home. Then they went to dinner, followed by his talk to the World Affairs Council at the University of Redlands.

*Galbraith and Willis, following his talk to the World Affairs
Council in Redlands, April 19, 1974 (courtesy **Redlands Daily Facts**.)*

The headline and text accompanying the photo read: "Famed economist talks at UR; John Kenneth Galbraith speaks to hundreds here. AMBASSADORS— Economist John Kenneth Galbraith (left), former Ambassador to India, wears in his lapel an orange blossom picked at the home of Frances Willis. She wears a silk scarf he gave her when she was Ambassador to Ceylon and he visited her there."

So Frances must have forgiven Galbraith for his publishing misadventures. They both are sporting rather dour looks, which for Galbraith is not surprising, considering the following aphorism ascribed to him: "Only the man who finds everything wrong and expects it to get worse is thought to have a clear brain."

The Stroke and its Aftermath

Following these events, Frances started plans for a round-the-world trip, revisiting old haunts, old friends and new places, starting in November, 1974. Her first stop was at the Hotel Roosevelt in New York, apparently the preferred choice of out-of-town U.S. diplomats. She had dinner the first night with her old Madrid FSO associate, Findley Burns, who reported the following events in a May, 2003, phone conversation with the author.

The next morning Frances was having breakfast and collapsed with a massive stroke. Two Secret Service Officers, also having breakfast but whose names are lost, recognized Frances and rushed her to a nearby hospital and into intensive care. They remembered that Frances had worked at the U.N., so contacted Harry McKee an FSO who was working at the U.N. McKee didn't know Frances but knew Findley and knew that Findley knew Frances. So he called Findley, who rushed over to the hospital to see Frances and notify the family.

Apparently Frances suffered a hemorrhagic stroke, which required hospitalization for about a month. But then she recovered sufficiently to return home under her own steam. She subsequently had two cranial operations in Redlands performed by her family physician, Dr. James Fallows, which led to a nearly complete physical recovery in the next six months. Unfortunately, her mental facilities did not recover as well, which accelerated her memory loss.

None of this stopped her, because by July, 1975, she had talked Dr. Fallows into clearing her to resume the trip. And in August she was again on her way, this time successfully around the world. Frances reported that she stayed in seven hotels and nine homes of resident diplomats. She also added a first stop at Martha's Vineyard to visit her cousin, Marion Sanger and her husband Richard in their summer home.

One letter from Frances survived her trip and reported that her visit to Ambassador Philip Crowe in Copenhagen coincided with that of Julia and Paul Child, and that her old domestic staff, Alberto, Livia and Adriana Gay, whom Crowe had hired after Frances retired, "were just as wonderful and loveable as ever."

So Findley Burns popped up yet again. As reported earlier, Frances first met Findley when he was assigned as her assistant administrative officer in Madrid in May, 1942—his first post as an FSO. They kept in touch throughout their careers as Frances said in her 1968 letter to the Department:

> There are a few people on duty in the Department now who have known me for many years and who have worked with me at different stages in my career. Possibly the one who has known me longest is Findley Burns.

The Department's Office of the Historian provided the following vita on Findley Burns, b May 4, 1917, Maryland:

Princeton AB, 1939
FSO, Feb 1942
Assistant Administrative Officer, Madrid, May 1942
Administrative Officer, Brussels, Oct 1944
Personnel Officer, Wash DC, June 1949
Harvard, Sept 1950
Political Officer, Vienna, July 1951
Foreign Service Inspector, Feb 1954
Political Officer, Berlin, Aug 1958
Special Assistant to Deputy Under Secretary for Administration,
    Washington DC, Aug 1960
National War College, Aug 1960
London Consulate, Administration Affairs, June 1962
Ambassador to Jordan, May 1966
Deputy Assistant Secretary for Management, Bureau of Inter-American
    Affairs, Jan 1968
Ambassador to Ecuador, Mar 1970
Retired, 1974; worked at U.N. until 1980

Along the way Findley received the Superior Service and Distinguished Honor awards. Frances undoubtedly had a hand in boosting his career during her tours on the Personnel Selection Board. But Frances' and Findley's careers physically intersected only that once in Madrid. The rest were planned encounters, for example that 1948 promotion party in Warsaw with Findley and Ned Crocker, her old Stockholm FSO associate. Findley died about a year after his conversation with the author.

Then back in Redlands Frances' memory loss began to accelerate. Nearly all her trouble lay in remembering nouns, which from a layman's viewpoint, had the symptoms of *verbal aphasia*, the loss of power to form words (nouns in Frances' case) orally or silently. It is often caused by a brain lesion, which Frances clearly suffered a year earlier. But no medical records diagnosing her condition survived, so that remains speculation.

These mental setbacks didn't deter Frances from her self-appointed missions to Johnston College, the annual Foreign Service Day in Washington DC and the Stanford Summer Alumni College. But her speaking engagements ended, because she didn't want to embarrass herself in the struggle to find words in front of her audience. Her press interviews also tailed off.[101]

Frances was clearly aware of her problem and was determined to fix it. So in 1979 she started speech therapy. It helped a little, but the decline continued, both in speech and writing, and Frances became more frustrated and now depressed. A letter dated September 7, 1979, from sister-in-law Enid responded to her agony:

> Bless your heart for your phone calls and then a lovely letter. Never worry if you do not have time to answer my letters to you—please. We are delighted you had two bridge games—and also all the rubbish removed from your grove and garden.
>
> Do not forget Stanford University for my sake, if no one else's. I want your lovely library and three flags, books and beautiful gifts from the countries you served those many years [to go there]. As your mother said to me when Ike announced you were now an Ambassador, "Frances climbed from the bottom of the ladder to the very top—on her own

---

[101] Winston Churchill struggled on occasion to find an appropriate word but converted it into an oratorical *tour de force*. Frances reported the effect in her "Spellbound" letter at the beginning of the London chapter.

brains and will power—no politics and no money." I will never forget the joy, Frances, for all of us when the word came out, and do not make small of this honor you earned!

Enid was clearly trying to placate Frances, especially in response to the disposition of her effects, which Frances obviously said that no one would want; so she was just going to throw them away. Not only that but both Enid and Belle identified the major accomplishment of Frances' career: climbing the Foreign Service ladder from bottom to top.

By now Frances' friends in Redlands had become alarmed over her aphasia, including her physician, Dr. Fallows, and the Rev. Henry Dittmar and his congregation at Trinity Episcopal Church. They called her nearest relative, Margot Pomeroy (grand-daughter of Frances' uncle George James) in Claremont, who immediately came, surveyed the situation and gently took charge. Margot found live-in, and most honest, housekeepers who could understand Frances and chauffeur her about town, including trips to Trinity Church and Johnston College.

Margot reported that during the last three years of Frances' life, she came to Redlands at least once a week to look after Frances. She also enlisted help from Avis Taylor, Frances' friend and CPA, along with the author, to help with Frances' finances. But it was a tough sell getting Frances to relinquish any of her finances, because she had been doing them herself for the last sixty years. Frances reluctantly agreed to these arrangements so that part of her life became orderly.

The family, with Margot in the van, came to see Frances when they could and Redlands friends stood solidly by her—just as the family knew they would when they moved to Redlands in 1916. It was that kind of small town then and continued that way through 1983.

Frances died at her home in Redlands July 20, 1983. Cause of death was recorded by Dr. Fallows as *Cerebral Artery Thrombosis* (cranial blood clot). She is buried with her mother Belle in Olivewood Cemetery overlooking Redlands.

Accolades

Frances' obituary and photo were carried in newspapers and wire services, including the *New York Times, Washington Post, Los Angeles Times* and the *San Francisco Chronicle*, along with all the local papers. The *San Bernardino Sun* printed a special editorial. And of course the *DACOR Bulletin* covered her death.

Three special obituaries follow, one capturing Frances from Stanford's point of view, one from her family's point of view and one from Redlands' point of view. The Stanford view was published in the 1991 *Centennial Issue of the Stanford Magazine.* The magazine was dedicated to short vignettes of significant alumni, including Frances:

THE FIRST LADY OF DIPLOMACY

The world was her home. Frances Willis, '20, PhD '23, served the U.S. Foreign Service in Chile, Sweden, Belgium, Spain, Britain, and Finland before she was named the first United States Ambassador to Switzerland in 1953. She was also the first American woman to achieve the rank of career ambassador.

Willis was an old hand at breaking new ground. For example, she and a colleague were the first women diplomats presented at the Court of St. James in London. The British newspapers noted with delight that this marked the first time U.S. officials had curtsied to the king.

Willis proved to be an extremely capable diplomat, able to quickly adapt to each new post. While serving in Belgium, she developed such an excellent network of sources that she was able to alert the U.S. government of Hitler's attack on Belgium 20 hours before it began.

When she was first selected by President Dwight Eisenhower to serve in Switzerland, some foreign diplomats expressed skepticism about the chances for success of a female ambassador in a country where women did not have the right to vote. But the Swiss government readily accepted her appointment, and she went on to serve with distinction. She skillfully managed to maintain good U.S.-Swiss relations even after the United States hiked the tariff on Swiss watches by 50 percent.

Willis became Ambassador to Norway in 1957. She was so popular there that when the State Department named her Ambassador to Ceylon (now Sri Lanka) in 1961, the Norwegian government requested, unsuccessfully, that she be allowed to stay on in Oslo. In 1964, after three [actually four] years in Ceylon—and more than three decades overseas—Willis retired and returned, at last, to the United States.

—Bruce Anderson

The family view is by the author's daughter, Sherene (Willis) Gravatte, who gave this five-minute talk at the 2006 Philately Convention in Washington DC, in which the U.S. Postal Service unveiled the Distinguished American Diplomats stamp series.

I am thrilled to be here today and in the words of my Great Aunt, "This is remarkable!" My name is Sherene (Willis) Gravatte, grandniece of Frances Willis. And although this is a remarkable occasion, Frances would have thought that such a distinguished honor was being bestowed upon her for work that she felt was her duty.

She was a modest, Christian lady, born in Illinois, brought up by unreconstructed Southerners in Memphis, schooled by a Mother Superior in Wisconsin, and polished by Stanford in California. Pride goeth before the fall was instilled in her throughout her life, and a credo that served her well in the Foreign Service. Furthermore, being recognized on a postage stamp as the first Career Woman Ambassador would have rankled her a bit. I say this because when asked her opinion on the adequacy of college training for women in 1933, her response was: "I believe women have in the past been handicapped by the fact that they have been educated as women. The things in education which I consider worthwhile are equally valuable to men and women."

You see, she was not part of the Woman's Suffrage movement. In fact, she very rarely joined any political organization. She was, in short, the consummate diplomat. She didn't see being a woman as a barrier; in fact she hardly noticed the barrier. She believed the best course was to do one's duty whole-heartedly and with the utmost dedication. The comment most cited in her Foreign Service annual efficiency reports— and encapsulated by her mentor Hugh Gibson, the Ambassador to Belgium in 1938—was, "She works too hard, which is tempered by the fact that she undoubtedly enjoys it." Most of her early efficiency reports from the 1920's, 30's and 40's included the phrase "doing good work, despite the limitations of her sex." The irony is she did not know nor take into consideration what others thought of her; she wanted her actions to speak for themselves.

Frances never defined herself as female diplomat. In an interview in 1958, she defined success in the Foreign Service as "largely a matter of temperament. You have to be adaptable without being a chameleon; live in, enjoy and understand another country without losing the American point of view; be part of a country without being absorbed. That takes the same temperament in a man or a woman."

This honor shows that she lived that ideal. Our family is proud of the legacy she has left us. As a mother of three daughters, I feel privileged to be able to pass on this legacy and her values to them. She has shown us that a dedicated life is truly "Remarkable."

—Sherene (Willis) Gravatte

The Redlands view was written by her old friend Frank Moore, editor of the *Redlands Daily Facts*. Both Frank and his brother Bill, publisher of the *Facts*, recorded Frances' career with precision, fidelity and humor over a span of fifty years. And that made the author's job much easier and certainly more entertaining, with many thanks.

*Frank Moore, circa 1982 (courtesy **Redlands Daily Facts**.)*

When Frances Willis was serving her country abroad she was "Madame Ambassador," but when she came home—as she loved to do—she was just plain "Frances." Astonishingly so. At Christmastime she would arrive at 503 West Highland Avenue to spend the holiday with her mother, Mrs. Bayard S. Cairns. Immediately she would start doing the chores, such as shopping.

Her favorite store was the A&P, which was situated on Redlands Boulevard at the present Bank of America site. When she had bought every item on the list for the day she would hitch a ride home. She might just encounter someone she knew and ask them to give her a lift. Or, she would talk to the manager, and ask him to ask one of his regular customers to give her a ride. Frances was the classiest hitchhiker we ever had in Our Town.

When a woman of such charm does not marry, people will inevitably wonder why. Now that she is gone, I guess it's all right to tell a secret. In 1917 she was going with a Redlands man, Harry Cook. Later, her mother would tell friends that Frances and Harry had been engaged, although there was no formal announcement. When America entered World War I, Harry joined the Army Air Corps and went to France. He survived his combat flights and would soon be home, or so it seemed. He never came back. He was killed in a train wreck in France soon after the armistice.

Frances, too, was to know war. That's when she was stationed in Belgium as a Foreign Service officer. America had not become involved in World War II. The Blitzkrieg swept across the low countries, bringing Hitler's panzer divisions into Brussels. That created pandemonium with which the American Embassy, of course, had to cope. In that crisis Frances kept her cool. She had her head screwed on as well as any man on the premises. She earned a reputation as a Foreign Service officer that was to stand her well in her future career.

Respecting international law, the Germans arranged for diplomats of non-belligerent nations to be taken out of Belgium by train [actually, she drove her own car.] Thus, she made her way to her next post, which was in Madrid. She liked Spain, with one exception—the late, late hours. An avid bridge player, she found that she had to swear off for the duration of that assignment—at least during the work week. "They wouldn't start playing bridge until 11 o'clock, or so," she lamented to me one time. "I couldn't stay up until 1 or 2 a.m. and be sharp on the job in the morning."

Various women of wealth have been appointed by presidents to ambassadorial posts. Harry Truman named his personable supporter, Perle Mesta —"the hostess with the mostest"—to Luxembourg. She became the topic of a popular musical, "Call Me Madame." Frances, on the contrary, was appointed on the basis of merit. She became the first woman Foreign Service officer to achieve the rank of ambassador. Her service, however, was not the stuff of musical comedies. She was appointed to Bern. The Swiss, at that time, were teed off with the U.S. because of our high tariff on their watches. Instead of just staying at the embassy, she circulated all over the country, explaining the policy of her country.

The strongest evidence that her peers held her in esteem came after her retirement. The United States needed the most experienced and able representatives it could find to negotiate what were then known as "The Kennedy Round of Tariffs." As a real pro, she was chosen for the first team. You can rest assured that tariff bargaining is no exercise in tea and cookies.[102]

As a public speaker, Frances was a disappointment to the home folks. They always wanted her to talk about the domestic affairs of the embassy. When there was to be a reception for 150 people, how did she manage? Did she decide on what food was to be served? Would the affair be in the garden or the house? Eschewing backstairs chit chat she would give a serious lecture on U.S. foreign policy and world affairs. She was, after all, an ambassador of serious purpose.

If you look in the files, however, you could find one Grain of Salt in which Frances gave out with the homely details. That was the time the Queen of England was a guest at the White House. Frances missed the telecasts, to her regret. I had taped them and she came up in my house for a replay. That certainly broke the ice. "Did you know the queen?" I asked. She laughed. "Sure, I knew her before she was the queen." As the reception in the White House Garden progressed on the TV screen, she was reminded of embassy days and for once, explained, how she would plan a party and work out the plan of operation with the butler [Alberto Gay.]...

Frances was a charmer. She entertained beautifully. But her talents were always directed toward representing the United States in the most effective manner. It's no wonder that she stood in such high esteem of her colleagues in the Foreign Service and the numerous Secretaries of State under whom she served.

---

[102] As reported earlier, Frances was head of the U.S. Delegation to the Fifteenth Session held in Geneva in October, 1966.

Maybe I should put the Frances that everyone wanted to know in a Grain of Salt book.

Perhaps this biography helps identify the Frances that Frank and everyone wanted to know.

APPENDIX 1

FOREIGN SERVICE HISTORY AND ITS ARCANE LEXICON

Early Twentieth Century History

UP to 1924 the Diplomatic Service and the Consular Service were separate U.S. offices in a foreign country. The Diplomatic Service did political work and the Consular Service did commercial and personnel work. Occasionally these domains would intersect, which apparently caused conflicts—even battles—with consequent embarrassment to their common boss, the chief of mission, and even the State Department. So the 1924 Rogers Act combined the two services into the Foreign Service, where political, commercial and personnel jobs could be done interchangeably. But it didn't immediately work out that way, because the two services were merely amalgamated in 1924, with both retaining their identities and ranks for many years afterwards. Furthermore, this new Foreign Service was still separate from the Department of State, and would remain so until they were integrated in 1954 upon recommendation of the Wriston Commission.

Frances provided a view of the situation in her May 10, 1967, post-retirement address, "Your Representatives Abroad:"

> For hundreds of years it was thought that the function of the consular and diplomatic services was so different that separate services were necessary. It was even argued that different types of persons were necessary to handle consular affairs, to deal with drunken seaman and less distinguished matters, and another type to conduct government to government relations and participate in the court life of the reigning sovereigns. I think there was something basically at variance with

American principles in this separation of the services. It was in fact the United States, which took the lead in merging the two services. There was considerable criticism of this action, which I am glad to report that four decades of experience have proved unfounded. It has in fact worked so well that a large number of other countries have followed our example and combined services.

Anthony CE Quainton described Foreign Service operation during these years in his 2001 article published by the *National Policy Association*, "Diplomacy in the 21ˢᵗ Century: Who Will Do the Work?"

> When the Rogers Act created the Foreign Service of the United States in 1924, the world was a much simpler place. The United States had only 50 or so embassies and less than a thousand diplomats. Today, the Foreign Service has over 5000 officers, and our embassy in Moscow alone has over 1000 diplomats.
>
> Diplomacy in 1924 was essentially a matter of bilateral government to government relations. The multilateral dimension of diplomacy was limited even for the powers who had joined the League of Nations. The America's network of bilateral relations was managed from the State Department at home and by the small cadre of Foreign Service Officers in the field. They were assisted by a handful of military attaches, trade specialists, and locally engaged staff, but the heavy lifting of diplomacy was the exclusive prerogative of the elite Foreign Service. That elite retained its monopoly of diplomacy until the end of the Second World War.

An article in the July, 1946, issue of *Fortune* magazine, titled "The U.S. Foreign Service," described this business in more entertaining terms:

> As a reporter, the service is expected to keep Washington posted on the strength of Franco's domestic opposition, the temper of the Swedish press, the influence of the Arab League, the health of Joseph Stalin, the Peruvian reaction to Peron's victory in Argentina, the market for U.S. refrigerators in India.
>
> As a spokesman for the U.S., the service is supposed to announce and

interpret to foreign governments the policies laid down in Washington; to bluster, wheedle, or stall, as the occasion may demand; to negotiate treaties or spring an American seaman from the Antwerp jail; to protect U.S. property abroad; to handle applications for American visas; to give foreign peoples a favorable picture of American life and institutions; to entertain visiting Congressmen and throw good parties on the Fourth of July.

With a few additions, that remained a decent characterization of the service through Frances' formal career (1927-1964). Nowadays, with near-instant global communications, much of the foreign interchange is controlled directly by the State Department.

Then as the bureaucracy evolved, Foreign Service duties became more rigidly defined. The Western Personnel Institute's 1946 brochure, "Foreign Service, An Occupational Brief," which was in Frances' effects, provides a formal description of the required activity in an American mission, depending upon the size and importance of the country:

A. Political: Negotiations, representation, protocol, reporting, biographic data, secretarial, clerical.

B. Economic and Commercial: Negotiations, trade protection and promotion, commercial intelligence, analysis and reporting of economic, finance, trade, legislation, labor, agriculture, mining, manufacturing, transportation, communications, commodities, etc.

C. Consular: Invoice services, citizenship work, visa and notarial services, seamen and shipping, protection and welfare.

D. Administrative: Supervision, property management, accounts, coding files and archives, mail, communications, personnel matters, administrative reports, etc.

E. Other: Information services, cultural relations, economic controls, library, secretarial, clerical.

Frances, in her 1967 "Your Representatives Abroad" address, commented on the protection job of the Consular Activity:

The classic functions of Consular Officers were and still are concerned with the protection of United States citizens abroad. [It] consists basically of seeing that they are not discriminated against or denied equal protection under the laws of the country where they happen to be. The protection does NOT mean, as some Americans abroad assume, that the Consul will get them off scot-free if they break the law.

The first four of the mission activities were later called Foreign Service *cones*. U.S. embassies were then organized around these cones, each ranked in a hierarchy. Ann Miller Morin in her 1995 book, *Her Excellency, An Oral History of American Women Ambassadors,* defined this cone hierarchy as first, political and economic, then consular, and last administrative.

Ann also reported that attachés and representatives of other agencies such as AID (Agency for International Development) and USIA (United States Information Agency) were separate entities within the embassy, except that these agencies were also ranked hierarchically, thus determining the standing of an attaché or agent within the embassy.

Late Twentieth Century History

Then large, but subtle, changes in the Foreign Service started after WW II, as described by Quainton in his 2001 article.

What passed largely unnoticed in the years of the Cold War was the shift of power and influence away from [the] Foreign Service toward a new array of bureaucratic players to win the competition with the Evil Empire: the covert information gatherers [Central Intelligence and National Security Agencies], the aid dispensers [U.S. Agency for International Development, Defense Security Assistance Agency], and the propagandists [U.S. Information Agency]. The Foreign Service, of course, did not cease to be involved in diplomacy, but its role became less central.

Quainton then documented a second wave of bureaucratic invasion in U.S. foreign missions, now for counter-drug and counter-terrorism work starting around 1980, including the FBI, Drug Enforcement Administration and

Customs. Consequently, the missions were getting pretty crowded with non-foreign-service diplomats. Frances clearly caught the first part of the first wave, but was mercifully spared the rest of these bureaucratic incursions during her career.

Even so, Frances reported in a February 8, 1967 *Claremont Courier* post-retirement interview with Frances Weismiller, titled "Touring the Foreign Service with a Lady Ambassador," that embassy operations had to be changed to accommodate the crowd:

> [The ambassador] must work very closely with the USIA, the military advisory agencies, the Peace Corps, the agriculture people, labor attaches. (There are many Labor governments abroad, and many powerful unions; Colombo's port involved 68. In a port tie-up, where ships hold perishables, confusion in authority can be incredibly costly. Labor attaches are essential.)
>
> Before the Bay of Pigs, "chaos had been almost imminent" due to the multiplicity of independent U.S. agencies in foreign countries. After that historic occasion, President Kennedy wrote instructing all ambassadors to provide leadership, to coordinate and supervise ALL U.S. operations in their countries.[103]
>
> There aren't those many hours in the day. So there evolved a new organization: the "country team." The top man from each agency is a member. The ambassador is chairman. All evaluations and policies are discussed and agreed upon at their meetings. The country team's recommendations go to Washington. For example in 1962 Ceylon took over, and did not promptly arrange to pay for, American property. Our law on such cases requires that foreign aid as such be withdrawn. But the question of other assistance (the Peace Corps, the Fulbright exchanges) arose, and on the country team's advice these were continued.

That's essentially where country teams stand today. Frances then talked about the cost of embassy operations:

> When Miss Willis entered the Foreign Service [1927] it ran on the equivalent of the fees it collected for such documents as passports, visas,

---

[103] Those instructions are quoted in the Ceylon chapter.

and bills of health. Ambassadors tended to be rich men without much background for their jobs. Now salaries are better and the custom of lavish entertaining has changed, so that only a few posts like London, Paris, Buenos Aires and Caracas [*sic*] require more money than a career ambassador is given, and must be headed by the independently wealthy.

The Fourth of July reception for Americans residing in a country can use up half the year's funds; it is being discontinued in many countries for this reason. The really important entertaining an ambassador does is of small comfortable groups of well-informed natives. People who know and trust you will explain things to you about the history, the culture and the real feelings of the people. This kind of entertaining must be done well, but it does not approach the costs of gigantic receptions—at which no one ever says anything worth hearing.

That comment about entertaining in "small comfortable groups" is vintage Frances and was a hallmark of most successful FSO's of her generation. And London, Paris along with Berlin, Moscow and Tokyo, weren't the only negative-cash-flow posts; Frances would have to dig into private funds for expenses incurred in at least her first ambassadorial post in Switzerland. And it was not an insignificant amount—equivalent to a year's tuition at her alma mater, Stanford University.

Foreign Service Ranks

After the 1924 Rogers Act amalgamated the Diplomatic and Consular Services into the Foreign Service, both services retained their own ranking system. Thus when Frances entered the Foreign Service in 1927 she was appointed a Foreign Service Officer-unclassified, a probationary rank for newly minted FSO's, which usually lasted a year. (In Frances' case it lasted over four years.) Then she was appointed Vice Consul in the Consular Service. Vice Consul was the first of nine consul steps, proceeding next to Consul Class VIII, then up to the top rank of Consul Class I.

In parallel, Frances was nominated Secretary in the Diplomatic Service, which required Senate confirmation and an oath, which she took in Washington DC in early 1932. The Diplomatic Service used only three ranks: Third, Second and First Secretary, which overlapped the Consular ranks and were separately appointed. So Frances wound up with two hats, Third Secretary and Vice Consul when she started her second post in Stockholm. These multiple hats could be worn at a mission, but not at a consulate.

For example in her fourth post Madrid, Frances arrived as a Second Secretary and Consul Class VI, then was promoted to Second Secretary and Consul Class V, then to Second Secretary and Consul Class IV, and then to First Secretary and Consul Class IV. Finally, when she reached the top of both ladders, she was appointed Career Ambassador, the absolute top of both services. Along the way she also held titles such as Consul, Counselor, Chargé d'affaires ad interim, Deputy Chief of Mission and Chief of Mission.

James Siekmeier of the Department of State's Office of the Historian said these latter titles are currently known as diplomatic titles. He said that all the old secretary and consul ranks were ultimately folded into these diplomatic titles. He added another set called functional titles, which include political, commercial, economic and visa officers. That meant, of course, that new Foreign Service ranks had to be invented to replace the old ones, which the Department did not once but three times: 1946, 1956 and 1980. An attempt to summarize this evolution and compare it to the more familiar—and more stable—military ranks is shown in the following table.

According to Siekmeier, FSO-unclassified now includes Vice Consuls of career, consular assistants, interpreters and student interpreters, as well as new appointees during their probationary period.

Normally the number two FSO in a mission is the Deputy Chief of Mission (DCM). But he—always a he until Frances came along—had also been called First Secretary, Counselor or Chargé d'affaires ad interim, or just Chargé d'affaires, or even just Chargé. More commonly, the Chargé is a subordinate diplomat appointed by the Chief of Mission to act for him when he leaves town.

It also seems that the DCM was (and is) always a career FSO; otherwise a politically appointed Chief of Mission wouldn't know what to do.

Military Service   *Foreign Service*

Navy	Army, Air Force, Marines	Rogers Act 1924 Consuls	Rogers Act 1924 Secretaries 3rd 2nd 1st			Foreign Service Act 1946	Amendments 1955-1956	Foreign Service Act 1980
(Midshipman)	(Cadet)	FSO-uncl.	FSO-uncl.					
Ensign	2nd Lt.	Vice	X			0-6	0-8	0-6
Lt., j.g.	1st Lt.	Class VIII	X				0-7	0-5
Lt.	Capt.	Class VII	X	X		0-5	0-6	0-4
Lt. Cdr.	Maj.	Class VI		X			0-5	0-3
		Class V		X		0-4		
Cdr.	Lt. Col.	Class IV		X	X		0-4	0-2
Capt.	Col.	Class III			X	0-3	0-3	0-1
Commodore (1 star)	Brig. Gen.	Class II			X	0-2	0-2	Counselor
Rear Adm. (2 stars)	Maj. Gen.	Class I			X	0-1	0-1	Minister Counselor
Vice Adm. (3 stars)	Lt. Gen.					Career Minister	Career Minister	Career Minister
Admiral (4 stars)	General						Career Ambassador	Career Ambassador

Equivalent Ranks of U.S. Military and Foreign Services

Column 3 cues the nine consul ranks to military ranks, with the three secretary ranks cued to the consul ranks using Frances' promotion schedule as a guide. Columns 5-7 are based on Ann Morin's book, Her Excellency. FSO-unclassified has no exact military equivalent. A rough equivalent would be a midshipman or cadet.

The 1980 Foreign Service Act also established a new Foreign Service designation: Career Member of the Senior Foreign Service (CMSFS). It goes with any of the flag ranks, counselor through ambassador. It parallels the Executive Branch's Senior Executive Service (SES) and the CIA's Senior Intelligence Service (SIS), which were established at about the same time.

Then to further compound the complexity, Ann Morin reported that there was a hierarchy of missions during Frances' days:

Until the reformations of the 1980's, there were four classes of missions, class 1 being the highest and commanding a higher ambassadorial salary and representational allowance and more lavish housing, official cars, and so on. Today there are no classes, each embassy being allotted the resources necessary to carry out its assigned mission. The only difference is that ambassadors to posts that were class 1 or 2 are paid at the salary of an under secretary, while those to former class 3 or 4 posts are paid at the salary of an assistant secretary.

Ann reported that Clare Boothe Luce was the first woman (politically) appointed to a class 1 mission in Italy. Then about a month later, Ike appointed Frances to Switzerland. A listing of countries in each class is not readily available but it's clear that Frances' posts, Switzerland, Norway and Ceylon, were not in class 1. By the way, Ann Armstrong, counselor to Richard Nixon and the highest ranking woman in the Republican Party, was the second female political appointee to a class 1 mission, the UK.

Old Diplomatic Terms

The following definitions of diplomatic terms, mostly from *Webster's New International Dictionary*, Second Ed, 1934, might help to clarify the early-to-mid twentieth century Foreign Service arcanum.

Consul: An official appointed by a government to reside in a foreign country to represent the commercial interests of their citizens and to protect their seamen.

Consul General: A consul of the first rank stationed in an important place or having jurisdiction in several places or over several consuls.

Counselor: A law officer assigned to an embassy or legation. Currently an FSO rank equivalent to a one-star military officer.

Secretary: One of the FSO's, forming with consul generals, the higher classes. When assigned as a law officer, called Counselor.

Political Officer: A representative serving as the only channel of communication between the native states and the government of

British India (as defined in Webster's, 1934.) Now probably an official in charge of political functions.

Comptroller General: An official (created by the 1921 Budget Act) charged with the settlement and adjustment of all claims made by or against the government, and with the investigation of all matters related to the receipt, disbursement and application of all public funds.

Diplomat: One skilled in conducting negotiations between nations without arousing hostility.

Diplomatic Agent: An agent employed by a state in its diplomatic service or intercourse or negotiation with other states. By regulations adopted at the Congresses of Vienna and Aix-la-Chapelle, which are conformed to by all states, diplomatic agents are divided in the order of their precedence, into four classes:

(1) Ambassadors, legates, nuncios

(2) Envoys, ministers, or other persons accredited to the sovereign, internuncios

(3) Ministers resident

(4) Chargé d'affaires.

Mission: A permanent embassy or legation, but not a consulate.

Consulate: The residence or official premises of a consul.

Chancery: The mission's office up to the early twentieth century.

Embassy: The ambassador's residence up to the early twentieth century; now the office of the ambassador and staff.

Legation: The office of the minister and staff.

Residence: Now the ambassador's or minister's residence.

Despatch: Variation of "dispatch"—and much preferred by diplomats.

Then the truly lowest consul rank—lower than a vice consul—recently surfaced, the honorary consul: a citizen of one country appointed (without pay) by another country to represent the latter country's commercial interests in the former country.

For example, in 2003 an American beauty contestant in Libya announced she admired Libya, so Muammar Gaddafi persuaded her to act as his honorary consul to the U.S. when she returned home. Another example is the socialite in Tampa, Florida, who entertained generals and diplomats at MacDill Air Force Base so well that she was awarded the rank of honorary consul by Korea circa 2010. Then she decided her work was so important that she promoted herself to "honorary consul general." It's not clear where that rank fits with the rest.

CAREER SUMMARY, HONORS AND AWARDS

Academic Career Summary

SCHOOL	LOCATION	DATES	DEGREE, MAJOR or POSITION
St. Mary's Grammar	Memphis, TN	1907 - 1911	—
Kemper Hall	Kenosha, WI	1912 - 1916	Diploma
University of Redlands	Redlands, CA	1916 - 1917	Latin, Mathematics
Stanford University	Stanford, CA	1917 - 1920	AB, History
Universite Libre de Bruxelles	Brussels, Belgium	1920 - 1921	Law, Government
Stanford University	Stanford, CA	1921 - 1923	PhD, Political Science
Goucher College	Baltimore, MD	1923 - 1924	Instructor, History
Vassar College	Poughkeepsie, NY	1924 - 1927	Instructor, Assistant Professor, Political Science

Foreign Service Career Summary

LOCATION	POSITION	START DATE	SUPERVISOR
Washington DC (FSO School)	Foreign Service Officer - unclass.	Sept 1927	Mr. Dawson
Valparaiso, Chile	FSO - unclass., acting as Vice Consul	Feb 1928	Carl Deichman
Santiago, Chile	Vice Consul	Feb 1931	Thomas Bowman

Stockholm, Sweden	Third Secretary & Vice Consul	Dec 1931	John Morehead, Laurence Steinhardt
Brussels, Belgium	Third Secretary & Consul VIII Consul Consul VII Second Secretary & Consul VI	Jun 1934 July 1934 Jan 1935 Apr 1937 May 1937 Apr 1939	D. H. Morris, Hugh Gibson, Joseph Davies, John Cudahy
Madrid, Spain	Second Secretary & Consul Consul V Consul IV First Sec'y & Consul	July 1940 May 1941 July 1943 Aug 1943	Alex Weddell, Carlton Hayes
Washington DC	Night Watch Officer to Secretary of State Ass't to Under-Secretary of State Consul III Ass't Chief, Div. of Western European Affairs Consul 3 (1946 FS Act)	Aug 1944 Dec 1944 Aug 1945 July 1946 Nov 1946	Cordell Hull, Edward Stettinius Joseph Grew, Dean Acheson Paul Culbertson, H. Freeman Matthews
London, England	First Sec'y & Consul Political Section Consul 2	Aug 1947 Apr 1948	W. J. Gallman, Julius Holmes and L.W. Douglas, J. L. Wenfield
Helsinki, Finland	Political Officer, DCM & Counselor FS Officer 1	Feb 1951 June 1951	John M. Cabot, Jack McFall
Berne, Switzerland	Ambassador Career Minister	July 1953 July 1955	John Foster Dulles
Oslo, Norway	Ambassador	May 1957	Dulles, C. Herter
Colombo, Ceylon	Ambassador Career Ambassador	Mar 1961 Mar 1962	Dean Rusk
Redlands, California	Retirement	Nov 1964	

Post-retirement Consulting Summary

POSITION	DATE	AGENCY	AUTHORITY
Alternate Representative	Sept 1965 to Jan 1966	U.N. General Assembly, Twentieth Session	U.S. Presidential Appointment
Head of U.S. Delegation	Oct 1966	Economic Commission for Europe, European Committee on Development of Trade, Fifteenth Session	U.S. State Department
American Specialist in Japan	1968	U.S. State Department: "Tour of Japan"	U.S. State Department
Consultant-Public Member, USIA Selection Panel	Jan 1974	U.S. Information Agency	U.S. Civil Service Commission

Frances' consulting work was formally sanctioned in a November 4, 1966, letter from William J. Crockett, Deputy Under Secretary for Administration, who started Frances' retirement process. Crockett enrolled Frances "...on the Department's Reserve Consultants Roster, a group made up of the retired senior officers [covering] the first five years after an officer's retirement." Crockett finished with, "We in the Department will look first to the members of this group whenever we need consultants."

Foreign Service Salary

One of the biographical documents in Frances' dossier listed her annual Foreign Service salary. It started at $2,500 in 1927 as an FSO-unclassified when she was attending the Foreign Service Officer School and an acting Vice Consul (VC) in Valparaiso, Chile. After four years of intense lobbying by Consul General Deichman, the Department raised it to $3,000 in April 1931—coinciding with her promotion to VC. She got no raise when transferred to Stockholm as Third Secretary in December 1931. Her next raise to $3500 came in July 1934 when she was transferred to Brussels and promoted to Consul Grade VIII.

Then as Frances slowly moved up the Foreign Service ladder, her salary rose in $100 to $500 steps, so that she was earning the handsome sum of $6,000 when she was promoted to First Secretary and Consul Class IV in Madrid in

1943. That amounts to a $3,500 raise in 16 years, or about $220 per year, a paltry rate today but not too bad during the Great Depression years.[104]

Finally the raises began to accelerate: $9000 when she became an Assistant Chief at the Department, 1946; $10,000 as First Secretary in London, 1948; $12,000 as Deputy Chief of Mission in Helsinki, 1951; and then a massive $13,600 as Ambassador to Switzerland, 1953.

Other documents in her dossier show that four months before retiring in 1964, her salary was increased from $22,500 to $27,000. She also earned that salary as an Alternate Representative to the U. N. General Assembly, Twentieth Session in 1965 and probably in her other post-retirement consulting jobs.

So Frances certainly didn't join the Foreign Service to get rich. She made this point in one of her retirement speeches forty years later, titled, "Your Representative Abroad:"

> The life is strenuous, but intensely interesting. No one gets rich in the Foreign Service. But the non-material rewards and the privilege of representing our country are far more satisfactory than making money.

The best news about her last raise was that $27,000 went a long way to set her retirement income—indexed to inflation—for the rest of her life. So she could live comfortably and leave a modest estate to the family and Stanford.

To complete the salary story, Frances reported in her application to the Foreign Service that she earned 50¢ per hour as a Corrector for the Economics Department as an undergraduate at Stanford, $1800 per year as an Instructor at Goucher, and $2000 as an Instructor and $2300 as an Assistant Professor at Vassar. She reported no salary for her Newfoundland work.

---

[104] As her brother Henry used to point out, a dollar was worth something in those days. For example, Stanford tuition was $200 per quarter when he was there in 1925 but had risen to $225 per quarter when the author started there in 1952. And Henry wasn't happy about that massive amount of inflation, which ran to just under a dollar per year.

Honors and Awards

HONORS AND AWARDS	ORGANIZATION	DATE
Phi Beta Kappa	Stanford University	1919
Fellowship to Univ. Libre de Bruxelles	Belgium Relief Commission	1920
Graduate Fellowship	Stanford University	1921, 1922
Woman of the Year (one of seven)	Los Angeles Times	1953
Dr. of Law	University of Redlands	1954
Dr. of Law	Western College for Women, Ohio	1955
Eminent Achievement	American Woman's Association	1955
Dr. of Law	Mills College, Calif.	1956
Dr. of Humane Letters	University of Rochester, New York	1960
Career Service Award	National Civil Service League	1962
20th Annual Grail Award	Redlands Round Table	1967
Hollins Medal (one of nine)	Hollins College, Virginia	1968
Dr. of Humane Letters	University of California, Riverside	1968
Woman of the Year	Soroptimist Club of Redlands	1968
Foreign Service Cup	American Foreign Service Association	1973

The graduate fellowship of $750 per annum appeared in a *Redlands Daily Facts* article pasted in a family scrapbook. (Frances' mother Belle never missed a thing.) Stanford did not award graduation honors when Frances received her AB in History in 1920. Honors were listed only for bachelor's degrees in 1923 when Frances received her PhD from Stanford, so again she got nothing.

Frances had lofty company when she received her Doctor of Law degree from the Western College for Women in 1955: A Doctor of Science degree was also awarded to Margaret Mead. The Honorable George Allen, Assistant Secretary of State for Near Eastern, South Asian and African Affairs, gave the graduation address, "U.S. Interests in the Near East," which with her Asian fascination should have tweaked Frances' interest.

The American Woman's Association, a private organization of business and professional women, presented their Eminent Achievement Award—a bronze medal—to Frances at the Waldorf Astoria Hotel in New York City. Again Frances found herself in lofty company. Past recipients included Jacqueline Cochran, Frances Perkins, Margaret Chase Smith and Amelia Earhart. They also recorded Frances' response, which she used in many speeches throughout her career.

> One of the primary tasks which faces us in the middle of the twentieth century is to keep the free world united and strong so that the liberties which we inherited may be passed on to future generations.

The University of California at Riverside, about thirty miles from Redlands, entered the local act by awarding Frances its Doctor of Humane Letters degree during its Charter Day Ceremonies in 1968. Charter Day celebrated the one-hundredth anniversary of founding the University of California.

Other colleges wanted to give Frances an award or have her give a speech, but couldn't connect schedules to make it happen. For example, Frances had to turn down Vassar's invitation to give the Kenyon Lecture, January 9-11, 1956, because while she was at the U.N. in New York in December, she had to return to Berne by January 1 "to call on the new President at the Bundesplatz." She also had to decline commencement address invitations at Ohio University in 1956 and Sweet Briar College in 1957 for the same reason: out of country.

Goucher College tried a number of times to confer its Honorary Doctor of Law Degree on her. On the second try Goucher wanted her to come June 11, 1961, for the ceremony with Milton Eisenhower giving the commencement address. But Frances had to refuse because she was leaving Washington DC for Ceylon in April.

Similar disconnects occurred with Bates College, Wheaton College and Russell Sage College. Rockford College wanted to award Frances its Outstanding American Woman Biennial Jane Addams Medal, but Frances couldn't break loose to attend the ceremonies. Rockford made the offer twice again, then gave up.

As reported in the Ceylon chapter, the Department of State nominated Frances for the prestigious Career Service Award in 1962, with the following citation:

> Perhaps the greatest confirmation of Miss Willis' outstanding performance in these important [ambassadorial] capacities is that, although the appointment of a woman as the U.S. ambassador initially has caused some misgivings in the countries of her assignment, her professional and

personal qualities have quickly won the respect and admiration of both officials and public alike.

Homer L. Calkin, in his book *Women in the Department of State*, added more detail, with his quotes taken directly from government citations:

> Willis was characterized as being "one of the outstanding women in the Federal Service and one of its most highly regarded officers in the Foreign Service." Long service as a Foreign Service officer has given her "an experience and knowledge of all phases of the various functions of the Service," with the result that she "is highly skilled in every aspect of her profession." Her outstanding performance as first secretary and consul in the U.S. Embassy in London from 1947 to 1951, "when coupled with the indication of her executive talent," led to her first executive appointment as Deputy Chief of Mission at Helsinki' in 1951.

Frances was only profiled in Calkin's book. She reported why in her October 22, 1968, response to Miss Myrtle Thorne of the Department, who had asked Frances for biographic information to be used in the book:

> You have put me in a difficult position. I want to be helpful to you personally in replying to your letter of October 15, 1968, but for two reasons maybe I cannot be.
>
> The first reason is that I do not have any organized material about my years in the Foreign Service. As long as my mother was alive she kept a scrapbook. Some of the articles it contains were far from accurate and there are so-called quotations of things I never said. In other words, the scrapbooks would not be useful (even if I could find them at this late date) without considerable editing.

The second reason is that she was "agin" articles about "Women in the Service," as detailed in Chapter 1. So Calkin and his staff had to rely on the standard-issue biographies, sundry photos and (inaccurate) press articles as source material for his book.

Then to drive home her point about inaccurate press quotes, Frances wrote

a second letter to Calkin's staff after she reviewed their draft. She first complemented them on the book—ever the diplomat—and said:

> One quotation of me which is inadequate: "Everything I taught was
> something I had read in a book." It should be "Everything I taught was
> something I had read or had learned from professors." Please do not
> object to my mentioning this.

The final version made this correction and even referenced her letter!

But that pales in comparison to this egregious misquote by Muriel Bowen in
the March 23, 1957, *Washington Post*, titled, "Envoy Willis Recalls The "Good
Old Days:'"

> Though she has found her job as Ambassador makes for "an extremely
> rewarding life," Frances Willis sounded a bit nostalgic last night when
> she referred to "the good old days."
>
> The new U.S. Ambassador to Norway was addressing a dinner
> meeting of the Chevy Chase Branch of the American Association of
> University Women at the Columbia Country Club, attended by 160
> clubwomen.
>
> "No longer does an ambassador get his instructions, set out in a sailing
> ship, and then pursue his independent course," she said. The telephone
> and airplane are tending to make "rubber stamps" out of ambassadors.

That misquote cranked Frances to the level of a phone call to Muriel the
same day, which Frances then summarized in a hand-written note attached to
the article:

> I did not say "the telephone and airplane are tending to make 'rubber
> stamps' out of ambassadors." I said just the contrary—that although
> some people claimed [that], I personally maintained the ambassador
> played a very important role.

Clearly, Muriel wasn't paying attention and Frances had grounds to get
grumpy. Frances did not say whether the *Post* issued a subsequent correction;
they probably just let it pass.

Then in 1973 the American Foreign Service Association and the Diplomatic and Consular Officers, Retired (DACOR) awarded Frances their Foreign Service Cup. Calkin reported the cup was a silver Paul Revere bowl with the following citation:

> Awarded on Foreign Service Day to a person who during his [*sic*] career has made an outstanding contribution to the conduct of foreign relations of the U.S..

Frances put up with that gender bias—*his career*—throughout *her career,* and even ten years after she retired. It died a slow death in the U.S. Foreign Service. Here is Frances' reply:

> It is with deep appreciation and high amazement that I receive this award. Since I heard it was to be conferred on me I have repeatedly said to myself mentally—not orally—I cannot believe it.
>
> After thirty-seven years in the Foreign Service and nine years in retirement I am still convinced that the Foreign Service has been and should be one of the great assets of our country. Service is its purpose and goal. In continued adherence to this basic principle I accept with deep but humble appreciation this great honor. And I say thank you personally to those who made the decision.
>
> It is also of great pleasure to have George Kennan my coordinate today.

Frances meant that George Kennan also received an award, the Director General's Cup. Kennan, a master architect of Cold War containment and Foreign Service critic, appears many times in this biography.

Following the ceremony Catherine Peterson, Conferences Division, Department of State, wrote a note to Frances returning check #17 for $7.50: "Ambassador Willis, It is our pleasure to return to you your check for the Foreign Service Day luncheon. Honorees are always guests!!" At this point, that is not a surprise; Frances was the straightest of straight arrows.

To this list of honors and awards, the State Department added a 1962 press release announcing Frances' appointment as a Career Ambassador:

Many distinctions have graced the long career of Frances E. Willis, a tall, slender woman with iron gray hair who has been Ambassador to Ceylon since 1961. One of the most highly regarded officers in the American Foreign Service, Miss Willis has, for more than three decades, been blazing a trail for the career advancement of women in diplomacy.

Skilled in every aspect of her profession, Miss Willis has established a number of important precedents in the U.S. Foreign Service. She was the first woman to serve as acting U.S. minister to a foreign country [Sweden, in 1932.] She was the first woman to be appointed to Class 1 of the Foreign Service and the first woman to achieve the rank of career minister to be held by occupants of certain key positions in posts abroad and positions of top responsibility in the Department of State. The new class of career ambassador was created in 1955. Persons appointed to this rank must have rendered exceptionally distinguished service to the Government.

Among all these now-familiar distinctions, the Department finally identified Frances' primary accomplishment; "blazing a trail for the career advancement of women in diplomacy." The press release also quoted various responses Frances made to these accolades, which are combined for effect:

It takes certain qualities to make a fair success in diplomacy. A diplomat's sex has nothing to do with it. Mostly, I think, it takes adjustability, intelligence and stability. The basis of diplomacy is to be tactful and sincere at the same time.

[The diplomatic life is] as interesting a life as it is humanly possible to have. Also immensely rewarding is the feeling of being able to contribute toward the solution of some of the world's problems, however small that contribution may be. I wouldn't have missed it for anything.

Two other awards were in the Hoover Archives. The first was a Knight of the Sauna certificate, awarded to Frances in 1952 by The Order of the Bath/Sauna-Seura, Waskiniema, Finland. That award was earned, because a bather comes out of a sauna parboiled and then must roll in the snow or jump into a very cold lake. The second was a truly tacky Honorary Citizen of the City of New Orleans certificate from the mayor, August 6, 1955. What Frances was doing in New Orleans was not recorded.

Finally, with all this adulation she was once quoted as saying, "I prefer not to be called Doctor." She elaborated on that quote in the May 11, 1969, *Los Angeles Times* interview with Ursula Vils:

> In academic circles, I'm "Doctor" but I've never used it. Until I became an ambassador I was always "Miss." I've been so many things in different countries. But in Redlands I was never anything but "Frances Willis."

INDEX